NEGOTIATING CHINA'S DESTINY IN WORLD WAR II

To Glenn,

With thanks,

Negotiating China's Destiny in World War II

Edited by
Hans van de Ven,
Diana Lary, and
Stephen R. MacKinnon

STANFORD UNIVERSITY PRESS

STANFORD, CALIFORNIA

Stanford University Press
Stanford, California

Printed in the United States of America on acid-free, archival-quality paper

Library of Congress Cataloging-in-Publication Data

Negotiating China's destiny in World War II / edited by Hans van de Ven,
Diana Lary, and Stephen MacKinnon.
    pages cm
  Includes bibliographical references and index.
  ISBN 978-0-8047-8966-0 (cloth : alk. paper)
  1. China—Foreign relations—1912–1949. 2. China—Politics and
government—1912–1949. 3. World War, 1939–1945—Diplomatic history.
4. World War, 1939–1945—China. I. Van de Ven, Hans J., editor of
compilation. II. Lary, Diana, editor of compilation. III. MacKinnon,
Stephen R., editor of compilation.
  DS775.8.N44   2015
  940.53'51—dc23   2014005256

ISBN: 978-0-8047-9311-7 (electronic)

Typeset by BookMatters in Sabon 10/12.5

Contents

Acknowledgments

We first wish to record our thanks and appreciation for the leadership of Ezra Vogel. The Chongqing conference of which this volume is the product was the fourth in a series of, so far, five conferences on the Second World War in China. The first four were held in Harvard (2002), Maui (2004), Hakone (2006), and Chongqing (2009). Each brought together Chinese, Japanese, and Western scholars; each has resulted in a conference volume. Ezra is one of the few Western scholars fluent in both Chinese and Japanese. He is a scholar deeply committed to fostering understanding based on serious research. His vision of a generally shared consensus on the war has not yet been fully realized, but his organizational abilities and his generosity of spirit have set us on the way to a much deeper appreciation of the extent to which China and much of Asia were shaped by the war. His enthusiasm and his ability to enlist the cooperation of colleagues have been critical to the project. Ezra has been an inspiration to us all.

The aim of the conferences was to bring Chinese and Japanese scholars together to discuss, jointly with Western scholars, the 1937–1945 Sino-Japanese War, still a disputed and often difficult topic in the relationship of the two countries. Without the enthusiastic and thoughtful cooperation of leading scholars in China and Japan, it would not have been possible to convene the conferences. Yang Tianshi in China and Yamada Tatsuo in Japan played a large role in finding the best paper writers.

We also wish to record our gratefulness to the Mellon Foundation. Without its support, this project would not have been possible. In addition, we thank Harvard University for making the publication of this book possible. We thank Yin Shuxi for providing excellent draft translations. The Chongqing government was generous in hosting the 2009 conference in the city that was the Chinese capital during the Second World War and doing so again four years later.

Contributors

MARIANNE BASTID-BRUGUIERE is a French historian who was educated at the École Nationale des Langues et Civilisations Orientales and Peking University. Her many publications include *Educational Reform in Early Twentieth Century China* (1988) and *L'Evolution de la Societe Chinoise a la Fin de la Dynastie des Qing, 1873–1911*. She has received honorary degrees from the Russian Academy of Sciences and Aberdeen University, and in 2010 she was named Grand Officer of the Legion of Honor.

CHANG JUI-TE teaches at the Chinese Cultural University in Taipei and holds concurrent positions at the Institute of Modern History of the Academia Sinica and at Taiwan Normal University. He received his PhD from the latter university. His publications include *The Management of China's Modern Railroads: An Analysis of its Political Dimension* (1974), *The Beijing-Hankou Railroad and the Development of the North Chinese Economy* (1987), and *The National Army's Personnel System during the War of Resistance* (1993).

DIANA LARY is Professor Emerita of the University of British Columbia. She was educated at SOAS, University of London, and was among the first British students to teach and study in the People's Republic of China. She has written on Chinese warlords and migration. Her publications relating to wartime China include *China's Republic* (2007) and *The Chinese People at War* (2010), and she has co-edited *Scars of War: The Impact of Warfare on Modern China* (2002).

LI YUZHEN is a Senior Research Fellow at the Institute of Modern History, Chinese Academy of Social Sciences. She learned Russian at the Beijing Foreign Studies University in 1959. After teaching there and at the Capital University, she moved in 1979 to the Institute of Modern History, Chinese Academy of Social Sciences, focusing on Chinese-Soviet and

CCP-Comintern relations. She has published *Sun Yat-sen and the Comintern* (1996) and *The Kuomintang and the Comintern* (2012), and she has translated a sourcebook, *The CPSU, the Comintern, and China* (1997).

XIAOYUAN LIU teaches Chinese history and international relations at Iowa State University and is also affiliated with East China Normal University. He has published *A Partnership for Disorder: China, the United States, and Their Policies for the Postwar Disposition of the Japanese Empire, 1941–1945* (1996), *Reins of Liberation: An Entangled History of Mongolian Independence, Chinese Territoriality, and Great Power Hegemony* (2006), and *Recast All Under Heaven: Revolution, War, Diplomacy and Frontier China* (2010).

STEPHEN R. MACKINNON was educated at Yale University and the University of California at Davis. From 1979 until 1981, he lived in China, teaching and researching at the Chinese Academy of Social Sciences. Since 1971 he has taught at Arizona State University. He has done extensive research on Chinese journalism and Republican history. His publications include *China Reporting: An Oral History of American Journalism in the 1930s and 1940s* (1987), *Agnes Smedley: The Life and Times of an American Radical* (1988), *Power and Politics in Late Imperial China: Yuan Shikai in Tianjin and Beijing, 1901–1908* (1980), and most recently *Wuhan, 1938: War, Refugees, and the Making of Modern China* (2008).

RANA MITTER is Professor of the History and Politics of Modern China at Oxford University. He also presents the BBC's flagship arts and ideas program, *Nightwaves*. Educated at Cambridge University, he has published *Forgotten Ally: China's World War II, 1937–1945* (2013), the widely used textbook *A Bitter Revolution: China's Struggle with the Modern World* (2005), and the monograph *The Manchurian Myth* (2000).

NISHIMURA SHIGEO is a Professor of Foreign Studies at Osaka University. His books include *Revolutionaries against Colonialists: A History of Northeast China, 1900–1949* (1993) and *On the Colonization of Northeast China and the Rise of Anti-Japanese Survival Movements* (1987). He has also written a biography of Zhang Xueliang (1999).

HANS VAN DE VEN: After earning a PhD at Harvard University, Hans van de Ven began teaching at Cambridge University, which he still does. His research has focused on Chinese military history as well as China's globalization in the 1850–1950 period. His publications include *From Friend to Comrade: The Founding of the Chinese Communist Party* (1991), *War and Nationalism in China* (2002), and *Breaking with the Past: The Global Origins of Modernity in China* (2014). He has been awarded the Philip Lilienthal Prize and the Annual Distinguished Book Award of the Society of Military History for *The Battle for China*, which he edited together with Mark Peattie and Edward Drea. Van de Ven is a Fellow of the British Academy.

WU SUFENG is a research fellow at the Academia Historica, Republic of China (Taiwan). She earned her doctoral degree from National Chengchi University. Her academic interests include the Chinese Civil War (1945–1949), political careers of Chiang Kai-shek and T. V. Soong, and modern Sino-Japanese relations, topics about which she has published more than thirty articles.

YANG KUISONG is a world leader in Chinese Communist Party history. After graduating from People's University, he worked at the Central Party School, editing *Research in Party History*. He has held positions at People's University and the Modern History Institute of the Chinese Academy of Social Sciences. He now teaches at East China Normal University and at Peking University. His many works include *Unbearable Solicitude: Intellectuals and Politics at the time of the 1949 Revolution* (2013), *A New Perspective on the Xi'an Incident: Zhang Xueliang and the CCP* (2012), and *Gratefulness and Resentment in Mao Zedong's Relation with Moscow* (2008).

YANG TIANSHI majored in the study of Chinese literary history when he entered Peking University in 1955. For sixteen years after graduation, he taught at secondary schools in Beijing while continuing his research. In 1972, he published a study of the Ming Dynasty philosopher Wang Yangming. He joined the Modern History Institute of the Chinese Academy of Social Sciences in 1978, focusing on Republican history. A prolific historian, Yang has also written on the philosopher Zhu Xi as well as on the history of Chinese literature. His most recent publications include *Searching for the True Chiang Kai-shek* (2008), *The End of the Imperial System* (2013), and *Strategy and Campaigns* (2009).

YANG WEIZHEN is Professor of Chinese History at National Chung Cheng University in Taiwan. His monographs include *A History of Modern and Contemporary China: A New Interpretation of the Rapid Rise of a Great Power* (2009) and *From Cooperation to Rupture: The Relationship between Long Yun and the Central Government* (2000).

TSUCHIDA AKIO is a Professor of Chinese history at Chuo University. He was educated at the University of Tokyo and has published widely on Chinese foreign relations. His latest books are *Studies on the History of International Cultural Relations* (2013) and *Chiang Kai-shek's Networks of Power and their Operation* (2009).

Introduction

DIANA LARY

During the Second Sino-Japanese War, China was transformed from a minor player on the international scene into a member of the elite club of the Allied powers. China, present at the Cairo Conference of November 1943, became recognized as one of the Big Four. It became a founding member of the United Nations and one of the five Permanent Members of the UN Security Council. This elevation was in stark contrast to China's international standing before the war. For most of the early Republic (from 1912 on), China was not taken seriously as an international player. At the Versailles conference, China was treated so disdainfully by the victorious states in the First World War that its views on the disposal of German territorial holdings in China and their partial transfer to Japan were not taken into account. China's international status did not improve in the 1920s and 1930s; China was considered by foreign countries to be weak and disunited. The reunification of China in 1928 under the Guomindang (GMD) did little to raise China's international standing. Some of the Western embassies even remained in Beiping after the capital was moved to Nanjing in 1929 by the new Nationalist government. Until the mid-1930s, the diplomats preferred the sophisticated and pleasing life of the charming old capital to the raw new capital with its awful climate.

After 1937 and the Japanese invasion of China, the violence of the Japanese forces produced sympathy and moral support for China from Western countries, but China's appeals for international assistance in stemming Japanese aggression received only a limited response, mostly of a moral rather than material nature. Germany had provided help to China in training its armies in the 1930s but broke off relations with China in the spring of 1938. The Soviet Union was concerned about China, since part of the avowed Japanese war aim was directed against the Soviets, from Manchuria. The Soviets provided military aid to China, including a large number of airplanes and the pilots to fly them. Marshall Zhukov's victory over Japan at the Battle of Nomonhan in summer 1939 put an end to the fear of a Japanese attack on the Soviet Union. Once the Second World War broke out in Europe in September 1939, China became important, especially to Britain and France with colonies on the borders of China, but at the same time, it became impossible for them to provide direct assistance. For the next two years, China faced the Japanese alone.

In late 1941, Japan attacked the United States. The world war that had started in Europe expanded into the Pacific. China became one of the major anti-fascist powers, thus gaining the equal status that it felt it had always deserved. China's participation on the Allied side was important. World War II could now be presented as a coalition of equals involving all countries opposed to German and Japanese aggression, rather than as a war of Asians against white imperialists, as Japan had been able to argue until Pearl Harbor.

Our book sees the war both as a period when much damage was inflicted on China, negating all the progress that had been made until then, and also as one in which China once again became a major presence on the world stage. During much of the Cold War, the rivalry between the Soviet Union and the United States obscured the significance of that change. It is only now, when China has begun to prosper economically, that we can gain a clear bearing on the importance of wartime China's strenuous efforts to enhance its international presence during the war. Our collection of essays suggests that its origins, as far as China's international position is concerned, lie in the Sino-Japanese War.

The chapters in this book are a selection of papers presented at a conference held in Chongqing, China's wartime capital, in September 2009. The central focus of the book is China's relations with its allies in the war against Japan and with its neighbors. Our coverage starts from before the outbreak of all-out war in 1937. This choice of starting point takes the time span beyond what has been the norm for discussing China's wartime foreign relations, a focus almost exclusively on China's relations with the United States after Pearl Harbor in 1941.

Our focus is on open, public international relations and on some of the major individual leaders involved in the war. Many of the articles rely on government records. Fascinating as it would be, we do not go into the murky world of secret negotiations and intelligence operations. Though they were a real and important area of wartime international relations, they are hard to document reliably.

Three Themes

During the conference a number of major themes emerged. We have organized the book along the lines of these themes, each of which seems to us to have been a major factor in the rise in China's international status, both then and in more recent times.

THE DEATH KNELL OF THE OLD EMPIRES AND THE RISE OF CHINA

The first section of the book deals with the impact of Japanese expansionism on Western imperialism in Asia and on Western colonies. In the early years of the war, China received little help from countries that, however well-disposed toward it, did not feel able to give material aid in resisting Japan. As the war went on, and the future inability of Western countries to defend their Asian colonies against Japan became clear, China came to be seen as a key ally, the last friendly holdout in a war that threatened to destroy European influence throughout Asia. The threatened colonies stretched from Hong Kong through French Indochina, Cambodia, Malaya, Singapore, Indonesia, Burma, and as far west as India, the British bastion in Asia, which, until late in the war, seemed vulnerable to Japanese attack. The threat of Japanese expansion was recognized in Europe, but the ability to react to it was severely constrained by the impact of the war in Europe on the home countries. Marianne Bastid-Bruguiere's chapter on French efforts to maintain a role in Asian politics and protect its colonial interests in Southeast Asia provides one illustration of the rapid decline of European influence. Rana Mitter's depiction of Britain's struggle to come to terms with the evaporation of its influence in East Asia forms another.

Nationalist sentiments in Asian countries in the 1920s and 1930s had been aimed against European, and particularly British, imperialism. The expansionist Japanese saw themselves as the destroyers of Western imperialism, and they justified their expansion in Asia in the name of establishing the Great East Asia Co-Prosperity Sphere, which would bring to an end European imperialism. The war in East Asia did bring the decline of Western empires in Asia, sometimes suddenly as in the case of Britain and at other times more slowly as with France. The European powers never recouped their prewar empires. By the 1960s European imperialism was gone, not just from East Asia but also elsewhere in the continent—with the exception of a few tiny colonial territories such as Hong Kong, Macao, and Goa. Thus, an Asian order that had emerged in the wake of the 1838–1842 Opium War and which had held sway for nearly a century, having an impact on East Asia and China at all levels, came to an end in World War II.

China's confidence in dealing with its neighbors, including the colonial territories, grew during the war. China started to plan seriously to reestablish its historical position in Asia. Ironically, the rise in the international status of China came at a time when the government of China appeared to be weak. After the Japanese occupation of northern and eastern China in 1937 and 1938, the area of China actually controlled by the Chinese government was dramatically reduced, to a large but poor and remote area of western China, governed from Chongqing, a city almost completely cut off from the rest of the world.

Chongqing's isolation changed the Chinese government's own view of China. The move to the west forced Chongqing to take greater notice of China's western borderlands and neighbors than the government had before. This involved working out where the borders of China actually were, and establishing the exact nature of its relationship with territories on the edge of the Chinese world. It became important to distinguish between sovereignty and suzerainty, an issue explored in Chang Jui-te's chapter on China's relations with Tibet, which of course remain a source of difficulty. Chongqing was keenly aware of the extent to which the war had destabilized traditional relations between China, its borderlands, and the neighboring states, and of the degree to which Japanese encouragement of "ethnic independence" was fostering irredentism among the peoples of China's periphery, including those of Mongolia, but also Xinjiang.

In terms of neighboring states, one of China's key relationships was with the Soviet Union, nominally friendly toward Chongqing. But the Soviet Union, as the leader of world Communism, was at the same time involved in a complex relationship with the Chinese Communist Party (CCP) in its remote capital at Yan'an. Its relationship with Moscow, channeled through the Communist International (Comintern), was dictated to a great extent by the twists and turns in the Soviet Union's relationship with Germany and Japan. Yang Kuisong analyzes CCP-Soviet relations in his chapter, "The Evolution of the Relationship between the Chinese Communist Party and the Comintern during the Sino-Japanese War," placing it in the contexts of the Soviet Union's wartime strategy and its alliance with the GMD.

In the world of wartime Chongqing, the relationship between China and the Allies became more intimate. The Western countries moved their embassies from Nanjing to Chongqing. The diplomats shared the miseries of the Chinese evacuees and lived through the same relentless Japanese bombing. Their reports from Chongqing, which spoke of the courage of the inhabitants under bombardment, kept the sympathy for China alive. Their descriptions of the heat, the noise, the smells, and the general discomfort of Chongqing gave the war in Asia a reality that reports from China had often lacked before.

The constellation of foreign representatives in Chongqing changed over time. Before Pearl Harbor there were a small number of official foreign representatives in Chongqing and a larger group of pro-China foreigners, including missionaries, academics, and journalists, from a number of different countries. After Pearl Harbor the number of foreigners in Chongqing grew, most of the incomers energetic and determined Americans who wanted to see the war won. Many of these men, most notably General Joseph Stilwell, made huge impacts. Diana Lary's chapter on Canada's relations with China draws attention to the impact of the war between China and less powerful countries that have not featured in "big history" but that are nonetheless worth examining to understand the changed nature of Chinese foreign relations brought about by the war.

NEGOTIATING ALLIANCES AND SOVEREIGNTY

China's wartime diplomacy was much more effective than would have been expected in the lead-up to the war, when China seemed almost bereft of active allies. Then its diplomats, though often skilled and personable, had been unable to make any inroads in the Western capitals. The League of Nations had declined to intervene on China's behalf and contain the Japanese occupation of Manchuria.

In 1937 there was a possibility that the outbreak of war could be prevented, or that the conflict could be kept below the threshold of formal war. In spite of expressions of disapproval of Japan's actions, unable to come to a common position and fearing the outbreak of war in Europe, European countries and the United States declined to intervene. Japan appeared to have got away with its occupation of China. Although the fighting was ferocious from the beginning, neither China nor Japan declared war. Although China would do so after Pearl Harbor, Japan never did so. Tsuchida Akio demonstrates that it was less the belief that such a declaration might trigger the activation of the United States' neutrality laws, which prevented the United States from providing assistance to any country at war, than domestic concerns that lay behind this situation.

Later in the war, the positions of the European states and the United States changed and polarized. Some became China's allies, others nominally its enemies. With the start of the European War in 1939, the Chinese government was able to link the war in Asia to the war in Europe, and to ally itself more closely with Britain, in the front line of fighting Nazi Germany. Chongqing was prescient and well-informed about the constantly shifting events in Europe. With Germany, Japan, and Italy joined together first by the Anti-Comintern Pact and then in the Axis, it was obvious that China's enemy was the enemy of those fighting the Germans and Italians, even though there was no formal British declaration of war on Japan until the end of 1941, after the attack on Pearl Harbor brought the United States into the war.

After Pearl Harbor, the dynamic in Chongqing between China and the Allies changed. The dominant foreign influence in Chongqing was now the United States, and the extent of the American involvement was enormous. Resources, advice, and financial aid poured into Chongqing from the United States. In his contribution, Xiaoyuan Liu analyzes the deliberations of US strategists about China's frontier regions and minorities. These were driven by the aim of finding a new configuration for East Asia that might enhance the stability of the region. Chiang Kai-shek was the central figure in Chongqing's international relations. He cultivated personal relations with several of the other global leaders, notably Roosevelt and Stalin. He also had a clear sense of who the rising leaders of Asia were. He put considerable effort into developing relations with them and securing their support for a new postwar international position for China. Yang Tianshi describes Chiang Kai-shek's visit to India and his meetings with Nehru. Li Yuzhen examines Chiang's requests to Stalin for active Soviet participation in the war, arguing that although these failed, both countries nonetheless profited from the limited cooperation they were able to achieve, which, in turn, was of fundamental importance to shaping the pattern of international alliances as it took definite shape after the Pacific War.

Chiang's skills at playing (and manipulating) the game of personal relationships, here in the international arena, underlined his central involvement in international affairs. He became, during the war, one of the first Chinese leaders to be elevated to the highest level of international awareness. In part his success on the international stage was due to the critical role of his wife and translator, Madame Chiang Kai-shek (Song Meiling). Chiang's diplomatic skills are one aspect of the major reinterpretation of his role in modern Chinese history, now underway in academic circles in China and abroad.

Sovereignty was a key issue in all of China's relationships with its neighbors and allies. It shaped Chongqing's view not only of the wartime present but also of the postwar world. The fundamental concern was the future extent of China and the nature of the relations between the Chinese center and the border regions. The end of the war was seen in Chongqing to involve not only the defeat of Japan and the end of foreign imperialism in China but also the emergence of a more strongly consolidated China, with its borders clearly demarcated and its "lost territories" reincorporated into the nation. In this sense, the views of the Chongqing government on the territorial extent of China were close to those later adopted by the Communist government. Nishimura Shigeo demonstrates in his chapter, "Northeast China in Chongqing Politics: The Influence of 'Recover the Northeast' on Domestic and International Politics," how China's Northeast (Manchuria) became regarded as an indelible part of China. By 1945 the GMD had invested so much political capital in this conceptualization of China that it became impossible for them to give it up in the civil war that followed, which, militarily, might have been the wiser option.

We do not deal with the collaborationist government in Nanjing. Though Wang Jingwei's government maintained some foreign relations, those relations did not amount to autonomous foreign relations. They were with allies of Japan and with countries that had fallen under de facto Nazi control, such as Vichy France.

ENDING WAR

Ending war is at least as complicated and difficult as starting it, although historians have paid little attention to this aspect of warfare. The end of the war in Asia came suddenly. After eight grim years of war, victory brought great relief to China, but it also brought its own problems. Chongqing was suddenly faced with enormous tasks—the resumption of control over areas occupied by Japan, the reconstruction of the economy, and the containment of the CCP, which had grown much stronger during the war.

One of the first issues was dealing with the defeated Japanese. Here, given how the Japanese had behaved in China and the terrible vengeance wreaked the year before when the Soviet Union's armies moved westward into Germany, China behaved with surprising moderation. In her chapter "The Nationalist Government's Attitude toward Postwar Japan," Wu Sufeng demonstrates that Chiang Kai-shek's policy of "repaying aggression with kindness" derived from the GMD assessment of the new realities that they believed would emerge in postwar Asia and the global international context.

China had to deal with the old empires, which showed signs of wanting to recoup former positions. There was little China could do about the Soviet Union in Manchuria. Soviet forces entered Manchuria in the last week of the war, effectively taking back control of cities created by the Russians only half a century before and lost to the Japanese in 1905. Eventually, the Soviet armies withdrew of their own accord in 1946, having removed much of Manchuria's moveable industrial equipment and facilitated the Communists' entrance into the region. China also had to deal with France over Indochina and with Britain over Hong Kong. Above all, Chiang Kai-shek needed to keep the United States involved in China's future, not least because of the Communist threat. This complex repositioning took place in the context of the deepening Cold War. Complementing Bastid-Bruguiere's chapter on the French attempt to maintain a role in Asian diplomacy before and during the war, Yang Weizhen reveals the internal contradictions in Chinese policy, involving the Ministry of Foreign Affairs, the Executive Yuan, local military commanders, and Long Yun, the governor of Yunnan Province, neighboring Vietnam. The result was that Chinese officials and officers entered Vietnam after the war to accept Japan's surrender but soon withdrew because of the need to cater to

France and the desire of China's Nationalist government to restrain local power holders.

The last chapter of the war did not come with the end of hostilities in 1945 but only with a peace treaty signed well into the Communist period. That treaty, ironically, was signed by a government that no longer had control over most of China but only of the island of Taiwan. The war had made China stronger internationally, but internally the war changed the balance of power; the Chinese Communists became strong enough to first challenge and then defeat the GMD government, in a civil war that started immediately after the Japanese surrender and that only came to an end four years later. Hans van de Ven shows that the treaty of peace between the Republic of China and Japan helped stabilize the political situation in East Asia, even though it was less a treaty of peace than an integral part of the United States' effort to create a pro-US Cold War front line in the region. The treaty recognition of China as one of the victors of World War II had ramifications that have lasted until today, and will do so for the foreseeable future. It also bequeathed to posterity a set of issues, including the status of Taiwan and Japan's war responsibility, which remain alive and might yet become destabilizing.

Part I

OLD EMPIRES AND THE RISE OF CHINA

1 France's Deluded Quest for Allies

SAFEGUARDING TERRITORIAL SOVEREIGNTY
AND THE BALANCE OF POWER IN EAST ASIA, 1931–1945

MARIANNE BASTID-BRUGUIERE

A review of French involvement in East Asia during World War II does not recast existing master narratives of the conflict in that area, viewed from China, Japan, or the United States. It can, however, illuminate how far the disappearance of France in the war in East Asia was the outcome of its 1940 defeat in Europe and its subsequent neutrality. And it does not obscure the lingering weight of French Indochina in shaping military and strategic issues in the confrontation with Japanese expansionism.

The French stakes in East Asia were seriously depleted by the First World War. The massive destruction and death toll at home, the heavy war debts, and the subsequent economic decline meant that French investment and power in the area, second only to Britain before 1914, fell.[1] France's main stronghold in East Asia was Indochina, with a population of 20 million; in 1940, 46 percent of all French private assets in its colonial empire were concentrated there.[2] Its assets in China and Japan, though diversified and not insignificant, were of direct concern only to a small lobby within the establishment, only some of whose members belonged to the larger coalition of interests involved in Indochina. In Korea, Thailand, and other parts of Southeast Asia, its vested interests were limited and linked to its nationals in Catholic missions and to the security of Indochina.

The fact that France's international role in East Asia rested primarily on its sovereignty over Indochina, which its military forces could not defend against any major aggression, induced France to base its policy in East Asia on safeguarding territorial sovereignty and the balance of power as conceived by the 1922 Washington conference. Though aware that Japanese expansionism threatened French dominion over Indochina, the French government was unable to win support for a consistent international stand against Japan after the coup in Manchuria in September

1931 (the Mukden Incident). It therefore decided after the Marco Polo Bridge Incident in 1937 to set aside French prejudice against the Nationalist government and to provide direct help to China by allowing arms and supplies to pass through Indochina en route to southern China. The Japanese took advantage of the French military collapse in Europe to impose on Indochina demands for logistical support for Japan and for cutting aid to China. In the face of a flat refusal of help from Britain and the United States, the Indochina authorities and the home government chose accommodation with Japan while staying on speaking terms with China and impeding as far as possible Japanese attacks on southern China from Indochina. This uneasy game lasted even after Chiang Kai-shek broke off relations with Vichy in August 1943. It ended only with the Japanese takeover of Indochina on March 9, 1945. Since 1941, local supporters of the Free French, led by General de Gaulle, had been trying desperately to get recognition and arms from China and its allies for their own resistance against the Japanese. De Gaulle's first emissaries arrived in Chongqing in December 1941. Only after Roosevelt had agreed to recognize de Gaulle's provisional government of the republic on October 23, 1944, did Chongqing take this step.

Neither in East Asia nor in Europe were the French able to impress any aspect of France's East Asian agenda on the minds of the Allies. In Indochina, the Japanese surrendered to the Chinese and British without a French representative present. The French chargé d'affaires was not invited to attend the Japanese capitulation in Beiping on September 14, although General Leclerc attended the formal surrender of Japan on board the USS *Missouri* on September 2, 1945.

The eclipse of French political power in East Asia after June 1940 can hardly be seen as enhancing the relative status of any of the Western Allies. The fact that none of the Allies came to the rescue of France at the end of the war suggests that such an eclipse suited them. The alternative options for a peace settlement embraced by the French were brushed aside. When, belatedly, in 1946, the British government and Ho Chi Minh gave them some thought, time had passed, and opportunities had been lost.

There were three different stages in the French shadow-play in East Asia. From 1931 to June 1940, the main themes ran from collective conciliation to a single partnership with China. June 1940 ushered in the confusion over Indochina's becoming a sanctuary. The last phase, from June to September 1945, saw the helpless abandonment of what the French had once called "the pearl of empire."

From the start, the French government did not have the slightest doubt about Japanese responsibility for the Mukden Incident. Reports of the local

French consul and the French minister in Nanjing stated that although the coup had been engineered by Kwantung officers, without the knowledge or direct orders from the Japanese general staff or government, many in these two bodies endorsed it.[3] Wilden, the French minister in Beiping , wrote that this affair was, for the Japanese military, "a fuse that would explode the gunpowder, long prepared."[4] But he recommended extreme caution to the two officers he sent to Manchuria to gather intelligence, stressing that "it is important that neither China nor Japan get the impression that we favor one or the other side."[5]

In the view of the French government, the best response was to bring into play the principle of collective security that had so far maintained peace in Europe. Japan had accepted the principle by signing the Briand-Kellogg Pact in August 1928. With the help of the nations that had signed the Nine-Power Treaty (1922), conciliation could be achieved between China and Japan. Given the growth of militarism in Japan, this meant a cautious and conciliatory attitude toward Japan in order not to jeopardize the position of its moderates. This was the policy of Aristide Briand, foreign minister in the government of Pierre Laval. His personal sympathy was with China, while the French press and Laval himself put part of the blame on China's disarray.[6] Briand's cautiousness has to be understood in the context of the prevailing opinion that the brutal lesson of the Japanese army would cool Chinese nationalist zeal against France. Vietnamese insurgents had received asylum in China after the 1930 Yen Bay uprising, and a violent anti-French campaign had been launched in March 1931.

Collective action for a peaceful settlement was the watchword of the French position. At the meeting of the Council of the League of Nations on September 22, 1931, the French delegate, Massigli, called for urgent intervention through an appeal to China and Japan to stop any action that could further impair peace and security and to implement an immediate troop withdrawal.[7]

The following day in Tokyo, the French minister, de Martel, participated in the joint appeal of the ambassadors of League members to Japan to stop further military action by the Kwantung Army. He added a warning against any movement of Japanese troops in Tianjin that could threaten the security of the foreign concessions.[8] However, France did not join the British in asking Washington to warn Japan to abide by the recommendations of the League.[9] De Martel advised that France not join concerted action directed only at Tokyo because it could "hurt Japanese self-esteem and make a settlement more difficult."[10] The result of this prudence was that the Japanese press claimed that France was siding with Japan.[11]

Further aggressive moves by Japan and growing outrage in Chinese public opinion threatened full-scale war. France agreed with Britain and the United States to separately urge Japan to implement the League of Nations resolution. De Martel visited Vice Foreign Minister Nagai on October 7 and got assurances on the retreat of Japanese troops by October 14.[12] After new Japanese provocations and the bombing of Jinzhou on October 8, France hastened to join Britain in warning Japan that its actions might push the League to actions that would favor China.[13] In China, the call for moderation was met with open disappointment.[14]

On October 13, Briand assumed the presidency of the League Council. The meeting was held in Paris because of his poor health. Briand's plan was to bolster the authority of the League by enlisting American cooperation. Through his personal prestige and persuasiveness, his suggestion was endorsed by the Council, against Japanese opposition, and was accepted by the US government.[15]

Although he was attacked in the press and by some senior officials in the Foreign Ministry for his "anti-Japanese stand," Briand tried to limit the Chinese response by refusing to declare Japan the aggressor. He had the Council dodge the issue of a deadline for the evacuation of Japanese troops.[16] Chinese diplomats understood his tactics and agreed on November 25 to withdraw Chinese troops to Shanhaiguan and to establish a neutral zone in Jinzhou.[17] He backed the establishment of an investigative commission, agreed to by the Council on December 10.

While critics in government circles argued that direct negotiation between the two protagonists would achieve better results than the League's slow procedures, Briand worried that Japan might withdraw from the League. Exhausted by his fruitless efforts and his illness, Briand was pessimistic over the prospect of lasting peace. Laval dismissed him from the cabinet on January 13, 1932, and he died soon after. His level-headedness had prevented escalation to full war, but he failed to obtain a return to the status quo ante.

Laval himself took over the Foreign Ministry. He had no special interest or knowledge of East Asia, but he sought, through bilateral relations and through the League , to focus on an international agreement on disarmament, for which France needed Japanese support. Consequently, France chose not to join British and American protests against the January 28 Japanese attack in Shanghai. Berthelot, the Foreign Ministry's secretary-general, argued that a joint protest would be reminiscent of past imperialist meddling in East Asian affairs; he warned that "China does not like conspicuous protectors."[18] The ambassador in Tokyo made a modest verbal protest to Foreign Minister Yoshizawa, stressing that "the French government attaches great importance to the international character of Shanghai and to its defense." As fighting came closer to the French Concession in February, Wilden was worried, but he got only small reinforcements of troops and arms from Paris.[19]

France offered its good offices to Nanjing on February 3 to broker an immediate cease-fire. The proposal was readily accepted by China but rejected by Japan.[20] Despite insistence by the Francophile Li Shizeng and by the Shanghai mayor that France was the only possible mediator, Wilden stressed that mediation could only be unofficial and coordinated with his British and American colleagues; unilateral intervention might antagonize one or the other belligerent.[21]

On February 5, Tardieu, war minister and French delegate to the Conference on Disarmament in Geneva, presented a bold and detailed plan to enact France's long-standing view that the organization of collective security must precede arms limitation.[22] The League would control a new international military force, made up of contingents from various countries. The plan was supported by Japan and China, among others, but vigorously opposed by the United States, especially President Hoover, and by Britain, not to mention Germany. Though it was not rejected outright, it was put on the back burner. To French policy makers it was clear that every effort had to be made to regain Anglo-American goodwill. In June France finally agreed at the Lausanne Conference to abrogate German reparations.

Since the attempt to check the development of the Sino-Japanese crisis through an international peace plan appeared to be deadlocked, Wilden was instructed to join any unofficial conciliatory steps with his foreign colleagues. A French proposal for the settlement of the Shanghai Incident was submitted to the League Council, accepted by China and Japan, and served as the basis for the agreement of May 5, 1932.[23]

Japan now tried to abort the growing international consensus to curb its ambitions. Since France was the main proponent of consensus and had the least vested interest in China, Japan tried to lure it away from the other powers. The attempt started with rumors of a "secret Franco-Japanese entente" that were spread in early February 1932 in the American, British, and Chinese press.[24] US secretary of state Stimson believed them so readily that Paris had to take great pains to counter them.[25] Repeated official and private denials succeeded in stopping the press campaign and in placating the State Department but not in removing the prejudice over Paris's alleged sympathy with Japan, which lingered in American and British leading circles until the end of the war, producing unwarranted and obnoxious outbursts.[26]

Enticing France into some kind of agreement and stoking Anglo-American prejudice against it through leaks about "secret deals" seemed good tactics to Japanese officers; many of them were French trained and had useful connections with the French establishment. A Japanese counselor in Warsaw suggested in March that as Japan was isolated in Asia, France was isolated in Europe; the two countries would benefit from a political alliance following a trade agreement.[27] On April 20, the Vice Minister of War Hata asked de Martel for a loan, which Paris quickly refused on the grounds that France could not finance war in China.[28] A new diplomatic offensive started in July 1932. On July 7 in Tokyo, the vice minister of war, General Koiso, asked again for a loan, which Foreign Minister Herriot refused "politely," on the grounds that the French money market was so tight that its resources had to be kept for domestic purposes.[29] On July 9 in Geneva, Colonel Kobayashi, military counselor of the Japanese delegation at the League , proposed an alliance with Japan, arguing that it would "protect France against Russia and Indochina against Communism," and he requested that General Claudel, the French member of the Lytton Commission, be instructed to favor Japan.[30] The French delegate, Massigli, explained that the requests ran counter to the principles of French diplomacy. He refused to transmit them to Paris but did report on them. Secretary-General Léger instructed Massigli by telephone that this was "unacceptable; any reply should be avoided."[31] At the end of July, the French consul in Harbin was offered a large sum for French interests in the Chinese Eastern Railway and privileged investment opportunities in Manchuria.[32] Again, in early September, War Minister Araki urged an alliance in a private talk with the admiral of the French Far Eastern naval forces, and Matsudaira, a close associate of the minister of foreign affairs visited the French chargé d'affaires for the same reason.[33]

On August 19, 1932, Yoshida, then ambassador to Italy, proposed to Herriot a formal alliance, but he was met with a firm refusal.[34] Japanese military attachés and diplomats spread extravagant rumors that France supported Japan and that if the French alliance failed, Japan would get German support. In the foreign press, the devastating image of a pro-Japanese France lingered, despite Herriot's strenuous efforts to kill it with official denials.[35]

France's resolute stance against an alliance with, or leaning toward, Japan was reiterated many times to the Japanese government in the months before the publication of the Lytton Report. In September 1932, Stimson traded the American position on German claims to equal rights at the coming disarmament conference for French endorsement of the United States' position on Manchukuo and Japan.[36] Soon after the Japanese recognition of Manchukuo (August 24), Herriot took steps to block loans floated for Japan or Manchukuo by small French banks.[37]

The United States did not demand French approval of the Lytton Report. The rejection was in line with the principled refusal to recognize Manchukuo, reiterated by French leaders and officials since February 1932. Keeping to that position was not to please the United States but to please the Soviet Union; France signed a nonaggression pact with the Soviet Union on November 29, 1932, and wanted the Soviet Union as a member of the League.[38]

Even while seemingly hewing closely to American or British positions, the French position was actually profoundly different. In international relations, Herriot, like Briand, opted for multilateralism and worldwide cooperation based on law and justice, enforced through the League , in association with the United States and the Soviet Union. He wished to prevent any return to national policies that would lead again to war. During his time in office, he was active on East Asian issues, about which he was knowledgeable through his long-standing friendship with Li Shizeng. His successors were far less involved because of overriding threats in Europe when Hitler became German chancellor on January 30, 1933. The response to the East Asian crisis was mostly left to the Foreign Ministry's permanent officials. The key figure was the secretary-general, Philippe Berthelot. He knew East Asia well, had traveled extensively there, and been a right-hand man to Briand. He was also the patient architect of the pact with the Soviet Union.[39] However, by spring 1932 his activity was restricted by illness; he was replaced by his trusted colleague and friend Alexis Léger, who remained in charge until his dismissal by Reynaud in May 1940.

Léger (better known as the poet Saint-John Perse) had been posted in Beiping for five years and had climbed the ladder as a close associate of Briand. He shared his faith in international solidarity as the basis of foreign relations. In his view, the primary tool to bring about such solidarity was the League , boosted by close cooperation with both the United States and the Soviet Union.

Shortly before the League met to consider the Lytton Report, the Foreign Ministry devised a skillful procedure that would give it credit and open the way to a workable settlement of the Sino-Japanese dispute, instead of the slow and cumbersome course envisaged by Britain, which was likely to lead to a costly dead end and to Japan's withdrawal from the League. The League of Nations Assembly would "adopt" the report and "approve" its conclusions with or without the two parties voting, and then invite those powers with special interests in the area (the Nine Powers plus Germany and the Soviet Union) to mediate locally between Japan and China along the lines of the report.[40] Because of Anglo-American refusal to bring in Germany and the Soviet Union, the French did not push this view but went with the general opinion.[41]

At the same time, a careful assessment was made inside the Foreign Ministry of the threat of Japanese and Chinese nationalism to French interests, in case of increased tension between Japan and the powers. The memo stressed that for a year Japanese policy had been "regressing" toward an "Asian *particularism*" or "an Asian Monroe Doctrine," away from "integration into the entente between the great world powers" and away from "the contractual system of the League." Japan was pursuing a "systematic program of wild imperialism." It did not respect international obligations. France should vote for sanctions. Its possessions in Indochina and the Pacific, and its special position in China, especially in Shanghai, were important and vulnerable, as evidenced by increased Japanese espionage activities and by attempts to buy Western shares in Chinese railroads. However, France's "general policy rests upon a network of international agreements the upholding of which is far more important for the safeguard of its interests." Since France's and Indochina's trade with Japan was small (27 million yen and 6 million yen, respectively), an embargo would affect French interests far less than British and American ones. In case of a Japanese attempt to retaliate in South China, the United States and Britain were likely to protect the Philippines and Hong Kong, so Indochina would not be under too great a threat.

The immediate danger for Indochina would be "the reorganization on its border, with or against Japan, of a united and disciplined China." France had to make sure that throwing the blame on Japan would neither appear as "unqualified approval of Chinese claims and methods" nor entail humiliation that would "push Japan to extreme solutions." There was some hope that Japan's dire economic and monetary straits would "sooner or later return Japanese opinion to a more realistic sense of opportunities and to a sounder appreciation of the need to collaborate with other big powers. French policy must aim at assisting such an evolution."[42] This policy applied until 1937.

The French government felt "relieved" that facing American refusal, Britain had dropped the idea of an arms embargo against Japan, a measure that Paris saw as damaging to everybody except Japan.[43] However, since Japan had left the League in March 1933, no need was felt to continue active diplomacy in East Asia. The main concern was to maintain a position of balance and impartiality. A growing worry was that in case of open conflict between Japan and the Soviet Union, France would have to support the Soviet Union because of its treaty obligations; Japan might threaten Indochina, which France could not defend.[44] France showed willingness to help China. France enabled the sending to China of Rajchman as technical delegate of the League, against strong Japanese opposition.[45] In late July 1933, T. V. Soong was warmly received in Paris. French experts participated in international cooperation projects on Chinese development initiated by the League.

In the wake of continuing Japanese encroachments in North China, the ambivalence of the Chinese government confirmed French policy makers in the assumption that taking bold or unilateral initiatives was useless and that "close collaboration and joint action of international powers must be continued."[46] Caution seemed wise, all the more so because the United States and Britain were taking the same position.

Domestic political instability (fifteen cabinets between September 1931 and December 1937) scarcely helped strengthen the French position in East Asia. After the Franco-Soviet Pact of Mutual Assistance was signed on May 2, 1935, some groups among the Japanese military campaigned for advances into South China. The murder of a Japanese shopkeeper in Beihai (Pakhoi) in September 1936 resulted in a Japanese naval display and in the reinforcement of marine and air forces around Hainan and in Taiwan. This was the first serious alarm for Indochina, especially because in Thailand factional struggles were leaning toward an alliance with Japan to recover territory lost to Indochina.[47]

Suspicions about extensive Japanese underground activities in Indochina were increased by the Anti-Comintern Pact signed between Japan and Germany on November 25, 1936, prompting a revision of French East Asian policies. Since 1935, officers of the Japanese general staff had been traveling regularly to Indochina, Singapore, and the Philippines to explore possible theaters of operations, warned the military attaché in Tokyo.[48] The ambassador to China wrote that there were more than ten Japanese intelligence agents in the major cities of Tonking and Cochinchina.[49] In the suitcase of a Japanese spy, Captain Endo, the Tonking police found a letter from Major Sato of the Tokyo general staff ordering him to collect books, directories, guidebooks, and maps about Indochina; he was also to gather intelligence on French business in the colony, important places, government services, population, ethnic groups and languages, religion and education, local products, trade, finance, transport and defense networks, and Guangzhouwan and the strength of its garrison.[50]

Indochina's strategic vulnerability was exposed by the military and colonial authorities and in the colonial press. Against those who advocated a firmer stand against Japan, divergent views were voiced inside the Foreign Ministry by Cosme, the new head of the Asia-Oceania desk. He stressed the "complexity of the situation" after the Xi'an Incident. "France must not take sides. It must defend its interests in China" without ignoring the Anti-Comintern Pact, a statement that implied that Japan was a more trustworthy protector of property and possessions than Stalin-supported China.[51] This was the first time that Japan's value as a bulwark against Communism was voiced in a policy paper on East Asia; Japanese use of this watchword in early 1932 to lure Paris into an alliance had been ignored. What motivated Cosme's warning in late 1936 was not the danger of a spillover of revolution from China to Indochina but the fear, largely shared by European opinion at the time, of a global Communist threat as a consequence of the economic crisis.

After the Marco Polo Bridge Incident, the opening of large-scale hostilities brought a new set of problems: handling international negotiations to limit, if not to end, the conflict; formulating a comprehensive response to Japan's action in China; defending French interests in China against Japanese troops; providing for the safety of Indochina.

It was soon clear to French policy makers that international action was powerless beyond limited protection of foreign interests in China. In international negotiations, French leaders were brutally confronted with the fact that they were standing alone in caring about Indochina's safety and in salvaging their Chinese interests. A new commitment to alliances in East Asia became the order of the day, enacted by discreetly strengthening links with China.

French ambassadors in Washington and London were instructed to contact the American and British governments with a view to joint conciliatory action that would "press for moderation" both in Tokyo and Nanjing. Such was Foreign Minister Delbos's first reply to Chinese ambassador Gu Weijun, who visited him on July 13, 1937, to ask him informally about the advisability of China bringing its case to the League or to the nine-power signatories of the Washington treaty. Delbos pointed to the risks and ineffectiveness of an appeal to the League.[52] In his telegram to Ambassador Corbin in London, Delbos asked if China had also approached the British government. He stressed that he wanted to "force the United States to take their share of responsibility" by using the Nine-Power Treaty procedure.[53]

The British response seemed encouraging at first, but Washington refused joint action in Tokyo and Nanjing. An early end to the illusion of possible international action came on July 21, when British foreign minister Anthony Eden told Corbin that he wanted joint action with the United States and France aiming at mediation, but since the State Department had refused, Britain would "rely only on general talks" as long as America kept that stance.[54] American isolationism and British vacillation on China left trying to limit the dangers of a Chinese appeal to the League as the only option.[55] On September 6, Massigli, now deputy head of the Political Department of the Foreign Ministry, urged Gu to refer the matter to the League 's Far East Advisory Committee.[56] Despite Japanese foreign minister Hirota's pressure to prevent Paris from presenting the Chinese request,[57] the French attitude at the meeting in Geneva was lukewarm, given the maneuvers and manipulations by China and other, smaller countries.[58]

In China, international cooperation worked somewhat more efficiently and achieved results, which by early December 1937 French diplomats deemed "satisfactory," about French interests in Tianjin, Shanghai, and the Chinese Maritime Customs, as well as the protection of Catholic missionaries.[59]

French initiatives were directed elsewhere. In late July 1937, the moderate-left Chautemps government decided to seek Chinese cooperation to protect French interests in China and Indochina, and to keep open the southern sea routes.[60] An agreement for a loan of 200 million francs was signed with Finance Minister Kong Xiangxi, who had approached the French government in early June, on his way to the coronation of George VI in London. The credit was to strengthen the Chinese currency and could not be used for war supplies. Because of shortages of military supplies for the French army, nothing could be bought from state-owned factories, but Kong was directed to private firms. A company was organized in Haiphong, with fifty trucks for road transport to Guangxi.[61] The Chinese government signed a contract with a group of French banks for a railway from Langson to Nanning that would eventually be extended to Hankou. Through agreement between Hanoi and the Guangxi military, a military training mission was sent to Guangxi, and a group of Guangxi officers was sent to Hanoi for artillery training.[62]

The Ministry of Foreign Affairs sought a Japanese commitment to Indochina's maritime security, through assurances on Hainan and the Spratlys and Paracels. But diplomatic clumsiness resulted in the Japanese muddying the issue with a demand to stop the transshipment of war supplies through Indochina, raising doubts in China about France's reliability. Some success seemed to have been achieved when, on September 24, 1937, the chief of staff of the Japanese navy minister declared to the French ambassador that Japan had no intention to occupy Hainan.[63] The ambassador also reminded the Japanese government of the sovereignty rights of Annam over the Paracels, even if contested by China, while secret Chinese consent was obtained for a French ship to lay lights and buoys on islands where the navy knew Japanese fishermen had settled, which France feared might be used by the Japanese navy to interfere with maritime traffic.[64]

On September 28, the Japanese counselor visited Cosme to ask about French arms sales to China and to tell him that if arms shipments through Indochina were not stopped, the Japanese air force would destroy the Yunnan railway and the line under construction in Guangxi.[65] This warning prompted Cosme to push for a quick decision between two mutually exclusive policies: to help China or to protect French possessions in Asia. He advised stopping arms transshipment through Indochina and wrote confidently that "there is no doubt that Japan is ready to recognize and respect our interests in return."[66]

On August 25, the Council of Ministers decided that since there was no declaration of war, arms exports to China and Japan should continue, but arms from French state industries were denied transshipment through Indochina. Arms transshipment through Indochina was forbidden, except for supplies ordered before July 15, 1937, or already at sea on October 13; the ban was provisional pending the Brussels conference decisions.[67] After a protest from the Air Ministry that aeronautics was private business, an exception was made for airplanes, which were to be delivered in kit form, assembled in Tonking, and then flown to China.[68]

The decision was passed on to Ambassador Gu Weijun by Léger on October 18, and to the Japanese ambassador. Li Shizeng, who arrived in Paris at Chiang Kai-shek's personal request to assist Gu in buying supplies through his French connections, said philosophically that they just needed to wait for the coming French elections.[69] But the French government was soon under an unexpected running crossfire of attacks from Japan and America.

On October 20, Charge d'Affaires Arsène-Henry was instructed to press for clear assurances from Tokyo against military action detrimental to France's interests in South China and the Tonking Gulf, given the ban on arms transshipment.[70] On October 20–22, in addition to bombing near Beihai, Japanese planes flew low over Moncai in Tonking, a blatant affront to French rights. Naïvely, in his subsequent protest to the navy and Foreign Ministries in Tokyo, Arsène-Henry argued that the ban on arms transshipment had to be "repaid" by written assurances against further Japanese action in South China; otherwise, it would be lifted.[71] He was sharply rebuked by Minister Delbos for putting France in a weak bargaining position.[72] Arsène-Henry denied the charge vehemently and claimed to have stressed only "continuing France-friendly attitude." He warned that the French situation in the Far East was "extremely vulnerable" faced with Japan's military power and "fierce egoism." He could only hope that "out of chivalry," the Japanese would not act against a trusted old friend, but if they could claim that France had turned against them, France would have no way to restrain them. Indochina's safety should be France's foremost concern in East Asia. If the ban on transshipment were lifted, the Japanese navy would jump at the chance to achieve its plans.[73]

The harm was done. Japanese officials and military linked the arms transshipment to Indochinese security, and for months pestered the French ambassador and the Foreign Affairs Ministry in Paris with detailed claims about breaches of the ban and requests to make local investigations of their own, accompanied by threats to occupy Hainan and to bomb railroads (eventually done at Nanning in early January 1938).[74] At the same time, they flatly refused to recognize French rights over the Spratly and Paracels Islands.[75]

Delbos's irritation at Arsène-Henry's clumsiness with the Japanese was caused by the sudden attack that the arms transshipment ban sparked against France from America. On October 22, 1937, Roosevelt conveyed to Chautemps his personal disapproval of the arms transshipment ban and his wish that the measure be reconsidered.[76] At the opening of the Brussels Conference ten days later, Foreign Minister Delbos was relieved that Norman Davis, Eden, and Spaak agreed that a "most benevolent attitude" be adopted toward Japan to let it accept mediation. However, a new bomb exploded under French feet when Davis rejected France as a member of the implementation subcommittee and as a participant in united naval action in case of Japanese military action against arms transshipment, but he did declare that the United States was ready to relinquish the Philippines for the sake of peace and that France should do the same with Indochina.[77]

The next day, a report of the visit of a former French colonial minister with Arsène-Henry to Roosevelt on November 6 gave the opposite view. Roosevelt mentioned that his message to Chautemps must have been "unpleasant," and said that France had "excessive fears" and should put security considerations behind "moral ones, which at the moment are the prevailing issue of the whole situation. Moreover, is France not aware that any Japanese attack against Hong Kong or Indochina or the Dutch Indies would equally be an attack on the Philippines? In this case, our common interests would be threatened and we would have to defend them together." He stressed his efforts to draw his country out of isolationism and his hope that the improving economic situation in Germany would turn the masses away from Hitler.[78]

Delbos reacted strongly to the confusing American positions. Ambassador Bullitt was summoned and asked about American intentions to relinquish the Philippines, which he readily denied. He was told that the Japanese threat was "not vague and remote" but immediate, with naval vessels around Hainan and the Paracels and an air base being prepared on Hainan. The ban on transshipment was only provisional and excluded substantial supplies already bound for China. Just as American opinion would not support actions based on international solidarity, French opinion would not agree to France taking more risks than other powers in East Asia, when it was excluded from the Brussels subcommittee.[79]

Arsène-Henry was summoned on November 9 by Secretary of State Sumner Welles, who had just seen Roosevelt and wanted to make clear the president's thinking, for fear that the French government would believe that the US fleet would defend Indochina. Roosevelt only meant that if Indochina were attacked by Japan, the United States would be "concerned." Arsène-Henry commented that Roosevelt was "impulsive" and that his words often went beyond his actual thinking; he frequently abandoned proclaimed intentions.[80] He delivered Chautemps's reply to Welles on November 10. Welles reiterated that the US fleet would not defend Indochina. He was not aware of any idea of giving up military protection of the Philippines, even less of France doing the same in Indochina. He declared that the only reason for American opposition to French membership in the Brussels subcommittee was that Italy would have demanded to be a member, and then inevitably the Soviet Union, meaning that Japan was bound to refuse any talks.[81]

Appalled by Roosevelt's attitude, the Council of Ministers decided on November 16 that the American government must be approached jointly by France and Britain to clarify its position in case Japanese reaction to decisions made in Brussels endangered the two countries' interests in East Asia. The ambassador in London was instructed to request Eden's agreement, pointing out that clarification on "readiness to enter the road of solidarity" was needed before the conference resumed its work, given that the Japanese ambassador in Brussels had warned that adoption of the present draft project would have "most serious consequences on Tokyo's relations with London, Washington, and other capitals.[82] Eden's unhelpful reply was that the United States would stay out of the conflict because of Congress's opposition.[83]

French evaluations of military forces in East Asia pointed up the overwhelming power of the Japanese Imperial Headquarters and its "totalitarian program." Though Japan remained dependent on American imports, the "ongoing organization of a totalitarian economy" would permit the warfare planned by the Japanese military. Soviet forces were limited, and Soviet neutrality in the Sino-Japanese conflict made their actual value doubtful. British forces could hardly defend Hong Kong.[84]

The Japanese marines' failed attempt to land on Hainan on January 19, 1938, stirred wide feeling in France. The Indochina Committee, a business lobby that since 1903 had gathered together all major firms and many colonial officials and politicians interested in trade and industry in Indochina and East Asia,[85] voiced loud alarm. Delbos instructed Arsène-Henry to deliver a firm protest to Tokyo with a threat to lift the arms transshipment ban.[86] The Japanese Navy Ministry replied that the Hainan operation was only a "visit and capture of Chinese junks carrying war supplies" and that *"at the moment* the Admiralty has no intention of occupying Hainan."[87]

Despite Arsène-Henry's belief that the ban could protect Indochina for a rather long time, Paris hastened preparations for defense. Although in December 1937 the National Defense Committee had discussed organization of military alliances and staff agreements only for the domestic and Mediterranean fronts, its February 1, 1938, meeting decided to make such agreements for the defense of "all the colonies."[88] A week later, a note from the National Defense Council gave a detailed analysis of current global strategic issues and of the military problems and needs of the French empire. Reinforcements of the most distant possessions had to stress sea communications, combine the defense of French and nearby foreign colonies, and prepare for joint action.[89] The General Plan for the Defense of the Colonies produced on February 17 suggested making East Asia agreements with Britain, the Netherlands, "and if possible" the United States to "guarantee the status quo regarding the possessions of those concerned powers" and military staff agreements to specify the modes of common action to safeguard sea communications and the integrity of their possessions against attacks by their common neighbors. A detailed proposal for a Franco-British joint operation to crush Thailand was ready if Thailand happened to side with the enemy in case of a conflict with Japan.[90]

Military staff talks were initiated in London with Chamberlain's approval, but after Eden's fall on February 20, they lacked the support of the Foreign Office.[91] There were exchanges of information about bombing targets in Germany and Italy, and of other intelligence.[92] However, Chamberlain declared to the House of Commons on March 7 that defense of the homeland was vital; losses overseas did not matter, since if the homeland remained unconquered, they could be recouped later. No illusion was left of military cooperation in East Asia.[93] France therefore insisted, over British and American quibbling, on maintaining limitations for Japan's navy at the conference on the London Naval Treaty in March.[94]

Positive action against Japan was taken in the South China Sea. In December 1937, in the Spratly Islands, where French possession had been established since 1930, a French ship ordered a Japanese fishing company recently established there to abide by Indochinese law and stop using its radio station. Firm protests were addressed to Japan and rejected, with no further action on Japan's side.[95] When a minelayer arrived there on August 8, French sovereignty over the islands was asserted in strong terms to Japan, in Paris and Tokyo, and rejected by the Japanese government on August 22, with a warning to evacuate, on the grounds that Japanese had been there since 1917.[96]

In the Paracels, where the French navy had also found Japanese fishermen with a radio, similar action was taken; Vietnamese fishermen and militiamen were settled there in the spring of 1938, without any communication to the Japanese government.[97] Despite threats by a Japanese cruiser on the spot, official notification of occupation in the name of Indochina was delivered to Japan in early July, with British support, endorsement from the US State Department, and secret Chinese consent.[98] An agreement was sought with London for joint action in the case of a Japanese attack on Hainan or of Thailand joining hands with Japan. The colonies minister added an additional 20,000 troops in Indochina, the largest increase since the time of conquest, and raised a 400-million-franc loan for the defense of the colony, especially for the air force, which was inferior to Thailand's 200 planes.[99]

Japan kept complaining about breaches of the arms transshipment ban. War supplies were in fact reaching China through Indochina; the tonnage of goods to Yunnan increased by one-third in 1938 and doubled in 1939, to nearly 200,000 tons.[100] Supplies were also transported along the Hanoi-

Lanson railroad and by trucks, small junks, carts, and human backs, thanks to the business acumen and patriotic zeal of the Chinese community in Tonking, and through the offices and companies set up by Chinese central and regional government and army services in Haiphong.[101] Receipts from Tonking transshipment taxes doubled in 1938 and increased fivefold by 1939, after the occupation of Guangzhou by the Japanese in October 1938 and the closure of the Yangzi River.[102] The governor general of Indochina did not stop supplies ordered after the ban; he just saw to it that conveying them remained "secret."[103] The Burma Road, opened in late 1938, had limited capacity (less than 10,000 tons in 1939).[104] Land routes through Xinjiang or Mongolia were precarious. Indochina was the essential channel for supplies to China.

Delbos decided to help China to get more. At the League's meetings, he pressed Eden to adjust the amount of help that China could get from individual nations and not limit aid to economic sanctions against Japan.[105] After Cordell Hull's public refusal of an alliance with any power, and of any unilateral supply of arms to China, supplemented with statements that the United States would protect only its nationals and its assets in China, Delbos tried to cool American irritation at the prospect of being drawn into commitment.[106] He nudged Eden to anodyne wording for the League's resolution, but he agreed with Eden and the Soviet Union to talk secretly with China about aid. He felt that France was regaining a position on a par with other big powers in East Asia.[107]

Diplomatic reports pointed out that despite popular emotion over the USS *Panay* Incident, no American military aid could be hoped for in Europe or Asia, except perhaps for some supplies to Britain and its allies. Unlike Hull, Roosevelt disapproved of Chamberlain's rejection of France to bargain with the dictators, but he was pessimistic about the French domestic situation.[108] Delbos was well aware that whether related to China or Europe, London and Washington distrusted the Soviet Union. In the foreign policy debate in the Chamber of Deputies on February 25–26, 1938, his line (which won by 439 votes to 2) was to maintain French loyalty to the League and to the Franco-Soviet Pact, to refuse a choice between London (meaning a four-power pact with Germany) or Moscow. He wanted collaboration with Britain, but as an associate, not a subordinate. As some diplomats put it, "Why should France be a satellite"?[109]

In late March 1938, seeing the German takeover of Austria as an opportunity to draw European democracies closer to China, Chiang Kai-shek directed Gu Weijun to approach the French government again for assistance, while Yu Hanmou, deputy chief of the Fourth War Area in Guangxi, made contact with the French military command in Indochina to discuss cooperation to prevent the Japanese from occupying Hainan.[110] Contracts were signed in April with French banks by the National Economic Commission for the building of railroads from Langson to Nanning and in Sichuan.

Since the American-trained Gu Weijun had not succeeded, Chiang Kai-shek made use of Rajchmann, the League's Polish expert, and his old acquaintance Li Shizeng. Rajchmann and Li were received separately by General Georges, adviser to Defense Minister Daladier. Both said that China was not asking for war supplies, knowing that France could not spare any, but for cooperation. China would guarantee the Indochina border and participate in its defense. In the event of a world war, China would provide France with workers and troops. In return, France would allow transshipment of war supplies, provide China with personnel to assemble and check equipment in Chinese arsenals, and send a military mission to China.

Li emphasized his lifelong friendships with Chiang Kai-shek, T. V. Song, and Sun Yat-sen; he was commissioned to "prepare behind the scenes Sino-French cooperation in the intellectual, economic, and military fields." The planes supplied by France should be assembled in Indochina, air communications from Indochina to South and Central China should be developed, and production of ammunition should be organized in Indochina, partly to stockpile it for future defense and partly to supply Chinese armies immediately. Funds were available from the United Group, which included the Bank of Paris and Pays Bas, the Indochina Bank, the Sino-French Bank, and the Lazare Bank. Regarding the military mission, since Chiang Kai-shek's relations with the Guangxi leaders were now good, it could be sent either to the central or regional command.

Li mentioned that he was soon leaving for China, but Rajchmann could pursue secret negotiations. Rajchmann telegraphed Li to give a positive impression of the talks.[111] Unfortunately, upon arriving in Hong Kong on May 27 and receiving Rajchmann's telegram, Li talked too much. On May 30, Arsène-Henry cabled that based on press reports from Hong Kong and Shanghai, the Japanese press was fulminating about an alleged Sino-French alliance.[112] A furious press campaign followed. The French ambassador received a flood of threatening anonymous letters and petitions. The Japanese navy bombarded Hainan on June 18. Officials returned to the attack on arms transshipment with demands for the French to investigate themselves in Indochina.[113] The diplomat Naggiar, who had used his skills for two years to convince Chiang Kai-shek that there was no possibility for bilateral commitment on the French side, warned strongly against any political pact with China. It would be devoid of substance, it would jeopardize all the efforts to safeguard French interests in occupied China, and it would antagonize China as well as Japan.[114] Bonnet made a negative assessment of the Chinese proposal. He pointed out that the Chinese embassy had not been involved in any way and that Li must be considered as acting privately, without official sanction. He then used Naggiar's arguments against the proposal.[115]

The arrival in Paris in late June of Sun Fo, president of the Legislative Yuan, revived the negotiations. Sun Fo, shrewdly advised by Li Shizeng, made contact only with Daladier, the Colonial Ministry, and the General Staff. On July 1, he secured a cooperation agreement based on the principle that "Chinese victory will guarantee everlasting integrity of Annam," and he got a secret agreement for the supply of personnel and of 10 million francs of heavy war materiel.[116] The ambassador in Moscow, Yang Jie, was sent to Paris in August to look after the financial implementation. Supplies were sent right away, much earlier than those from Britain, which started only in the spring of 1939.[117] In the final agreement, reached in January 1939, supplies were to be paid for by Chinese deliveries of tungsten and other rare minerals to be purchased by the American and British militaries, for a total of £40 million, guaranteed by the Soviet Union. This would meet war needs for two years. The war materiel was to be shipped to Haiphong and carried into China by the French colonial army.[118]

The French military mission of seven officers, headed by General Berger, a highly qualified air officer, arrived in March 1939 and stayed until october 20. According to Chinese testimony, the officers were highly appreciated. They did a good job of training at various military schools and barracks in several military regions and of advising staff on organization, tactics, strategy, and technical skills.[119]

The Japanese takeover of Hainan and the Spratlys in February and March 1939 prompted Chiang Kai-shek to attempt to get more cooperation from a now sympathetic France. He instructed Yang Jie to explore the possibility of a military agreement. A draft from the Military Commission used the main points of Li Shizeng's proposal. China offered ten to fifteen divisions, for which France would provide heavy equipment, for Annam's defense. France would permit transshipment to China, open larger arsenals, and stockpile arms and ammunition in Annam. It would provide China with a large loan.[120] A military cooperation plan was discussed in Hanoi by a delegate of the Liangguang government.

The text sent to Chongqing on May 16, 1939, seemed to the Military Commission too vague on detailed commitments. Further negotiations were held, but they collapsed upon the start of war in Europe in September 1939.[121] The Chinese consul in Hanoi reported obstructions to the transshipment of arms.[122] His complaints were rejected by Berger in November 1939, as rumors spread of local Chinese officials embroiled in illicit profit seeking.[123] Indochina had been helping the transshipment, with large investments to increase transport capacity. The defense minister and colonies minister had pledged to increase supplies to China and to extend a large credit that China could repay with tungsten.[124]

In 1938, French diplomats and policy makers had advanced the idea of a "democratic front" with Britain and America to restrain Japan in China, always careful to let the other two take the formal lead.[125] The United States had belatedly accepted the idea in November 1938, after seeing the damage caused to US trade by Japan's blockade of the China coast and the Yangzi, and by its control over the foreign concessions. Paris endorsed the joint protest about the Yangzi blockade enthusiastically, and other diplomatic efforts, even a show of force at Xiamen, in 1939.[126] France suffered less than the British in their concessions in China, but many of its nationals left. Most French troops in North China were withdrawn in November 1939. On January 25, 1940, a decree gave permission to the Indochina Bank to open branches in London and Yokohama. The London branch was needed to facilitate deals in sterling. The Yokohama branch started operation only in April 1943.[127]

French military and colonial authorities in Indochina were strongly committed to helping China as the only safeguard for the colony. The Plan for General Defense of Indochina adopted in October 1938 focused on defense against Japan and Thailand, instead of against China, as was the case before.[128] American and British inaction over the Japanese takeover of Hainan and the Spratlys and the Singapore conference with British commanders (June 1939),[129] which called for sending troops from Indochina to protect Malaysia but gave no hope of British naval intervention if Tonking was attacked, confirmed the French authorities in support of China through the spring of 1940, despite worries about the defeat of the Guangxi troops near Nanning (November 1939) and Japanese bombing of communication lines in Tonking.

The Nazi-Soviet Pact (August 1939) brought a reversal in policy. Like the British ambassador in Tokyo, Craigie, French diplomats saw Japan as isolated and ripe for detachment from the totalitarians. Cosme, who was appointed ambassador to China in November 1938, suggested in early September that in view of Chongqing's poor military performance and French military weakness in Indochina, the best course in East Asia would be an "entente" with Japan and the Wang Jingwei government. It would guarantee the integrity of French possessions in East Asia, consolidate French interests, and further oppose Japan to the Soviet Union. Chauvel, the head of the Asia-Oceania desk, who hated Cosme, refuted the latter's argument as a "purely theoretical view." He made many points: Wang Jingwei had as yet no government and wanted to annul the unequal treaties; Japan would occupy French concessions; South China belonged to Chongqing; Japan did not want to get involved in the European conflict and would not oppose Russia; France could not reverse its policy because of its ties with Britain and America.[130] Nevertheless, a few days later, the Ministry of Foreign Affairs published a communiqué accommodating Japan, which triggered strong protests from China.[131] Daladier set things right. On September 24, he telegraphed Cosme that Wang Jingwei's government would be "only another Manchukuo." The United States supported Chiang Kai-shek. There should be a union between Wang and Chiang.[132]

However, steps to appease Japan, whose ambassador in Paris had been withdrawn after the occupation of Hainan, were taken. In early September, Tokyo was notified of French willingness to solve some pending issues and to hold talks on more general problems. The Japanese government agreed and appointed Sawada Shigeru as ambassador to Paris, "the best candidate that France could have thought of." Sawada's instructions were limited. He could only renew demands to stop supplies to China, with Japanese bombings adding local pressure. In February and March 1940, the Japanese government seemed to be considering a nonaggression agreement. Although talks went on for some time, the approach met with an unfavorable reception in Paris and Hanoi.[133]

A major crisis came with the French collapse on the Western front. On June 16, 1940, Roosevelt's brief and evasive reply to Reynaud's pathetic call for help left no hope.[134] Sumner Welles and Roosevelt sternly advised the French not to hand over their fleet to Germany and to continue the fight from their colonies. As for the French islands in the Pacific and Caribbean, if local governments were not given extended powers, American public opinion would demand that they be put under American trusteeship.[135] At the Foreign Affairs Ministry, Secretary-General Charles-Roux told American ambassador Biddle that the United States, a noncombatant, should keep silent. Minister Baudouin instructed the ambassador in Washington to proclaim that "France is not a culprit, but a victim."

Baudouin had extensive experience in East Asia as general manager of the Indochina Bank; his wife was half Vietnamese. On July 1, 1940, his instruction to ambassadors in Shanghai, Tokyo, and Bangkok was that the armistice did not apply to East Asia; the German Reich had told Japan of its lack of interest in Asia. French action in the region "may keep a certain autonomy from developments in Europe." It must maintain as far as possible French positions there until there was a general peace. Each problem should be approached empirically, taking into account the particular facts in East Asia: that there was "actual solidarity with Britain" and that the United States wanted to maintain the status quo. France "should fall in with arrangements that might divert the Japanese threat" while keeping "close ties with Britain and the United States" and getting Chongqing to understand.[136]

France did not have much leeway to negotiate. On June 14, 1940, the day Paris fell to the Germans, General Catroux, the governor general of Indochina, was advised by the French embassy in Tokyo that Japan was preparing a combined land and sea attack. Heavy bombing of transport routes resumed, as did demands from the Japanese army that the border with China be closed completely. On June 16, he decided on his own to forbid all transshipment of gasoline, and he notified Japan through the embassy in Tokyo, to no avail. On the evening of June 19, the day the French government appointed its delegates to negotiate an armistice with Germany, two telegrams from the Tokyo embassy conveyed to him the Japanese ultimatum for a complete ban of transshipment of war supplies to China; the deadline was June 20. On the advice of Arsène-Henry that it was "the only possibility to perhaps save Indochina," Catroux accepted. The colonies minister was shocked by Catroux's surrender and by his blunt explanation of his independent action.[137]

Indochina's troops had been increased from 32,000 in 1937 to 90,000; most were infantry, and only 14,500 were Europeans. Many of the officers were inadequate, and their loyalty could not be fully trusted. Naval forces totaled three small vessels; air defenses, seventeen planes.[138] Catroux claimed that he had no forces to resist, that communication with the government was too slow and uncertain for him to wait, that he was determined to keep Indochina for France, and that he was trying to avoid war with Japan by negotiating and playing for time.[139] At the meeting of the Council of Ministers on June 25, it was decided to replace Catroux with Admiral Decoux, commander of the Far East Naval Force in Saigon.[140]

The reasons for Catroux's summary dismissal seem to have been mixed: fear of disobedience; recent bad experiences with de Gaulle; distrust of his proclaimed pro-British feelings; and retribution for what some thought was an unnecessary surrender. Decoux took over from Catroux on July 20. On June 28, Decoux and Catroux met in Saigon with the British commander, Admiral Noble, who agreed to safeguard French shipping east of Singapore and enable Indochina to continue trading. In the hope of a formal guarantee of Indochina's integrity under French sovereignty, Catroux made on his own several important concessions to the head of the Japanese mission, General Nishihara: He agreed to stop all traffic from China to Tonking, even having a portion of the track lifted on the Yunnan railroad. He provided supplies and assistance for the Japanese army in Guangxi. On July 10, Catroux informed Arsène-Henry that Nishihara had offered a military alliance.[141] Japanese sources show that the idea of a defensive alliance against China, in exchange for a Japanese pledge on the territorial integrity of Indochina, was raised by Catroux on July 4. On July 7, Nishihara received agreement from Tokyo, on condition that Japanese troops be stationed in Indochina and use military facilities. Negotiations were conducted with Catroux, then Decoux, who both refused stubbornly to give in.[142]

An internal note from the Asia-Oceania desk, dated July 13, suggests a clear line: there was no need to worry about American convenience, since Washington was now focused on Europe and would not give France any guarantees in East Asia; Britain was now hostile and hampering Indochina's trade; the road was open for talks with Japan on the basis of Nishihara's proposal, even if the Japanese general had probably acted without government permission; it should be made clear to the Japanese ambassador that no general agreement could be obtained in Indochina; Japan did not want a proper alliance with any foreign power, but France could obtain a nonaggression pact including mutual recognition of the two parties' interests in East Asia. France had to be careful that even if Japan was now a "decisive factor" in the area, China was the "neighbor and hinterland" of Indochina and the "permanent element." And "no Chinese would ever be grateful to France in the future for furthering Japanese military operations in China." Only "negative measures" should be taken, such as an embargo on transshipment. On "positive measures" such as opening Indochinese territory to Japanese military transport, a pledge for the future should be obtained in exchange for facilities. And, finally, Japanese were looking for contacts in the economic field. A Japanese economic mission would visit Hanoi. Economic collaboration with Japan was necessary for Indochina because of the interruption of trade with China, the British colonies, and Europe, even to the extent that Indochina be integrated into the Japanese economic system including Manchukuo and occupied China.[143]

The note shows that frustration about American and British policy had accumulated for several years, exacerbated by the British destruction on July 4, with Roosevelt's loud applause, of the disarmed French fleet at Oran.[144] Combined with distrust of the Soviets and magnified by the German-Soviet Pact, the frustration produced among well-informed French policy makers the illusion that Japanese partnership could be an alternative. Baudouin met Ambassador Sawada on July 15, 1940. Foreign Minister Matsuoka started the negotiation with Arsène-Henry in Tokyo on August 1 with harsh demands and threats.[145] Desperate but hopeless, the French appealed for help to Washington. On August 30, an agreement was signed in Tokyo. According to the agreement, the Vichy government recognized Japan's political and economic predominance in East Asia, gave Japan preferential economic treatment in Indochina, and agreed to the stationing of Japanese troops in Tonking. Japan promised to "respect" French sovereignty over Indochina and to preserve the territorial integrity of the country. On September 22, an agreement between Decoux and Nishihara allowed for the establishment of Japanese air bases in Tonking, with Japanese garrisons to protect them. When Thailand attacked

Indochina, Japan imposed its mediation in February 1941, with the result that a large section of territory in Laos and Cambodia was transferred to Thailand. In July 1941, under the threat of outright conquest, Japan compelled the Vichy government to accept the establishment of air bases in Cambodia and Cochinchina, and of naval bases at Camranh and Saigon, as well as the stationing of troops in southern Indochina.

Just after Pearl Harbor, on December 8, 1941, the Japanese extracted from Decoux an agreement to cooperate in the "common defense" of Indochina. It guaranteed the preservation of public order and the security of Japanese communications in the country. The Japanese forces were entitled, if necessary, to assist in this task. Decoux was able only to avoid giving direct assistance to Japanese military operations and subjecting French forces to direct subordination to Japanese command. Japanese civilians in Indochina were subject to French law and jurisdiction. Free France had relentlessly criticized Vichy policy in Indochina, but it had not declared that it was at war with Japan. Only after Pearl Harbor did it do so.

Conclusion

Partnership had quickly turned into grievous, but accepted, subjection, a situation that isolated France further from the ABCD (American, British, Chinese, and Dutch) front and isolated Indochina, both militarily and politically, in the war theater, turning it into a field of disputed allegiance and sovereignty among the victors.

Since 1931, French policy had been involved in the Sino-Japanese conflict out of rational motivation, not out of any emotional drive nurtured by nationalism. Even when the Japanese embassy in Paris paid lavish sums of money to journalists, Japan received limited coverage and seldom aroused displays of protest or sympathy in public opinion. There is no evidence from archival records that business lobbies put special pressure on the government regarding any particular issue. Decisions were prepared in the administrative sphere, by civilians and military personnel, metropolitan officials, and personnel en poste; often they were simply endorsed by political figures in government. These personnel had a relatively large network of information and had frequent exchanges with leaders of civil society; they did integrate various private interests into their thinking, whether financial, industrial, or commercial. An important consideration for the top policy makers in the Foreign Affairs Ministry and Colonies Ministry, though rarely explicitly stated, was the fact that Indochina played a substantial part in France's national economy. Although its finances were heavily in deficit and depended on metropolitan allocations, its trade had a large surplus which compensated for part of the metropolitan trade deficit at the time. Keeping Indochina under French sovereignty was not simply a matter of political prestige but also a matter of making a profit in a global economy.

Domestic political instability and economic depression during the 1931–1941 period seriously impeded the emergence of any imaginative French political action in East Asia, even more so than in Europe. The pacifist trend of collective security died after Herriot's last cabinet. The common front with the Soviet Union was blocked both by Stalin's reluctance and by American and British opposition. Neither Chinese nor Japanese partnership elicited wide and lasting support among French officialdom itself. All these factors combined together to mitigate against France taking a strong and consistent position during a period when China and Indochina were increasingly threatened by Japanese expansion.

2 British Diplomacy and Changing Views of Chinese Governmental Capability across the Sino-Japanese War, 1937–1945

RANA MITTER

On October 18, 1946, M. E. Dening, assistant undersecretary of state at the British Foreign Office, sent a memo to Ernest Bevin, the foreign secretary:

> Up to the outbreak of the war in Europe in 1939 Great Britain may be said to have occupied the dominant position in China. Since then, a great change has taken place and our place is now occupied by the United States, to whom China looks primarily alike in the cultural, diplomatic, economic, financial, and military fields. We ourselves abandoned our privileged position in China with the signature of the Treaty of 11 January 1943, renouncing extraterritorial rights and ancillary privileges, and our interests in China today are purely commercial and cultural. As a result of the war therefore the US have replaced the United Kingdom as the Western Power capable of exercising principal influence and pressure in China. We are interested in the political situation in China only insofar as unstable conditions hamper the development of our trade and cultural relations, and also to the extent that, if China were to come under the domination of the Soviet Union, this would be liable to threaten our position in South East Asia where there are large Chinese communities and also in Burma and India.[1]

Dening's note to Bevin seems to summarize the extent to which Britain's status in China had fallen by the end of World War II. At the outbreak of war in 1937, Britain was a world empire that had undoubted power in China, whether through extraterritorial rights, volume of trade, or institutions such as the Maritime Customs Service or the Shanghai Municipal Council. By 1945, these realities had either disappeared or crumbled significantly. The eight years of total war between China and Japan had changed the balance of power in East Asia beyond recognition.

The end of the war with Japan meant the rise of two great new empires in Asia, those of the United States and the Soviet Union, and the end of two others, those of Japan and Britain. Within the field of Chinese studies, the start of the war and the end of the Japanese empire have been well documented. The ending of Britain's role has been far less widely examined. Britain's role in China has been regarded as secondary to its imperial role in India or in Africa, and the story of Indian independence in 1945 to 1947 has seemed far more central to Britain's own sense of identity than the loss of status several thousand miles further east. From the Chinese side, the story of Britain's downgrade in status has been a minor footnote in a narrative that leads to the victory of the Chinese Communist Party in 1949.

It would be unfortunate to lose sight of the significance of the shift that came between 1937 and 1945. For it was through conflict with the British, not just Japanese imperialism, that much of the narrative of modern Chinese nationalism had been formed, from the Opium Wars to the May Thirtieth Movement. British attitudes in the eight years from the war's start to its end reveal a more complex and nuanced set of views than has been realized.

This essay uses one particular set of views: those of British Foreign Office officials serving in the 1930s and 1940s. Although the analysis of these views must be differentiated from those of the settler community or the Maritime Customs Service, it gives insight into the ambivalence that marked the "official" British mind as it moved from the attitude of widespread contempt for China that marked the aftermath of the Boxer Uprising to an ambivalent acceptance of China as one of the Big Five powers only four decades later. Not surprisingly, perhaps, analysis suggests that there was no smooth movement from contempt to acceptance.

What is also clear is that the war with Japan was crucial to the shift in attitudes. This chapter compares British attitudes in the very first months of the war and the very last months and the aftermath. In 1937, Britain was developing a change of attitude toward China that was still shaped along a largely British agenda, despite the new power of Chinese nationalism. By 1945, it was clear that American and Soviet attitudes, along with those of a more prestigious China, meant that Britain could no longer call the shots. The war in China was a turning point in Britain's sense of itself as an imperial power.

The Outbreak of War

British attitudes at the outbreak of war reflected an ambivalence toward Chiang Kai-shek, present since 1927. From 1926 onward the British had been among the first to see that the nature of the Western interaction with the Chinese would have to change. As will be seen, there were variations of opinion in how far and how fast those changes should come. The outbreak of war in summer 1937 saw a continuation of the ambivalence on the part of the British officials about the nature of the Nationalist regime and of Chiang Kai-shek as leader.

First Secretary Robert Howe sent a message from the British embassy in Nanjing on October 5, 1937, relating to the Japanese peace terms on offer at the time. The terms were rejected, but the description Howe used of Chiang was indicative: "It is a difficult matter to gather definite impression from a Chinese of Chiang Kai-shek's stamp who is slow to make up his mind. . . . Madame Chiang Kai-shek . . . is of a more volatile temperament."[2] This sort of language, even from an official sympathetic to China, suggested a continuation of stereotypes about the Chinese character from the mid-nineteenth century onward.

There was also an early, if grudging, realization that the policy of resistance to Japan was real. Howe noted, "The difficulty which I found in Nanking was that no-one in authority appeared to be able or willing to formulate terms which would serve as a basis for an approach to the Japanese either for an armistice or peace."[3] On November 27, Howe went on to say that "the unwillingness to surrender is practically confined to the military and intelligentsia, whilst the agricultural and mercantile mass of population are apathetic and would welcome peace on almost any terms."[4]

Part of the sensitivity was that the outbreak of war put British power and goodwill on the spot. Nationalist China wanted assistance from Britain but seemed unlikely to get it. One embassy official wrote to Foreign Minister Eden from Hankou on December 17, 1937, that the Chinese government showed "resigned acceptance of the unpalatable fact that there is no immediate hope of foreign intervention. In no case have I heard a sharp criticism of England's attitude. . . . Regret is nevertheless expressed that we should not be in a position to defend our vital political and economic interests in the Far East which Chinese are convinced will be entirely obliterated once the Japanese gain control over China." A memo the next day debated the wisdom of sending the Royal Navy to the Far East:

Had there been a powerful British fleet in Far Eastern waters in July, Japan would never have dared to ride rough shod over all our established rights in Shanghai for the purpose of attacking and destroying the Chinese Government. . . . Japan was admitted to share in these privileges [within the International Settlement, by the British and the Americans] and His Majesty's government are entitled therefore to insist that she does not grossly abuse them.

This assessment went on to review the deteriorating situation in China in terms of British interests. It noted that the situation in the Yangzi Valley was to be treated as part of an international situation. However, in southern China, and particularly around Hong Kong, it was made clear that "it will be necessary to regard the matter solely from the standpoint of British interests." In particular, the establishment of "puppet governments" in the surrounding areas was a major concern to the Foreign Office. The summary went on to state that Britain should "restore the status quo in the Yangzi Valley and South China, . . . namely a regime under the control of the Chinese Government providing for the open door." In addition, Britain should "protect particular British interests in North China, but otherwise stand aside."

On January 24, 1938, Sir John Pratt, who would become known as a deeply pro-Chinese figure during the Cold War era, reflected on the balancing of Britain's interests in China and Japan. He saw the main aims of British policy as being "to defend threatened British interests while the conflict lasts" and also to make sure that any settlement should "afford the maximum opportunity to British trade, industry, and finance." Pratt did not give much credence to Japanese assurances that they would maintain the open door in an occupied China. Britain's opportunity, he observed, would come from hoping that China would look to the United Kingdom as one possible "counter-weight" against Japan. He condemned those members of the Shanghai settler community who either praised the Japanese action or at least found themselves angling for influence after an assumed Chinese defeat. "Great Britain desires to see a prosperous and united China," Pratt noted; this made British interests wholly at odds with those of Japan. He deplored the desire in 1935, at the time of the Leith-Ross mission, to "hunt with the hare—develop China—and ride with the hounds—co-operate with Japan."

Pratt was unusual among British officials in arguing that "national honour" was at stake in China; most officials regarded the conflict as marginal to core British interests. Yet his comments are part of a wider tone of alarm that Britain was unable to defend its own interests. The Foreign Office was operating in the context of an increasingly worrying world for the British Empire: Germany was becoming dominant in Europe, and policy on India had made the subcontinent a sensitive subject in domestic politics. A crisis in China had become a test of British willingness to stay engaged.

Attitudes toward the Nationalists had to take into account the reality that understandings of the nature of the Chinese government had had to change in the past decade. Douglas MacKillop, then on the Foreign Office's Far Eastern staff and later to become head of its Refugee Department in the aftermath of the war, wrote to Eden from the temporary capital at Hankou on January 24, 1938, stating that he believed that the territory the Nationalist government would be able to hold on to was limited and unlikely to bear the cost of waging modern war. Another key term was "rationally": MacKillop doubted that "the task of rationally organising remaining territory" was possible for the Nationalists.[5]

MacKillop's assessment may seem a straightforward comment on the damage being done to the Chinese state by the war. But it is important to remember how recently British attitudes had come around to the idea that modern and rational government was even a possibility for China. Thirty years previously Britain had been involved in crushing the Boxer Uprising, which lived on in British (and Western) memory as a deeply irrational attempt to defy the natural order of imperialism and openness to trade. The Republic of China itself had only a quarter century of history behind it when war broke out in 1937, and the Nationalists themselves were regarded with great apprehension by the Western powers. The context means that the achievement of the Nationalists in forcing the British to take them seriously in the years leading up to war was a significant one. It also meant that the new attitude, which sought to assess the Nationalists as a meaningful and powerful government, was shot through with elements of the older, more contemptuous, attitude that had still not been fully cast off.

This tension between new and old attitudes is sometimes visible in the writing of the same person, as in the follow-up note on January 31, 1938, from MacKillop at Hankou:

My personal view goes further. The strongest impression which one forms here is of the supineness, incapacity, disunion, irresponsibility and ill-founded optimism of the Chinese Government—optimism based almost wholly on hope that other countries including prominently our own will be willingly or (?unwillingly) involved in war and that a great catastrophe will save something out of the wreck for the Chinese government.

It can be stated fairly in their defence that their machinery of government and even their centre of gravity has been forcibly displaced, that they have never before been called upon to discharge full normal obligations of centralised sovereignty over this territory, that it is a difficult country to administer on modern lines, and that they are deprived of foreign advice and of the wealth of Shanghai to which they formerly had access. But the real question for us is surely not respective deserts of blame or sympathy but whether they are capable of existing. . . . In my opinion answer is that they will disintegrate as soon as they are forced to leave Hankow. . . .

I have spoken of Chinese Government and not of China. Latter unlike the former is probably indestructible.[6]

This frustrated note contains a variety of themes that show the contradictory attitudes of British officials. The adjectives used—supine, irresponsible, ridiculously optimistic—do not, on first glance, seem to relate to specific complaints but rather to reflect a long-standing assumption that Chinese governments were incapable of acting in a responsible way. The final statement, that China would last while its government did not, while seemingly positive, is in fact a typical example of the idea that in some way modern government was alien to a more traditional and unchanging China. The idea that the Nationalist government was an indigenous product of a new, modern Chinese identity still seemed hard to swallow.

However, the second paragraph does reflect a change in view that recognizes that the problems of the Nationalists were not all of their own making. Dealing with a specific issue—the forced evacuation of the government to the interior—MacKillop made a more specific set of criticisms: that a would-be modernizing government had been forced to abandon its sources of finance and foreign expertise. However, this threw him onto uncomfortable ground because it devolved blame from the Nationalist government and pointed out the inadequacies of the British response. In effect, MacKillop was finding excuses for British inaction.

Perhaps the most important thing to note was that MacKillop's assessment was wrong. The Nationalist government may have been weak for all the reasons outlined, but it did withdraw from Wuhan (Hankou) successfully, and it did survive at Chongqing for the next seven years, even though it was almost destroyed in the process. In practice, one can see why the British government would have been unlikely in early 1938 to offer any sort of practical assistance to China. The European situation was darkening, and in a few months, prime minister Neville Chamberlain would make his ill-fated trip to Munich to appease Hitler. The last thing Britain needed was a war in China. But MacKillop's note, precisely because of its self-contradictory tone, betrays the unease in the mind of the diplomats on the ground.

The British military attaché in Hankou, W. A. Lovat-Fraser, sent a similarly worded note on February 2, 1938, which warned that the "Chinese army is irreparably smashed and air force is eliminated"; that the government, "most of whom are men with unsavoury records" was trying to draw out resistance so as to attract British help; and that

the Chinese are not serious about fighting our war and have done nothing but harm to our interests having brought about serious international situation in Shanghai and gravely jeopardised our commercial interests in Central China.

The Central Government should therefore receive no encouragement to continue.[7]

The idea that the Chinese defense should be assessed in terms of its effect on British trade interests was no doubt widespread but proved too much for Howe in Shanghai, who noted to Eden: "While I feel that you should be in possession of these views I do not agree with them." Howe's views, which were generally more favorable toward Chiang, found favor within the Foreign Office (for instance, with Charles Orde, the head of the Far Eastern section). Howe's note of February 3, 1938, suggested that the Guangxi generals would be likely to try and resist even if Chiang sought agreement with the Japanese, and that such a government continuing to resist a largely occupied China would make "rational organization" of this territory possible for a rump resistance government. His suggestion was not to supply "special facilities," but also not to let neutrality restrict the Nationalists' ability to receive arms.

The difference among British officials about how to assess Nationalist China's wartime effort was represented by the views of MacKillop, who was more negative about the Chinese government's chances, and those of Howe, who remained more positive. The division in their views became clear in messages sent on February 4 and 7, 1938. MacKillop declared openly the contradictory element in British policy that had been implied in his earlier assessment:

The vice of our postwar China policy has been its duality. We have been fellow members with China of League of Nations and at the same time we have exercised within her territory "simulacrum" of sovereignty which has been incompatible with such fellowship and yet has never been . . . based on a force sufficient to make it in fact what it purported to be.[8]

Howe retorted:

Duality is more apparent than real. . . .
    Extra-territorial system (Mr. MacKillop's "simulacrum of Sovereignty") was imposed on China when she was not in a position to resist it. That is in fact the only condition under which extra-territoriality can endure. We have, since the war, not only been adopting a more liberal attitude on moral grounds, but have been uncomfortably aware that China was growing up and that her continuous subjection would need the use of force which we did not want to use. We have been gradually relaxing our grip as a result of the policy deliberately adopted in 1926. . . . Our China policy is perfectly consistent and coherent.[9]

Howe's views found favor over MacKillop's at the Foreign Office, as Eden made clear on February 10, 1938. On March 1, 1938, Howe took over from Orde as head of the Far Eastern Department. In general, attitudes continued to waver, but grudging admiration for Chinese resistance began to emerge in the documents sent as the war spread. The following note from Sir Archibald Clark Kerr, the British ambassador in China, to the new foreign secretary, Lord Halifax, on April 29, 1938, gave grudging credit to Chiang Kai-shek at the outbreak of conflict:

[Chiang] has now become the symbol of Chinese unity, which he himself has so far failed to achieve, but which the Japanese are well on the way to achieving for him. . . . The days when Chinese people did not care who governed them seem to have gone. . . . My visit to Central China from out of the gloom and depression of Shanghai has left me stimulated and more than disposed to believe that provided the financial end can be kept up Chinese resistance may be so prolonged and effective that in the end the Japanese effort may be frustrated. . . . Chiang Kai-shek is obstinate and difficult to deal with. . . . Nonetheless apart from Dr Kung and his follies they are making in their muddling way a good job of things in extremely difficult circumstances.[10]

Clark Kerr's comment is typical of the mixture of dismissal and respect that marked British attitudes. Britain had come around to the realization that the old imperialist ways were no longer acceptable. The ambiguity was also because China occupied an odd status in British eyes. Unlike India, it had its own sovereign and autonomous government, yet like colonies, it was not wholly sovereign, with extraterritoriality and the maintenance of the Foreign Concessions in Shanghai as part of the continuing imperial presence.

The End of War and Its Aftermath

The war both exacerbated and smoothed out these tendencies. The performance of Chiang's armies had not impressed the British, which led them to come down hard on Chiang for reasons that often had as much to do with propaganda as with military performance.[11] A sense of realism also propelled them to understand that a postwar China could not be expected to reestablish many of the trappings of imperialism that had continued to hold firm all the way to Pearl Harbor in late 1941. In that sense, the war was indeed the making of a sovereign China, even while it was the unmaking of Nationalist China. The turning point was the signing of the new treaties of 1943, which ended extraterritoriality, abolished the foreign concessions of Shanghai, and finally established that a postwar China would be sovereign and equal: 101 years after the Opium Wars, the "century of humiliation" had finally come to an end.

British leaders did not share the American conviction that a newly sovereign China should be seen as a powerful actor in Asia. Both Churchill and the new prime minister, Attlee, expressed their doubts about the future role of China.[12] Yet the post-1945 settlement meant that Britain now had to deal with China as a sovereign power with equal status in the United Nations. Britain had also suffered the humiliation of its power being visibly lost during the Japanese occupation of Southeast Asia from 1941 to 1945.[13] In this atmosphere, attitudes toward Chinese participation in the new international order had to change, yet the ambiguities of the prewar era remained, and there was controversy within the Foreign Office about how postwar policy toward China should proceed.

Even before the war in Asia had ended, J. C. Sterndale-Bennett, head of the Far Eastern section at the Foreign Office, submitted a long memorandum in favor of active British engagement with China in a way that would take account of the newly powerful role of the United States.[14] Sterndale-

Bennett was keen to stress that Britain should maintain an imperial role and make it clear to the United States that it did so for supposedly unselfish reasons, picking up the pieces after the Japanese surrender. His views provide a useful insight into the way in which attitudes had changed with regard to China.

The general assessment of China's record late in the war shows some of the ambivalence visible in 1937–1938. Sterndale-Bennett seemed to show a certain pleasure in recording American views of the Chiang regime as "a moribund and reactionary regime" by late 1944, after the Ichigo Campaign had taken over large parts of central and southern China, but he also admitted that the "Chinese Government reacted not unsuccessfully" with a series of ministerial reshuffles.[15] Sterndale-Bennett's note used a quotation from Sir Eric Teichman (who had had long service in the British consular service) in which he stated explicitly what had become true during the course of the war:

Comparing China's foreign policy in 1943 with her attitude of ten years earlier, nothing is more striking than her dependence on America and acceptance of American leadership. . . . China looks primarily to America, not Britain, to defeat Japan . . . and to build up the great new China after the war is won. On our side, because we are not in a position to do otherwise, we have accepted this condition and have abdicated from the position of leadership which we have occupied in China for the past hundred years.[16]

It was probably an exaggeration to suggest that Britain had had the "leadership" role in China even prior to the 1930s. To suggest that the country would fall easily under US leadership was to misunderstand the nature of the Nationalist government and of Chiang's postwar intentions. Chiang did not seek to replace British influence with American influence: rather, he sought to create an independent China that would balance the newly emergent American and Soviet empires against each other.[17] Yet much of the discussion did seem to be along the lines that some sort of return to the status quo ante could be achieved. There were aspects of the China market in which "British firms, having greater experience and commercial goodwill, could successfully compete with America." Sterndale-Bennett believed that there was a specific "political and strategic interest" for Britain in China, and that an "unfriendly" China could cause immense problems in Southeast Asia. He seemed convinced that Chinese attitudes toward Britain would be warm because of Britain's "continued support of the Kuomintang Government, from 1926 when we took the lead in meeting China's claim to Treaty revision, down to 1943, when the treaty relinquishing extraterritorial rights was signed." However, Sterndale-Bennett also detected a "latent xenophobia" in postwar China and felt that Britain should seek to counter it.[18]

These views are an intriguing combination of recognition that a new situation had arisen in China and a blind set of assumptions that at some level, very little had changed. The idea that the British presence was, overall, regarded as a benign one that had been instrumental in modernizing China was based on a set of presumptions that few Chinese would share. Reaction to the record of British imperialism, after all, was central to the development of Chinese nationalism, whether it was in Shanghai's streets or in remembrance of the many *guochi* (national humiliations) that marked the Chinese republican calendar. Chiang had, of course, sought British assistance to play off Japan before 1937, and after that date in the hope that China would gain military support. However, the wartime period had been marked by poor relations between the British commanders and the Chinese, and while British figures such as Joseph Needham had made significant contributions to the war effort, Britain was seen as an unreliable ally at best. The distance between being an imperialist conqueror and a wartime ally was simply too great to overcome in such a short time. The note did put forward ways in which the United Kingdom could help the postwar Chinese state: from Royal Air Force collaboration to provision of consumer goods, to looser credit, to technical scholarships. These had some attractiveness but were relatively limited in comparison with the massive crisis that China faced. The hope that they could provide "assistance in the rebuilding of the Chinese customs service," where "British influence was previously predominant"[19] seems to fly in the face of reality: the inspector general, L. K. Little, was an American, and it was clear that the days of foreign influence within the customs were numbered.

China as a Great Power?

British diplomatic documents from the end of the war echo a strong sense in the British newspapers that the status of China as a major power was "unreal," and this sense recurred frequently in British statements emerging from the negotiations in the immediate postwar period. For the British, there was a difference between the admission of China into an equal status with other states and its emergence as a power of global significance in terms of Roosevelt's concept of the "Four Policemen." Even during the Potsdam Conference in July 1945, before the war in Asia was over, the Foreign Office made it clear that China's new status was something they found problematic:

The introduction of China into the detail of European peace making is very questionable. . . . China is not a party to the Four-Power assumption of supreme authority over Germany. . . . The Soviet Government are unlikely to agree to her inclusion as a principal party on the Council for all purposes. It was suggested instead that China should be "nominally a member of the Council" [and] she should not have a vote on final decisions about Germany, although she might take part in the discussions.[20]

Opposition to the involvement of China in the European talks was not total. On August 11, the Foreign Office even declared that China "is likely to be more of a help than a hindrance" on European matters.[21] However, the new prominence of China did raise hackles elsewhere. On August 1, 1945, days before the end of the war, the Australian prime minister, Ben Chifley, wrote to Viscount Addison, Attlee's dominions secretary, complaining that the inclusion of China (and also France) at the top table for discussion of the postwar settlement meant that Australia should also be allowed to participate: "Australia can fairly stand alongside either of these Powers, and in terms of European war commitments and postwar interests in Europe has more than equal right to effective participation than China."[22]

There was still an undeniable sense of the colonial about some of the British suggestions. On August 30, 1945, L. H. (Leo) Lamb, in the embassy at Chongqing, wrote to G. V. Kitson, head of the China Department in London, and suggested that it would be wise to "try and take advantage of the chaotic state in which the Ministry of Foreign Affairs is likely to find itself to force the pace while they may be too disorganised by the move."[23] Kitson also noted on August 14 with asperity that the American desire not to be seen as engaging in "collusion" with the British over carving out new trade rights in China was somewhat hypocritical considering that the "extra'lity" [extraterritoriality] treaty had also been done under "collusion." Kitson further argued that the Americans were taking over the British commercial position in China but refusing to acknowledge British interests in the process.[24] Views on the role of China as a market to be carved out, rather than as a trading partner, had not yet disappeared.

Kitson sent a memo to the Foreign Office on March 1, 1946, in which he acknowledged that the war had deeply disrupted the old British network of consulates in China. He advised waiting to see how the postwar geography developed:

Until a trend away from the big cities and back to the interior towns becomes sufficiently marked to consider re-opening Consulates in some of the interior places, the most we can probably do is (a) to encourage British firms in China to send their representatives on frequent visits to interior places to spy out the land and collect orders; and (b) to send members of the staff . . . in the existing posts on frequent tours of interior places to report on trade possibilities and to recommend, where necessary, the opening of a new consular post.[25]

In particular, Kitson saw Manchuria as an area where new consular posts would be needed after the thirteen-year gap, not least to prevent the monopolizing by Russia of the trade in the region. His words and tone seemed to echo an older British attitude.

The inability of the empires to place a non-European people within the higher councils of world development proved problematic. Ironically, this was an echo of the situation that Japan had found itself in. In the early twentieth century, Japan's status as the only non-Western empire of substance meant that it found itself simultaneously admired, feared, and despised in the West. China was now to find itself in a similar situation.

The New Cold War World: Britain and China

British attitudes to the newly sovereign Nationalist China were shaped in the last months of the war, and its immediate aftermath, by the election of a Labour government with Ernest Bevin as its foreign secretary. The change of government coincided with the first jockeying of the Cold War era for influence in Europe and Asia, and British actions during the time were heavily influenced by the idea that their presence in China might be used to find a position of advantage between the United States and the Soviet Union. China also became a symbol of how the British found dealing with both powers, but particularly the Soviet Union, increasingly difficult as 1945 turned into 1946.

On September 16, 1945, T. V. Soong and Wang Shijie joined Bevin at Chequers, the prime minister's country residence, for lunch and conversation. In general, their conversation seems to have reflected the changing priorities of the Cold War world. The report made by Foreign Office officials noted that "Dr Wang showed much interest in the atomic bomb, which he thought had undoubtedly brought the Japanese to surrender. It had been for that reason greatly welcomed in China."[26] The two sides went on to share their impressions of the Russians, with Bevin (who had always been a strong anti-Communist) declaring his resentment at the way in which Soviet foreign minister Molotov had tried to pressure Britain, and Soong noting that his own negotiations with the Russians had been "very tough," although he claimed to be satisfied with their outcome.

The Molotov question became more and more significant in the autumn of 1945 as the Council of Foreign Ministers, set up to deal with the problems of the postwar settlement, started to get to work. Repeatedly, it appeared to be the Soviet Union and not the Western powers that was attempting to downgrade the importance of China. This provided the British with an unexpected opportunity to see themselves as de facto allies of the Chinese, despite their reservations about whether China could be seen as a country of genuine significance. At the London meeting of the Council of Foreign Ministers in Lancaster House on September 22, 1945,

Molotov had declared that "China had nothing to do with Finland or the Balkan countries" and therefore should be excluded from discussing them.[27] Molotov applied the same strictures to France. He objected strongly to the idea that France and China should join the Big Three in the postwar settlement. A Foreign Office memo on September 23, 1945, sent in the name of Attlee and Bevin and marked "top secret," took issue with Molotov's position. The memo noted that "M Molotov considers that the decision of the Council on September 11th was a violation of the Potsdam agreement . . . and that in future . . . China would be excluded altogether and France from all the treaties except the Italian."

The memo went on in Attlee's voice: "This does not accord with my understanding of the spirit and intention of the decision arrived at Potsdam" and noted that such a reversal of the decision would not only be hard to achieve but would also "cause grave offence to France and China and be completely misunderstood here by the public and Parliament." The note ended waspishly with the observation that "after all it is peace we are endeavouring to establish, which is more important than procedure."[28]

The matter was followed up in cabinet. The cabinet ended up with a "general agreement that we should not yield to the Soviet demand for the exclusion of France and China, and that nothing would be gained by prolonging the present Conference." This was followed by a suggestion that a new UN conference, in which the dominions could have a voice, would be an acceptable alternative, not least because it would "strengthen our position vis à vis the United States." The wider point was made that "we should make it clear to the United States Government that it was impossible for us to work with them if they constantly took action in the international sphere, affecting our interests, without prior consultation with us."

The reluctance of Moscow to countenance China as a serious power was reflected again in a note on October 27, 1945. It was reported that in conversations with Averell Harriman, Stalin had at first suggested that "Russia, America, China and [the United Kingdom]" should discuss the "Far Eastern issue," but "came round to the view that as the difference was between the Americans & the Russians the best course would be conversations between the two governments," a position as offensive to the British as to the Chinese. Stalin then proposed a detailed explanation of which countries in Europe might take part in the second-stage conference but noted that "China of course was excluded." Harriman, putting forward the US position, which wished to boost the importance of China, argued that "this was a far cry from the United Nations organization," but "Stalin said that was a thing of the future, whereas the peace treaties were to bury the past."[29]

Particularly interesting was a side note on the position of India. Harriman had argued on behalf of the United States and United Kingdom that

India should participate, but Stalin declared that as a colony, it was not eligible and that he would have no hesitation in opposing a formal American-British statement on behalf of India, on the grounds that it would "give him the opportunity for which he had long been waiting to make a statement on India, showing that British policy there was hypocritical and that we had no serious intention of changing the colonial status of India." One official took this seriously: "In the light of growing criticism in the Soviet Union about British policies since Potsdam, we should I think pay serious attention to this outburst about India." Memories of Chiang Kai-shek's wartime visit to India, when he had called for Indian independence, were no doubt still fresh in British official minds, and any encouragement to Chiang's postwar regime to act against British interests was to be discouraged.

Bevin became more concerned about the situation in China inasmuch as it reflected a hardening of the incipient Cold War and a further exclusion of British influence. On November 8, 1945, a memo from Bevin on the "Foreign Situation" took a wider view of the world in terms of diminishing British influence, and in particular, reflected on developments in Asia in terms of rising American, rather than Soviet, influence:

The United States have long held, with our support, to the Monroe Doctrine for the Western hemisphere, and there is no doubt that notwithstanding all the protestations that have been made they are attempting to extend this principle financially and economically to the Far East to include China and Japan, while the Russians seem to me to have made up their mind that their sphere is going to be from Lubeck to the Adriatic in the west and to Port Arthur in the east. Britain therefore stands between the two with the western world all divided up, with the French and British colonial empire[s] separated and with a very weak position in what is called the western group.[30]

Bevin's note went on to point out how the emergence of spheres of influence left the British Empire curiously vulnerable, and most of its content deals with European questions. But the case of East Asia was on his mind. It is worth remembering: in autumn 1945, the likely scenario in Asia appeared to both the United Kingdom and Soviet Union to be an East Asia entirely dominated by the United States, in China and Japan, with marginal Soviet influence in North Korea and remaining British influence in Southeast Asia. The ultimate scenario with a Communist, pro-Soviet China, was not thought of as impossible, but was regarded as much less likely. As Bevin observed later in his note: "Just as there may be a clash between France and Russia over who is to get control of the German people, so there are all the makings of a still more dangerous conflict between the United States and Russia over the body and soul of China." Bevin worried that "we in Great Britain . . . will be left to take sides either with one or the other."

By December 18, as the foreign ministers of the Big Three met in Moscow, it became clearer that the United States and the Soviet Union would disagree strongly about the role of China. The US secretary of state, James Byrnes, agreed to exclude China from the drafting of the treaty, but he "insisted on China and France, as permanent members of the Security Council, being allowed at least to express their view on any peace treaty agreed upon"; he also stressed that the whole conflict should be regarded as "one war." Even Byrnes was willing to use sleight of hand when justifying the treatment of China, noting that "China had agreed that her Allies should wage war in Europe at the expense of the war against Japan," a rather optimistic reading of Chinese attitudes toward the Allies. Molotov, in turn, had stated with simplicity that "China had not fought in Europe."[31]

France and China occupied a rather similar place in the minds of the Big Three, jostling for influence in autumn 1945; they were symbolic of the type of uneasy questions that the postwar situation had forced upon the Allies. Both were weak countries that had been catapulted to great-power status. China also marked the most obvious case of a non-European power whose contributions meant that it had to gain greater status but with no clear answer as to how that status should be defined. For Britain, which clung explicitly to empire, there was an additional problem in treating the Chinese as equals while maintaining dominance over much of Africa and Southeast Asia.

The Challenge of Communism

The appearance of the Chinese Communist Party (CCP) as a major factor in postwar China coincided with a new approach toward world Communism on the part of Britain. Bevin and Attlee were both strongly anti-Communist and were deeply suspicious of Moscow; they were also influenced by trying to put down the emergence of Communist-influenced nationalist movements in Southeast Asia. For Bevin, it became a top priority to work out what exactly the role of the CCP was in the new post-1945 China. Sir Horace Seymour, the British ambassador in Chongqing, wrote to Bevin on October 25, 1945, to assess the CCP's role and its relationship with the Soviet Union. Unstated was a comparison between the role of the Communist parties in Europe and that in China. Seymour stated:

It would probably be safe to say that it is at present a movement *sui generis,* having sprung from orthodox Soviet Communist seeds, and aiming eventually at orthodox ends, but having in its present phase matured into a hardy Chinese product. . . . The Communists in China may therefore be classified rather in the light of an opposition or rebel element in the internal life of China than as a subordinate or associated group in a wider field under the captaincy of a nominee from Moscow.[32]

Seymour noted that there was currently an accord in which the Soviet Union agreed not to provide assistance to any government other than the Nationalists, but he also noted that Soviet desire for influence in Xinjiang and Mongolia might lead them to an alliance with Yan'an. He noted that the Nationalists themselves were also as much "an outcrop of Soviet political theory as . . . the Communists of Yenan," an insightful observation that few in London fully understood in assessing the nature of Chinese politics. This statement concealed a wider debate within the Foreign Office, which echoed the argument taking place in the United States as to the true nature of the Communist Party; for instance, a memo from Kitson argued that the CCP was made up of "agrarian reformers" rather than adherents to Marxism-Leninism, and that they were viewed in contrast to the "Kuomintang and its armies, which have usually robbed and oppressed the peasants."

A subsequent message from Chongqing on November 1, 1945, showed Seymour in a despondent frame of mind:

The general picture in China is, I am afraid, rather gloomy. We hear of the troubles of British subjects in getting possession of their properties, and it makes one wonder what the emissaries of Chungking are doing to their own people who have been under Japanese occupation. It seems to me they may easily get into the position where the Chinese public begins to say that the Japanese were no worse than Chungking, and if we do get this then the Communist troubles will take on a much more serious aspect. This may, however be an unduly gloomy view. The rapid rise of the pound sterling in Shanghai does suggest that there is a great deal of nervousness about.[33]

Seymour's note reflects that "we still remain dreadfully short-handed, especially as regards people with Chinese experience"; although consular posts at Tianjin and Guangzhou were being reopened, he "unfortunately cannot improvise Chinese-speakers."

By December, the question of China was being discussed among the foreign ministers of the Big Three, not just in terms of Chinese participation in the European treaties but also with regard to advice that "democratic" elements should be encouraged to take part in the Nationalist government.

Sterndale-Bennett advised against demanding this on December 27, "since it was in effect interference in the internal affairs of China," a statement which was a remarkable alteration of tone even compared to a decade previously.[34] Yet even seasoned observers did not tend to think that the Communist challenge might be serious enough to topple the Nationalists and therefore pose a threat to British interests. One such observer was Lord Killearn, who as Sir Miles Lampson had been British minister in China from 1926 to 1933. On June 11, 1946, he wrote to Sargent from Singapore declaring that "China is in a mess—politically, militarily, financially, socially." He went on to say that "Chiang Kai Shek today is, to my mind, what he has always been—the only man in sight to run China. The engineer, so to speak, is first class, but I suspect the machine may be worn out, and makeshift patching and repairs which served well enough in war time are not good enough now." However, he did continue to view the major issue as being the balance between US and UK interests, arguing that the Chinese had always wanted to "play off the No 2 of the moment against the No 1" and that Britain should "take our chances" if the opportunity came to "regain our position and trade to some considerable extent."

Lampson's conclusion reads deeply ironically in retrospect:

I went to China with one dominant thought in my mind—the importance of keeping her out of the Russian orbit and inside ours. . . . Well, I am now pretty clear from my talks with Chiang Kai Shek and T. V. Soong that there is little present prospect of any "get together" with the Bear: on the contrary, there is heavy dislike and suspicion. So that the nightmare of any concerted action between China and Russia in the Far East does not seem to me at all likely.[35]

Killearn was relieved on these grounds, as he thought a Sino-Soviet alliance was likely to lead to a "subversive effect" in Southeast Asia. Within four years, of course, his fears would become much more substantial.

The short periods around the outbreak of war in 1937 and the end of war in 1945 were both crucial ones for the British. They were not crucial because the British presence in China was central to the overall British international position: China was important, but it did not hold the place of India in British minds, nor was it a popular source of anxiety as Nazi Germany or the Soviet Union were. Furthermore, the domestic situation in Britain meant that politics had to look at domestic issues such as mass unemployment and postwar reconstruction.

But China did provide a microcosm of changing British views of their own roles in an imperial and postimperial world. And is clear that those attitudes were nuanced. Britain had taken steps to adjust its own view of China's Nationalist government as early as 1926, yet the continuing reality of racial doctrine and imperial attitudes colored those progressive steps all the way through the war and beyond. As it turned out, the Nationalist government had only four years left on the mainland in 1945. But it is still worthwhile to look at how China's eight long years of total war, four of them with Britain as a formal ally, changed the way in which the world's largest empire looked at a country with which it had had more than a century of deeply unhappy interaction.

3   An Imperial Envoy

SHEN ZONGLIAN IN TIBET, 1943–1946

CHANG JUI-TE

In October 1943, the Nationalist government appointed Shen Zonglian, councilor of the Supreme Defense Committee, as director of the Mongolian and Tibetan Affairs Commission's (MTAC) office in Lhasa. After the announcement, Chiang Kai-shek emphasized to Shen the importance of the mission in Tibet. He asked Shen to undertake several tasks, without arousing the suspicions of the British in India.

First, Shen was to stress the central government's authority and its determination to unify China, noting that China, the United States, Britain, and the Soviet Union were allies. Second, Shen was to emphasize that the central government had always been friendly and respectful to Tibetans. He should let them know that Britain was threatened by the Indian independence movement and had no capacity to support Tibet. Tibet could have a bright future only if it strengthened its ties with China. Third, Shen was to ask the Tibetan administration to agree to the construction of the Xikang-Tibet Road. Once the war was over, the road would be built rapidly and would connect Tibet to China. Fourth, Shen was to try to improve the welfare of the Tibetans. The Chinese government planned to establish telegraph offices, banks, and hospitals in Lhasa and to increase the number and size of primary schools in Lhasa.

Chiang granted interim funds to cover Shen's outlays for operational expenditures and gifts. Shen was authorized to select his own staff, an authorization confirmed by the MTAC. Shen was also permitted to send officials already in Tibet whom he deemed incompetent back to China. For confidential issues, Shen was permitted to contact Chiang directly, without going through the MTAC. He was assigned his own secret password.[1]

Shen Zonglian's appointment to Tibet was high profile, though he used the nominal title "director of the Tibet Office of the MTAC." If the title "special envoy" had been used, the British administration in India and the Tibetan administration might have been suspicious.[2] On receiving notification of his appointment, the Tibetan regent Taktra sent this telegram to Wu Zhongxin, the commission's director:

Shen Zonglian is well respected. He is well trusted by Chiang Kai-shek. When he arrives in Tibet, China and Tibet definitely will resume their friendship. I am very satisfied and grateful. To show Sino-Tibetan friendship, Tibetan soldiers have already been sent to the Sino-Tibetan border as an escort. The Tibetan administration has already arranged ceremonies to welcome Shen Zonglian.[3]

British officials in Lhasa also noted that Chiang Kai-shek was trying to improve relations with Tibet by sending his protégé to Tibet.[4]

There has been little study on Shen's performance in Tibet.[5] Using the archives of the MTAC and memoirs, I look at Shen's appointment and performance, to shed light on modern Tibetan issues and on frontier administration. I also examine the pros and cons of Chiang's use of a special envoy to resolve problems.

Chiang Kai-shek's appointment of Shen had a specific historical background. In January 1941, the regent, Reting Rimpoche, who was pro-Chinese, resigned, and the pro-British Taktra Rimpoche assumed power. Sino-Tibetan relations were at a stalemate.[6] The international situation had also changed. Some Indian Congress Party members were secretly in touch with Japan. Japan had made dramatic advances in Southeast Asia. Nepal, Bhutan, Sikkim, and Tibet were threatened, as was the security of southwestern China. In 1942, Chiang Kai-shek and his wife visited India. They tried to persuade Congress leaders who were hostile to the British, such as Mahatma Gandhi and Jawaharlal Nehru, not to let themselves be used by Japan but to support the Allies.[7] Chiang believed that Britain was exhausted from dealing with the Indian independence movement and had no capacity to manage Tibetan affairs. He wanted to build the Xikang-Tibet Road to help the Allies, to control Tibet, and to help China's rear areas.

Kong Qingzong had not done well. He thought of himself as the almighty mandarin from the center and tried to replicate the prestige of a Qing minister in Lhasa. His arrogance and chauvinism aroused strong antipathy among local officials.[8] Nevertheless, his work went well when Reting Rinpoche was in office, but after Taktra Rinpoche took power, his pro-British line meant that he was unfriendly to the Chinese government. In September 1941, he refused permission to build the Xikang-Tibet Road. In July 1942, he set up the Tibetan Bureau of Foreign Affairs. In April 1943, he closed the pack animal route to China. Kong asked the

Chinese government to resolve the disputes by force, but this tough line contradicted the policy of stressing political measures and using military measures only as a fallback.[9]

An incident in September 1942 inflamed the situation. A Chinese injured a Nepalese resident in Tibet and then fought with police. He fled to the Tibet Office, where guards detained the policemen who followed him. The Tibetan administration negotiated for the policemen's release for five months, without success. The Tibetans demanded Kong's recall and cut off supplies to the office.[10] The MTAC at first assumed that the incident was a ploy by the Tibetan administration to test China's bottom line on Tibetan independence and would not compromise, in the belief that if it gave in and recalled Kong, his successor would run into the same problems.[11] However, Chiang Kai-shek did decide to compromise. The MTAC then proposed to recall Kong and appoint Luo Shishi as director. There was military intelligence that the Tibet Office had serious problems with budget and personnel. It was suggested that Chiang send an envoy to investigate; after some time, Kong would be recalled, and the envoy would replace him.[12] Ultimately, Chiang Kai-shek did not appoint Luo Shishi, his decision influenced by Wellington Koo (Gu Weijun), the Chinese ambassador in Britain, who in April 1943 advised Chiang to appoint a senior diplomat to Tibet. Chiang agreed. He chose Shen Zonglian, who was nominated by the senior Guomindang (GMD) figure Dai Jitao.[13]

Shen had graduated from Qinghua University and had studied in the United States. He held an MA in economics from Harvard. He was able and had a capacity to think strategically. He had been in charge of the General Office of the Ministry of Foreign Affairs (MFA) under Guo Taiqi.[14] At the end of 1941, Guo lost his position as foreign minister after accusations of corruption were made against him. Chiang Kai-shek himself served as the foreign minister for a while, though in reality the director of the Second Bureau of Chiang's staff office, Chen Bulei, filled the post. Chen appointed personnel from the staff office to the MFA and brought Shen into the staff office.[15] Shen suggested that Chiang strengthen ties with Tibet. Chiang appreciated the advice. Shen accompanied Dai Jitao to Burma and India. Dai reported to Chiang that Shen was thoughtful and knowledgeable.[16]

After his appointment was announced, Shen Zonglian formed a team to accompany him to Tibet. Chen Xizhang was named Tibet Office secretary and First Bureau director (in charge of general affairs, paper work, and personnel).[17] Yunnan University sociology professor Li Youyi was made the Second Bureau director (in charge of politics, religion, education, and construction). Shen set up a third bureau for public affairs and investigation, headed by Zong Renjie, who had worked under Kong Qingzong.

From Kong's staff, Shen kept Li Guolin, a Tibetan. He also appointed Kang Gangmin as consultant on Tibetan newspapers; Kang had worked at the Bureau of Mongolian and Tibetan Education at the Ministry of Education and knew Tibetan. He put an expert from the Geology Institute of the Ministry of Economics in charge of exploration in Tibet. He invited two doctors from Chongqing to take charge of medical clinics.

Shen invited two engineers from the Sichuan-Xikang Road administration to investigate the construction of the Xikang-Tibet Road. The Central Trust Bureau appointed an officer to examine the feasibility of setting up financial institutions in Lhasa.[18] Shen selected more than twenty attachés, including an English secretary, an interpreter, a transcriber, a chef, and several servants, all designated as diplomatic staff, and paid salaries higher than those of regular officials, and in foreign currency not affected by the depreciation of the Chinese currency.[19] Shen Zonglian's team was larger than that of his predecessor. The changes, inconsistent with the Tibet Office's existing regulations, were made at Shen's discretion, then reviewed by the MTAC and accepted.[20] The power of the office was increased.[21]

Before Shen's departure, attention was given to what gifts to take with him. There were to be many recipients: the Dalai Lama, the regent, the Living Buddhas, ministers, the Dalai Lama's parents and servants. Shen sent people to Chengdu and elsewhere to buy more than a hundred gifts, including silk, gold, silver, and jewelry. He purchased lacquer ware and ceramics from Fujian and Jiangxi.[22] When he reached Calcutta, he bought toy trains and motion picture projectors from Europe and the United States as gifts for the Dalai Lama, who had not yet reached adulthood.[23] At the farewell banquet organized by his colleagues, Shen stated that "for this trip, I have spent a lot of money. This is extravagant, but I have to deal with a Tibetan upper class that is backward, authoritarian, and closed-minded. I have to use power and gifts to win them over. Otherwise, they would look at me with scorn."[24]

Shen's staff was to fly from Chongqing to India in two groups and enter Tibet via Sikkim. Their passports were issued, and they applied for visas at the British Embassy in China. Shen and the first group of his staff promptly obtained visas. However, the British in India and Lhasa suspected that Shen's arrival would be detrimental to British-Tibetan relations, and they asked the British Embassy in China not to issue visas to the second group of Shen's staff. They also asked the Tibetan administration to limit the size of his staff.[25]

In mid-April 1944, Shen Zonglian and his staff flew from Chongqing to Calcutta. Shen visited Delhi at the invitation of the Indian government, from May 6 to May 14. He had five talks with the Indian foreign secretary, Sir Olaf Caroe. Caroe told him that British policy was to maintain Britain's existing territory; Britain had no ambitions on Tibetan territory. British economic connections with Tibet were insignificant. However, as Tibet was a security buffer for India, Britain wanted Tibet to be autonomous. In the Tibetan people's perception, Tibet was an independent country and had been so de facto for the past thirty years, but China regarded Tibet as part of China. These two perceptions differed fundamentally and could hardly converge. Britain wanted to compromise. On the one hand, the British did not want to make Tibetans unhappy. On the other hand, they recognized China's suzerainty.[26] Shen emphasized that what China exercised in Tibet was sovereignty, rather than suzerainty. The two disagreed about the meaning of *sovereignty* and *suzerainty.* Caroe invited Shen to check the *Encyclopaedia Britannica,* where they found the definition of *suzerainty* was flexible; they could not discern a clear difference from *sovereignty.* Finally Caroe stated, "To my understanding, when a country is powerful, suzerainty can be a synonym for sovereignty. However, if a country is not powerful enough, sovereignty is a different concept."[27]

Caroe's interpretation of suzerainty left Shen optimistic. In the report that he sent to China, he wrote:

From Sir Olaf Caroe's interpretation of suzerainty, we realize that Chinese-Tibetan relations depend on our efforts. If we have the power to strengthen our control over Tibet, Britain seemingly would hardly create obstructions. When the right time comes, based on the concept of suzerainty, the Chinese central government may take over Tibet's foreign affairs. This option is not impossible.[28]

This optimistic attitude became a driving force behind Shen's work in Tibet. British documents reveal that Caroe formed a good impression of Shen. He regarded him as a pleasant and eminently reasonable individual.[29]

On July 1, at the invitation of Sir Basil Gould, British political commissioner in Sikkim, Shen visited Gangtok, the capital of Sikkim, for three days. He attended a banquet given by the Prince of Sikkim. He had several private talks with Gould. Gould believed that the Simla Convention (1914) had laid a solid foundation to resolve the Tibet problem. Shen pointed out that the convention had not been ratified by China and therefore could not serve as the basis for negotiation. Gould argued that in discussing the Tibet problem, Tibetan representatives should be present. Otherwise, Tibet would definitely not accept any resolution. The failure of the China-Britain-Russia Convention (1907) was an example. Shen argued that as suzerain of Tibet, China could represent Tibet. Gould hoped that the Tibet problem could be resolved before Indian political turmoil erupted again.[30]

British documents indicate that Gould was impressed by Shen's ability and thought him candid and flexible. Senior officials in the British administration in India normally had poor impressions of Chinese officials; Gould's good impression of Shen was rather rare. Yet Gould also implied that Shen might be detrimental to British interests in Tibet.[31]

While Shen was in India, the MFA negotiated with the British Embassy in China over the visas for the second group of Shen's staff. The British and Tibetans did not want China to have a large office in Tibet. They feared that the Chinese officials, once in Tibet, would be difficult to evict. The British administration in India had promised to support Tibetan autonomy in foreign affairs and wanted good relations with Tibet, so they refused to grant visas to Shen's staff.[32] The second group of Shen's staff had to abandon their travel to Tibet.

On August 8, 1944, Shen Zonglian reached Lhasa. Two hundred Tibetan officials and soldiers lined up to welcome him, along with British, Nepalese, and Bhutanese officials in Tibet.[33] After his arrival, Shen, accompanied by Li Guolin, who had worked as Tibetan secretary in the Tibet Office for many years, visited senior officials of the Tibetan administration, the three major monasteries (Drepung, Sera, and Ganden) and the Living Buddhas. He distributed gifts and gave banquets. He made donations to the monasteries. His generosity impressed the elite in Lhasa and improved Sino-Tibetan relations substantially.[34] On Chinese National Day (October 10), Shen invited a theatrical troupe to give Peking Opera performances. He held a sumptuous banquet for the Tibetan elite and invited Sir Basil Gould, who happened to be in Lhasa; the British representative in Lhasa, George Sheriff; and Nepal's representative in Lhasa.

These activities cost a lot of money and caused a sensation; 28,300 lamas from the major monasteries in Lhasa and Shigatse received gifts. Under Kong Qingzong's tenure, each lama had received 2.5 Tibetan taels in silver and money for tea. Under Shen each lama received 3 taels.[35] Besides the gifts from his office, Shen put pressure on the Chinese merchants in Tibet to make donations. The British, who did not have the tradition of making donations, lost out.[36]

In Lhasa, Shen Zonglian strengthened ties between China and Tibet, activities that had a great impact in Tibet and aroused suspicion in the British in India. Sir Basil Gould suggested sending a delegation to Tibet to counter China's propaganda work in Tibet and to strengthen ties between India and Tibet. He also suggested that India should host a permanent Tibetan representative in India. He encouraged the Tibetan administration to send a special envoy to the United States to meet President Roosevelt and to increase Tibet's international visibility. The Foreign Office in London did not want Tibet to strengthen diplomatic relations with the United States or India and ordered Gould not to make any commitments to the Tibetan administration; it did not want to challenge China by protecting Tibet militarily, or to support Tibet's desire for independence.[37] In this atmosphere, Gould paid a visit to Lhasa in August 1944. Chen Zhiping, the consul in Calcutta, reported to the MFA:

On August 8, the director of the MTAC's Tibet Office, Shen Zonglian, arrived in Lhasa. On August 31, the British political officer Sir Basil Gould arrived in Lhasa. Our government sent Shen Zonglian as director to Tibet to improve Sino-Tibetan relations. Yet Britain became suspicious. It ordered the Tibetan administration to limit the number of Chinese government staffers in the Tibet Office staff, and it ordered Gould to go to Tibet. Gould took a lot of gifts for important persons in Tibet. He advocated Tibetan independence and the stationing of troops in a Tibetan area close to Bhutan. Gould had been in Sikkim for more than twenty years and is regarded by the British as an expert on Tibet. Last year, he reached the age for retirement, yet his tenure was prolonged. He is conservative and unable to fit in to the modern time. The British administration in India has a well-planned policy, carried out discreetly by Gould. Director Shen entered Tibet with our government's gifts for the Dalai Lama. He planned to set up a hospital. Gould also came to Tibet with a lot of gifts. The original clinic that Britain set up in Lhasa was shabby, but recently it has been refurbished and equipped with updated facilities. All these measures went against our policy. As Sino-Tibetan relations improved, Britain increasingly stepped up her activities. This is worrisome for China's Tibetan administration.[38]

British archives indicate that Gould's activities in Lhasa were not so limited. Gould informed the Tibetan administration that the British administration in India was determined to strengthen control over territories south of the McMahon Line. He also proposed a series of plans for financial and diplomatic aid. The British administration in India would give financial aid to the Tibetan administration and monasteries to compensate for the loss of tax revenue after the region south of the McMahon Line was ceded. This aid would strengthen the Tibetan administration in countering the Chinese government's increasing influence.[39]

The British government supported the Tibetan administration in maintaining the status quo, though Gould seemed to be advocating Tibetan independence. Gould told the Tibetan administration that Shen was trying to turn Tibet into a Chinese province, though according to international practice, any country that had twenty-five years of autonomy met the qualification for independence. Tibet had been autonomous for almost thirty years and so could be independent. On Gould's advice, the Tibetan administration contacted the British administration in India, expressing the desire that Britain support Tibetan independence. The Foreign Office refused, stating that China was Britain's ally. The British administration in India instructed Gould to tell the Tibetan administration that it could use only diplomatic measures to help Tibet to maintain her autonomy and could not guarantee military support.[40] This outcome was a blow to the Tibetans.

China and Britain were wartime allies, but in Tibet they competed to win the friendship of the Tibetan administration. In 1945, when Robert Ford, a British telegrapher, arrived in Lhasa, he was shocked by the mistrust and hostility between the local British and Chinese; they were in a state of cold war.[41] As Chinese-British competition in Tibet intensified, both sides gradually adopted cash diplomacy. Since Gould's tenure, the British had given money directly to important persons in Tibet. In the 1940s, British officials in Lhasa started to record the donations. And since the early 1930s, China had gradually increased the value of donations.[42] In 1943, the Chinese government donated 39,900 Indian dong to monasteries in Lhasa.[43] In 1945, the amount was increased to 50,000 dong.[44] During the 1930s and 1940s, the donations from both China and Britain exceeded traditional ethical limits.

Chinese donations to Tibetan monasteries had historical precedents. Britain had sold arms that challenged Chinese authority over Tibet for years.[45] In money diplomacy, Britain could not rival China, but it could supply materials that Chinese and Tibetans lacked, such as kerosene and sugar, and it offered duty free import to commodities coming via India, saving the Tibetan elite who relied on imports from China and India a lot of money.[46]

In July 1945, the MTAC submitted a report to the Fourth Plenary of the Chinese National Convention. It cited the following achievements of the Tibet Office under five headings, as follows:

1. *Political.* After the appointment of Shen Zonglian as the Tibet Office director, relations between the central government and Tibet had improved gradually. The Tibetan administration had received Shen well. It had immediately resumed supplies to the Tibet Office. In regular matters between the central government and Tibet, Shen negotiated with the Tibetan prince regent and the Tibetan administration directly, no longer via the Bureau of Foreign Affairs. On Chinese National Day in 1944, a campaign was launched in Lhasa to have each county donate an aircraft. In total twenty-five aircraft were donated, valued at 5 million yuan.[47]

2. *Education.* The central government had set up a primary school in Lhasa, but the school had insufficient teachers and funding and barely functioned. Chinese and Uighur students were disappointed and went to Tibetan language schools. At the end of 1945, the school had only fifty to sixty students. In early 1946 the school obtained a large amount of funding from the Bureau of Frontier Education. Faculty and facilities improved dramatically. The student body had increased to 206 by the autumn of 1946.[48]

3. *Health care.* The Tibet Office's clinic offered medical treatment to Lhasa residents. Doctors and nurses had come to Tibet with Shen. The clinic purchased medicines and equipment in India. Each day

around fifty people came to the clinic for treatment. This number rivaled the number of visits to the British clinic.[49]

4. *Legal.* The MTAC had held discussions with the Ministry of Justice and drafted outlines for the Tibet Office to resolve legal cases involving Tibetan, Uighur, and Chinese people. The outline was ratified by the Executive Yuan and forwarded to the Legislative Yuan for approval.

5. *Religion.* For two years after Taktra had seized power, the Tibetan administration had not followed historical precedent in choosing new Living Buddhas; this had involved nominations from the central government. In early 1945, it reverted to historical precedent and to government nomination. The Sera Monastery, one of the three major monasteries in Lhasa, had been hostile to the central government since its skirmish with the Chinese army in 1912. Under Shen, the monastery presented religious objects to the central government to show loyalty.[50]

Shen Zonglian won respect from the elite in Lhasa, including those who had no sympathy toward China. He was cautious and avoided involvement in Tibet's domestic affairs. For instance, he forwarded legal cases involving Tibetans and Chinese or Uighurs to the Tibetan administration.[51] Earlier Chinese officials in Tibet had often referred to the Qing Dynasty, under the mistaken belief that Tibetans had liked Qing governance.[52] Shen, however, contrasted the Qing's brutal rule in Tibet with the policies of Republican China. He told Tibetans that Chinese had been persecuted by the Qing government as the Tibetans had been. In *Zhongguo zhi Mingyun* (China's destiny), Chiang Kai-shek mentioned that Tibetans were the descendants of the Yellow Emperor.[53] Shen tried to avoid this topic. He emphasized that under the Republic all ethnic groups should live in harmony and equality. The friendship between Tibet and China could be restored. The trouble with the Xikang-Tibet border was caused by a few ignorant officials. All problems were easy to resolve, provided that Tibetans negotiated with the central government.[54]

Besides taking open measures to strengthen Chinese-Tibetan ties, Shen collected intelligence. There were a lot of government agencies collecting intelligence in Tibet. Besides the Tibet Office, the Bureau of Investigation and Statistics, the Military Headquarters, and the GMD Organization Department all collected intelligence on Chinese and Uighurs, but they had insufficient sources of information on British activities in Tibet, for instance, on British arms sales.[55] To make things worse, the intelligence agencies did not cooperate with one another. Shen's efforts to control and monitor the various operatives encountered resistance and were abandoned.[56]

Under Shen's leadership, the Tibet Office collected intelligence about Japanese use of lamas to conduct covert activities in Tibet, about British activities, and about Tibetan customs. The work on Tibetan customs was productive. The scope included politics, the military, culture, religion, and local customs, and it produced important reports, such as *Changdu xilie baogao* (a series of reports on Qamdo).[57]

The information collected by the Tibet Office was circulated to various organs, and edited versions were published in newspapers and journals. Liu Shengqi worked the hardest on research on Tibet. During his tenure, he wrote three English-language commentaries on China-Britain-Tibet relations and a report on the Reting Incident (1947), all published in newspapers and journals in Shanghai.[58] He and Shen wrote a report entitled *Xianshi zhi Xizang* (Contemporary Tibet); the report was published in 1952 as *Tibet and Tibetans*.[59] Liu became a renowned expert on Tibet.[60]

Because communications were so poor, Chinese had little understanding of Tibet. Until 1948, official correspondence from the central government to Tibet often had strange addresses, such as "Tibet province government" and "Tibet city parliament." The Bureau of Frontier Education at the Ministry of Education specialized in frontier affairs, yet it once mistakenly sent a communication for a primary school in Tibet to Suiyuan.[61]

In the year after Shen came to Tibet, Sino-Tibetan relations improved. On August 14, 1945, when the news of China's victory in the Resistance War came over the radio, the Tibet Office set off firecrackers. The national flag was raised on the roof, surrounded by colorful bunting. More than four hundred Chinese and Uighurs in Lhasa rallied at the Tibet Office. A torch-lit parade was held that night. It circled the Jokhang Temple. The next day, Shen held a banquet. The Tibetan elite all came, as did British and Nepalese representatives in Lhasa.[62]

Nevertheless, the impact on Tibetans was minor. According to a British report on August 14, the celebration by Chinese in Lhasa was so noisy that it aroused antipathy in some Tibetans. The director of the Tibetan Bureau of Foreign Affairs met Shen and demanded that all Chinese flags, bunting, and photos of political leaders be taken down. On the day of Shen's banquet, all the flags raised the previous day were gone, except the national flag of the Republic of China on the roof of the Tibet Office.[63]

The Tibet Office under Shen Zonglian performed better than it had under Kong Qingzong. China-Tibet relations improved, but Shen was not complacent. He wanted to make a breakthrough on Tibet. After serious deliberation, he drafted some suggestions and sent them by confidential telegram to Chiang Kai-shek.

Shen made two bold suggestions. First, to boost ties with Tibet so that

Tibet would not lean toward the British in India, the priority should be building the Xikang-Tibet Road. To carry out such a big project, the central government must eliminate warlord Liu Wenhui's control over Xikang and completely reorganize the Sichuan provincial government. Xikang should be merged into Sichuan. A senior official (such as Wu Zhongxin) should command Central Army troops in Chengdu, Xichang, and Kangding. The troops would construct the Xikang-Tibet Road. Some of Hu Zongnan's troops could be used. Second, China should use the impact of Chiang Kai-shek's India visit and push for India's independence at the United Nations. Meanwhile, the GMD should send an envoy to negotiate with the Indian Congress Party to reach a gentleman's agreement that would recognize Tibet as a part of China's territory.

Chiang read the telegram and gave it to Chen Bulei to study, along with Song Ziwen, Dai Jitao, Chen Guofu, and Zhang Qun. Later, Song went to London, where he inquired about the British stance on Tibet. The response was that Britain was focused on Indian independence and had no time to worry about Tibet.[64]

In fact, it was Chiang who did not have time to worry about Tibet. After the end of World War II, Chiang was reliant on the United States to mediate between the Chinese Communist Party (CCP) and the GMD and to prevent civil war. In the short run, he planned to resume the campaign of extermination against the CCP. There were worrying problems in Manchuria, Xinjiang, and Mongolia. Chiang did not have much energy left to deal with Tibet. And he could hardly challenge Liu Wenhui's control over Xikang.[65] Therefore, Chiang had Chen Bulei respond to Shen that the domestic situation was complicated and the status quo in Tibet should be maintained. "No achievement is a great achievement." Shen realized that nothing could be done and thought of resigning.[66]

In order to promote Tibetan independence, the Tibetan administration sent a delegation to China, Britain, and the United States. The delegation leader was Thubten Samphel, and the deputy leader was Dzasak Khemey Sonam Wangdu. Other members included Tsewang Dundul, Dorje Ngodrub Changngopa, and an interpreter.

The central government (now back in Nanjing) decided to convene the National Representative Conference in 1945. The Tibet Office of the MTAC asked the Tibetan administration to send representatives to the conference. The office let it be known that the Tibetan representatives could make proposals that the government would try to accommodate. The Tibetan administration saw this as an opportunity to raise Tibet's status, and it enhanced the existing delegation by adding several members.[67] The delegation planned to go to India first to pay its respects to the British and American governments, then to Nanjing to attend the National Representative Conference.

To prepare for the conference, the Tibetan administration convened an all-Tibet conference and drafted a report to submit to the conference on behalf of all Tibetans. The report carried the seals of the administration and of the three major monasteries. The report laid out the position that China-Tibet relations had always been relations between donor and recipient, and that it was hoped that these relations would be maintained. Tibet was an independent country and would operate independently in the future. In the past, China had used force to seize territories that obviously belonged to Tibet linguistically and culturally, such as Qinghai and Xikang. These territories should be returned to Tibet. Tibet had always been an independent country. It should manage its own domestic, foreign, and military affairs.[68] The Dalai Lama had the power to name Living Buddhas, appoint officials, and carry out reforms. China and other countries should not interfere. The Chinese government should apply for visas from the Tibetan administration for any Chinese who wanted to enter Tibet. Many countries had achieved great fortune and power, but only one country was dedicated to the well-being of mankind: Tibet. So Tibet was extremely important for world peace and happiness. If a foreign country invaded Tibet, Tibet would ask China for help, based on their historical relationship.

The Tibetan delegation had a strategic plan. If Chiang Kai-shek responded to the report before the conference started, the Tibetan delegation would leave China. If Chiang did not respond before the conference, the Tibetan delegation would attend the conference as observers rather than as formal representatives.

Sir Basil Gould, the British political officer in Sikkim, had already retired. Arthur Hopkinson had taken over the position. He learned that a Tibetan delegation would attend the National Representative Conference, and he contacted the Tibetan administration: participation in the conference would be in contravention of Article 4 of the Simla Convention and would jeopardize Tibet's autonomy. The Tibetan administration stated that it had no plan to attend the conference.[69] The Tibetan delegation members did not carry the Tibetan government's report with them, to keep it secret from the British. Messengers took the report to Nanjing via Xikang and gave the report to the delegation in Nanjing.[70] An extensive round of calls was planned so that after the delegation had submitted the report to the Nationalist government, the delegation could promote its ratification.[71]

Before they left Lhasa, the delegates were instructed to say that their visit to Nanjing was to recognize the Allied victory; they should keep secret the fact that they were attending the conference and presenting a report.[72] Chiang Kai-shek knew from intelligence reports that before the delegation's departure the prince regent, Taktra, had convened a meeting and asked the delegates to try to maintain the status quo and not to speak recklessly, which might fuel the Chinese government's determination to use force to resolve the Tibet issue. If the government took a conciliatory position, the delegation should demand Tibetan independence, or at least total autonomy. If the demand was met, the China-Tibet border delineation should follow the lines of the Simla Convention.[73]

At the end of January, the delegation's eight official members left Lhasa. Three weeks later, they reached Gangtok, the capital of Sikkim. They were welcomed by the king of Sikkim and by Arthur Hopkinson. Hopkinson accompanied the delegation to New Delhi, where it stayed for two weeks. The members met the viceroy, Lord Wavell, and passed on letters from the Dalai Lama and the prince regent, Taktra. They presented gifts, including scrolls embroidered with Buddhist images, silver ware, and Tibetan carpets. The delegation visited George Merrell, interim US chargé d'affaires in India, and passed on letters from the Dalai Lama and the prince regent to President Truman, with photographs of the Dalai Lama. The embassy held a banquet and showed a movie.[74]

Hopkinson did not take a public position on the delegation's trip to Nanjing, but he was clearly unhappy with its intention to participate in the National Representative Conference and tried to delay the trip, suggesting that the delegation travel to China by sea. In the hot and humid climate, some delegates had developed prickly heat. Hopkinson exaggerated the skin disease as a serious infectious disease that needed prompt treatment. The delegation asked the Chinese government's Tibet Office for help and moved into the Chinese Consulate in Calcutta.[75]

Shen Zonglian had persuaded the Dalai Lama's brother, Gyalo Thondup, and brother-in-law, Phuntsok Tashi, to go to Nanjing. They secretly entered India. Shen sent a telegram to Nanjing, stating that the Tibetan administration had decided to send two senior officials to Nanjing. As the matter was important, he would accompany the Tibetan officials. On April 4, the delegates, the attachés, and the Dalai Lama's relatives, in total almost thirty persons, accompanied by Shen, flew to Nanjing via Kunming. The news of their journey reached Lhasa and shocked the pro-British Taktra.[76] The British saw this maneuver as a political coup for Shen.

On April 7, the delegation reached Nanjing and was welcomed by the MTAC. At that time, the Nationalist government was still in the process of moving from Chongqing to Nanjing. In May Chiang Kai-shek arrived in Nanjing. The Nationalist government held a ceremony to celebrate victory in the Resistance War. After the ceremony, Chiang Kai-shek and Madame Chiang held a banquet for the delegation and Gyalo Thondup and Phuntsok Tashi.[77] After the celebrations, the Tibetan delegation sent the report (already translated into Chinese by the Tibetan administration's office in Nanjing) to the MFA, which refused to accept the report, as Tibet was not a foreign country. The delegation had to submit the report to the MTAC. It expressed the wish to get some comments on the report before the conference convened. The commission replied that the report was worth detailed discussion, as it concerned important issues. It suggested that the Tibetan delegation should attend the conference and state its views there.[78]

The National Representative Conference started on November 15, 1946. It was called the Constitution Drafting Conference, because the major task of the conference was to make a new constitution. The Tibetan administration's representatives included eight officials and two incumbent officials from the Dalai Lama's office in Nanjing. The Panchen Lama sent six representatives. Gannan, Qinghai, and Xikang each had a Tibetan representative.[79]

Having heard no comment on the report from the Chinese government, the Tibetan delegation followed the Tibetan administration's instructions and did not formally register for the conference. It claimed that its members came as observers, not as formal delegates. The government assigned Bai Chongxi, who was familiar with frontier administration, to deal with this issue. Bai invited the Tibetan delegates to his residence and made the following speech.

You refuse to take delegate cards. You state that you are here as observers. This stance is not appropriate. Tibet is the territory of the Republic of China. Now we have won the war. Delegates from all over China have come to attend this conference. Tibet is no exception. In our country, ethnic groups live in harmony. You are one of the ethnic groups. Why will you not attend the conference? You should attend, although you are from a frontier region. You should know that at the end of the Qing Dynasty and the beginning of the Republic, Tibet was not on good terms with the central government. The split was stirred up by Britain and was harmful to both Tibet and mainland China. At the beginning of the Republic, Yin Changhong from Sichuan resorted to military force to suppress the Tibetan army's rebellion. He failed. At that time, supplies were difficult to obtain, and he did not go all out. Now the situation is different. In 1938, the Tibetan Authority refused to raise the Chinese national flag at the Tibet Office. I was ordered to open an airport in Yushu County, Qinghai. Then you backed down, as you feared that bombers might bomb Lhasa. The central government has to take such measures if there is no alternative. Please immediately send a telegram to the Tibetan administration. You must change your position. You cannot be troublemakers. The conference will not accept your request to be observers at the conference. You may suffer if you do not enter the conference venue. Do not fall into the trap instigated by the British. Cooperation with the central government will be beneficial to your development, and education and causes no harm. Why do you struggle for separation? Please send a telegram to Tibet to report. That will be good for you.[80]

After Bai's speech, the Tibetan delegates sent a telegram to Tibet asking for instructions. The Tibetan administration permitted the members of the delegation to attend the conference as delegates. The delegation leader,

Thubten Sangpo, was elected as a member of the conference presidium. Some Tibetan delegates were elected as members of the constitution drafting committee.[81]

Throughout the conference, Tibetan delegates meticulously followed the Tibetan administration's instructions. Twice they sent telegrams to the administration asking for instructions. One reply stated that the Tibetan delegates should not applaud and should not vote. Another instruction was that the Tibetan delegates should try to make sure that Tibetan issues not be included in the conference resolutions.[82] In group discussion, Tibetan and Mongolian representatives were in the same group, chaired by Bai Chongxi. They discussed the constitutional draft sentence by sentence. One article was on the autonomy of Tibet and Mongolia. Following instructions from Lhasa, the Tibetan delegates remained silent. After the session ended, they told Bai that Tibetan issues should not be included in the constitution. Bai repeated his opinion that ethnic groups should live in harmony. "Our country is a big country, like a big company. There are Han Manchu, Mongolian, Uighur, and Tibetan. We are all masters in this big company. Ethnic groups live in harmony. The article has no flaws." The Tibetan delegates made no further comment.[83] After the conference, Tibetan delegates assumed that there would be a signing ceremony. They left Nanjing and went to Shanghai for a week, to avoid signing. They were wrong; there was no signing ceremony.

The conference passed the new Constitution of the Republic of China. The constitution clearly articulated Tibet's status. Article 168 states: "The state guarantees the status of ethnic groups at the frontier and renders special support to their regional autonomy."[84] After the conference, Chiang Kai-shek and Madame Chiang invited the Tibetan delegates and the Dalai Lama's relatives (twenty-two people) to a banquet. The MTAC arranged for the delegates to visit various places. The delegates did not leave Nanjing for Tibet until May 1947.

For six months, there was no feedback on the report. The Tibetan delegates inquired a few times. The reply was that the government had set up a group led by the MTAC to investigate and resolve the issue. Two Tibetans sent an agent to buy gold bars and bracelets in Nanjing, to try bribery to push for the report's ratification.[85] Finally, on Chiang Kai-shek's instruction, the commission responded. One of the report's demands was that the Nationalist government return territories that historically had belonged to Tibet. The Tibetan administration was asked to send senior officials to Nanjing for negotiation.[86] The Tibetan delegation realized that nothing would be achieved if negotiations took place in Nanjing. However, if negotiations took place in Lhasa, progress might be possible. It telegraphed Tibet for instructions. The Tibetan administration replied, agreeing to negotiate later.[87]

In April 1947, the MTAC was reorganized. Xu Shiying became director. Reviewing the files, he found that the report contained the sentence "Tibet is a holy place for Buddhism and an autonomous country." If this statement was not refuted, the Nationalist government would effectively recognize Tibet as a country. On Chiang Kai-shek's instruction, Xu refuted the whole report.[88] The Tibetan administration's efforts and schemes at the National Representative Conference were finally over.

The Tibetan administration had suffered a severe blow. It had failed to enhance its political status, to resolve the territorial disputes, or to alter the constraints of the constitution. The delegation's participation in the conference and constitution making was widely reported in the media, publicity that helped the Chinese government when the United Nations General Assembly discussed Tibet. The Chinese government won a victory by persuading the Tibetan delegation to participate in the conference and constitution making. It increased the legitimacy of the Chinese government and put Tibet within its constitutional framework.[89]

Shen Zonglian accompanied the Tibetan delegates and Gyalo Thondup to their meeting with Chiang Kai-shek. Before the meeting, Shen had visited Dai Jitao and Chen Bulei and talked about the situation in Tibet over the past year. He felt that not much could be achieved there. He could not stay longer in the cold climate on the plateau, as he suffered from heart disease. He asked Chen to pass on his wish to resign. Chiang agreed that he should rest for a while and then work elsewhere later. In early 1947, Shanghai mayor Wu Guozhen appointed him general secretary of the city government.

One day, some colleagues who had worked at the staff office had a reunion. Talking about Tibet, Shen Zonglian sighed, "Our country is not strong enough and is split. We can do nothing about Tibet."[90] This remark sums up his Tibet experience.

During Shen Zonglian's tenure in Tibet, the Tibetan administration and Tibetan officials improved their attitude toward the Chinese government. Nevertheless, Shen was not able to make any breakthroughs. First, the frontier administration had a poor understanding of the situation in Tibet.[91] The MTAC specialized in frontier administration, but had no power. Second, the personnel system was unsatisfactory. British officials in Tibet normally worked in Tibet for long terms; they were familiar with Tibet. Their work impressed the Chinese government's staff in Tibet, who often rotated every two or three years and could hardly develop expertise. Much more seriously, China was alienated from Tibet.[92] Before the war, a Chinese official wrote a book, *Kang Zang* (Xikang and Tibet), which describes Tibetans as follows:

Tibetan people were once strong, brave, and skillful in fighting. They adopted Buddhism and believed blindly in nemesis. Then over time they became simple and kind. They are honest and disciplined, but crude and naïve. They are closed-minded. They love their homeland and do not want to move. Moreover, they have no determination and often follow blindly like sheep.[93]

Even Chinese officials working on Tibet had prejudicial impressions of Tibetans. The mass media often made discriminatory remarks about Tibetans. It was common to say that Tibetans had syphilis and gonor-rhea. In general, Chinese people regarded Tibetans as ignorant, greedy, lazy, closed-minded, and uncivilized, people who urgently needed civilizing projects to raise their economic, educational, and cultural levels to Chinese standards.[94]

Second, Tibet stuck to its desire for autonomy. After the Republic was established, Tibetans had de facto independence, but they were not able to establish a nation. They did not try to build their own imagined community and did not develop a concept of citizenship, moves that would change the existing relations between monasteries and the general population.[95] Nevertheless, since the Chinese government had pulled out of Tibet at the beginning of the Republic, Tibet had had complete autonomy. The Tibetan administration was powerful, but civilians were enslaved to grasping noblemen. Tibetans believed in Buddhism and donated so much to monasteries that they were impoverished. The Dalai Lama had ruled Tibet for more than twenty years. His foreign policy and his instructions before his death were to maintain Tibet's autonomy and be friendly to both China and Britain.

Therefore, the Tibetan administration kept a careful distance from both the Chinese government and the British in India. It twice welcomed Chinese government envoys at the enthronement ceremonies of the two successive Dalai Lamas and allowed the Chinese to set up offices, a radio station, hospitals, and primary schools in Lhasa. It also had its own representative in China. After the war, it sent representatives to the National Congress, the friendliest gesture toward the Nationalist government and the most significant achievement of Shen Zonglian's work in Tibet. However, the Tibetan administration still would not allow Chinese to enter Tibet freely. The Tibetan Bureau of Foreign Affairs, set up during the war, still existed, and the Tibetan administration effectively rejected the Chinese government's initiative to negotiate border issues. It also allowed the British in India to set up offices, a radio station, hospitals, and schools in Lhasa. It purchased or borrowed weapons, money, and other commodities from the British authority but disregarded Britain's request for more economic and political power. And it would not allow Britons to enter Tibet freely. This was Tibet's delicate balance.[96]

Third, China and Britain both defended their national interests and would not compromise. From the Simla Convention in 1913 to Indian independence in 1947, British foreign policy was to maintain its existing territories. Britain did not support Tibetan independence. However, as Tibet was India's defense shield, Britain hoped that Tibet could maintain autonomy and serve as a buffer between India, China, and Russia.[97] In early 1942, when the United States, Britain, the Soviet Union, and China signed a declaration for the United Nations, China became one of the four major world powers; it later helped the Korean and Vietnamese independence movements and sent troops to fight in Burma.[98] These demonstrations of China's responsibility toward its neighbors aroused suspicion in the British in India and in the British government at home.

For the British in India, China's threat to Britain's colonial governance in Asia was perhaps more serious than Japanese jingoistic threats to the Far East and Hitler's threat to Europe. The British believed that given the fast-growing Chinese presence in South Asia, a future China would claim power, unity, and international prestige and pose serious threats to British colonial rule in India and Southeast Asia. So it decided to counter China on issues such as Tibet and the China-India border. British diplomats even believed that if Chiang Kai-shek asked Britain to grant independence to India, the Chinese government should agree to Tibet's independence from China.[99]

China persistently insisted that Tibet, like Mongolia and other border regions, was a part of China's territory. In 1933, with Japanese support, the Mongol prince Demchugdongrob (De Wang) demanded autonomy.[100] Chiang Kai-shek stated in public that China could grant autonomy to frontier peoples, to make a country where ethnic groups lived in harmony.[101] After the war, with Outer Mongolia already independent, Chiang Kai-shek was asked to agree to grant a high degree of autonomy to Tibet.[102] Both China and Britain insisted on their own vested interests and would not back down. As it turned out, the British position was soon negated by the independence of India, while China's insistence that the border regions were an integral part of China has continued to this day.

4 The Evolution of the Relationship between the Chinese Communist Party and the Comintern during the Sino-Japanese War

YANG KUISONG

In September 1935, after being driven to a desolate plateau in the southwest, the Chinese Communist Party (CCP) Central Committee and the Red Army's First and Fourth Front Armies split over their future direction: south or north? This was the largest split in the history of the CCP. For about a year, there were two CCP Central Committees, two central governments, and two military committees. The split occurred after the CCP had lost contact with Moscow. It was largely resolved when the northern part of the army unexpectedly reconnected with the Comintern.[1] The southern part was much stronger than the northern, but since it was out of contact with Moscow, it was the loser in the split.

Liaison officers from the Comintern reached the northern army's base in northern Shaanxi, and passed on instructions from the Comintern regarding the new United Front. The CCP was no longer isolated and could now form an alliance with one group or attack another. By using the conflicts between military factions of the Guomindang (GMD), the CCP found space to survive. As the United Front started to work, the CCP began to believe that it could unite with forces opposed to Chiang Kai-shek to overthrow his government in Nanjing. This belief was fiercely criticized by the Comintern, and the CCP was forced to negotiate with the Nanjing government.

Between the end of 1935 and the beginning of 1937, the CCP was strongly influenced by the Comintern politically, militarily, and financially. In the autumn and winter of 1936 the CCP concentrated all its forces to break through the government encirclement in order to receive shipments of military equipment from the Union of Soviet Socialist Republics (Soviet Union). It lost 20,000 to 30,000 soldiers, and the army fell into despair. To help the party and army get through the difficulties, the Comintern tried to secure nearly US$1 million from Moscow. But when the CCP aligned with Zhang Xueliang and Yang Hucheng to precipitate the Xi'an Incident and held Chiang Kai-shek and others hostage, the Comintern stepped in to prevent the CCP from harming Chiang. He was freed.[2]

The relationship between the CCP and the Comintern changed radically; the CCP Central Committee was then subordinate to the Comintern. The CCP was under remote control from Moscow. The telegraphed orders were often belated. But while the Chinese Communists were physically isolated, Moscow occupied center stage in world politics and had wider perspectives and a more acute political judgment. It was hard to say whether the relations were good or bad. Before the Sino-Japanese War broke out, the help from the Comintern was much greater than the negative effects. However, during the Sino-Japanese War, as the environment and the conditions of the CCP changed drastically, clashes, conflicts, and changes inevitably occurred in the relationship.

The First Disagreement

Before the Sino-Japanese War broke out, Moscow had little confidence in the leaders of the CCP. Major CCP leaders had made "mistakes." From 1931 on, the leadership of the CCP was volatile; its composition changed rapidly, and the leaders became younger and younger. After the start of the Long March, Moscow lost all contact with the CCP Central Committee. In January 1935, the CCP changed its leadership on its own initiative. This was significant for the Comintern, which always tried to control foreign Communist parties closely. When the Second United Front between the CCP and the GMD began, the Comintern was in direct contact with the CCP Central Committee, and it quickly resolved to send the CCP leaders in Moscow back to China in order to strengthen its own influence. This precipitated the first disagreement between the CCP and Moscow after the war broke out.

On July 7, 1937, the Lugouqiao Incident took place, and the war with Japan broke out. Then negotiations between the CCP and the GMD focused on the operational control of Communist troops and the CCP's status as a regional government. As the war expanded, the GMD government was forced to make concessions to the CCP. From the start of the negotiations, both parties mistrusted the other. The gap between the military strength of the two forces was tremendous. The CCP had only 20,000 to 30,000 soldiers, and its means of survival was still perilous; its attitude to using these troops was cautious. Chiang Kai-shek authorized the reorganization of the Red Army as the Eighth Route Army of the

National Revolutionary Army. It had three divisions and a headquarters unit. Zhu De was commander, and Peng Dehuai, deputy commander. The majority of leaders on the CCP Central Committee considered sending troops to fight the Japanese, but Mao Zedong and a few other leaders were wary.

Mao Zedong had two major concerns. First, the nearly 1 million GMD soldiers had been unable to halt the Japanese invasion. The Communists troops had poor equipment and only 20,000–30,000 soldiers. They had no possibility of winning on the North China battlefields. Communist troops were not good at defensive warfare. Even if they fought hard, they would not be able to reverse the situation. The CCP might lose invaluable assets. Second, in terms of social class, the GMD and CCP were enemies of each other. Chiang Kai-shek might use the Communist troops as he had used other regional troops. He would be happy to see the Communist troops eradicated on the battlefield. Mao believed that "we have to be defensive and on the alert." The CCP should not passively obey Chiang's order and throw its forces into the war. On August 1, 1937, with Zhang Wentian (also known as Luo Fu, the Central Committee's new leader chosen at the Zunyi Conference), Mao sent a telegram to Zhou Enlai and others who were in charge of negotiations with Nanjing. Mao asked them to pursue the following objectives:

First, as the strategic guideline, we should carry out independent and dispersed guerrilla warfare, not positional or concentrated warfare. We should not be limited in military tactics.

Second, according to these principles, the Red Army should at first send one-third of its forces. Large bodies of troops are not suitable for guerrilla warfare and are vulnerable to attack. Other units of our forces should be utilized later as the war develops.[3]

On the different opinions in the party and army, Mao clarified his concerns:

The war will be long and brutal. The warlords are independent from Chiang Kai-shek. Chiang Kai-shek demanded that all Red Army units should go to the frontlines. Furthermore, Shaanxi and Gansu provinces are our only viable rear areas behind the frontlines. Chiang Kai-shek still has ten divisions in Shaanxi and Gansu provinces. If we send all our troops to fight, Chiang Kai-shek could occupy our rear areas.[4]

He continued:

The schemes of the GMD are obvious. Their goals are as follows. First, the GMD will send all Red Army units to the battlefield. Second, the Communist troops will be dispatched along different routes and cannot be concentrated as a single unit. Therefore, they will have to follow orders [from the GMD]. Third, after the Red Army is dispatched, it will become subordinate to Chiang Kai-shek. Chiang will be in command and will resolve issues about the CCP and the border regions.

The CCP will not be allowed to make any protests. The soviets in China will be eradicated.[5]

To win over people with different opinions, the Central Committee convened a special meeting in Luochuan (northern Shaanxi) on August 22, 1937. At the meeting, Mao Zedong outlined his position explicitly:

All our work should follow the principle that the party and Red Army are central in the war and China should make the transition to a democratic republic with a worker-peasant-capitalist alliance. Therefore, the party should try all means to preserve and expand the Red Army. On the one hand, the army should avoid losses, on the other it should try to grow. The main function of the army right now is not to concentrate to fight but to scatter to mobilize the masses.[6]

Mao stated that the Red Army should cooperate with other military forces, but this cooperation was strategic and long-term, not tactical and short-term. Specifically, for the moment, if they concentrated their forces to fight the Japanese, they could not mobilize the masses; if they mobilized the masses, then they would not concentrate to fight. The only way to defeat the Japanese enemy and to help the Communists' allies was to disperse to mobilize the masses. If they concentrated their forces and fought right away, they could achieve no significant outcome.

This guideline obviously was different from Moscow's expectations and requirements. The strategy of the Comintern was based on the interests of the Soviet Union. The major objective of Soviet policy toward China was to push China to fight so that Japanese aggression would be directed south and reduce the threat to the Soviet Far East. The powers were reluctant to help China fight Japan. In fact, the Soviet Union was almost the only nation that offered aid to China. Stalin was willing to help the Chinese government build up its own military industry and equip GMD troops with modern weapons so that China could counter Japanese aggression in the long-term.[7] Given these circumstances, the Comintern would naturally ask the CCP to focus on maintaining the United Front and to fight Japan with all its strength. When the Comintern sent the Chinese representatives to the Comintern back to China, its message was to emphasize that the CCP must stick to three principles. First, fighting Japan was the supreme mission. Second, every policy should be made through the United Front, and every action should follow the United Front's decisions. Third, the CCP and GMD should share "joint responsibility and joint leadership."[8]

It is noteworthy that the instructions that Comintern general secretary Georgi Mikhailovich Dimitrov and Joseph Stalin gave to Chinese leaders were inconsistent. For instance, Dimitrov repeatedly underlined that "cooperation with the GMD will probably cause some trouble and dangers to our Chinese comrades and CCP. Chiang Kai-shek has his own secretive encirclement strategy." The Comintern even passed a resolution asking the CCP Central Committee "to increase revolutionary alertness to the utmost." The GMD was not to be allowed to use divisive tactics or espionage to sabotage the CCP and its army.[9] On the one hand, Stalin encouraged the CCP to take part in the general struggle for national liberation; on the other hand, he emphasized that the CCP must assume leadership in the fight. On the one hand, he declared that the Soviet Union would try its best to help Chiang Kai-shek build up China's own military industry; on the other hand, he was dissatisfied that the CCP had only three divisions. He held that the Eighth Route Army must have thirty divisions, not just three. He proposed that the Eighth Route Army should establish reserve units to expand its numbers. As the army still did not have modern equipment, its strategy should not be to attack directly but to harass the enemy and lure it in deep and attack the enemy from the rear. It should focus on destroying the Japanese transport lines and railway bridges.[10] Obviously, Wang Ming and other leaders did not heed these suggestions, with the result that they put themselves in disadvantageous positions in the later disputes.

Wang Ming, Kang Sheng, Chen Yun, and other leaders flew in to Yan'an on a Soviet airplane on November 29, 1937. They landed at the makeshift airport. Soon after they had settled in, they heard about the disputes going on inside the Central Committee on the strategic guidelines for the war. In the enlarged meeting of the Politburo from December 9 to December 13, Wang Ming came out clearly against Zhang Wentian and Mao Zedong, the major figures on the Central Committee. Wang stated that there was a clear standard to distinguish between enemies and friends: whether you fought the Japanese or not. Chiang Kai-shek was the formal leader of the Chinese people. If the CCP did not align with Chiang, it would effectively help Japan. He argued that GMD-CCP cooperation had several goals. First, it should unify all the various parties. Second, it should establish a unified national army. Third, it should establish a unified national authority. Now all these goals were being reached. This showed that China was heading in the right direction. Of course, in the United Front, clashes were inevitable. But in its struggle, the CCP should not scare off the GMD. It must acknowledge that the GMD was superior in national authority and military strength; this was a fact. It should not vainly claim that the proletariat should be superior to the capitalists. And it should not recklessly divide the GMD into left wing, middle, and right wing, or into fighters and capitulationists. It should not criticize the GMD for fighting without mobilizing the masses. Otherwise, the GMD would come to believe that the alliance with the CCP would fail. On the military front, the CCP should support unified leadership. The Eighth Route Army should obey Chiang Kai-shek's orders. It must not oppose unified military discipline, combat plans, or logistics. The independence of the Red Army was manifest as follows. First, it had leadership from the CCP. Second, it exercised leadership through its cadres. Third, it had established its own educational and political work. Fourth, it had created a model for winning victory. Moreover, it must have legal status now. Therefore, all Communist regulations must stick to the current format so that the GMD was not antagonized. Only in this way could the CCP achieve the objective of "joint responsibility and joint leadership." Only by building good relations with the GMD could China and the Red Army receive more Soviet assistance.[11]

Wang Ming had worked in the Comintern for many years, and he had a special status as inspector general. Consequently, the instructions that he passed on from the Comintern and his criticism of the previous work of the CCP Central Committee naturally received support from the majority of the conference delegates. Zhang Wentian made a self-criticism. Mao Zedong did not acknowledge that the strategic guidelines laid out at the Luochuan conference were wrong. He emphasized instead that the Red Army was slow to act because Chiang Kai-shek was tardy in issuing his commands. But he did admit that due to his lack of experience, some of his formulations and methods were wrong.[12]

Following the resolution of the Politburo, Zhang Wentian and Mao Zedong underlined CCP-GMD cooperation in the United Front. They made it clear that the CCP did not want to contest the so-called leadership in the cooperation. The GMD led by Chiang had already taken leadership. The CCP wholeheartedly supported the GMD government. To achieve the goals of the United Front, under the slogan of joint responsibility, joint leadership, and mutual help in development, the CCP must try to win consent and cooperation from the GMD. For issues where no compromise could be reached in the short run, the CCP would concede rather than act alone or play tricks.[13]

Wang Ming had returned to China with a dual mission. First, he was to execute the Comintern's policy in China. Second, as a new presence familiar with the international situation, he was to guide the CCP Central Committee. The first part of his mission was executed smoothly. But the second part of his mission did not go well. He had worked as a Comintern Executive Committee member and Presidium member for a long time, in charge of work in Latin America. He had also worked as the leader of the CCP delegation in the Comintern. He was used to giving orders to the CCP in China. He often used the name of the CCP Central Committee to issue instructions to party organs in China.

With this background, after he returned to China, Wang Ming often behaved in an overbearing fashion. At the Politburo meeting in December 1937, he criticized Zhang Wentian and Mao Zedong without mentioning their names explicitly. After the meeting, Wang went to Wuhan to meet Chiang Kai-shek. He stayed in Wuhan for a long time, in the name of party secretary of the Yangzi River region. He used the name of the CCP Central Committee to issue statements. He also used the names of leaders in Yan'an, such as Mao Zedong. He acted unilaterally, such as requesting that the Central Committee's official journal, *Jiefang ribao* (Liberation daily) be moved to Wuhan. Soon major leaders in Yan'an such as Zhang Wentian and Mao Zedong were dissatisfied with Wang Ming's behavior.

At that time, Wang Ming followed the Comintern principle that "fighting Japanese aggression is supreme." He tried to build good relations with the GMD and to carry out "joint responsibility and joint leadership." But his efforts were not successful. The GMD refused to legitimize the CCP and would not allow Communists to join the Nationalist government. Moreover, the GMD's propaganda organ proclaimed "one party, one principle." It declared that the GMD was superior to all other parties. Other parties were not qualified to talk about equality with the GMD.[14]

Wang Ming had thought that Zhu De, Peng Dehuai, and other leaders stood beside him, but as the CCP bases expanded rapidly, these leaders were forced to break with the policy that all administrative regulations in the Eighth Route Army region had to keep to the old format. They acted without formal permission and established governments in the border area of Shanxi, Chahar, and Hebei. Wang opposed these moves, condemning them as practically validating the rumor that the world would belong to the Communist Party after China won the war. He claimed that these measures would be detrimental to the United Front. But he could do nothing to stop them.[15]

Wang Ming's efforts to carry out the resolutions of the Comintern ran into major problems with the GMD. Thus, when the Central Committee convened a Politburo meeting at the end of February 1938, issues about the independence and leadership again became key topics of discussion. Zhang Wentian explicitly noted that after a few months' experience, it was obvious that the CCP and GMD were indeed struggling over leadership. The GMD needed the CCP, but at the same time it feared that the CCP would get too powerful. Conflicts were inevitable. Mao Zedong underlined the role of the CCP, stating that victory in the war depended on the strength of the CCP and the Chinese people under its leadership. He did not believe that the GMD forces could guarantee victory. On the contrary, he held that the CCP must pay attention to the strategic importance of guerrilla warfare in the expanded national revolutionary war.[16]

Wang Ming's disagreement with Zhang Wentain and Mao Zedong was fully revealed in March 1938. On March 25, the CCP Secretariat, headed by Zhang and Mao, drafted a telegram to the GMD Provisional National Congress. It demanded that the GMD convene a congress that could truly represent national popular opinion, pass guidelines for the United Front to fight Japanese aggression, and devise detailed measures for the guidelines' implementation. Patriotic people with goodwill, credibility, and ability from all political parties should be brought into the government. Local governments should be reorganized. Corrupt officials should be removed. Elections should be held in districts and towns. The GMD should promulgate democratic laws on freedom of speech, assembly, publication, and religion.[17] Wang Ming suppressed this telegram. Without authorization from the Secretariat, Wang, in the name of the Central Committee, submitted a rather modest and general proposal to the congress. He advised the leaders in Yan'an, "What you wrote cannot be sent to the GMD. I hope that nowhere will you publicize your second proposal, since it would have a very detrimental effect inside and outside the party."[18]

In April 1938, Ren Bishi went to Moscow to report on the Central Committee's work in carrying out the Comintern's instructions. He also reported on the conflicts between Wang Ming and the CCP leadership in Yan'an. On the one hand, the report affirmed the Comintern's instructions. On the other hand, it stated that the GMD was trying to maintain a one-party system and using any means to weaken the CCP. It had prevented the Eighth Route Army from obtaining grain or raising money locally to replenish losses in men and weapons. It was also determinedly preventing the CCP from expanding its influence over the masses. In its propaganda, it stuck to "one principle, one party, one leader, one army, and one government." However, the Eighth Route Army had continued to carry on guerrilla warfare, had expanded its base, and was developing considerably. It had established many bases behind the Japanese lines. The situation was complex: the CCP and GMD were in cooperation and in conflict.[19]

Before Wang Ming returned to China in 1937, Dimitrov and Stalin emphasized two principles: the CCP should strengthen the United Front, and at the same time it should focus on independent development and expansion. Moscow was pleased with what the CCP had achieved in less than a year. Ren reported that the Central Committee had stuck to the line that "resisting Japanese aggression is supreme" and to "joint responsibility and joint leadership." This suggested that the CCP had met Moscow's demands. But just at this time Pavel Mif, Wang Ming's key supporter in the Comintern, became a target in the purges. Wang then had no chance for promotion; indeed the Comintern decided to abandon Wang and support Mao Zedong. Dimitrov told Wang Jiaxiang and others who were heading back to China that the CCP and Red Army should strengthen internal unity and support Mao Zedong.[20] Although Wang Ming believed that he had faithfully carried out the orders of the Comintern, the Comintern believed that Mao could carry out the Comintern's orders and also had strong military and political leadership capacities. Only Mao could guarantee that the CCP could flourish in so complicated an environment as the War of Resistance and the United Front.

The Second Disagreement

In September 1938, Wang Jiaxiang returned to Yan'an with new orders from the Comintern.[21] The CCP convened the Sixth Plenum of the Sixth Central Committee and endorsed Dimtrov's statement that the CCP should unite around Mao Zedong. With this affirmation from the Comintern, Mao expressed his support for the Comintern's guidelines on the United Front. He reiterated the Comintern's instructions on support for Chiang Kai-shek and its belief that the GMD had made progress and that war could allow all forces in China to grow. The CCP should consider measures that could alleviate the GMD's concerns. For instance, they should not recruit GMD members, set up branches inside the GMD, or hold secret activities or organize secret organs. The CCP should also submit to the GMD the list of CCP members who had joined the GMD.[22]

Following Mao's proposal, the Sixth Plenum passed a resolution to support the Three People's Principles, Chiang Kai-shek, and the GMD government. The resolution also stated that the CCP would not establish secret units inside the GMD or the army. The meeting made a declaration to publicize the resolution. Meanwhile, Mao Zedong asked Zhou Enlai and other leaders to propose to Chiang Kai-shek to reorganize the GMD to accommodate the GMD-CCP cooperation and strengthen ties between the two parties.[23] However, the proposal received no active response from Chiang Kai-shek. After the fall of Wuhan, the GMD government was forced to retreat to Chongqing. Half of China had fallen to the Japanese.

The GMD fell into great difficulties, militarily and politically. In contrast, as the Japanese troops advanced, the Communists seized opportunities and expanded their bases in the enemy's rear. The Communist forces and their influence grew significantly. Chiang Kai-shek was horrified. When Wang Ming, Zhou Enlai, Bo Gu, and other Communist leaders presented him with the resolution of the Sixth Plenum, which was intended to promote CCP-GMD cooperation, Chiang Kai-shek was noncommittal. He claimed that his responsibility was to merge the CCP into the GMD, and thus he would encourage Communists to leave the CCP and join the GMD or have the CCP give up its name and join the GMD en masse. But CCP members could not join the GMD as individuals. Nor was the CCP allowed to expand among the masses. This issue went to the GMD's very existence; if these goals were not reached, he would not die in peace. Even if the GMD won the war with Japan, the victory would be meaningless.[24] Representing the Eighth Route Army, Peng Dehuai asked to reorganize the administrative zones in North China according to the actual situation and to match senior officers to the new administrative zones, in order to decrease clashes. The Eighth Route Army was even willing to give up some regions as a sign of goodwill. But Chiang Kai-shek would not concede.

Between January 21 and 31, 1939, the GMD convened the Fifth Plenum of the Fifth Central Committee. The meeting formally rejected the CCP suggestions. Instead, it made policies to prevent or limit CCP growth. Subsequently, the GMD in various regions took steps to implement these policies. To win control over villages in the enemy's rear, Chiang Kai-shek dispatched large numbers of GMD troops to restore the GMD's political presence in the rear. This measure inevitably caused a series of military clashes with Communist forces.

The skirmishes and conflicts between the two parties in China paralleled the tensions in Europe. Since 1933, seeing the rise the Nazi Germany, the Soviet Union had tried to sign collective security treaties with Western democracies such as the United Kingdom and France in order to reduce the danger that Germany and Italy would start a war. But the United Kingdom and France were suspicious of the Soviet appeals. On September 29, 1938, the United Kingdom and France suddenly adopted policies of appeasement. They acceded to Germany and Italy at Munich and agreed to cede Sudetenland to Germany in order to ease Germany's threat to Czechoslovakia, which was an ally of the United Kingdom and France. Germany got the Sudetenland, but it still went on to occupy Czechoslovakia (March 1939). Hungary had allied itself to Germany. Germany's expansion into Eastern Europe convinced Stalin that it was a British/French conspiracy to push Germany to move eastward. On March 10, 1939, Stalin condemned the United Kingdom and France as warmongers. He tried to push Germany westward. On August 23, the Soviet Union and Germany signed a nonaggression pact, agreeing to secretly delimited spheres of influence in Eastern Europe and a Poland divided between themselves. On September 1, 1939, German troops stormed into Poland, an ally of Britain and France. The United Kingdom and France had to declare war on Germany.

The change of Soviet policy toward Britain, France, Germany, and Italy altered the Comintern's United Front policy in Europe, and the change in the Comintern's policies toward the capitalist European countries inevitably influenced its attitude toward the tensions between the CCP and GMD in China. On May 20, 1939, after hearing from Ren Bishi and Lin Biao, Dimitrov stated that the GMD repression of the CCP was part of a capitulationist plan and proposed to focus its strength on attacking GMD capitulationists.[25] In a telegraphed instruction sent after Dimitrov's speech, the United Front was still emphasized, but the message stated that the major danger was that the GMD would surrender. The CCP should be alert to the possibility that the GMD would surrender and to its conspiracy against the CCP.[26] This corresponded to the concerns of Mao Zedong since the Luochuan conference in 1937.

Mao Zedong had analyzed the international background to the GMD's change of policy. He suspected that Chiang Kai-shek would organize a

Munich-type conference in Asia and, relying on the United Kingdom and the United States, make concessions to Japan. He believed that the recent CCP-GMD clashes were related to British and American policy.[27] The instructions from the Comintern confirmed his judgment. His assessment of the international and domestic situations had changed. Previously, he had been optimistic about the international situation; now he stressed the dangers of concession and capitulation. Previously, he had held a positive attitude toward Western democracies such as the United Kingdom and the United States; now he condemned the anti-Communist, anti-Soviet nature of imperialism. At the Sixth Plenum, he had seen a bright future for the GMD and had proposed to support Chiang Kai-shek and the GMD government wholeheartedly; now he pointed out the shortcomings of the GMD and withdrew unconditional support for Chiang. He asked the CCP to be ready to deal with GMD capitulation and the chaos that would follow. The CCP would then be the savior of the Chinese people, who would see the CCP as a star; they would have faith in the Soviet Union too, and in international revolution.[28]

After war broke out in Europe on September 1, 1939, Mao Zedong made a public speech. Following Moscow's instructions, he defined the war in Europe as an unjust war between imperialist groups. He went further to claim that the CCP should turn the imperialist war into a revolutionary domestic war and build up the people's United Front against the imperialist war to overthrow the counterrevolutionary fortresses. The CCP would use revolutionary war to defeat the imperialist war, overthrow the warmongers, and topple the capitalists. He claimed that the capitalist economy had reached its end and the time for great changes and revolution had come.[29]

From the spring of 1939 to the beginning of 1940, the cooperation between the CCP and the Comintern was flawless and mutually beneficial. At this time, Communists in Europe faced great difficulties. In particular, Communists in countries that faced German and Italian aggression had to deal with the issue of how to relate to the capitalist governments and parties that resisted fascism. Some Communist organizations were not capable of "correctly managing" this issue according to Moscow's requirements; they were forced to disband, after they were abandoned. The Comintern itself fell into confusion.

The Comintern supported the CCP in the military skirmishes and clashes. At the beginning of 1940, the Secretariat of the Comintern Executive Committee repeatedly condemned the GMD's secret plans to capitulate and expressed concern over the future of the United Front. The condemnations claimed that the counterrevolutionaries inside the GMD were more dangerous than ever. They were trying to get the GMD to act against the Communists and to cause clashes and conflicts between GMD troops and the Eighth Route Army. Their aim was to eradicate CCP governments and disband the Eighth Route Army. This would be implementing Japanese schemes to use Chinese to suppress Chinese. The Comintern resolutely supported the CCP in rejecting GMD proposals that might isolate or weaken the Eighth Route Army and the New Fourth Army and might threaten CCP governments. The Comintern supported the CCP's struggle against counterrevolutionary forces.[30]

In the spring of 1940, German armies crushed those of France and the United Kingdom in a stunning blitzkrieg. In June 1940, France surrendered. Three months later, on September 27, Germany, Italy, and Japan suddenly declared a military alliance. Stalin realized that the Soviet Union was again imperiled. Then, the Soviet Union might be attacked from the west and the east. In this new situation, Moscow wanted the GMD to fight fiercely, as its key ally. On September 29, Chiang Kai-shek sent a telegram to Stalin in which he stated his willingness to cooperate with the Soviet Union and fight together.[31] Stalin promptly replied that the Soviet Union would continue to give significant aid to the GMD government if Chiang could exclude the possibility of negotiating with Japan.[32] Moscow resumed its plans to aid China providing a large amount of military aid, including 150 fighters, 100 bombers, 300 cannons, and 500 vehicles. The Soviet government selected Vasily Ivanovich Chuikov as the chief military adviser to China. Stalin told Chuikov that "the CCP and working class are still too weak to become the leaders in the war against the invaders. It takes time to win over the masses. It is hard to tell how long it will take." They would support Chiang Kai-shek fully to make sure that the Soviet Union could avoid fighting on two fronts if Germany attacked the Soviet Union.[33]

Moscow's attitude toward the GMD had changed, but the CCP did not know this. Mao Zedong still looked at the domestic situation and CCP-GMD relations on the assumption that the GMD was going to surrender to Japan. On July 16, 1940, the GMD issued an order to the Eighth Route Army and New Fourth Army to move north across the Yellow River and concentrate in Hebei and Chahar provinces. Mao was puzzled. At that time, the CCP forces had expanded to 470,000 soldiers, and there were rear-area Communist bases in ten provinces in North and East China; in these GMD troops were inferior to Communist troops. Mao could not find a reasonable explanation for Chiang Kai-shek's sudden order. He assumed, therefore, that there was a hidden agenda, connected to the world war. His conclusion was that Chiang intended to surrender to Japan. Chiang wanted the CCP troops to move into Hebei and Chahar so that GMD and Japanese troops could attack the CCP's forces on both flanks. Mao Zedong was extremely worried. He decided to act preemptively. His plan was to muster 150,000 superior troops, under the banner of "exterminating the pro-Japanese clique" and attack from North China toward Chongqing through northwest China, to crush Chiang Kai-shek's plot to destroy the Communists. This measure involved great political risk. Mao could not decide impetuously. On November 4, he sent a long telegram to Dimitrov, asking Moscow to consider this option and to give instructions.[34]

By this time, Moscow no longer believed that Chiang Kai-shek was plotting to surrender to Japan and attack the CCP troops. In his reply, Dimitrov stressed this. He stated that Chiang Kai-shek and his clique were different from pro-Japanese cliques. They were vulnerable to being trapped by the pro-Japanese cliques into surrender, but provided that the CCP did not act aggressively and persistently showed support for Chiang, the GMD, and its troops, the risk of surrender and split could be avoided.[35]

This was Moscow's view, and Mao could not find evidence to prove that Chiang was indeed plotting to join Japanese troops in attacking Communist troops. The Central Committee accepted Moscow's judgment. From December on, the committee issued inner-party instructions stating that the danger of a GMD surrender was over. "The major danger is still Left Extremism." From now on, to avoid upsetting the GMD, "we should not emphasize anti-capitulationism as we did on October 11."[36]

The Central Committee and Moscow believed that the anti-Communist wave in the GMD had passed and that a serious danger no longer existed. They did not anticipate the New Fourth Army Incident (South Anhui Incident), which started on January 6, 1941. As nearly 10,000 soldiers of the New Fourth Army in southern Anhui marched northward, they were ambushed. More than 7,000 soldiers were killed, commander Ye Ting was captured, and party secretary Xiang Ying died as he tried to break through the encirclement. The incident was sparked by mutual mistrust and suspicion, not by a planned conspiracy. Nevertheless, for the CCP, which suffered major losses, the incident seemed to be a machination that Chiang Kai-shek had planned for a long time. Moreover, based on his previous estimation that Chiang and the Japanese might attack the CCP troops on both flanks, Mao concluded that it was part of the GMD's conspiracy to exterminate the CCP army. Mao sent repeated telegrams to the Comintern. He described how, as the New Fourth Army marched northward, they were encircled by GMD soldiers. They fought fiercely for several days and nights. Meanwhile, the GMD had concentrated 300,000 soldiers and was attacking the CCP in the Shaanxi/Gansu/Ningxia border region. The Red Army was in danger of being exterminated. Guerrilla bases in Jiangsu, Shandong, Anhui, and Hubei were also under attack. The GMD might soon launch a wave of arrests and assassinations all over the country. The counterrevolutionaries were aggressive, but the CCP was ready to counterattack.[37]

These urgent telegrams from Mao Zedong shocked Dimitrov. He immediately informed Stalin: "Obviously Chiang Kai-shek believes that now is the best time to launch a general attack on the Communists. His military commanders have shamelessly attacked the New Fourth Army and are fighting the Eighth Route Army and the Communist border regions." "The Communists are in an extremely difficult and dangerous situation. They have to launch a counterattack against Chiang's aggression and conduct self-defense." "If Chiang does not stop this aggression, a civil war is inevitable." "To avoid a civil war, the Soviet Union must adopt measures to influence Chiang. It should urge the United States, the United Kingdom, and other countries to take similar measures. This would put pressure on the GMD government and influence Chinese public opinion."[38]

Soon Dimitrov received information that the situation was not as bad as Mao claimed. On January 17, 1941, news came from Chongqing. Chiang Kai-shek asked Zhang Chong to pass on a message to Moscow: "The event that took place between the Third War Zone and the New Fourth Army should be regarded as a local military incident. . . . It will definitely not affect the relations between the central government and CCP." On January 21, Dimitrov talked with Stalin. Stalin had received reports from the Soviet ambassador and the military attaché in Chongqing. He noted that the New Fourth Army had received an order to move north but had instead moved south, into the defense region of the Third War Zone. He did not support Mao Zedong's opinion but on the contrary criticized Ye Ting as an undisciplined guerrilla fighter. He believed that Ye had provided a pretext for the GMD army's attack.[39]

Mao Zedong was unhappy that Moscow did not support him immediately. On January 20, he sent angry telegrams to Zhou Enlai and other CCP leaders. "The current CCP-GMD relations are not working for us or for the revolution. The deterioration was initiated by Chiang Kai-shek. This is an opportunity for us." "The problem is that the Far Place [that is, Moscow] has a policy that runs against our policy. Over three months we have not resolved the dispute. So we will go on the offensive politically. But militarily we have to be reserved. We have to be prepared for aggression. We hope to have the strength to go on the attack in four to six months."[40]

One week later, the CCP Politburo passed an important resolution. It stated that the New Fourth Army Incident was the point at which the GMD turned from revolution to counterrevolution. The CCP's previous policy toward the landlords and capitalists headed by Chiang Kai-shek was to struggle on the one hand and to unify on the other. This policy no longer applied. The CCP had to abandon the alliance and take up the fight. In the present international and domestic situation, the process might take a long time, but Chiang's movement toward a split was clear.[41]

The Comintern immediately expressed its disagreement with this resolution. Dimitrov sent a telegram to Mao. "We believe that the split with Chiang Kai-shek is not inevitable. You should not prepare for a split. On the contrary, the CCP must rely on people who want to preserve the United Front and use all measures to avoid a split. Please reconsider your position and inform us of your thinking and proposals."[42]

Mao was reluctant to agree with Dimitrov, but unexpectedly Japanese troops attacked GMD troops in Henan, so he had to readjust his decision to move to a split. On February 7, his instructions changed to acknowledge that the CCP and the GMD again had grounds for mutual concessions. Chiang Kai-shek's plan to exterminate the Communists had failed. A civil war could be avoided. It was possible to use the conflict between Japan and Chiang Kai-shek to push Chiang into being pro-Soviet and to making peace with the Communists.[43] The Central Committee did not give up the fight. It protested when the GMD had erased the name of the New Fourth Army and continued the imprisonment of Ye Ting. When Japanese troops attacked the GMD base in Zhongtiaoshan in the southern part of Shanxi Province three months later, the Soviet adviser insisted that the Eighth Route Army units nearby should aid the Nationalist troops, but the CCP refused. The Central Committee informed the frontline commanders that they should not ignore Soviet suggestions, but they need not follow them too precisely. The current guideline was to attack Japanese troops, but they should not fight too fiercely. If they did not fight, the GMD would blame them, and neutral people would also have strong feelings. But if they fought too fiercely, they would run the risk that Japanese troops would seek revenge, and the GMD would take advantage and attack the CCP.[44] The basic guideline was to unite and help the GMD to fight. But they should never rise to the GMD's provocation. They should scrupulously consider the conditions and give well-planned assistance.[45]

This time the disagreement between the CCP and the Comintern was far more serious than the previous time. Obviously, Dimitrov had to stand beside the Soviet Union. He subtly criticized the CCP's actions. On June 5, he stated in a telegram, "Although there are many difficulties, you must take all possible measures to actively resist Japanese attacks."[46] However, Dimitrov never understood that: Mao believed that only by following his own ideas could the CCP bring about the Chinese people's liberation and that the CCP's future was in its own hands. This was the largest and most insurmountable division between the two sides.

The Third Disagreement

The CCP and Moscow were sharply divided over the New Fourth Army Incident, but there was no open breakdown in relations. On June 22, 1941, Germany suddenly invaded the Soviet Union, a huge catastrophe. The CCP still asked for economic aid from Moscow.

Economic aid was an important means of maintaining the Comintern's supervisory relationship over the CCP. From the founding of the CCP in 1921 to the early 1930s, the Comintern had provided monthly funding to the CCP. In the early 1930s, when the CCP Central Committee withdrew from the cities, economic aid changed to a four-stage process: application, examination, ratification, and allocation. Once the two sides reestablished telecommunications in 1936, the process was that the Comintern reviewed the CCP's funding applications and transmitted them to the Soviet Communist Party Central Committee, which would authorize the Comintern to instruct relevant departments to allocate funding to the CCP.[47]

The requests submitted by the CCP would normally be cut. This occasion was no exception. The CCP asked for US$2 million for military equipment and logistics. Dimitrov cut the budget in half and submitted it to the Soviet leaders Molotov and Malenkov. The next day, the two leaders granted the request. Dimitrov notified Mao that US$1 million had been approved and would be paid in several tranches.[48]

After the German invasion, the Soviet military repeatedly asked the CCP Central Committee to provide intelligence about the Japanese army on the Soviet-Mongolian border. The Soviets hoped that the Eighth Route Army would launch an attack to distract Japanese troops from massing on the Soviet border. The CCP did provide some intelligence to Moscow. This was the context for asking for increased financial aid. Since its foundation, the CCP had always promoted defending the Soviet Union. With the German invasion, Moscow did call on the CCP for help.

On July 2, 1941, ten days after the Soviet-German war broke out, Mao Zedong sent his first order on defending the Soviet Union to frontline commanders:

A Soviet-Japanese war is very likely to erupt. Sino-Soviet relations will improve. If Japanese troops attack the Soviet Union, they will strengthen their suppression in North China to secure the rear. Our army must prepare immediately to fight with the Soviet forces. When the time comes, we will act at once. This cooperation is long-term and strategic, not short-term and tactical.[49]

These guidelines were similar to the instructions Mao gave about cooperation with GMD troops in fighting Japan after the Sino-Japanese War broke out. Mao did not order the Communist troops not to cooperate, but the cooperation had to be based on strategic considerations, on long-term objectives, and on preserving the Eighth Route Army's strength. The CCP would not blindly follow Soviet orders. The cooperation that the CCP Central Committee envisaged was mostly collecting intelligence and destroying the enemy's transport lines. Mao did not want to sacrifice the Eighth Route Army for the Soviet Union, and he was not convinced that Japan would attack the Soviet Union. A few days later, Mao told Zhou

Enlai, who was in Chongqing, that the Soviet situation might be stabilizing, and that Japan would not attack the Soviet Union. Intelligence that the Japanese were concentrating in Manchuria had not been confirmed. Mao asked Zhou to inform Soviet diplomats that the Communist military headquarters in North China was ready.[50]

By early July 1941, according to Soviet intelligence, Japan was ready to act. Japanese troops were massed in Manchuria and would attack the Soviet Union. The Soviet Union was withdrawing major plants and personnel into Siberia. Japan's attack would force the Soviet Union to fight on two fronts, an impossible task. Moscow was afraid of this outcome. It expected the Chinese troops to draw off Japanese troops. But the GMD troops were in southwestern China and unable to move to North China or Manchuria. Moscow could rely only on the 200,000 to 300,000 Eighth Route Army troops. The Soviet Communist Party Central Committee and the Comintern telegraphed the CCP Central Committee to ask the CCP to aid Soviet resistance to the German invasion by attacking Japanese forces along the Soviet-Mongolian border.

The telegram from Moscow was transmitted to the CCP Central Committee through the Soviet representative in Yan'an and its embassy in Chongqing. On July 15, 1941, Mao Zedong made an official response. In his telegram to Zhou Enlai, Mao made his opinions clear:

Concerning military operations, since the Soviet-German war broke out, we increased reconnaissance and are ready to sabotage transport lines to distract the Japanese enemy. We are determined to help the Soviet Red Army as much as we can in current conditions. However, over the past four years, the Japanese have built strong defenses in the cities, along railway lines, and in mines. The gap in military equipment between the enemy and us is simply too great. We have increasing difficulties with labor, materiel, and weapons. If Japan attacks the Soviet Union, we are afraid that we cannot offer too much military assistance. If we act unconditionally, we are likely to collapse and will not be able to hold our bases for long. This would be very bad for us. We should consolidate our base in the enemy's rear and carry out extensive guerrilla warfare. Our policy should be for a long-term fight, not gambling. If we had more armaments, machine guns, cannons, and explosives, our operations would be more effective. Bullets are essential; we have only twenty bullets for each rifle. We have few machine guns, even fewer cannons. We have no TNT.[51]

In the official telegram to Moscow, Mao Zedong deleted the sentences "we are afraid that we cannot offer too much military assistance" and "if we act unconditionally." The telegram emphasized only that with current equipment, the Red Army would try its best to prevent Japanese forces from moving from North China to attack the Soviet Union. The Communist army would focus on destroying the enemy's transportation network. The telegram asked most urgently for military equipment and ammunition. Molotov followed the Soviet Communist Party's suggestions and expressed agreement to the reply from China, but he did not make any specific promises on the request for ammunition.[52]

In the event, Japan decided to attack south and occupy the British, French, and American colonies in Asia. On December 8, 1941, the Japanese attacked Pearl Harbor and provoked the United States into declaring war on Japan, Germany, and Italy. Japan did not attack the Soviet Union. The CCP did not come to a direct clash with Moscow over defending the Soviet Union but stuck to a self-interested line. On October 7, 1941, Dimitrov telegraphed Mao Zedong and the CCP Central Committee with fifteen pointed questions. One was: if fascist Germany continued its attack on the Soviet Union, what measures would the CCP take to launch an offensive against Japan on the China front in order to prevent Germany's ally in Asia from opening a second front against the Soviet Union? Such questions were echoed by a few Chinese leaders such as Wang Ming. At a meeting of the Central Committee, Wang directly questioned Mao's policy. But Mao stuck to his policy. On November 7, after Japanese troops started a prolonged extermination campaign in North China, Mao, in the name of the Central Military Committee, reminded leaders in various bases that they should focus on preserving their strength and avoid provoking the enemy. The struggle had entered a new and fiercer stage, in which the policy was protracted struggle and dispersed guerrilla warfare. To deal with the enemy, they must use all means (from violent combat to the most peaceful revolutionary ambivalence). They should preserve their military and popular strength and wait for the appropriate time.[53]

Mao's pragmatic policy was focused on winning the revolution in China, a policy not acceptable to the Comintern. Moreover, inside the CCP, there were a few leaders such as Wang Ming who were used to standing beside the Comintern. To consolidate his status and his political line, Mao had to launch an ideological remolding campaign from top to bottom within the party.

In May 1941, Mao Zedong proposed to his senior colleagues that they should rid themselves of the subjectivism that ignored the objective reality of the Chinese revolution and the dogmatism that blindly copied foreign experience. He ordered the compilation of party history documents (since the Sixth Party Congress). The compilation studied the party's successes and failures and reviewed experiences and lessons to be learned so that people would know that the Chinese revolution had developed well under his leadership. From September 10 to October 22, he convened an expanded Politburo conference. He stressed the serious damage to the party that had come after the people who came back from the Soviet Union had assumed leadership, including the serious mistakes that Wang Ming made at the Politburo conference in December 1937, just after the Sino-Japanese War erupted.[54]

Mao had resolved the ideological division between the party's leadership and other leaders. Only he could lead the Chinese revolution. He launched the Rectification Campaign targeting party cadres. He still insisted on using the basic theories of Marx, Engels, Lenin, and Stalin as guidelines, and he designated the articles and documents to be studied. He was still respectful of Dimitrov and the Comintern. His fundamental objective was that party members should grasp basic revolutionary theories, and then, based on the specific realities of the Chinese revolution, as analyzed by himself, the party would pursue Marxism in a Chinese style.[55] At the beginning of the Rectification Campaign, the Communist daily newspaper, the *Jiefang ribao,* published an article which stated that the party and the army must get rid of the rubbish of subjectivism, dogmatism, and sectarianism and should believe the following in unanimity:

Comrade Mao Zedong's theory and strategy is the application and development of Marxism-Leninism theory and strategy in colonies and societies that are half colonial and half feudal. Comrade Mao Zedong's theory is China's Marxism-Leninism. Therefore, if you want to become a Chinese Marxist-Leninist, you must study and grasp Comrade Mao Zedong's theory and strategy and be its loyal disciple.[56]

In the year after the campaign was launched, Mao established absolute prestige and authority from the top to the bottom of the party. On March 20, 1943, the Politburo appointed Mao as Politburo chairman and chairman of the Central Committee Secretariat, with the final say in all questions discussed at Secretariat meetings.[57]

Mao Zedong used all means to consolidate his status and power, but he did not break with Moscow or the Comintern. We notice that even during the Rectification Campaign, Mao was still respectful to Moscow and valued the Comintern's instructions. However, he chose to implement only those instructions that benefited the CCP. For instance, on June 16, 1942, Dimitrov sent a telegram to the CCP instructing them to make all efforts to improve their relations with Chiang Kai-shek and consolidate the United Front.[58] Mao Zedong followed the instruction without hesitation. He talked with the GMD liaison person and asked Zhou Enlai to pass on a message that he was willing to talk with Chiang Kai-shek in person about GMD-CCP relations.

As it turned out, in 1943, two months after the Politburo granted supreme control to Mao Zedong, Stalin decided to disband the Comintern, which had been in operation as the organization for global Communists for twenty-four years, in order to push the British and American governments to open a second front. On May 21, Dimitrov sent this message to the CCP Central Committee. On the next day, the Comintern Executive Committee Presidium announced the news in the Soviet newspaper *Pravda.* On May 26, the CCP Politburo passed its own resolution, agreeing to dissolve the Comintern. On June 9, the Presidium of the Comintern Executive Committee declared formally that the Comintern and its affiliated organs were to disband on that day.

It is not hard to imagine what meaning this decision from Moscow had for Mao Zedong and the CCP. The CCP was not reluctant to accept the dissolution of the Comintern. It rated the action highly.[59] Immediately after getting the message from Dimitrov, Mao expressed this view inside the party. He claimed that the Comintern had been disbanded because this kind of international organization was no longer suitable for the complicated and fast-changing situation; the Comintern could not give timely and correct instructions given the complicated situations that Communist parties in various countries faced. Revolution must be organized by the Communist parties in their respective countries. The complicated situation of the Chinese revolution at the time was different from the historical situation of the Russian Revolution. The dissolution of the Comintern would help Communist parties in other countries to become more home based and make it easier to find revolutionary paths that suited their national characteristics and specific conditions.[60]

During the Sino-Japanese War, relations between the CCP and the Comintern changed several times; the relationship was complex and delicate. The Soviet Union backed the Comintern. It was the headquarters of the international Communist movement and the source of orthodox ideology, a powerful force that the CCP had to respect. For the CCP, the Comintern played multiple roles. By maintaining good relations with the Comintern, the CCP gained ideological sanction and economic and military benefits. Hierarchical subordination and concrete benefits were key elements in the relationship.

However, the Soviet Union controlled the Comintern. Instructions and help from the Comintern reflected the needs of the Soviet Union. The major recipient of Soviet aid was the GMD government. The CCP would have become subordinate to the GMD if it had strictly followed instructions from Moscow. In the CCP's handling of relations with the Comintern during the war, we see that without Mao Zedong, the CCP would have suffered by catering to the self-interest of the Soviet Union. As long as Mao was in charge in the CCP, the party grew by using the wartime opportunities as its relationship with Moscow inevitably moved toward detachment and even conflict.

Of course, Mao Zedong was still a Communist. He ultimately had to get ideological legitimacy from Moscow. No matter how much he upset Moscow in the interests of the CCP, he had to demonstrate his loyalty to Moscow, something that would not change even after the Comintern ceased to exist.

On November 29, 1943, the CCP Central Committee passed a resolution sternly condemning the line of Wang Ming and Bo Gu. "Essentially they are the representatives of the GMD in the CCP. They are the presence of landlords and capitalists among the proletariat."[61] Dimitrov expressed disagreement. Mao Zedong did not show disrespect, even though the Comintern had been dissolved and Dimitrov no longer had any status with the CCP. On the contrary, Mao tried to let Dimitrov believe that he deeply respected Moscow. "Comrade Stalin and the Soviet Union are highly respected by the CCP." "We have the same thoughts and feelings as you do."[62]

5 Canada-China Relations in Wartime China

DIANA LARY

The Japanese invasion of China in 1937 produced convoluted responses from states well-disposed toward China. There was a general sense, at the government level, that there was little to be done. The League of Nations' condemnation of Japan after the annexation of Manchuria in 1931 had been futile—Japan withdrew from the League. The deep economic depression in the West made involvement in another war seem foolhardy, and there was a widespread resistance to involvement in another war so soon after the Great War. The only state to come to China's aid was the Soviet Union. Elsewhere, there was some official hand-wringing, some sympathy for China, some criticism of Japan, but little concrete help.

The reaction of many Westerners living in China was very different. Resident missionaries and journalists rushed to China's aid, launching vociferous campaigns in support of China and providing asylum and practical help to refugees. Businessmen in China were less enthusiastic in their support for China. Few were pro-Japanese, but they had a grudging respect for Japanese efficiency, and they feared that a long war would spoil business, as it did. As time went on, the brutality of the Japanese invasion produced an increase in the influence Westerners in China had on their home governments, whose policies toward China came to be shaped in part by the sympathies and actions of their nationals in China. These people used long-established connections within their home communities.

Canada and China

Wars are key periods for the growth of nationalism and national identity. For Canada, the two world wars of the twentieth century were the generators of a growing sense of autonomous national identity. Ironically, though Canada's participation in the wars was predicated on the historic attachment to Britain, both wars helped to accentuate the separation from Britain. Canada showed a growing reluctance to be the handmaiden of Britain, and it fought in the wars on its own terms. At the same time, Canada's early involvement in both wars marked a clear divergence of policy from its neighbor, the United States, which entered both wars much later than did Canada.

Since the First World War, Canada had moved out of the shadow of the imperial umbrella and had gradually come to determine its own foreign policies and priorities. Much of its foreign representation was still through British offices, and much foreign policy was still made in London, but Canada set up its own diplomatic offices abroad, first in London and Washington and then, in 1929, in Tokyo, a post responsible for all of Asia. The Tokyo opening was a sign of the importance that Canada assigned to Asia.

Canada had no diplomatic representation in China until well into the Second World War, except for a trade office in Hong Kong, but this did not mean that China was ignored in Canada. Quite the contrary, China had a special place in the hearts of Canadians, established long before the outbreak of war in China in 1937. In the decades after Canada achieved dominion status (1867), the country's main foreign interests, after the United States and Europe, were in China. Canada was regarded there as a relatively friendly, helpful country, unlike the rapacious European powers. The relationship was expressed most publicly through the missionary movement; more Canadian missionaries went to China than to any other foreign country. The missionary movement connected Canada to China by close bonds of faith and a sense of service. At the same time, the growing numbers of Chinese Canadians, especially on the Pacific Coast, were tied to China by blood and by identity. These two groups made up the fabric of relations between Canada and China.

MISSIONARIES

From the late 1890s on, Canada sent thousands of missionaries to China. Almost all Christian denominations were represented in China, supported by numerous parishes and missionary organizations at home. The home churches held prayer meetings and funding drives to support the work of missionaries in China. The missionaries' reports on the work in China, and on the situation in China, were distributed to the faithful.

The largest number of Canadian missionaries came from two denominations, the Presbyterian and Methodist, later amalgamated as the United Church. In the late nineteenth and early twentieth centuries, these two denominations set up large and well-funded missions in Henan and in Sichuan. The missionaries were educated and pragmatic, given less to proselytizing than to practical work, as doctors, teachers, engineers—and dentists. Missionaries in Chengdu established the first dental hospital in China, a practical endeavor that endeared them to every level of the local population; toothache knows no class barriers.

The missionaries lived most of their lives in China; many were born there. They had a strong sense of community and close personal and family ties with one another, which produced several missionary dynasties, for example the Endicott, Small, and Menzies families. They kept in close touch with their native land, through letters and periodic furloughs. Most were also well connected by birth and education (usually at the University of Toronto) to the administrative and commercial elites of Canada, including Ottawa mandarins and church leaders.[1] During the years after the start of the war in China, the missionary connections took on a new importance, both in rallying public support for China and in forming Canadian policy.

One mission was distinct from the mainstream of Canadian respectability. The China Inland Mission (CIM), to which one of the largest groups of Canadian missionaries was attached, represented a very different form of Protestantism. The CIM missionaries were holy rollers , fervent, intrepid, careless of their own creature comforts, and often successful evangelists. They came from less educated backgrounds, most were never ordained, and many of them were women. The CIM started in England, but Canada, especially Ontario, was a fertile recruiting ground. The missionaries were often recruited at religious revivals and went straight off to work in China. They had little political influence at home and almost no connection with the other Canadians in China.[2]

Canada had a Francophone mission in China, in Xuzhou (Jiangsu Province) where dozens of Jesuit priests manned a string of rural churches. The Xuzhou Mission came under French protection, as part of the *Missions Étrangères*, which had its headquarters in Paris, but the priests had a strong self-identity as Canadien. This was Quebec's only mission abroad; for decades it received dedicated support from what was then a poor province. The missionaries were remarkably homogenous, intelligent, hardworking, intrepid, and uncomplaining. They accepted the adversities they encountered working in a poor and backward region.[3]

The Anglican Church of Canada was less prominent than other denominations in the mission field. The chief Canadian Anglican missionary in North China, the bishop of Henan, William White, was more interested in Chinese artifacts than in Chinese souls. He acquired, by obscure and sometimes dubious means, the bulk of the fabulous collection of Chinese antiquities in the Royal Ontario Museum during his years in the mission field.[4] White's reputation in China could not be more different than that of the Presbyterian missionary James Menzies, who worked for years in

Anyang (Henan) and played an important role in the discovery and interpretation of the oracle bones found in the Wastes of Yin.[5]

Canada also had missionaries in Japan, Korea, and Taiwan, most of
them Presbyterian. Some espoused local causes. George Leslie MacKay is
still remembered in Taiwan for the school he founded at Danshui, near Taipei, and for the hospitals named in his memory. Herbert Norman was born
into a missionary family in Japan. He became a diplomat and author and
was Canada's leading expert on Japan. Norman remains important, not
only for his writings but because of his death. He killed himself in Cairo
in 1957, while Canadian ambassador there, after years of accusations from
the United States that he was a Communist agent.[6]

OVERSEAS CHINESE

The Cantonese communities in British Columbia were among the oldest nonnative communities there. The first Chinese settlers arrived in the
1850s and for a while made up a large proportion of the nonnative population on the West Coast. The community had a long tradition of support
for the revolutionary movement in China. The freedom that being outside
China gave the Chinese Canadians led them to call for political change at
home. Kang Youwei, Liang Qichao, and Sun Yat-sen, their fellow Cantonese, were all received and generously supported by the communities
in Victoria and Vancouver. The revolutionary association continued after
1911. The Guomindang (GMD) was a leading Chinatown organization; it
promoted Chinese culture and political loyalty to China. From the early
1930s on, the GMD and other bodies organized anti-Japanese campaigns,
in response to events in China. These often overflowed into hostility and
even brawls with the neighboring Japanese Canadian community in Vancouver. Bond drives to support the Chinese war effort were successful,
especially after visits by anti-Japanese heroes such as Cai Tingkai, the
commander of the resistance in Shanghai in 1932.

The identification with China grew at a time when it was difficult for
Chinese to enter Canada. The increasingly tough restrictions on the immigration of Chinese, which had started in the 1890s, ended with a complete
ban on immigration from China in 1923. Those who were already living
in Canada kept close ties with their families at home, frequently traveling
across the Pacific and maintaining at least part of their families at home
with remittances. The war changed their situations dramatically. Connections to home became difficult and then impossible. The Canadian Chinese communities rallied to their ancestral land and sent major financial
donations. The concern for China peaked in mid-1938, with the occupation of much of coastal Guangdong (the homeland of almost the entire
Chinese Canadian community) and the savage bombing of Guangzhou.

These events aroused furious passion. Behind the passion was a sad recognition that the war would bring the isolation of most Chinese Canadians from their home communities.

World War II

Diplomatic relations between China and many Western states were transformed by the start of World War II in 1939. Diplomatic relations between Free China and the Axis powers broke down,[7] while China developed extensive relationships with the Allies. China's connections to Britain and to other Allied countries (Australia, Canada, Free France, India, New Zealand) were strengthened during the war. When the United States came into the war in 1941, China came into the forefront of the war, as one of the major Allied powers.

After 1938, and especially after 1941, foreigners poured into Free China, both people who already lived in China and newcomers. They included soldiers, diplomats, journalists, and aid workers. Wartime Chongqing was filled with colorful, often vociferous foreigners, all committed to China's victory. The fetid climate did little to improve their tempers, and their diaries and memoirs are full of frank accounts, often highly critical of the Guomindang (GMD) government. One of the best-known figures was General Joseph Stilwell, a peppery Yankee who was the most vocal critic of Chiang Kai-shek and the GMD. Stillwell's relentless criticisms, which made him a folk hero in certain circles in the United States, are now under reappraisal.[8] Another dramatic figure was Joseph Needham, the British biochemist and sinologist, who cut a dashing figure in wartime Chongqing.[9] John King Fairbank, the leading American sinologist and developer of the China studies field, was in Chongqing and left a vivid account.[10] Robert Payne, the poet and polymath, wrote at great length about Chongqing.[11] Theodore White, the American journalist, was a scathing critic of the GMD. Han Suyin, the Sino-Belgian novelist, wrote a romantic account of her first marriage and of her epic journey from Wuhan to Chongqing.[12] Diplomats also wrote their memoirs, one of the best by the Indian government's representative, K. P. S. Menon.[13] These wartime accounts by foreigners give a glimpse only of life in Chongqing, not of foreigners working elsewhere in China. Another group left out of the Chongqing-centered accounts were the overseas Chinese, who though far away from China felt completely identified with its suffering.

Canada's wartime diplomatic relationships with China evolved from existing bilateral relationships: through trade, education, missions, and family connections. The wartime relationships were far more than simply government-to-government relationships, conducted by diplomats and politicians. They involved a fluid collage of connections. China's wartime relationship with Canada coalesced previously distinct relationships, brought together by the emergency of the war. The stories of these relationships are usually told separately—as diplomatic, military, missionary, ethnic, political, and personal. Here the stories are linked together, as they were during the war, when the crisis of the war, and its extraordinary demands for service and sacrifice, brought many Canadians who cared about China together and blurred their previous differences.

In Ottawa, paradoxically, Canada's entry into World War II, in September 1939, brought a shift in focus. The start of the war in Europe underlined the close ties Canada still had to Britain. Over the next two years the focus of the country was almost entirely on the war in Europe, to which Canada made major military and air force contributions. The shortage of resources and of soldiers meant that decisions had to be made carefully. Europe was closer, not just in distance but also in historical ties.

There was a curious aspect to these careful wartime decisions and to the policies of which they were a part. They were made largely by the long-time prime minister, McKenzie King, a sound, cautious, gray man, and a confirmed bachelor. His policies gave all the appearances of being derived from his sober personality. Later revelations in his diaries (published thirty years after his death) showed that he took advice on critical issues during the war from his mother. This was not simply an act of filial respect for the wisdom of a parent. It involved a venture into the spirit world, since his mother was long dead. His unorthodox source of advice turned out to be quite as sound as advice from more pedestrian sources such as civil servants and soldiers. Asia did not occupy much of King's attention for the first three years of the Second World War. Only in late 1941 did Asia reappear as a major concern. The attack on Pearl Harbor precipitated the Pacific War. Canada was drawn into it immediately.

In mid-November Canada had shipped two infantry battalions to Hong Kong to strengthen the critically weak British garrison there. They were doomed. By the end of the year, the men were dead or prisoners of the Japanese. Almost 300 of the 2,000 men who had landed in Hong Kong a few weeks before were killed in the fighting in Hong Kong, and about the same number later died as prisoners in Japan, of malnutrition, disease, and maltreatment. The survivors have never been compensated, or fully recognized in Canada. They are now commemorated in a number of sites in Hong Kong, in official cemeteries, and in the opening of battle sites as parks.[14]

The Australian losses in Malaya and Singapore were even more disastrous. The news of the Australian and Canadian losses aroused fierce emotions at home: fury at the Japanese; fear (particularly in Australia, though enough in Canada to intern all Japanese nationals) of a possible Japanese invasion; and barely disguised bitterness toward the British for having sent "colonial troops" to fight a war the home country had already conceded. These feelings all had the effect of intensifying sympathy for China.

This was the end of Canada's active war in Asia but not of its sympathy for China. The various facets of this sympathy can be seen in the lives of four Canadians, all closely involved with China.

Four Canadians and the War in China

Four men encapsulate the nature and scope of Canada's relations with China in wartime. They represented major aspects of the country that produced them. Victor Odlum was a senior army officer who became Canada's official representative in Chongqing. Robert McClure was a missionary doctor who in the early years of the war organized international relief for refugees in the Yellow River Valley. Norman Bethune, a surgeon, died in 1939 while working with Communist forces in Shaanxi. Quan Louie, son of one of Vancouver's best-known Chinese families, was killed late in the war, when his plane was shot down over Germany.

During the war, the first two men were well-known in Canada. They were deeply embedded in the sober, Protestant world of the Anglo-Canadian establishment, the personification of the values prized in Canada at the time: hard work, energy, Christian rectitude, and indifference to discomfort and difficulty. From China they were in close touch by letter with their families and their constituencies at home. They were admired and respected in Canada, men serving the war effort in a distant and difficult place. They were similar to the large group of missionaries who stayed in China throughout the war, most caring for their flocks, some, like Chester Ronning, working in the Chongqing embassy.

Norman Bethune, by contrast, was almost unknown at home while he was in China. He had cut his ties with a world that he found stultifying and narrow-minded. He left his medical position in Montreal, first going to Spain to work with the Republicans in the Spanish Civil War and then on to work with the Communists in China. Those who did remember him thought of him as a difficult, willful character who had thrown off the traces of his sober upbringing and chosen a radical, socialist life out of character for a Canadian of his time and status.

Quan Louie was a teenager when the war started, and he was still very young when he enlisted in the Royal Canadian Air Force. He was one of a large number of young Chinese Canadians who volunteered for the armed forces to show their patriotism. His death in early 1945 was one of the tens of thousands of wartime deaths of young men who died on active service. When he died, his family mourned him as so many other Canadian families were mourning their sons. It was not clear then that his sacrifice would come to represent a key step in the amelioration of the situation of Chinese Canadians and, by extension, a change in one part of the Canada-China relationship that was eventually to become a dominant one—the relationship based on immigration and blood ties.

In historical memory, the wartime situation has been reversed. The first two of the four men are now almost unknown, in Canada and in China. Bethune is a hero in China, the only foreigner mentioned by name in the works of Mao Zedong aside from Marx, Lenin, and Stalin. There are six separate commemorative sites dedicated to him in China.[15] He has been described as the best-known Canadian in the world—and in numerical terms he undoubtedly is, given the size of the Chinese population. He has been commemorated in Canada, but only decades after his death, under insistent prompting from Beijing. In 1976 his birthplace, the Presbyterian manse in Gravenhurst, a small lake town north of Toronto, was made into a museum. There is also a statue of Bethune in Montreal, and a college named for him at York University in Toronto.

Quan Louie did not emerge into historical memory until quite recently. Over the past decade, however, he has been widely commemorated in Chinese Canadian communities, by people, many of them veterans themselves, who are interested in the history of their community and its emergence during the war from the racism of the 1920s and 1930s. A lake has been named for him just north of Vancouver.[16]

The first three men had much in common. All were the sons of fathers who were deeply committed to a particular form of Christian life, stern Presbyterianism. Odlum's father was a professor of religion, Bethune's a minister, and McClure's a missionary in China, where he himself was born. They were the products of sober religious upbringings. They were imbued with a concept of service, down-to-earth and hardworking. All had a strong sense of internationalism. They were tough, practical men, able to cope with hardship, almost disdainful of the soft lives of people who had not grown up in the harsh physical environment of the Canadian winter. They were oblivious to the discomforts of wartime China and highly adaptable. McClure pedaled his way around war-torn North China on a bicycle, virtually the only way to get around a region in which other forms of transport had broken down. Odlum was a martyr to prickly heat in the three summers that he spent in Chongqing. "I broke out in prickly heat and look as if I had the measles over most of my body," he said, but he did not let it slow him down.[17] He made no complaints about the winter chill of Chongqing but adapted to it in a practical but unexpected way; he was probably the only ambassador to wear a long, padded Chinese gown. And Bethune managed to perform surgical operations in the most difficult of conditions, despite the lack of medical equipment that he would have been used to as a surgeon in Montreal.[18]

The fourth man, Quan Louie, was completely different from the other three. He grew up in a Chinese Canadian community beset by poverty and racism, almost completely separate from the white world. His family, however, had already taken some steps toward economic success. Quan had a comfortable upbringing in (relatively) warm Vancouver. His was a generation of Chinese Canadians that was about to make its mark on the world. He was educated at the University of British Columbia and became a star athlete. His older brother, Tong Louie, went on to create one of the largest family businesses in western Canada, the London Drugs Chain. Quan Louie never went to China; he lived most of his short life in Canada and died in Europe in 1945.

The Louie family was a key part of the British Columbia Chinese community, one of the first nonnative communities to be established in the province. From the 1850s, it grew slowly and quietly, struggling to survive in a hostile, racist environment but making major economic contributions to the forest and fishing industries. The Chinese Canadian community began to come into its own during the war, emerging from the shadows of prejudice and discrimination to play a role in the war effort. The Louie family's story was very much part of Canada's wartime relations with China, a story that involved deep social and personal connections to the ancestral country—and a desire to serve in a war that had started in China.

The Chinese Canadian experience in war was also part of the story of overseas Chinese in other countries. People who had been somewhat separated from China during the Depression became deeply involved with China in the early stages of the war, collecting money, demonstrating, and even, in some cases, going back to China to fight in the war. The Vancouver community mirrored many other overseas communities.

VICTOR ODLUM

In 1943 Canada appointed its first ambassador to the Republic of China. The official announcement of the exchange of ambassadors was made in August 1941, but the implementation was slow, much slower than the appointment of the Chinese representative to Canada, Liu Shi-shun. The choice of ambassador was unorthodox. Rather than appointing a professional diplomat, the Canadian government at first thought of appointing a Canadian already in China, that is, a missionary, given how difficult it was to send anyone to China during wartime.[19] In the end, in November 1942, it was decided to send Victor Odlum, who had fought in the Boer War and risen to the rank of brigadier general in the First World War.

Odlum's appointment (and his brief stint in Canberra that preceded it) may have had more to do with altercations at the top of the Canadian military than with the feeling that he was the best person to send to China.

At the start of the war, Odlum was appointed to a position he loved, as commander of the Second Canadian Division, stationed in England. Suddenly, in late 1941, he was told that he had passed a (new) retirement age and was to resign. This was a bitter blow.[20]

Odlum's knowledge of Asia was limited. He had spent several years in Japan as a child, where his father was a missionary educator, but he left Japan at the age of six after his mother died, and nothing else connected him to Asia. He was not a diplomat. His passion was the military, though he had an interwar career in radio and print journalism. His two interests crossed. While chairman of the Canadian Broadcasting Corporation early in the war, he ordered the launching of martial music broadcasts, including "The Army Sings" and "A Day in the Life of a Recruit."[21] These uplifting programs promoting the military could not redeem his killjoy reputation in the Canadian forces; during the First World War he had cut out the alcohol rations of the troops under his command, something the Canadian military has never forgiven him for.

Odlum arrived in Chongqing in May 1943 and set to work with a degree of eagerness that must have startled a Chinese and foreign community that after six years of war was already jaded. Ottawa's wartime China policy was vague and long-term, to prepare the way for postwar trade and investment.[22] Odlum's ideas were different. He conceived of one of his tasks in China as offering his services as an honest broker and mediating between the United States and Britain over their policy toward China. He wanted to prevent the divisions he perceived between Canada's closest allies from being used by the GMD government:

China, for various reasons, had been trying to play Britain against America and this did not suit Canada's book. So, instead of merely talking about the matter, Canada had decided to do something. That something was to establish the Canadian legation in China and to send me as the first minister. My own judgement was that I was not suited for the task, but having come I would do my best.[23]

He appointed himself to the mission of formulating Canadian policy toward China and, bold and uninvited, to offering Chiang Kai-shek military advice. These were tasks that no one had asked him to undertake, and they were ones that he was ill-equipped, in terms of status, accommodations, and financing, to fulfill. He was at the head of a three-man operation, working without a chancellery, a residence, or even a vehicle. His first task after he arrived in Chongqing was to find accommodations. He moved into the United Church hospital compound and spent much of the next few months looking for permanent quarters.

Odlum's grandiose aims say more about his own predilections than about policy made in Ottawa. In fact, Ottawa officials found his frequent messages exasperating. In late 1943 one of the senior members of the

Department of External Affairs, Norman Robertson, had this to say of Odlum: "His assurance and his confidence in his own judgement is rather frightening." Strong words for a diplomat.[24] But Odlum had one advantage that civil servants did not; he communicated directly, by personal letters, with MacKenzie King, someone whom he regarded as a friend and an equal. He also made an impression on other diplomats in Chongqing.

Major-General Odlum is one of the most hard-working and self-assertive person-alities in Chungking [Chongqing]. By the time a normal person is awake, Odlum has already done two hours' work—he rises at 4—and continues to work right through the day. He likes to air his views on all things in heaven and earth. He used to irritate the Chinese but they now credit him with a heart of gold.[25]

This assiduity could not make him popular—the urbane Menon was quietly appalled by such dedication. Nor could it do much to make him an effective ambassador. At the diplomatic level, Canada's relations with China could not compare in significance to China's relations with the other Allied powers. His country had little to offer the Chinese government of immediate material value or military aid, and his main duty was to set up the mechanisms for postwar trade, not an activity that a country at war would regard as of top priority.[26]

Odlum's views on China had the brisk certainty characteristic of a military man. His views on the military were clear, concise—and often critical. So were his views on the political situation. In these views he was led by the Canadian missionaries in Chongqing, most of whom shared the view that the government, for all its weaknesses, should be supported. He listened to other views, notably those of James Endicott, a China-born United Church missionary who went against type and was already strongly critical of the GMD. He and Endicott talked whenever Endicott was in Chongqing, and when he was not, they wrote long letters to each other. Even so, their paths diverged. Odlum had some sympathy for Endicott's position and a real respect for the CCP leaders, such as Zhou Enlai, whom he met in Chongqing. He wrote about his political sympathies with (for a diplomat) disarming frankness:

As a matter of fact I nearly ran off in the Yenan [Yan'an] direction, through pure human sympathy coupled with a natural ideological inclination. At home I hover on the boundary between left Liberal and C.C.F [Cooperative Commonwealth Federation, a moderate left-wing party]. But just when I was about to make what I now think would have been my first serious error, I suddenly realized that my duty was to the government to which I was accredited.[27]

He was convinced too that he had got the measure of Chiang Kai-shek, whom he met often. In the Canadian context, Odlum had come down on the right, cautious side, unlike Endicott, who went on to take a radical path. He headed the Canadian Peace Congress in the 1950s and 1960s, was an avid "friend of China," and was a vocal critic of the purported use of germ warfare during the Korean War.[28]

NORMAN BETHUNE

Canada had a special connection with the Chinese Communist Party in Yan'an, through Norman Bethune. His successful career as a doctor and surgeon in the United States and in Canada was interrupted twice, the first time when in 1926 he was forced to take a year off to recover from tuberculosis, and the second time a decade later. By then his relations with his colleagues at the Royal Victoria Hospital in Montreal had turned sour, his impetuousness and strong political ideas disturbing to his sober colleagues. He was disgusted by the state of Depression-era society, and he turned sharply to the left. He resigned from his job in 1936 and went to Spain to work for the Republican side in the civil war. The medical work that he did in Spain in developing first aid and blood transfusions was revolutionary.

Bethune did not stay in Spain until the tragic end of the war; instead, he returned to Canada in 1937 and spent the rest of the year speaking to anti-fascist audiences throughout the country—and attracting the attention of the Royal Canadian Mounted Police (RCMP), who regarded him as a dangerous agitator.[29] In early 1938, he went on to China and went straight to work with Communist forces in the Jinchaji border region. He worked there for almost two years, treating wounded soldiers, organizing medical services, and improvising medical and surgical care. He died of blood poisoning in November 1939.

A few weeks after his death, Mao Zedong wrote one of his most famous essays, "In Memory of Norman Bethune" (*Jinian Bai Qiuen*). The thrust of the essay was to commemorate Bethune and to use him as an example of self-sacrifice:

Comrade Bethune's spirit, his utter devotion to others without any thought of self, was shown in his great sense of responsibility in his work and his great warmheartedness towards all comrades and the people. Every Communist must learn from him. There are not a few people who are irresponsible in their work, preferring the light and shirking the heavy, passing the burdensome tasks on to others and choosing the easy ones for themselves. At every turn they think of themselves before others. When they make some small contribution, they swell with pride and brag about it for fear that others will not know. They feel no warmth towards comrades and the people but are cold, indifferent, and apathetic. In truth, such people are not Communists, or at least cannot be counted as devoted Communists. No one who returned from the front failed to express admiration for Bethune whenever his name was mentioned, and none remained unmoved by his spirit. In the Shanxi-Chahar-Hebei border area, no soldier or civilian was unmoved who had been treated by Dr. Bethune or had seen how he worked. Every Communist must learn this true Communist spirit from Comrade Bethune.[30]

Though the essay is at least as much about criticizing Chinese Communists as praising Bethune, it catapulted him to fame in the Communist world in China. Mao Zedong wanted to imbue his own people with the same sense of service that he saw in Bethune. The image of the dead doctor was promoted as a model of dedication, with a strong critical message built in: if a foreigner can behave so well, what is wrong with you Chinese?

Bethune's fame did not extend to Canada, where only two small memorial meetings were held for him, in Winnipeg and Montreal. Both were dutifully attended by members of the RCMP, intent on gathering information on the Canadian Communist Party. There was Chinese representation. The United Front between the GMD and the CCP was still in force at the end of 1939, and the Chinese consul general, Dr. C. Y. Shih, attended the Montreal meeting.[31] For the next forty years, Bethune's name was scarcely heard in Canada.

Meanwhile, in China Bethune's fame grew and grew, and after 1949 it extended to the whole of China. His energy and idealism became a model for generations of Chinese.

ROBERT MCCLURE AND OTHER MISSIONARIES

The disparate missionary endeavors in China by different denominations and different countries of origin came together in the wake of the Japanese invasion in 1937. In Henan and in Jiangsu, almost all missionaries rushed to provide emergency aid and sanctuary to tens of thousands of refugees. In many cases, they also provided medical aid to wounded soldiers. Robert McClure moved out of the Henan hospital where he was a surgeon and coordinated work for relief in Henan as field director of the International Red Cross.

With relentless energy and passion, he started organizing businesses, schools, missions, and temples to provide relief for the refugees he knew the conflict would bring. For the next eight months, he worked like a whirlwind, crisscrossing the region by train and bicycle, sometimes pedaling a hundred miles a day. The need became greater and greater as Japanese troops advanced westward on the south bank of the Yellow River in the spring of 1938, and even more serious when Chinese forces opened the dyke of the Yellow River at Huayuankou in June 1938. The war and the horrible need it provoked stimulated McClure to the greatest work of his entire career, and to a work whose impact on the lives of individual Chinese outstripped that of any other Canadian.[32]

McClure's path crossed with Bethune's only once, in early 1938 at Dongguan, on the Yellow River. Bethune was going north to join the Communists in Yan'an, and McClure was working his way along the LongHai line on his relief work. Bethune had disappeared, on a "rural pub crawl." His Chinese minders asked McClure to find him. When he did, Bethune was quite far gone on the same local home brew that McClure used to sterilize his instruments for surgery. Despite their almost identical backgrounds, the meeting so far from home did not go well. McClure was cheerful, resourceful, and completely at home in China. Bethune was doctrinaire, angry, drunk, and out of his depth in a strange new world. The two found "no single point of contact," and they never met again.[33]

The Quebec missionaries in northern Jiangsu also rose to the challenge and the terror of the war. The Japanese occupation of their region came in May (1938), Mary's Month.[34] Most of the priests worked on their own, in small towns and villages quite remote from each other. They too were dependent on bicycles to get from place to place. As Japanese troops advanced, the priests opened up their compounds to thousands of terrified refugees. They sent home graphic descriptions of the invasion and of the brutal behavior of the Japanese armies.[35]

Missionary letters and reports were read from pulpits throughout Canada. When missionaries returned to Canada on furlough, as many did in the early years of the war when trans-Pacific travel was still possible, they preached and spoke across the country in support of China's cause. Their views also came to the attention, through personal connections, of the highest levels of government. They intensified the identification with China in Canada.

Most of the missionaries stayed at their posts, even in the occupied areas. Those who were doctors and engineers were of greatest help to China. Their work went on, usually without fanfare or celebration, year after year, until well into the Pacific War. Norman Bethune's work was replicated by that of other Canadian doctors. The Anglican medical missionary Richard Brown actually worked with Bethune for four months. But Bethune died in the service of the anti-Japanese cause and the cause of socialism, and he won the badge of martyrdom.

The Canadian missionaries played a major role in forming wartime public opinion on China. At a time when organized religion played a powerful role in public life, and when those who attacked religion were godless Communists, churches exerted a great deal of influence in their communities. In a time of war, this influence grew. The churches saw men off to war, and they organized prayers for them while they were away. The warmth of feeling toward China in the churches in Canada gave China a special position among the Allies that other Allied countries, such as the godless Soviet Union, could never share. The Jesuit priests, who might have been compromised in their sympathy for China by the fact that they were under Vichy French protection and thus caught in the complicated web of Vatican relations with the Axis, did not appear to have been influenced by these concerns and criticized Japanese brutality quite openly in their reports home, which were regularly read from the pulpits of their home churches.

The early years of the war were the high point of the Canadian missionary venture in China. Missionaries were able to give real practical help to those suffering from the war. Conversions rose, hymn singing became immensely popular, and some missionaries even had influence with the GMD government, helped by the overt Christian faith of Madame Chiang Kai-shek (Song Meiling). These successes came, ironically, in the last period in which missionaries would work in China. Though they did not know it at the time, their days of working in China were numbered and would end within a decade.

QUAN LOUIE

Quan Louie died young, a life cut short. There is little to remember him by, but as a story of the Chinese Canadian involvement in the war, his life has much to say. Well before the start of the war, Chinese Canadians were deeply concerned about the looming threat to China from Japan. There were propaganda campaigns, and fund-raising drives raised money for China. Some young men even went off to China to fight with the Chinese or to work in areas where their knowledge of English could help the war effort.

After 1938 and the occupation of southern Guangdong, this concern for China was intensified by deep anxiety for the relatives that most Chinese Canadians had in the occupied areas. The anxiety increased after December 1941 when, with the fall of Hong Kong, all contact with family members at home was lost. The anxiety fostered a great desire in the young men of the community to fight. For the first time, Chinese Canadians had a sense of being involved in a common cause with all Canadians, of really belonging in Canada and of being accepted. They continued to make generous contributions to the war effort in China, and at the same time, they engaged in the Canadian war effort.

A number of young Chinese Canadians went into the armed forces. This was the first time they had been allowed to contribute to their country, and they reveled in the chance to serve. They were sent off to war by their community with pride and excitement. Many of them served overseas, most as ordinary soldiers and some as interpreters.

Military service was a huge breakthrough for young Chinese Canadians. They found to their surprise that in the armed forces the prejudice and discrimination they were used to in civilian life did not exist. A clear sign of the acceptance of Chinese Canadians in the armed forces is the obituary for Quan Louie in the *Vancouver Sun*. His picture appeared in the company of three white Canadian airmen, also shot down; they were treated equally as fallen heroes.[36]

The war had a diametrically opposite effect on Japanese Canadians in terms of their relationship with Canada. Japanese Canadians who lived in the coastal areas of British Columbia (the majority) were interned in 1942 and shipped to camps in the interior of the province for the duration of the war. They were dispossessed, they received no local sympathy, and, until 1988, no apology for their maltreatment. Studies of the internment usually put it down to systemic racism, an interpretation based on a comparison between the wartime treatment of white Canadians of German and Italian descent, which did not involve harsh measures. The institutional racism argument, which points to deep anti-Asian sentiment in British Columbia, is undercut by the sympathy for China in Canada and the wartime emancipation of Chinese Canadians.

The end of the war was the beginning of a new era for Chinese Canadians. The joy at the defeat of Japan was matched by a determination to change the status of Chinese Canadians. In 1947 after considerable pressure from the community, the Chinese Immigration Act, which had prohibited Chinese immigration, was repealed. Even though it would take a long period for full equality to be achieved, the explicitly racist policy was gone.[37]

One long-term effect of the war for Chinese Canadians was a permanent division between families. The families of Chinese Canadians who were caught by the war in China were not treated by the Japanese as enemy aliens and were never interned. But they suffered great privations, not least because they lost their source of income from Canada; remittances were cut off after 1941. The family of Chan Sam (consisting of a wife, two Canadian-born daughters, and a son born after one of Chan Sam's visits home) was in Taishan when Guangdong was occupied. They received no remittances for the duration of the war, nor were they able to send news to Canada, even when Nan, one of the daughters, died in mysterious and undoubtedly tragic circumstances after she encountered a Japanese patrol. The family was never reunited. Chan Sam never saw his son, who was born after he returned to Canada. His third daughter, Way-hing, born to his second wife in Vancouver, did not meet her sister and brother until the 1980s, when it was finally possible for her to travel to China.[38]

This was a typical story for a Chinese Canadian family, of a permanent divergence between the two branches of a family, at home and abroad, precipitated by the war and prolonged by the civil war and the Communist ascendancy. It became so entrenched that many of the younger generations growing up in Canada were barely aware that they had close relatives in China. This led to some awkward situations when, in the 1970s and

1980s, young people went to China and discovered unknown relatives, the children and grandchildren of their grandfather's "China wife"—whose identity was kept hidden in officially monogamous Canada.[39]

Two of the men we have discussed here survived the war. Victor Odlum went home and into a comfortable retirement in Vancouver. Robert McClure also went home and became a much loved and respected figure—the moderator of the United Church, the most senior position in Protestant Christianity in Canada. He was a spell-binding preacher.[40] Of the two who died in the war, Norman Bethune was remembered at home only in the minuscule Communist Party of Canada and in other leftist circles. Ted Allen, a fellow veteran of the Spanish Civil War, wrote a glowing tribute to him, *The Scalpel, the Sword*, which later was the basis for the script for a movie about Bethune's life.[41] Quan Louie was remembered by his family and, eventually, by his native province; in 1996 Louie Lake was named for him.

Canada, China, and the Postwar Period

Though Canada's military participation in Asia was limited, what happened to the soldiers who did serve in Asia became a key part of the narrative of the war. The government of Japan finally apologized to the Canadian prisoners of war taken in Hong Kong in December 2011, when the few survivors were already in their late eighties and early nineties.

There has been no apology to civilians. Most of the Canadian civilians in China who had not moved into Free China were interned after 1942, some in Weixian (Shandong Province), others in Shanghai. The Jesuit priests were corralled late in the war in Shanghai, at the Jesuit house in Shanghai, but before that happened, three Jesuit priests were shot to death in Fengxian (northern Jiangsu Province), in 1943. The circumstances of the shooting have never been made clear.

The war fostered nationalism in China. At the start of the war, the high tide of nationalism stimulated resistance against all the odds. By the end of the war the focus of nationalism had shifted, away from the government led by the GMD and toward the CCP.[42] This shift was tacitly accepted by most Canadian missionaries and official representatives in China, who had come to see the GMD as corrupt and inefficient.

In 1949 the Canadian government differed at first from the United States in its approach to recognition of the new Communist government, coming close to diplomatic recognition, but it was eventually forced to concur with the US decision to outlaw the People's Republic. The difference of opinion did not save the Canadian missions in China. One by one they were closed, and the missionaries returned to Canada. Gradually China disappeared from the Canadian consciousness.

The Chinese Canadian communities, after a few brief years in which there was some contact with their families in Guangdong, were once again, after 1949, completely cut off from China until after the establishment of diplomatic relations between Canada and China in 1970. After that, some family members in China were allowed to move to Canada, a flow that increased after China opened up in the 1980s. During the years of separation, Chinese Canadians' sense of home shifted, from the China to which they were denied access to Canada, where they lived.

In the 1950s and 1960s, the Christian involvement of many Canadians in China was forgotten, especially as, over time, the influence of the Protestant churches declined in an increasingly secular Canada. In Quebec the Quiet Revolution of the 1960s completely undermined the role of the Roman Catholic Church. But the change of policy in China after 1980 produced an unexpected twist to the missionary story. The mission enterprise turned out to have sown seeds—which finally flowered in the 1980s and 1990s. Many of what were once thought to be abandoned parishes are now flourishing. The church of James Menzies in Anyang now has Sunday congregations of up to 5,000. In Quebec interest in the province's devoutly religious past is minimal, in a now secular world, but in China the three dead Jesuit priests are commemorated in Feng xian. The church has been restored, and a large memorial has been erected to the murdered priests. A campaign is underway at the moment to have one of them, Father Prosper Bernard, canonized by the Roman Catholic Church.[43] Canonization is a complex process and one that sometimes takes centuries; the wheels of the Vatican bureaucracy grind slowly. Should it succeed, it would be important for Canada, a country where the Catholic Church has a long history but to date has produced few saints.

The wartime role and influence of the states friendly to China that did not have the great-power status might seem insignificant when compared to that of the heavy hitters. That does not mean that they were not involved in China's war, and in planning for the postwar conflict, which all realized was coming. The role of the second-tier Allies was often deeply committed, more carefully thought-out (given the limitations of resources), and less prone to flamboyance and grandstanding. Canada managed its relationship with China at different levels, always in a cooperative way, never in a domineering or confrontational way. The warmth toward China in Canada persisted long after the war, as did the positive feelings toward Canada in China.

Part II

NEGOTIATING ALLIANCES
AND QUESTIONS OF SOVEREIGNTY

6 Declaring War as an Issue in Chinese Wartime Diplomacy

TSUCHIDA AKIO

According to modern international law, a declaration of war is a necessary act that must be taken when a state initiates a war with another state. After the declaration of war, the state of war between the combatant states is recognized, and wartime international laws are applied. Wartime international law covers a wide range of topics, including rights and obligations such as blockading the ports of the enemy, searching ships from neutral states, public administration in occupied territories, the protection of prisoners of war, and the neutrality of noncombatant states.[1]

For the first four years, from 1937 to 1941, the Sino-Japanese War remained an undeclared war, despite the fact that combat escalated on all fronts and evolved into protracted comprehensive warfare. Only after Pearl Harbor did the Chinese government finally declare war on Japan, as well as on Germany and Italy. This essay explores the debates over this issue within the Chinese government and suggests, contrary to the prevailing view among Japanese historians, that domestic politics shaped Nationalist thinking, rather than concern about US activation of the Neutrality Acts. Japan, on the other hand, which would never issue a formal declaration of war, did fear that a formal declaration of war would lead the United States to proscribe exports to Japan under the acts.[2]

After the Marco Polo Bridge Incident of July 7, 1937, Chiang Kai-shek, as chairman of the National Military Committee and the director of the Executive Yuan, issued a written command on July 9 to Defense Minister He Yingqin and Chief of Staff Cheng Qian: "The Japanese enemy has provoked us. No matter what the enemy's intentions are, Chinese troops must be fully prepared. Troops all over China must be put on high alert. We will start procedures for a declaration of war."[3]

This written command is the first document that mentions a declaration of war. A few days later, on July 13, Chiang Kai-shek sent a telegram to General Song Zheyuan.

The conflicts at the Marco Polo Bridge cannot be resolved peacefully. We are determined to go all out in resisting Japanese aggression. We are willing to make the necessary sacrifices to defend our country and our dignity. . . . The Chinese Nationalist Party is determined to declare war on Japan. I am willing to join all your commanders and soldiers to sacrifice our lives in the struggle.[4]

In fact, at that time, the Nationalist Party's Central Committee had not formally decided to go all out militarily or to declare war on Japan. Nevertheless, Chiang Kai-shek had expressed his determination to declare war on Japan. Moreover, by demonstrating his determination to fight resolutely, Chiang Kai-shek showed the people inside and outside of the Nationalist government that he would not surrender to Japanese aggression. He hoped that such a tough confrontational stance would strengthen national unity and prevent Song Zheyuan from seeking a compromise with Japan. Chiang asked the government to make a statement concerning Japan's aggression toward China. However, during the Central Military Conference on July 14, He Yingqin proposed that the government state the hope for peace rather than declare war. The military committee members could not reach agreement. In the end they decided not to declare war.[5]

On July 16, at a meeting of the Executive Yuan, Education Minister Wang Shijie stated the following:

The government should decide guidelines for the future as soon as possible. . . . Should the central government still regard the fighting as a local conflict (similar to the Mukden Incident on September 18, 1931, or the skirmishes in Shanghai in January 1932)? Or should the central government consider China and Japan to be in a state of war and formally sever diplomatic ties with Japan?

At the meeting, it was decided that the Foreign Ministry, the Defense Ministry, and the Executive Yuan appoint experts who would jointly discuss the issue and solicit the opinion of the Chiang Kai-shek.[6]

On July 17, representatives of the Foreign Ministry, including the Deputy Foreign Minister Xu Mo; representatives of the Chinese military, including Xu Zuyi (the director of the Second Bureau of the General Staff); and experts on international law held a meeting. They made the following recommendations in a formal document concerning a declaration of war and the severance of the diplomatic ties with Japan.

1. After the start of hostilities, the Chinese Foreign Ministry will immediately issue a formal declaration stating that China has to defend itself against Japanese aggression. A draft of the declaration has been completed.

2. We should think about whether to sever diplomatic ties with Japan.

After the severance of diplomatic ties, Japan and China are in a state of war. Now the Japanese navy holds absolute supremacy. As a combatant nation, Japan will notify world nations and prohibit all military necessities and raw materials from being imported into China. The impact will be large. It is unlikely that China can become self-reliant in terms of necessities.

3. After China severs diplomatic ties with Japan, Japanese residents in China and Japanese who live in Japanese concessions would move to British or French concessions. They can still engage in activities such as spreading rumors, causing disturbances, and espionage. Their activities would be protected by the British and French authorities. The Chinese government has no way to expel or arrest these Japanese. However, the Chinese government cannot protect Chinese citizens living in Japan. They would be expelled or even arrested. China does not have sufficient numbers of ships to carry these Chinese citizens back to China. Balancing the pros and cons, if China cuts off diplomatic ties with Japan, Japan can still exercise the rights as a combatant nation, while China cannot enjoy these. Therefore, after total war breaks out, China should not severe diplomatic ties with Japan. China should maintain the diplomatic status quo as it did during the Mukden Incident on September 18, 1931.[7]

Surprisingly, during the meeting, the issue about whether or not the United States would follow the Neutrality Act if war was declared was not discussed.

After the Marco Polo Bridge Incident, the leaders of the Nationalist government were not sure about the stance of the Japanese government. Did it want to prevent the skirmishes from escalating? Or was it determined to go all out with the invasion of China?[8] As the situation developed, the Nationalist government could not hesitate any longer. On July 28, the Japanese troops stationed in northern China attacked Chinese troops. On July 30, they conquered Tianjin. On August 4, they occupied Beiping. On July 31, Chiang Kai-shek issued the "Letter to All the Commanders and Soldiers Resisting Japanese Aggression." He appealed for unity. On August 1, at the Central Military Academy in Nanjing, Chiang delivered a speech on how the "whole nation must prepare for the war."[9]

On July 26, concerning the issue of a declaration of war on Japan, Chiang Kai-shek sent a telegram to Kong Xiangxi, who was visiting the United Kingdom. Chiang stated, "Large-scale war has started. The hope for peace is dashed. I have decided that we will sever diplomatic ties with Japan and then declare war on Japan."[10] However, this statement was made merely to demonstrate his strong determination. On July 28, Information

Minister Shao Lizi told foreign journalists that the Chinese government had no intention of cutting off diplomatic ties with Japan.[11]

As the situation moved toward total war, people inside and outside of the Chinese government disagreed on whether China should resist, or seek peace with Japan. Privately, Chiang Kai-shek thought that negotiation with Japan might be possible. As the supreme military commander, he advocated a resolute stance and sternly rejected all activities suggesting accommodation.[12] Chiang won popular support, including from soldiers in regional armies and left-wing intellectuals. His firm nationalist stance strengthened his leadership.[13]

On August 9, fighting broke out around the Hongqiao district of Shanghai. Hostilities rapidly escalated. On August 12, more than twenty Japanese warships arrived in Shanghai, and more than 10,000 Japanese marines landed. A war between China and Japan was obviously inevitable. On the same day, the Central Standing Committee of the Chinese Nationalist Party held a secret conference. It decided that from that day forward China was in a state of war. Following the proposal from Lin Sen, Chiang Kai-shek was appointed as the generalissimo. But these decisions were not publicly announced.[14]

On August 13, the Chinese and Japanese troops stationed in Shanghai engaged in fierce combat. With the battle for Shanghai, the war expanded from northern to central China. On August 14, the Chinese Supreme National Defense Council, which was the supreme decision-making body during the Sino-Japanese War, held its first session. According to the diaries of Wang Shijie, the following resolutions were passed: (1) The Chinese government would stay in Nanjing for the time being. (2) The Chinese government would not declare war on Japan or sever diplomatic ties with Japan for the time being. (3) The Chinese government would continue to negotiate with the United Kingdom, France, and Russia and report the issue to the League of Nations for resolution.[15]

On August 15, the Japanese government declared: "We will take stern measures to punish vicious Chinese troops and force the Nationalist government to reflect on its mistakes." On the same day, the Nationalist government issued a Declaration of Self-Defense and Resistance to Japanese Aggression. "Forced by Japan's unconstrained aggression, China must defend itself and resist aggression."[16]

Although the fighting between China and Japan became intense, the two states nonetheless maintained formal diplomatic and commercial ties. Both China and Japan kept open the embassies and consulates in each other's country. The treaties signed between China and Japan remained valid, with the result that Japan still enjoyed special privileges in China, such as extraterritoriality. An editorial at the time in the Shanghai edition of the *Da Gong Bao* newspaper fiercely criticized the government.[17]

On August 26, the Nationalist government convened the Supreme National Defense Council. During the meeting, the council carefully reviewed the proposals from the Central Political Committee and made the following decisions:

1. All Japanese employees in the Chinese Maritime Customs Service will be dismissed immediately, as the first step to take back the administrative control over the customs service.
2. The extraterritoriality enjoyed by Japanese citizens in China will be revoked immediately.
3. The issues listed above do not affect whether we will cut off diplomatic ties with Japan.[18]

Thus, the Nationalist government decided to maintain formal diplomatic ties with Japan, but at same time it would abolish Japan's special privileges in China.

Japan's policy toward China was to cease to recognize the Nationalist government as the legitimate representative government of China. China's policy of maintaining a diplomatic presence was obviously irreconcilable with this policy. Consequently, Sino-Japanese relations in reality were close to severance. After the declarations of August 15, the Japanese government moved its embassy from Nanjing to Shanghai. It closed consulates in places such as Suzhou, Chongqing, and Guangzhou, and it shipped Japanese citizens in China back to Japan.[19] These measures demonstrated that the Japanese government had entered into a state of war in terms of diplomatic and consular affairs.

On December 9, the Chinese Foreign Ministry speculated that if Nanjing fell, Japan might refuse to recognize the Nationalist government, forcing the Nationalist government to close the Chinese embassy in Japan. If so, China would ask the American embassy in Japan to preserve the archives of the Chinese embassy and to protect Chinese interests. The American government was secretly asked about its position on the matter.[20]

After Nanjing fell, Japan destroyed China's embassies and consulates in various places. In Korea and Taiwan, which were Japanese colonies, Japanese soldiers, police, and thugs prevented the Chinese embassies and consulates from displaying the Chinese national flag. They forced them to fly the five-color flag of the early Republic. They prevented the movement of consular officials, attacked overseas Chinese, and even occupied Chinese embassies and consulates.[21] As the situation deteriorated, some Chinese diplomats and overseas Chinese, headed by Fan Hansheng, the Chinese consul general in Tokyo, chose to support pro-Japanese regimes. The betrayal made the operation of the Chinese embassy and consulates in

Japan more difficult. On January 10, 1938, the Supreme National Defense Council decided to recall Chinese ambassador Xu Shiying while at the same time to keep open the Chinese embassy and consulates in Japan. On January 16, the Japanese cabinet, headed by Prime Minister Konoe Fumimaro, made a declaration of "not regarding the Nationalist government as the Japanese government's legitimate counterpart" and recalled the Japanese ambassador to China, Shigeru Kawagoe. Obviously, the Japanese government had adopted a policy of cutting off diplomatic ties with the Nationalist government. On January 20, Xu Shiying departed Yokohama and returned to China. From January to early February, Chinese consulates in Japan, Korea, and Taiwan ceased to function, and their staffs returned to China. The Chinese embassy in Japan was closed on June 11.[22]

All these events hindered the containment of the war or the resolution of the conflict through negotiation. In fact, the Chinese government was concerned that Japan might declare war on China first. On January 15, in his diary, Chiang Kai-shek wrote, "In this week, the Japanese enemy has used all measures to intimidate us. It threatens to declare war on China, to refuse to recognize the Nationalist government, and to continue military operations."[23] On January 26, the Chinese ambassador to the United States, Wang Zhengting, asked the American secretary of state, Cordell Hull: "Now that Japan's declaration of war on China is imminent, what is the American government's stance?"[24] At the Supreme National Defense Conference on February 26, Education Minister Wang Shijie asked, "What are China's countermeasures if Japan declares war on China?"[25] Wang Shijie was an important adviser to Chiang Kai-shek. His remarks had considerable impact, more than the proposals from Foreign Minister Wang Chonghui.[26]

During the Sino-Japanese War, the Office of Counselors of the National Military Council (*junshi weiyuanhui canshishi*) played an important role in the making of China's foreign policy. The office was an advisory body for National Military Council chair Chiang Kai-shek. It was in charge of researching diplomatic issues and reporting to Chiang Kai-shek with analysis and proposals. The first director of the Office of Counselors was Zhu Jiahua. The second director was Wang Shijie. Many experts on international affairs staffed the office.[27] The possibility of Japan's declaration of war on China became a high-priority topic for discussion at a meeting in March. During this meeting, Wang Shijie said that Japan's declaration of war depended on the British stance:

If the British-German negotiations fail, Europe will become turbulent, and Japan will act recklessly and will declare war on China. Different people have different views on whether Japan's declaration of war on China is beneficial or detrimental.

I believe that it would be more harmful than beneficial. All China's sea transport would be cut off.

Wang Shijie emphasized that the Chinese government should prepare diplomatic countermeasures to deal with Japan's potential declaration of war. Chiang Kai-shek was even clearer. "According to my observation, if Japan wants to declare war on China, it will do so in the next two months. . . . Therefore, the period before June will be the most dangerous time for China."[28]

From March 29 to April 1, 1938, the Provisional National Congress of the Chinese Nationalist Party *(Linshi quanguo dahui)* was convened at Wuhan. The Nationalist government was reorganizing after the defeats and chaos of the early Sino-Japanese War period. Greater unity was achieved. Consequently, concerns about Japan's potential for declaring war decreased. In the summer of 1938, the Japanese Foreign Ministry renewed a discussion about declaring war on China. It was proposed that Japan should declare war on China in order to cut off China's routes for receiving foreign aid and thus force the Nationalist government to surrender. However, the Nationalist government did not respond to the rumor of the proposal.[29]

In the fall of 1938, Nationalist leaders debated again the idea of China's declaration of war on Japan. Chiang Kai-shek then argued for a declaration of war, but Wang Jingwei (vice president of the Chinese Nationalist Party) and Kong Xiangxi (vice director and treasurer of the Executive Yuan) firmly opposed the idea. Why did Chiang Kai-shek change his stance and feel that it was necessary at that time to declare war on Japan? In order to explore these questions, we need to understand the military situation, the changing international environment, and the political confrontation brewing between leaders of the Nationalist government who advocated compromise and those who advocated resistance.

On August 22, 1938, Japan began a siege of Wuhan. And, farther south, to cut off China's supply routes, it launched an attack on Guangdong Province. On October 21 and 25, Guangzhou and Wuhan fell, respectively. This put the Nationalists in a difficult military and economic situation. The Nationalist government hoped that the Western powers would intervene. However, the Western powers were cautious and tried not to get involved in the Sino-Japanese War. Chen Bulei angrily wrote in his diary, "Western powers such as the United Kingdom and France did not respond to the Sino-Japanese War. I cannot express my fury sufficiently."[30]

After the fall of Wuhan and Guangzhou, military defeat and international isolation created an atmosphere of hesitation and pessimism inside the Nationalist government. Leaders inside the Nationalist government who favored negotiating with Japan for peace became more active.[31] In the middle of October in 1938, it became widely known that Wang Jingwei had dispatched staff to Shanghai to negotiate with Japan. On October 22, 1938, Reuters reported from Shanghai on Wang Jingwei's proposed conditions for peace.[32]

Earlier, from September to October 1938, Japan had proposed various peace plans to people close to Chiang Kai-shek. Chiang rejected these plans. He stuck to the position that the situation before the Marco Polo Bridge Incident should be restored.[33] In the face of the military crisis, given Japan's proposal offering compromise and the hesitation of other senior leaders in the Nationalist government, Chiang decided to declare before the Chinese people and the world his determination to fight Japanese aggression. On October 27, Chiang Kai-shek wrote in his diary, "The Japanese enemy did not scale back its ambition. And it is trying to lure us into compromise. I have decided to issue an open letter to the Chinese people so as to demonstrate my determination to fight."

On October 28, Chiang Kai-shek wrote again in his diary about the pros and cons of declaring war on Japan. Chiang made clear his advocacy of a declaration of war and his firm stance of resistance in order to counter others around him who advocated compromise.[34] On the same day, he sent a telegram to the opening ceremony of the National People's Consultative Congress (*guomin canzheng hui*) in Chongqing. "The war has entered a new stage. The situation has become increasingly difficult. All parties in China must continue to make great efforts. Our national policy of resistance will ultimately succeed."[35] On October 30, Chiang Kai-shek sent a telegram to Kong Xiangxi and Wang Jingwei:

We must investigate the pros and cons of a declaration of war on Japan. We should not be worried about the impact a declaration might make on China's overseas transport, as all ports in coastal China are blockaded by Japan. If China declares war on Japan and then the United States enforces the Neutrality Act, the Japanese enemy would be cut off from their sources of steel and petroleum, and the consequences will be detrimental to the enemy. We should carefully investigate the impact of a declaration of war on China's relations with the League of Nations and with other world nations. We will instruct our ambassadors abroad to investigate the issue.[36]

The next day, Chiang Kai-shek issued "An Open Letter to All Chinese People Concerning the National Army's Retreat from Wuhan."[37] He called on all Chinese solders and civilians to make further sacrifices in the struggle against Japanese aggression. Meanwhile, the letter was publicized overseas in order to inform the world about China's determination to fight Japanese aggression.[38]

However, Wang Jingwei disagreed with Chiang Kai-shek. On November 1, in his telegram to Chiang Kai-shek, Wang argued:

1. It is unclear whether the United States will grant loans to China. If China's declaration caused the US government to invoke neutrality, it will not grant loans.

2. If the League of Nations and its member states stay neutral because of China's declaration of war, they will stop aid going to China, and transport links through Vietnam and Burma will be closed. Before making a decision, should we not cable Chinese ambassadors abroad to investigate these two issues?[39]

Chiang Kai-shek did not change his mind, but he suggested: "Can we mobilize some members of the council to submit a proposal suggesting a declaration of war by the People's Political Council?"[40] The People's Political Council was a consultative body representing a wide range of political views. It had considerable impact on public opinion at the time. Wang Jingwei was its chairman. Most representatives disagreed with him, firmly advocating continuing the war. In November, the People's Political Council passed a resolution supporting resistance and opposing compromise.[41]

Wang Jingwei continued to object. In two telegrams to Chiang Kai-shek he was blunt:

This morning, Wang Chonghui showed me his telegram to you. He says that according to his investigations, declaring war on Japan is harmful rather than beneficial to China. I wonder whether you have read the telegram. The Japanese enemy is well prepared. After China declares war on Japan, the world's nations will declare neutrality and no longer offer foreign aid to China or apply sanctions against Japan. . . . I have discussed the issue with Chinese Nationalist Party leaders Ye Chucang, Chen Gongbo, and Chen Lifu. A declaration of war would lead Japan to be cut off from sources of steel and petroleum, but meanwhile China's hope of getting loans from the United States would be dashed. The composition of the People's Political Council is extremely complicated. Even if we do not make a decision on the proposal submitted to the congress concerning China's declaration of war and do not publicize the proposal, we cannot stop the circulation of the news out of the conference. Then if the Chinese government does not declare war on Japan, it would be criticized, as people would say that the Chinese government actually does not have the determination to fight. So by making the proposal, we actually hurt ourselves.

Chiang Kai-shek's rejoinder was no less firm:

Your view is certainly right. Nevertheless, the Chinese Nationalist Party Central Committee should study harder the pros and cons of a declaration of war. We hope that the declaration would cause changes in the international situation by turning the Sino-Japanese conflict into a global affair. Thus, a declaration would be beneficial to China. Please do assign experts to investigate the issue further.[42]

From this exchange of telegrams in early November, we know that Chiang Kai-shek's proposal was opposed at high levels. Most of the senior figures in the Nationalist government argued that China's declaration of war on Japan would be harmful. Nevertheless, Chiang Kai-shek still insisted that they should discuss the issue further, along with possible future changes in the international situation.

Chiang Kai-shek told the British that China intended to declare war on Japan, and he hoped that he would receive a supportive response from the United Kingdom. On November 4, Chiang met with the British ambassador to China, Archibald Clark Kerr, in Yueyang, Hunan Province. He argued that since Japan occupied Guangzhou, British interests and authority in the Far East faced a severe threat. He asked whether the British government would side with Japan or China. He stated that if the British government rejected China's request for aid, China might go ahead with a declaration of war on Japan.[43]

On November 3, Konoe's cabinet in Tokyo declared its intention to construct the New Order in East Asia and welcomed the participation of a reorganized Chinese government. In other words, if Chiang Kai-shek resigned and the Chinese government gave up resistance, China and Japan could achieve a negotiated peace. The Japanese government wanted to increase the split inside the Nationalist government and encourage a move toward cooperation with Japan.[44]

Although Chiang Kai-shek remained resolute, others inside the Nationalist government concluded that the Japanese cabinet headed by the Prime Minister Konoe was now willing to recognize a reorganized Nationalist government. This meant that prospects for Sino-Japanese peace negotiations were bright. Tao Xisheng was one such person.[45] Others who were close to Chiang Kai-shek, such as Kong Xiangxi, Chen Lifu, and Jiang Zuobin, considered the Japanese declaration important enough for the Chinese government to make a statement in response.[46]

Hearing this news, Chiang Kai-shek sent a telegram to Kong Xiangxi on November 10. He forbade Kong from circulating the remarks made a few days earlier at a ceremonial meeting of the Executive Yuan in which Kong discussed the issue of the Japanese declaration.[47] On the next day, in anticipation of a forthcoming visit of the British ambassador to Chongqing, Chiang instructed Kong Xiangxi and Wang Chonghui, the foreign minister, to make known China's intention to declare war on Japan to the British ambassador.[48] On November 18, following the instructions of Chiang Kai-shek, during his meeting with the British ambassador, Wang Chonghui explicitly stated, "Now our government is planning to formally declare war on Japan."[49]

In response, on November 17, Wang Jingwei vigorously opposed Chiang Kai-shek's proposal to declare war on Japan in a long statement, focusing on four reasons. First, he argued that the activation of the Neutrality Act would hurt China. Second, China had no navy and so would be unable to break Japan's blockade. Third, a declaration would confuse the people of China, as the fighting had already lasted sixteen months. And, fourth, the declaration of war would prevent the free flow of trade at important ports like Shanghai.[50]

Chiang Kai-shek wanted a declaration of war for a variety of reasons. Internationally, he wanted to influence the United States and Britain by globalizing the Sino-Japanese War—hoping for an international coalition against Japan. Domestically, Chiang wanted to confront and suppress the opinions of those advocating compromise with Japan—people like Kong Xiangxi and Wang Jingwei. He considered Wang Jingwei's Neutrality Act argument a red herring. The Chinese People's Political Council had criticized the idea of negotiating with Japan and passed a resolution in support of Chiang Kai-shek's position. Regional military commanders such as Bai Chongxi, Li Jishen, and Feng Yuxiang also asked Chiang Kai-shek to declare war on Japan and to expel those who were not determined to fight from the Chinese government.[51] In other words, a declaration of war on Japan would certainly boost Chiang Kai-shek's political authority and deal a heavy blow to his political rivals such as Wang Jingwei.

At this point, Wang Jingwei defiantly went ahead and carried out negotiations with Japan for a compromise. His intention was to reverse his declining political status and to wrest control of the leadership of the party and state away from Chiang Kai-shek by seeking a cease-fire between Japan and China. But others, like Kong Xiangxi, who agreed with Wang on the issues, had no intention of challenging Chiang Kai-shek's authority. On December 18, Wang Jingwei left Chongqing and intensified his contacts with the Japanese toward the goal of a negotiated cease-fire. Eventually, at Nanjing he established a puppet national government that cooperated with Japan.

On January 1, 1939, the Central Standing Committee of the Chinese Nationalist Party formally revoked Wang Jingwei's party membership. Others who advocated compromise also left the government and joined Wang Jingwei.[52] The opinions of those who sought compromise with Japan became unpopular in Chongqing.

After these events, Chiang Kai-shek never mentioned declaring war on Japan again. The reasons are obvious. In the autumn of 1938, Chiang Kai-shek insisted on declaring war on Japan as a political tactic to counter the peace movement being advocated by rival leaders like Wang Jingwei. In reality, Chiang Kai-shek was never fully committed to a declaration of war on Japan. He understood and accepted the view that "declaring war on Japan is not necessarily beneficial to China," a position that had been held by the Nationalist government since the autumn of 1937. With Wang Jingwei gone, the subject was dropped—until Pearl Harbor.

*   *   *

After the summer of 1939, the international situation changed radically. With the United Kingdom and France engaged in a war of survival, both sought compromise with Japan. They became hesitant to continue to aid China, so China turned to the United States. China hoped that the American government would adopt a more active policy in the Far East and help it fight Japan. On July 26, 1939, the United States announced the abolition of the commercial treaty between the United States and Japan. The United States gradually stepped up economic sanctions against Japan. The big question for China was how would Japan react? The US sanctions might cause Japan to declare war on China. And if this happened how would China get commodities or foreign aid from other governments? The question loomed high on the foreign policy agenda of the Chongqing government.

On November 1, 1939, the Office of Counselors of the National Military Council revisited the question.[53] On January 26, 1940, following the order from office director Wang Shijie, Zhang Zhongfu, the chief staff for the office, drafted a memo for Chiang Kai-shek. Zhang Zhongfu was a scholar of international politics who had studied in the United States and had taught at Peking University. In the memo, Zhang Zhongfu made the following suggestion. If the American government pursued economic sanctions against Japan, the probability of Japan's declaration of war on China increased. The sea routes for shipping military supplies into China might be completely cut off. Thus, the Chinese government should draw on loans from the United Kingdom, the United States, and the Soviet Union as soon as possible to purchase supplies and transport them through Burma and Vietnam for storage. These military necessities could be used after Japan declared war on China. Economic sanctions from the United States would hit Japan hard, he believed, and might cause it to collapse politically.[54]

Chiang Kai-shek did not act on this suggestion. But a year later, he changed his mind and returned again to the declaration of war issue. On February 4, 1941, the Nationalist government received information from the Japanese Domei News Agency that Japanese foreign minister Yosuke Matsuoka had told the Japanese parliament that the Japanese government was discussing how best to exercise the rights of a combatant nation toward China.[55] Chiang Kai-shek responded promptly. On February 8, he queried Wang Shijie: "What are the pros and cons of Japan's declaration of war on China? What should be China's countermeasures?"[56]

On February 11, 1941, Zhang Zhongfu submitted a report entitled "Memo on the Issue of Japan's Declaration of War on China." In great detail, the report discussed the status quo of the Sino-Japanese War, the possibility and consequences of a formal Japanese declaration of war on China, and China's countermeasures. In summary, Zhang made the following points. First, the probability of Japan's declaration of war on

China had significantly increased. Second, the route through Burma was an important supply line. If the port at Rangoon was cut off or disturbed because of Japan's exercise of its rights to inspection, the disruption would be a heavy blow. The Japanese navy would confiscate all military supplies. China should try to get the United Kingdom and the United States to intervene with Japan on China's behalf. Failing this, at the very least China should persuade the American government to promise that China could purchase on credit American products and raw materials (such as trucks, airplanes, and gasoline) needed for China's resistance. Alternatively, the United States could lease the products and raw materials in the way that was stipulated in the American Lend Lease Act. The amount of supplies should be enough to meet China's needs for one year. The products and raw materials should be shipped to Rangoon in the shortest possible time. From there it would take longer to transport the supplies inland into China. Zhang added that China should be careful about its foreign policy toward the Soviet Union. If Soviet aid to China continued overland, Japan might believe that declaring war on China would not have much benefit for Japan.[57]

Chiang Kai-shek ratified the memo, and the Chinese government began to implement the proposals promptly. On February 21, Wang Zhengting and Zhang Zhongfu met with Lauchlin Currie, the special envoy sent to Chongqing by Franklin Roosevelt. Wang and Zhang urged the following countermeasures:

1. The United Kingdom and the United States should try to prevent Japan from exercising the right of inspection on the high seas on the grounds that Japan had violated the Kellogg-Briand Pact (also called the General Treaty for the Renunciation of War) and the Nine-Power Treaty.
2. If Japan exercised the rights of inspection on the high seas, the United Kingdom and United States should ban Japanese imports and exports, and British and American warships could escort commercial ships.
3. In the shortest possible time, the United States should supply a large amount of military materiel to China via Rangoon and then overland to Sichuan.[58]

From this point on during 1941, senior leaders in the Nationalist government closely followed US-Japanese negotiations. China hoped that the United States would apply strong economic sanctions such as an embargo on petroleum products. China was concerned that the United States might make concessions and sacrifice China's interests.[59] Finally, on November 26, the US State Department rejected a compromise and sent a strong memorandum to Japan.[60] The Nationalist government was relieved, as it observed that the probability of US-Japanese concessions had disappeared, and the United States and Japan were heading for war. On December 1, Jiang Tingfu, the provisional general secretary of the Executive Yuan, stated that China might declare war on Japan if war broke out between Japan and the United States.[61]

News of the Pearl Harbor attack reached Chongqing at 3:30 a.m. on December 8, 1941. At 10 a.m. on the same day, the Chinese Nationalist Party Central Standing Committee convened in a special meeting, chaired by Chiang Kai-shek. Japan's declaration of war on the United States and United Kingdom was discussed in detail. At the meeting, Executive Yuan director Sun Ke proposed that the Nationalist government should declare war on Germany and Italy. Foreign Minister Guo Taiqi agreed. However, three persons, including the Chinese Nationalist Party Organization Minister Zhu Jiahua, opposed declaring war on Germany and Italy. Examination Yuan director Dai Jitao argued that the Nationalist government should carefully discuss the issue of a declaration of war on Japan. Wang Shijie proposed that the Nationalist government declare war on Germany, Italy, and Japan immediately and should invite the American, British, and Soviet ambassadors to demand that all anti-aggression countries should act in unity and declare war on the Axis jointly. The Soviet Union should declare war on Japan, with the United States declaring war not only on Japan but also on Germany and Italy.[62] Chiang Kai-shek summarized the discussion and insisted that China should declare war on Japan. However, the declaration of war should be made after soliciting the views of the Allies, because Chiang Kai-shek wanted to maximize the use of the declaration of war to promote his grand strategy, which was the formation of an anti-Japanese alliance composed of China, the United States, the United Kingdom, and the Soviet Union.[63]

That afternoon, on December 8, Chiang Kai-shek met with the American, British, and Soviet ambassadors to China, insisting that China, the United Kingdom, the United States, the Soviet Union, Australia, the Netherlands, Canada, and New Zealand sign an agreement that none of the Allies would sign a separate truce treaty with Japan.[64] At 7:30 p.m. on December 8 (Chongqing time), at a press conference for Chinese and foreign journalists, Chinese foreign minister Guo Taiqi and information minister Wang Shijie stated that the Chinese government had decided to declare war on Germany, Italy, and Japan. The declaration of war on Japan was announced in fact before the declaration itself had been formally drafted and adopted.[65] On December 9, *Zhongyang ribao* (Central daily) used a whole page to report the Chinese government's decision.[66] Personal messages of support to Chiang Kai-shek from President Roosevelt and British Prime Minister Churchill arrived by telegram.[67] The Chinese government declared war on Japan after having received the news that the United States and Britain had done so. At 5:00 p.m., December 9, Chiang Kai-shek convened the Supreme National Defense Council, which finally declared war on the Axis powers.[68] On December 10, the Chinese government formally announced the decision to the Chinese people and to the international community.[69]

Chiang Kai-shek appealed to the Soviet Union through diplomatic channels and military representatives. Moreover, through Song Ziwen, China's representative in the United States, Chiang Kai-shek asked the United States for help.[70] But despite these efforts, the Soviet Union did not change its policy of not declaring war on Japan.[71] On December 12, on behalf of the Chinese government, Wang Shijie proposed that all Allied nations should form a military alliance and establish a unified leadership body to facilitate joint combat.[72] On December 14, Roosevelt responded. "An extremely important measure is to act immediately to prepare joint campaigns to resist our common enemies." Franklin Roosevelt proposed that before December 17, the Chinese government should convene a joint military conference of representatives from China, the United States, the United Kingdom, the Netherlands, and the Soviet Union in Chongqing. Based on the preparatory conference, he argued, unified military plans and standing leadership bodies might be created.[73] Roosevelt informed the Soviet Union and United Kingdom of these proposals.[74]

On December 23, the first military cooperation conference was held in Chongqing. During the meeting, topics such as defending Burma and the cooperation of the air forces were discussed.[75] Only the Soviet Union refused to attend the conference as an observer, arguing that the objectives of the conference were unclear.[76] Chiang Kai-shek was appointed as the Allied supreme commander of the China Theater.[77] China could send its representatives to the supreme command of the Allies based in Washington. And China signed the Allied declaration of January 1, 1942.[78] The outbreak of the Pacific War had helped China at long last to globalize the Sino-Japanese War.

At the first stage of the Sino-Japanese War, the Chinese government's policy toward Japan was not to declare war, a policy to which it adhered until the outbreak of the Pacific War for the following reasons: A formal declaration of war would entitle Japan by international law to blockade China's ports and cut off its supply lines. In argument with Wang Jingwei, Chiang Kai-shek was not concerned with the United States' enforcement of the Neutrality Act. After Nanjing fell, the Nationalist government felt that the probability of Japan's declaration of war on China had increased.

Countermeasures were prepared, but Japan never did declare war, in part because that would have meant that Japan took Chongqing seriously as a combatant and negotiating partner. In the autumn of 1938, the fall of Wuhan made Wang Jingwei and a few other leaders even more pessimistic about China's prospects in the war. They urged compromise with Japan and clashed with Chiang Kai-shek, who advocated declaring war on Japan. Chiang was adamant. His position had the desired effect of consolidating his power by forcing political rival Wang Jingwei and associates out of the government. Yet, afterward, for two more years, Chiang Kai-shek held off for strategic reasons from issuing a formal declaration of war—until Pearl Harbor in late 1941. The event globalized the war, a development that, needless to say, was warmly welcomed by Chiang Kai-shek.

7 Chiang Kai-shek and Jawaharlal Nehru

YANG TIANSHI

Jawaharlal Nehru was an important leader in the Indian national liberation movement, and he was independent India's first prime minister. During the Sino-Japanese War, as chairman of the Congress Party, he had close relations and frequent interactions with Chiang Kai-shek. In this chapter, I analyze the relationship from Chiang Kai-shek's side. The two men established a personal connection based on mutual respect and anti-imperialism. Chiang struggled to balance sympathy for the Indian national liberation movement with the effort to stop the Japanese and win the war. This required continuing cooperation with the British, India's colonial masters.

From the Marco Polo Bridge Incident in July 1937 to June 1939, China independently resisted the Japanese invasion for two years. During this time, various political parties and regional divisions in China achieved unprecedented unity. The Chinese Communist Party and Nationalist Party—bitter enemies—found a way to reconcile differences and jointly fight the Japanese invaders. The situation appealed to patriotic freedom fighters in India, which had been a British colony for a long time, in their effort to overcome ethnic splits and partisan political and religious divisions.

Jawaharlal Nehru represented the left wing of the Indian national liberation movement. Soon after the Sino-Japanese War broke out, Nehru established a China Day, when people would convene all over India and condemn the Japanese invasion. In 1938, Nehru also proposed that medical teams be sent to aid China. The next year, 1939, Nehru began to plan a trip to China. On June 15, 1939, he published an article titled "China," emphasizing China's importance to the world, Asia, and India. In the article, he particularly praised China's resistance:

She [China] is news because of her heroic resistance and the way she has overcome the tremendous difficulties she had to face. Only great people could have done that; a great people, not merely because they are the heirs to a great past, but because they have established their claim to the future. . . . Behind the war and inhumanity and violence, there is something happening in China which is of vital significance. A new China is rising, rooted in her culture, but shedding the lethargy and weaknesses of ages, strong and united, modern and with a human outlook. The unity that China has achieved in these years of trial is astonishing and inspiring. It is not merely unity in defence, but a unity in work and in building up. Behind the war fronts, in the vast undeveloped hinterland of China, there are vast schemes afoot which are changing the face of the country.[1]

Before Nehru's visit to China, various associations in China had already formed a committee to welcome the Congress Party leader. On August 23, 1939, the *Central Daily News* (Zhongyang ribao) published an editorial praising Nehru for his grand vision of liberating India, for giving up personal enjoyment, and for spending so much of his life in prison.[2] Zhu Jiahua, Chen Mingshu, and Liu Chi represented the Guomindang's (GMD's) Central Committee and ninety-three associations in China in welcoming Nehru at the airport. Wu Zhihui stated, "We are fighting a war for our survival, but also for the future of East Asia, and for world peace. China and India are major countries that represent oriental culture. We share a grand vision." Nehru responded:

In China's resistance to invasion, on behalf of the Indian people's leader Gandhi, Congress Party chairman, and poet Rabindranath Tagore, I bring supreme respect. For my trip to China, I have two tasks. First, I want to pass on the message of Gandhi to Chinese leaders. Second, I want to make the Indian people's efforts to aid China more practical.[3]

On August 25, at a press conference in Chongqing, Nehru stated that under the leadership of the Congress Party, the majority of the Indian people were engaged in activities that helped China and resisted the Japanese aggression.[4] Immediately upon arrival at Chongqing, Nehru visited Chiang Kai-shek and discussed cooperation. In the afternoon, he attended a conference chaired by Kong Xiangxi, head of the Executive Yuan.[5] On August 28, Chiang Kai-shek invited Nehru to his official residence on Huangshan, Chongqing. They discussed the Indian independence movement. That night Japanese airplanes bombed Chongqing three times. In an air-raid shelter, by candlelight, Chiang and Nehru spoke at length. Nehru was talkative. Their dialogue became a monologue, with Chiang listening most of the time. Nehru was eager to introduce the Congress Party to Chiang. He criticized the British government for trying its best to prevent India from achieving independence. Moreover, he informed Chiang that Italy and Germany were eager to build ties with India. He agreed to Chiang's proposal that China and India must go beyond mutual understanding and cooperate closely.[6] Chiang noted in his diary how well the two men got along.[7]

The next day, Nehru sent a long proposal to Chiang Kai-shek on developing India-China relations, with this preface:

Unfortunately, our contacts with China have been limited. It was the intense desire to add to these contacts and to learn from what was happening in China that brought me here. It has given me the greatest satisfaction to find that the Generalissimo shares this desire with me to add to our contacts and to develop Indo-Chinese relations. . . . China today has to face a mighty problem—how to resist Japanese aggression and hurl it back and establish her complete freedom. That is her chief and primary concern and all else is secondary. So also in India we have the primary problem of securing our freedom, all else is secondary. . . . We in India were differently situated and we adopted different tactics and methods [than Chinese resistance to the Japanese]. . . . We did it peacefully by mass organization and mass action. . . . The British imperialists have tried all means to destroy us (and failed). I firmly believe that China can benefit from our experience.[8]

Nehru then made seven suggestions. Besides the establishment of an effective and permanent organization for the exchange of information, he proposed the exchange of experts, contact at the university level, the dispatch of a Chinese delegation to the upcoming annual conference of the Congress Party, as well as direct contact between quasi-governmental groups such as the Chinese Industrial Cooperatives and the Indian Agricultural and Industrial Association. Finally, China and India should have a common policy for dealing with the European powers. China wanted to prevent Britain and Japan from reaching accommodations or even agreements that would harm China. The Indian nationalist leadership of course was focused on independence. China should send delegates to a small-scale anti-aggression regional conference in India to be organized in the near future. Such an anti-aggression meeting would promote India-China cooperation.[9]

Pleased, Chiang Kai-shek sent the proposal to Zheng Yanfen, Li Weiguo, and Ye Suzhong, who crafted a response expressing enthusiasm and support for the proposal. Political ties between the two parties should be cloaked in the name of cultural cooperation. After negotiations, a document called "The Preliminary Outline for India-China Cultural Cooperation" was prepared. Professors and students would be exchanged, books in Chinese and Hindi would be translated. The Central Chinese News Agency would establish branches in Calcutta and Bombay, as would the Bank of China and the Bank of Communications. Chinese delegates would attend the Congress Party conference in December. And the India-China Association would be expanded.[10]

On August 31, Nehru flew to Chengdu, and he returned on September 2. He had intended to stay in China for half a month. He was just about to fly to Guilin and had accepted the invitation from Mao Zedong for a visit to Yan'an. But war broke out in Europe on September 1, 1939.

The Congress Party urged him to return as soon as possible. Chiang Kai-shek bade Nehru farewell. They had succeeded in laying a basis for closer India-China cooperation. Chiang Kai-shek gave Nehru a photograph. In his diary, he noted that "Nehru's thoughts and behavior are reasonable."[11] On September 5, Nehru returned to India. Before his departure, on behalf of India he thanked the Chinese people for their warm welcome and stated that for the future of Asia, India-China cooperation was essential.[12]

The Chinese consul general in Calcutta reported that Nehru was deeply impressed by the war-mobilization efforts of China, especially the efforts in resistance and nation building.[13] Afterward (1940), Nehru published the pamphlet *China, Spain and the War*, whose introduction stated: "What impressed me was the tremendous vitality of the new China. I was no judge of the military position, but I could not imagine that a people with this vitality and determination, and the strength of ages behind them, could ever be crushed."[14]

In October 1939, the Congress Party convened its annual conference. To avoid misunderstandings with Britain or the opportunity for Japan to separate China and Britain, the Nationalist Party decided to send a nonparty member, Fu Sinian, who was the director of the History and Linguistics Institute at Academia Sinica. Unfortunately, Fu was not able to make the trip.[15] Dai Jitao, a leading Nationalist Party member and a Buddhist, was sent instead. Chiang Kai-shek gave Dai detailed written instructions, stating that he must be sincere, treat equally all ethnicities, religions, and social classes, and express China's hope that India would become more unified spiritually and politically. A unified India was the key to the improvement in India-China cooperation. On this last point he was as subtle as possible.[16]

In a letter handed over by Dai, Chiang addressed Nehru as "comrade":

Last year you visited our country. I was honored to talk with you a few times. Our country is still resisting Japanese aggression. The whole nation is determined. The key point for the world in moving from turmoil to peace is the Asian people's common struggle against Japan. To defend each nation's freedom, we have first of all to rid Asia of the Japanese enemy. The leaders of India know the world situation well. Our missions are identical.[17]

The Congress Party's primary objective was the overthrow of British rule. But Britain was also an ally. Therefore, Chiang Kai-shek highlighted Japan's ambitions and asked the Congress Party to place resistance to the Japanese enemy also as a primary concern in their struggle for freedom.

Not surprisingly, the British were alarmed. On October 25, the British foreign minister met with Guo Taiqi, the Chinese ambassador to Britain. He emphasized that China should not just show favor to the Congress Party. Instead, China should also be in contact with Muslim leaders and princes of various states. China should develop its business and economic ties with India. Political cooperation should be avoided.[18] Chiang asked Guo to reply that Dai Jitao's visit to India was to make contacts and persuade various political parties in India to cooperate with Britain. Economic issues were not on the agenda.[19]

But British-Indian tensions were high. A month earlier, Britain had declared war on Germany without consulting Indian leaders. On September 14, 1939, the Congress Party passed a resolution drafted by Nehru condemning Britain for having declared war on behalf of the Indian people and arguing that India should stay neutral. On October 13, Gandhi proposed a nonviolent resistance movement to the war. On November 10, Nehru was arrested for making antiwar propaganda. Thus, by the time Dai Jitao arrived in India, Nehru was in prison. Dai visited Nehru's family. He passed on Chiang Kai-shek's message to Nehru's sister, Vijaya Lakshmi Pandit, that the Congress Party should make the best of wartime opportunities.[20] Nehru did not respond to Dai's visit and the letter until after he was released from prison in mid-December.

Whatever has happened, and whatever may happen, it will not shake my firm conviction in the triumph of your cause, just as I am equally convinced of India's bright future, though the way to it may be long and dark. I realise fully, as you do, that all our problems in Asia and Europe are inextricably connected, and we have to follow closely world developments. . . . I think his [Dai's] visit has helped greatly in making the Chinese struggle even more real to our people and in drawing India nearer to China.[21]

A year later after the Pearl Harbor attack of December 1941, with agreement from the British and Dutch governments, President Franklin Roosevelt established the Allied Supreme Command of the China/India/Burma Theater, naming Chiang Kai-shek as commander in chief. Chiang then needed to consider resistance to Japan not only in China but in Asia as a whole, and especially in Southeast Asia. On January 2, 1942, Chiang instructed the Chinese ambassador to the United States, Hu Shi, to sign the four-nation declaration of war and noted in his diary that he was proud, nervous, and excited.[22]

On January 23, 1942, Chiang Kai-shek began planning a visit to Burma and India. In his diary, he wrote that the visit would lay a foundation for China's postwar policies toward British colonies.[23] The chief aims of the India visit were to urge the British and Indians to cooperate, to persuade India to contribute more troops and labor to the war effort, and to persuade Britain to grant India autonomy.[24]

As Chiang considered the situation in Asia, India was a high priority. But at the same time, India made Chiang nervous. China and Britain were allied against fascist Germany, Italy, and Japan. The Congress Party opposed British colonial rule in India and refused to support Britain's war effort. The German, Italian, and Japanese governments were eager to take advantage of this situation. They were trying to woo the Congress Party over to their side. In the Congress Party, there was a dangerous tendency among some to be in contact with the Axis powers and use them to cast off the yoke of British rule. This is why Chiang Kai-shek decided that the primary goal of the India visit was to persuade Britain and India to compromise and fight Japan together. Some of those around him saw the venture as hopeless. Dai Jitao and Chen Bulei tried to persuade Chiang Kai-shek to postpone his visit. Chiang retorted, "You do not understand the big picture. If 450 million Chinese and 350 million Indians cooperated, how wonderful that would be!"[25]

On February 9, 1942, Chiang Kai-shek and his wife, Song Meiling, arrived in New Delhi via Lashio, Burma. Chiang was eager to meet Gandhi and Nehru, but the British were not happy. In the early morning of February 10, the British ambassador to China, Archibald Clark Kerr, told Chiang that Lord Linlithgow, the viceroy, insisted that Chiang not visit Gandhi's residence at Wardha. Such a meeting would increase Gandhi's status and reputation and cause Britain to lose face. Also, Clark Kerr proposed that Chiang first visit the viceroy before meeting Nehru. Chiang was disappointed. He had to ask Madame Chiang to go ahead and meet Nehru before he did.[26] During the visit with Linlithgow, Chiang suggested that Britain immediately announce India's status as a dominion. In return, Indian leaders would temporarily postpone their campaign for full independence.

The next day Chiang himself met Congress Party chairman Maulan Azad along with Nehru. Azad stated that the Indian people were sympathetic to China's resistance against Japanese invasion, but India was governed by the British. The Indian people would help in the war effort only after Britain had granted independence to India. Chiang opined that India should go through a few transitional stages before getting full freedom. He suggested that India should use indirect methods and political tactics to gain freedom. Azad rejected Chiang's suggestions out of hand. There could be no intermediate stage to independence. Chiang asked whether it was possible that India could be granted dominion status first and then independence. Nehru replied that the Congress Party would consider this option only if there was a real transfer of power.[27]

After the meeting, Clark Kerr came again and passed on the viceroy's suggestion that Chiang Kai-shek not go to Bombay to meet Gandhi. Chiang should ask Gandhi to come to New Delhi. Otherwise, Gandhi would have the same status as the viceroy; the viceroy would lose face and be punished by the British government in London. Chiang was displeased and felt rebuffed. He angrily responded that he would rather return directly to

China. Late that night Clark Kerr indicated that it was agreed that Chiang could go to Bombay.[28]

On February 14, Chiang Kai-shek lamented in his diary: "I have tried my best to make constructive suggestions."[29] That evening, Chiang received a letter and telegram from Gandhi, who expressed great sorrow for the circumstances over which the Indian people had no control. A country's loss of freedom had many long-term implications.[30] Chiang was deeply saddened by the correspondence. He decided that one way or another he would meet Gandhi.

On February 15, Chiang summoned Clark Kerr for a talk. He said that he must meet Gandhi before his departure from India. He pointed out that he might be able to change Gandhi's attitude toward Britain. He chose the International School outside Calcutta as the meeting place. In the afternoon, Chiang told Nehru that he wished to meet Gandhi; otherwise this visit would be wasted. Moreover, Chiang stated that the current revolutionary strategy for India should be one of gradual progression rather than extreme moves. Nehru promised to telegraph Gandhi and arrange a meeting place.[31] In the evening, Nehru informed Chiang that Gandhi had to attend a friend's funeral and would meet Chiang Kai-shek at Calcutta.

While he was in India, Chiang Kai-shek had meetings with the governor of Bengal, Sir John Herbert, the viceroy, various other British administrators of the Indian government, the Nepali prince, Congress Party chairman Azad, Gandhi, Moslem League leader Mohammed Ali Jinnah, and leaders of the princely states. But mostly he met with Nehru.

When Chiang Kai-shek asked about Azad's rejection of his proposal that India might first gain the status of dominion, Nehru stated that the Indian people must be granted substantive power and be free to decide on their own what kind of government they would build.[32] Chiang learned that Gandhi had stated in a letter to the British that he would be satisfied if the Axis powers drove the British out of India. He also knew that Nehru had similarly attacked the British government in conversations with Indian journalists. Chiang was surprised. He thought that Gandhi's message was too radical and Nehru's position also too extreme, leaving no room for China's mediation.[33]

Chiang and Nehru had a long three-hour conversation. Chiang tried to persuade the Congress Party leadership to seize the opportunities presented by the world war. By fighting with the Allied powers, India would win worldwide sympathy. In terms of domestic policy, Congress should seize the opportunity presented by the British inability to effectively govern India. It should develop education, cultivate military and political personnel, and make active preparations to assume government. If India stuck to noncooperation (the Quit India campaign), the Indian revolution would suffer great losses. If India did not cooperate actively, India would lose the sympathy of the Allied powers. Chiang emphasized that the cooperation that he proposed was not cooperation with Britain but with the worldwide democratic front. "Britain would certainly change its India policy. If the revolutionary party in India would change its attitude and join the worldwide democratic front in the fight against fascism, it would greatly help the front to achieve victory. The outcome will be beneficial for India, if we judge the situation objectively."[34]

In response, Nehru denounced the British oppression of the Indian people and supported the Quit India independence movement. He stated that Britain had ruled India for around 160 years. British behavior had not been much different from that of the Japanese and German aggressors. Eighty years ago, the British harshly suppressed the Indian uprising in a fashion that was just as brutal as Hitler's cruel measures. During the First World War, India had been promised freedom after the war, but there was less freedom after the war than before the war. In 1919, the Congress Party organized a mass rally in Amritsar. The British government sent troops that surrounded the place, opening fire and killing more than 2,000 people. Gandhi rejected cooperation because of these bitter realities and created a nonviolent movement of great strength that frightened the British. The conversation ended with Chiang Kai-shek asking, "Is it possible that you would consider temporarily stopping the offensive against the British government in India?" Nehru answered, "No, I am afraid not, because it is our only weapon."[35]

Finally, on February 18, Chiang Kai-shek met Gandhi in Birla Park (Calcutta), with Nehru in attendance. Nehru did not speak throughout the conversation. Chiang proposed that China and India struggle together and seek common ground for bilateral cooperation. Gandhi did not answer. He just continued to spin cotton on a spinning machine. In his diary, Chiang wrote, "He loves only India. He cares only about India. He does not consider other people."[36]

A few days later, Nehru addressed the subject of the Sino-Japanese War directly. He began by stating that some leaders had proposed that the Indian leadership should be neutral. Others, like the former chairman of the Congress Party, Subhas Chandra Bose, believed that Japan and Germany would do less harm to India and that India should not oppose Japan and Germany. Bose had sent representatives to Japan to lobby for Japanese and German recognition of India's independence. If the Congress Party took part in the war, people sympathetic to Bose would leave. Nehru asked Chiang to pass on a clear message to the British that if they wanted the Indian people to join the fight, Britain had to let the Indian people know that the war was their own war by allowing them to form a national government. It would not be a national government controlled solely by the Congress Party.

The talk concluded with Nehru and Chiang Kai-shek discussing relations between the Chinese Nationalist Party and the Congress Party. Nehru repeatedly emphasized that if Indians could establish a national government, they would offer further cooperation. Under the existing circumstances, they could provide only moral support for China's resistance to the Japanese.

Nehru was not willing to move further than "sympathy." So Chiang Kai-shek changed the subject. He highlighted the importance of a China-India alliance. He stated that both countries had vast populations and large territories and suffered from foreign occupation. If the two nations really united, white people, no matter how closely they cooperated, could not suppress them. In contrast, if the two countries could not build strong ties, they would be surrounded by aggressive imperialists and never have hope of independence and freedom. Chiang criticized Gandhi's methods as too slow. India would have to wait for twenty or even thirty years for independence. Now was a good time for the party to adopt methods that did not contradict Gandhi's principles and would push forward the Indian revolution.[37]

On February 20, Nehru accompanied Chiang Kai-shek and Madame Chiang to visit the International School established by Rabindranath Tagore at Santiniketan. Chiang Kai-shek donated 50,000 rupees to the school and 30,000 rupees to the China Institute. In the car, Chiang said to Nehru that he hoped that the Congress Party would value diplomacy, especially diplomacy with China. He was unhappy when Nehru answered only that the situation was complicated. He criticized Nehru in his diary, "Nehru still does not pay attention to diplomacy."[38]

On February 21, Chiang Kai-shek drafted his "Letter of Farewell" to the Indian people. He made a final appeal to the various political parties in India and to the British government in India. China and India had related interests and similar futures. He called on the Indian people to join the anti-Japanese struggle. Then India would appear on the battlefield for a free world and obtain its final victory. At the same time, Chiang appealed to the British government: "I firmly believe that our ally Britain will promptly grant Indian people substantive political power."

After lunch, Chiang and Nehru continued their conversation. Nehru criticized the Atlantic Charter for having too many contradictory and confusing points. Chiang answered, "All political issues are confusing. Politics is about reality. We should use everything that would help us, even if it is our enemy's policy." Chiang advised Nehru to carefully consider the current opportunities. Nehru remained silent. Chiang thought that Nehru was being emotional and kept silent at the moment because he was greatly concerned about the future and was reluctant to say good-bye.[39]

After Chiang returned to China, on March 3, 1942, he sent Shen Shihua as China's special commissioner to India with the purpose of strengthening ties with Indian leaders. On March 7, the Japanese captured Rangoon, driving the British out of southern Burma. On March 11, Churchill sent Sir Stafford Cripps to India to propose the granting of dominion status and the promise to write a constitution after the war. But the talks failed. Nehru explained to Chiang in a letter that the British had been willing to go no further than adding Indian representatives to the viceroy's Executive Committee. Nehru said the Quit India movement would continue.[40] Chiang Kai-shek then asked Nehru how China could help India. Nehru answered in a letter to Madame Chiang that he found it hard to answer the question because Britain was bound by its self-made constraints. The most appropriate measure would be for the Allies to recognize Indian independence.[41] In a later note, Nehru added that after the failure of negotiations with Cripps, India was split between hatred of the British government and the hope that, although unarmed, Indians would succeed in resisting Japan. On March 12, Chiang declared India Day from Chongqing.

Chiang Kai-shek and Madame Chiang continued to labor to persuade Gandhi and Nehru to reduce anti-British sentiments. In May Nehru sent this message to Chiang Kai-shek, "Soon Gandhi will launch a large-scale anti-British mass movement. Anti-British sentiments are at an unprecedented height. The movement will involve non-cooperation, such as strikes."[42] On June 14, Gandhi sent a letter to Chiang Kai-shek, stating that he would demand that the British leave India immediately but promising that he would oppose a Japanese invasion. He was willing to allow Allied troops to stay in India and use India as a base.[43]

In the struggle with the British government, Chiang Kai-shek took the side of the Congress Party. On July 14, the Congress Party Working Committee passed a resolution to demand that the British leave India and threatened a disobedience movement. On July 27, Chiang convened the Supreme National Defense Council and the Nationalist Party Standing Committee. Wang Shijie proposed that the Nationalist Party should make a statement about the Indian situation. Chiang agreed. China should warn Britain not to take tough measures.

On July 28, the *Central Daily News* published an editorial titled "On the India Problem" by Wang Shijie. The article asked the Congress Party National Committee not to launch the disobedience movement, while making no demand on Britain. Chiang Kai-shek was furious and criticized Wang Shijie for failing to understand revolution and showing unnecessary concern for Westerners. He asked Chen Bulei to draft an article, titled "Second Statement on the India Problem," which declared that the resolution of the Indian-British tension depended on Britain. On July 29, Chiang Kai-shek wrote in his diary, "The British combine propaganda and conspiracy with penetrating effect. Propaganda Minister Wang Shijie fell into their trap unawares. It is truly evil."[44]

At the same time during 1942, Chiang Kai-shek lobbied the American government about India through Song Ziwen in Washington. He asked Roosevelt to mediate in the Indian-British standoff. He was worried that if the British government did not completely change its policy, it would lead to the Japanese occupation of India.[45]

On February 26, 1942, Chiang Kai-shek asked Song to suggest to Roosevelt that China and the United States jointly persuade Britain. "Future success in the Pacific Ocean and Mediterranean Sea depends on the reasonable and timely resolution of the India problem."[46] On April 23, Madame Chiang wrote to the American presidential envoy, Lauchlin Currie, warning that the failure of the Cripps mission had intensified anti-British sentiment in India.[47] On June 14, Gandhi made public a letter to Roosevelt, asking the United States to take a stand on the India problem. On June 17, Madame Chiang passed on the contents of a telegram from Nehru to Chiang Kai-shek. Gandhi was willing to ally with Britain, but he was unwilling to have India be subordinate to Britain. Her telegram claimed that India's independence was the only way to mobilize India in the battle for freedom.[48]

During the summer of 1942 the situation went from bad to worse. In June 1942, British and American troops began to arrive in India. The British government worried that Gandhi would launch a new movement demanding that the British and Americans leave India. Therefore, the government prepared to suppress it. On June 25, the British ambassador to China, Horace Seymour, visited Chiang Kai-shek, stating that the British government would "confine" Gandhi. Chiang Kai-shek warned that Gandhi had too many followers. On June 26, Chiang Kai-shek asked Gandhi for his views on the current situation. He reminded him that the priority should be to resist Japan.

Roosevelt did not want to see a clash between the Indians and the British. He felt that Gandhi was not a practical person. He asked Chiang Kai-shek to persuade Gandhi not to take extreme measures. On July 6, Chiang telegrammed Shen Shihua, asking him to request of Nehru that he act with restraint. However, Gandhi told Chiang that clashes seemed inevitable.

Nehru had predicted that if Britain did not change its policy toward India, Indians would become even more hostile to the British. His prediction proved correct. In August 1942, the Congress Party demanded British withdrawal from India. On August 9, sixteen persons, including Gandhi and Nehru, were arrested. Quit India ferment swept the nation.

From prison, Nehru authorized the Chinese Central News Agency to publicize his "Letter to the Chinese People" of August 8, 1942. In the letter he expressed his respect for Chiang Kai-shek and Madame Chiang.

He admired China's bitter five-year struggle of resistance. He claimed that he worked with the sole aim of gaining independence for India. He was willing to go all out to struggle against the invaders of India and China. A free India could fulfill this mission, while a restrained India could not.[49]

Chiang Kai-shek continued to worry that the situation in India would worsen. On August 8, in a weekly section in his diaries called "Reflections on Last Week," he wrote, "The situation in India has been stagnant. How will it evolve?" On August 10, Chiang Kai-shek learned that Gandhi and Nehru had been arrested. He told Chen Bulei, "The Soviet Union will stand by, and the United States will not necessarily be sympathetic. If China does not stand up for justice, there will be no justice in the world."[50] He condemned British brutality.[51] He once more appealed to Roosevelt, arguing that people would say that the Allies were suppressing liberty. Chiang also sent supporting telegrams to Gandhi and Nehru, stating "I have learned that you are in prison, and I am concerned. Please take care of yourself for the nation. I send this telegram to convey my sympathy."[52]

Publicizing this telegram became an issue. After the message of consolation was drafted, Chiang Kai-shek ordered that it not be sent. But three journalists already knew of its existence. Deputy Minister of Propaganda Dong Xianguang (Hollington Tong), held back the message itself from these journalists. Chen Bulei suggested that the publication of the message should be postponed. Wang Chonghui stated that Roosevelt had advised Chiang Kai-shek not to make an explicit statement and that British officials were discussing the idea that Madame Chiang and Vice President Henry A. Wallace might mediate. Wang proposed that they should wait for the appropriate time to make the telegram public. Finally, Chiang ordered that his message be released publicly. And he asked Lord Linlithgow to pass on the telegram to the prisoners, but his request was turned down.[53] On that day, Chiang left angry remarks in his diary accusing Britain of being extraordinarily cruel.[54]

The next day, on August 11, Chiang Kai-shek ordered Shen Shihua to hand his telegram to Nehru in prison so Nehru would know that China's attitude toward their Indian friends had not changed. On the same day, the *Central Daily News* published an editorial that expressed concerns about the collapse of British-Indian relations. The editorial expressed the hope that the Indian government would adopt a more tolerant spirit and seek political reconciliation.[55]

Chiang met the British ambassador, Seymour, in Chongqing on August 11, and he stated that he was prepared to go to London personally to mediate.[56] Seymour told Chiang that Churchill had expressed the desire to visit Chongqing. Chiang wrote in his diary, "Churchill might use this visit to show that he supports China. I do not want to accept this favor.

Therefore, I disregard Churchill's intention to visit."[57] On August 20, the British minister responsible for India met Ambassador Gu Weijun to ask China not to interfere in Indian affairs.[58]

In the relationship between Chiang Kai-shek and Nehru, there was another important issue that is not well-known. In 1942, as part of the plan to join forces with Japan, Nazi Germany planned to attack India. Hermann Goering asked his trusted subordinate Jahnke to contact General Gui Yongqing, who had studied in Germany. Gui was contacted three times. Goering wanted Chiang Kai-shek to betray the Allies and join Germany in attacking India. Chiang Kai-shek rejected the German overtures.[59]

Chiang Kai-shek remained sympathetic and supportive of India's independence movement. He pursued pro-Indian and anti-British policies. The year before, in August 1941, he and Madame Chiang met an Indian woman revolutionary, who talked about the tragedies India had experienced after it became a British colony. Chiang Kai-shek was moved. He wrote in his diary, "I am very sad. I am aware that resisting foreign invasion is important. Otherwise, our descendants may suffer from the tragedies that India experienced. My wife and I both believe that we should live free or die. . . . After China gains independence and liberation, China must help India win independence."[60]

During his 1942 visit to India, Chiang Kai-shek tried to persuade the Congress Party to stop its anti-British movement. He wanted India first to join the world war against the Axis powers together with the Allies. Independence would come after the war. Chiang felt caught between the British imperial rule and India's independence movement. He hated the British and was sympathetic to Nehru and India. Although the worldwide anti-fascist war was his chief concern, he also wanted to support the liberation of the people of Asia from the yoke of imperialism.

On November 26, 1942, Madame Chiang left for the United States. Before the trip, Chiang Kai-shek gave her a list of key points to be raised in conversation with Roosevelt. The fifth point stated that if India could not become independent, world peace and equality for mankind could not be achieved. He proposed that India must become independent, but to save Britain's face, there should be a transitional period.[61]

A year later, at the Cairo Conference, Roosevelt, Churchill, and Chiang Kai-shek discussed the war and postwar issues. Chiang and Roosevelt had discussions about the future of colonies such as Korea and Vietnam. Chiang proposed that they should become independent. He also raised the subject of India's independence. Roosevelt stated, "We should not discuss it now, not until after the war. Churchill is a conservative person. You will get nowhere by discussing it with him. After the war, Britain will have a new government which will surely resolve the India issue." Chiang accepted Roosevelt's advice.[62]

At the end of 1943, Congress Party leader Subhas Chandra Bose established the Indian National Army in collaboration with the Japanese to fight in Burma and then liberate India. Bose established a government in exile in Singapore and appointed himself prime minister. But in India Nehru remained in control of the Congress Party and persisted in trying to help China resist Japanese aggression.

In 1945, when the Sino-Japanese War ended with China's victory, Nehru congratulated Chiang Kai-shek in a telegram. Chiang thanked him. In September 1946, when the Indian Provisional Government was established, China's Nationalist government immediately recognized it. On February 28, 1947, Luo Jialun was appointed as the first Chinese ambassador to India.

Unfortunately, at this point the friendly nature of the Chiang-Nehru relationship began to change. Nehru inherited Britain's position toward Tibet and tried to solidify and expand Britain's privileges in Tibet. In July 1947, Chiang Kai-shek complained in his diary that immediately after gaining independence, India maneuvered to consolidate control over Tibet. "Such arrogance was unbelievable" were his words.[63] In his diary, Chiang Kai-shek condemned Nehru's Tibet policy and the Indian government a number of times.[64] Communication between the two leaders ended.

In March 1951, the Tibetan administration sent a delegation to the new Communist government in Beijing to negotiate the peaceful liberation of Tibet. Chiang Kai-shek was happy when he heard the news in Taiwan. He wrote in his diary, "This time the Dalai Lama was not stopped by Britain and India. He has sent delegates to Beijing. India's plot has failed."[65]

Thus, the once cordial wartime relationship between Nehru and Chiang Kai-shek ended on a sad, bitter note. The misunderstanding of each other's national interests proved too deep. Strange indeed how a similar scenario in which cordiality and overblown rhetoric turned sour was repeated a decade later with the breakdown of Premier Zhou Enlai's relationship with Nehru—a breakdown that led to the border war of 1962.

8 Chiang Kai-Shek and Joseph Stalin during World War II

LI YUZHEN

During World War II, Chiang Kai-shek and Joseph Stalin dominated relations between China and the Soviet Union. Previous history had left a legacy that was not conducive to their cooperation, with Chiang Kai-shek having evicted Soviet advisers during the 1920s when he launched the 1926 to 1928 Northern Expedition that unified China. Chiang had continued to fight the Communists, whom Stalin could not abandon unless he was willing to give up his claim of directing a worldwide Communist movement. Just one sign of the deep animosity between the two was that Stalin kept Chiang Kai-shek's son, Chiang Ching-kuo, as a hostage in the Soviet Union.

As the threat of Japan to China increased, and that of Germany and Japan to the Soviet Union, China and the Soviet Union moved gingerly toward an accommodation. While Chiang hoped for Soviet material aid and actual Soviet military involvement in China's war with Japan, Stalin's strategy was to trap Japan in China so as to be able to concentrate on Europe and avoid a war with Japan on its eastern frontier. Stalin had the best cards, including a far more powerful army. He resisted Chiang's pressure to throw Soviet forces into China's war with Japan until the last two weeks of the war. Stalin was motivated less by aiding China than by ensuring Soviet involvement in the defeat of Japan and securing a postwar Soviet role in the Pacific and in China. Even though Stalin essentially sat out the war in China, Chiang was compelled to accept Soviet joint management of the China Eastern Railway, Soviet access to the ice-free harbors of Dalian and Lüshun, and Soviet control over Outer Mongolia.

However, this did not mean that Stalin's support for the Nationalists had no real meaning. Soviet pressure on the Communists had been critical in securing Chiang Kai-shek's release during the December 1936 Xi'an

Incident. Without Stalin's pressure, the Communists would never have accepted Chiang Kai-shek as China's wartime leader. Soviet financial and military aid was instrumental in sustaining China's war effort during the first years of the war against Japan. Even though it is fair to say that the Soviets gained the most, the accommodation between Stalin and Chiang Kai-shek paid dividends for both sides.

This chapter provides a close examination of the evolving relationship between Chiang Kai-shek and Stalin during World War II. It is virtually entirely based on Soviet and Chinese party and government documents, maintaining a sharp focus on the policies and underlying strategies both pursued. It draws much less on memoirs and diaries, which are often useful but can also frequently be misleading. It argues that both wartime leaders based their policies on a rational calculation of the strategic interests of their countries and their assessments of the international political situation. Both were committed to defeat the Axis powers of Germany and Japan. Had the two not developed a minimum level of cooperation necessitated by the strategic interests of their two countries, it is highly debatable whether either could have joined in the titanic struggle against Germany and Japan, with all the consequences of that. War necessity compelled two men who had every reason to distrust each other to overcome a long history of mutual suspicion and animosity to find common ground.

Détente: From the Xi'an Incident to the Sino-Soviet Nonaggression Pact (December 1936 to August 1937)

Chiang Kai-shek's decision in 1927 to order home Soviet advisers and his suppression of the Communists during the 1926 to 1928 Northern Expedition soured Sino-Soviet relations. In 1929, Nationalist China broke off foreign relations with the Soviet Union when Zhang Xueliang, the warlord in charge of Northeast China who was nominally allied with the Nationalists, attacked the Soviets in a bid to end their control over the China Eastern Railway. Japan's decision to seize China's Northeast Provinces, or Manchuria, in 1931, however, changed the strategic situation. The Soviet Union and the Nationalists then faced a common enemy along a border many hundreds of miles long.

The quiet resumption of diplomatic ties was the first step. Neither Stalin nor Chiang Kai-shek wanted to draw attention to this, not only so as not to alarm Japan but also because the Nationalists were still fighting the Chinese Communists. In June 6, 1932, the Central Committee of the Chinese Nationalist Party agreed to the normalization of diplomatic relations as well as an eventual nonaggression pact. On December 12, 1932, while attending the Geneva Conference on arms reduction, Chinese representative Yan Huiqing and Soviet Diplomatic Commission representative Maxim Litvinov exchanged diplomatic notes, which was followed the next day by a formal declaration by Foreign Minister Luo Wengan in Nanjing.[1]

The many differences between the Nationalists and the Soviets, including the issue of the Soviets' recognition of Manchukuo, prevented any serious cooperation. So did Japan's determination to keep foreign countries from providing support to China. Japan left the League of Nations when China lodged a complaint against Japan, accusing it of aggression. Japan, in turn, objected to foreign aid provided to China, arguing that any such aid "inevitably had political significance."[2] In August 1935, the Japanese commander in North China, General Hayao Tada, announced that Japan's policy was to remove Guomindang (GMD) influence from North China.[3] On August 4, Japan demanded that China join Japan in the "mutual defense against Communism" and cooperate with Japan economically and politically.

Chiang Kai-shek rejected these demands. As early as 1933, Chiang Kai-shek stated to the Soviet ambassador in China, Dmitri Bogomolov, that "China regards the Soviet Union as a friendly neighbor. If war erupts unexpectedly, China will support the Soviet Union. And China will use all its strength to prove this friendship."[4] Three years later, Chiang Kai-shek rejected Japan's demand to join the Anti-Comintern Pact out of hand. The day it was signed, the Chinese Nationalist Party stated that it would rely on its own strength and did not need to negotiate with any third party.[5?]

Chiang instead worked to improve relations with the Soviets. In 1935, he asked Deng Wenyi, an attaché in the Chinese embassy in Moscow, to contact Wang Ming, the representative of the Chinese Communist Party to the Executive Committee of the Comintern, the Communist International, in Moscow. Chiang asked Deng to relay the message that he hoped to come to an agreement with the Communists. This was prevented at the time by the demand that the Chinese Communist Party recognize the authority of the Nationalist government, which was unacceptable to the Chinese Communist Party.[6]

The historian and diplomat Jiang Tingfu played an important role in improving Sino-Soviet relations after Chiang Kai-shek sent him to Moscow as China's ambassador in 1936, instructing him to find out more about Soviet attitudes toward closer cooperation.[7] Jiang told Boris Stomonyakov that many people favored this—referring to important GMD figures such as Kong Xiangxi, the minister of finance; Sun Ke, Sun Yat-sen's son; and Song Meiling, Chiang Kai-shek's wife—and that "at this stage, Chiang Kai-shek's foreign policy does not represent or reflect the Chinese people's attitude."[8] Jiang told Stomonyakov that "under no circumstances shall China side with Japan against the Soviet Union," and asked him for suggestions on how their two countries might achieve a closer collaboration.[9]

The fraught relationship between the Nationalists and the Chinese Communists formed a major obstacle to an improvement in relations between the Nationalists and the Soviets. Chiang Kai-shek had repeatedly declared that he could not work together with the Chinese Communists as long as they had their own independent military forces, while the Communists were not willing to give up their army. However, the rise of fascism and a Soviet change in policy paved the way for closer ties. In 1935, the Seventh Congress of the Comintern decided that Communists around the world should participate in national united fronts against fascism rather than concentrate on overthrowing imperialism: it called for cooperation of socialists and bourgeois capitalists in popular fronts against fascism. The Chinese Communist Party published "An Open Letter Calling on Compatriots to Fight the Japanese Enemy and to Save China." This was the famous August 1 Declaration, which called for an end to civil war and joint resistance to the Japanese.

It took time before a new united front involving the Communists and the Nationalists became a reality. For their own reasons, both Stalin and the Chinese Communist Party (CCP) had opposed Chiang Kai-shek. Stalin was the first to become convinced of the importance of Chiang Kai-shek in resisting Japan's expansion into Northeast Asia and securing the eastern flank of the Soviet Union. He was convinced that the most important condition for an effective resistance to Japan was a united China.

In China, forces opposed to Chiang Kai-shek remained active. The CCP attempted to unite them under its banner. For instance, it attempted to ally with the Northeast Army of Zhang Xueliang and Yang Hucheng. Together, they requested a monthly allocation of US$3 million from the Comintern to support the Red Army and the Northeast Army, and in the spring of 1936 the Communists began negotiations with Zhang Xueliang about military and administrative issues.[10]

The Guangxi Clique led by Li Zongren was another force that the Communists attempted to bring into an anti–Chiang Kai-shek alliance. In June 1936, when Chiang Kai-shek abolished the Southwest Political Council to end southern autonomy, the Guangxi Clique contacted the Chinese Communists in the hope of bringing about a common front against Chiang Kai-shek and to secure Soviet aid. But the incident was resolved without fighting and would come to nothing.[11] The Communists, finally, also turned to Chen Mingshu, who in 1933 had led his Nineteenth Route Army to rebel against Chiang Kai-shek and who had briefly presided over a "Fujian People's Government." In May 1936, from Hong Kong where he had sought refuge, Chen Mingshu submitted a proposal to the Comintern, arguing for a CCP-led alliance to overthrow Chiang Kai-shek and resist Japanese aggression.[12] Within weeks after receiving Chen Mingshu's proposal, the Comintern sent a secret instruction to the CCP in which it described Chen as an unscrupulous warlord. It contained no mention of opposition to Chiang Kai-shek, arguing that the only use Chen Mingshu could possible have was to mobilize support among overseas China and insisting that the CCP should sign no agreement with Chen.[13]

During most of this time, the CCP and Moscow were not in contact. After communications links were reestablished in June 1936, Dimitrov became aware of what had been going in China and held discussions with Stalin about it. They decided that the CCP should reduce its anti–Chiang Kai-shek propaganda. On July 23, at a meeting of the Secretariat of the Executive Committee of the Comintern, Dimitrov argued that the CCP should change, and he argued that "a question has emerged in the CCP, namely to what extent its policy toward the Nanjing government and Chiang Kai-shek is correct." Even Wang Ming was criticized.[14]

In this way, Dimitrov ended the policy favoring the expansion of CCP areas in China. He argued that the CCP should stop calling for the overthrow of Chiang Kai-shek. "At the present moment, the priority is not the expansion of soviet areas or of the Red Army. Instead we must put forward concrete ways and develop appropriate slogans to unite the great majority of the Chinese people for resistance to Japan."[15] Stalin and Dimitrov agreed on two measures. The first was to relieve Wang Ming from his responsibilities in connection with guiding Communist parties in Central and South America and to send him back to China.[16] The second was the dispatch of a telegram on August 15 to the CCP that insisted that the CCP abandon its hostile stance toward the Nationalists and instead seek to join an alliance with it to resist Japan. It argued that it was "wrong" to believe that "Chiang Kai-shek and the entire GMD were the allies of the Japanese." Because the priority was to resist Japan and because "it was impossible to resist Japan and oppose Chiang at the same time," the telegram instructed the Communists to cooperate with the Nationalists. The telegram argued that the CCP should stop land confiscations of small landowners as well as of all soldiers and officers who participated in resistance to Japan. It instructed the Chinese Communists to drop the slogan "Declare war on Japan immediately" and instead to use "Chase the Japanese invaders from China." It argued that the CCP should call for a "democratic republic" in which all soviet areas would be incorporated. The telegram at the same time insisted that in negotiations with the Nationalists, the CCP should demand that the Nationalists halt all civil war and release political prisoners. In addition, the Red Army should be under a unified command, be granted a certain level of armaments, and be stationed in its own area.[17] In short, Moscow instructed the CCP to abandon the policy of bringing about an anti–Chiang Kai-shek alliance and instead to work toward a united front with the Nationalists against the Japanese. Because of the requirement of Soviet security, Chiang Kai-shek's position improved greatly.

The Xi'an Incident of December 1936 provided an opportunity for a radical realignment, in conformity with Stalin's wishes, of CCP-GMD and Sino-Soviet relations. During the incident, Zhang Xueliang took Chiang prisoner when he was in Xi'an to press Zhang to continue to fight the Communists. Stalin's intervention was key to the unwinding of the incident. When Stalin learned of Zhang's action on midnight, December 14, Stalin immediately phoned Dimitrov, asking, "Did the incident in China erupt with your approval?" Dimitrov denied this. Both concluded that Chiang's capture, and likely death, would be to the great benefit of Japan. Stalin suspected Wang Ming had been behind the incident. Wang had wanted to send a telegram calling for Chiang Kai-shek's execution.[18]

Stalin had an article published in *Pravda* which stated that Zhang had been manipulated by Japan and denied any involvement by the Soviet Union.[19] Stalin moved so aggressively on the issue because he feared that the Japanese would conclude that the Soviet Union had been behind the incident, hoping to remove Chiang Kai-shek to bring about an anti-Japanese united front led by the CCP and Zhang Xueliang. For the same reason, Stalin instructed the Comintern Executive Committee to request the Chinese Communist Party not to raise the slogan "Ally with the Soviet Union."[20] Moscow also brought pressure on the CCP to release Chiang, which was done.

After the Xi'an Incident, the Soviet foreign commissar, Maxim Litvinov, asked Jiang Tingfu to inform Chiang Kai-shek that the Soviet government supported him.[21] Moscow criticized the CCP for following an erroneous policy of trying to split the GMD and refusing to cooperate with it against Japan. Stalin criticized even Wang Ming.[22] On February 10, 1937, the Chinese Communist Party Central Committee proposed to the Nationalists that in return for an end to civil war, joint resistance to the Japanese, and policies to improve economic conditions, it would publicly announce the abrogation of its policy calling for the overthrow of the Nationalists, change the name of its soviets to special zones, and formally incorporate its forces in the national army.[23] These measures helped provide the right conditions for bringing about substantive cooperation during the war.[24]

Chiang remained highly critical of the Chinese Communists for dividing Chinese society at a critical period in its history. In late February, the GMD Central Committee passed a resolution that took a hard-line view and vowed to put the Red Army out of action.[25] However, Song Qingling (Sun Yat-sen's widow), Sun Ke, and He Xiangning (the widow of GMD elder Liao Zhongkai) called for a return to what they stated had been Sun Yat-sen's policy in the mid-1920s of allying with the Soviet Union, toleration of the CCP, and support for peasants and workers. They argued that after these policies were jettisoned, "revolution had failed and foreign aggression arrived."[26] To resist Japan and unite the country, they argued, it was necessary to return to those policies.

After fighting between Chinese and Japanese forces broke out on July 7, 1937, the Soviet Union moved quickly to ensure the Nationalists of its support. In an important symbolic gesture, the Soviet Politburo agreed to release Chiang Ching-kuo,[27] with Dimitri Bogomolov, the Soviet ambassador to China, making the arrangements.[28] It made available a loan of 50 million Mexican dollars for the purchase of airplanes, tanks, and other military equipment. It agreed to train pilots and tank operators in the Soviet Union for China. A delegation of artists was dispatched to China as an indication of moral support.[29] Finally, on August 21, Foreign Minister Wang Chonghui and Bogomolov signed the Sino-Soviet Nonaggression Pact in Nanjing. The treaty stipulated that neither would offer assistance of any kind to an aggressor attacking China or the Soviet Union.[30] It also stated that China would not join an anti-Communist alliance and that the Soviet Union would not sign a nonaggression pact with Japan.[31]

For much of the 1930s, Chiang had kept his options open, and some in the GMD had indicated that they favored participation in an anti-Communist pact. The Sino-Soviet Nonaggression Pact was important, then, in foreclosing the option of either nation joining in with Japan, completely isolating the latter. If it might be thought the Soviet Union was unlikely to collaborate with Japan, it should not be forgotten that two years later Stalin had no qualms in signing an agreement with Ribbentrop that led to the invasion of Poland. This history underscores, too, that the final pattern of alliances which emerged in the course of World War II was not foreordained.

Chiang Kai-Shek's Appeals for Soviet Red Army Involvement after the Outbreak of War

As important as Soviet support was to Chiang Kai-shek, what he really needed was the active involvement by the Soviet Red Army in the fighting. Chiang would make three attempts to convince Stalin to agree to this, but he would fail each time. Stalin was convinced that Germany posed the main threat to the security of the Soviet Union, and he was therefore determined to avoid being dragged into China's war with Japan. He had no compelling reason to take the risks such a step would involve, especially not at a time when his purges had weakened the Soviet Red Army and when the international situation remained highly unpredictable. Britain,

France, and the United States remained deeply suspicious of the Soviet Union.

Soon after the beginning of war between Japan and China, Chiang made a first cautious effort to secure Soviet, as well as British and American, involvement. At the November 1937 Brussels international conference called by the nine countries that had signed the 1922 Washington treaties pledging support for the integrity of China, China's delegation, led by Gu Weijun (Wellington Koo), hoped for condemnation of Japan as an aggressor state in conformity with League of Nations treaties. Anticipating defeat, Chiang instructed Gu to attempt to secure UK and US support for the use by the Soviet Union of its forces against Japan.[32] The conference was not prepared to go any further than to call for a temporary halt to military action so as to make a peaceful settlement of the disagreements between China and Japan possible. Soviet representative Litvinov suggested the creation of a collective security mechanism, but this was unacceptable to the United Kingdom and the United States.

In October 1937, as large Chinese and Japanese armies battled at Shanghai, Chiang Kai-shek instructed Yang Jie, who was leading a delegation to the Soviet Union to make arms purchases and who would succeed Jiang Tingfu as ambassador to Russia,[33] to ask Stalin directly whether he would be willing to deploy troops in China in case the Brussels conference failed.[34] On November 1, Yang met with Soviet national defense commissar Kliment K. E. Voroshilov. Arguing that China's resistance at Shanghai was near collapse, Yang stated, "If the Soviet Union can maintain peace in the Far East, no war will break out in the West," adding that Chiang Kai-shek hoped that the Soviet Union would join the war against Japan as soon as possible.[35] Voroshilov made clear that while the Soviet Union would provide support to the Nationalists, it would not mobilize its forces against Japan, as it could not risk a war on two fronts.[36] Soviet policy was to help China resist Japan but not involve itself directly in the fighting.

To leave no doubt of Soviet support for Chiang Kai-shek, Voroshilov also stated to Yang that he believed that Chiang should take firm control in China and act decisively against anyone disobeying his orders, and even to execute people. Such a determined attitude, according to him, was necessary to unify China at this time of war. Voroshilov added that Stalin wanted Yang to relay this message to Chiang.[37] Stalin wanted Chiang to have no concern about any possible repercussions his actions against the Communists might have on Sino-Soviet relations. When Stalin met Yang personally, he told him that all parties in China should follow Chiang Kai-shek, that he hoped that the CCP's and the GMD's forces would be unified under one command, and that he would provide as many airplanes as the Nationalists desired.[38] China had virtually no air force, with the result that the Japanese had been able to establish air control within weeks of the beginning of the fighting. Stalin made plain, though, that he would not dispatch Red Army forces. "Even if Japan defeats China now, China should seek revenge in the future. Great nations never perish."[39] He had no doubt, he stated, that China would be able to defeat Japan by itself.

After the Japanese took Shanghai and Nanjing, Chiang Kai-shek wrote a personal letter to Stalin pleading for Soviet involvement:

China and Russia are two great nations and the two pillars of peace in East Asia. As China is close to collapse, I have to state the truth. China has tried its best to survive and meet its international responsibilities, but we have been forced to withdraw from our capital, Nanjing. China sincerely hopes that China's friendly neighbor the Soviet Union will aid China. I hope that you will be able to act decisively and send troops to reverse the calamitous situation in East Asia.[40]

Stalin turned down Chiang's request.

Soon after, Chiang tried again to secure Soviet participation, in a personal letter for Stalin carried by Sun Ke, who replaced Yang Jie as China's special envoy. Chiang thanked Stalin for the Soviet Union's moral and material assistance "during the past months" and expressed the hope that the Soviet Union and China would collaborate in preserving the peace in East Asia.[41] To bring further pressure, Lin Sen, the Chinese Nationalist government chairman, also gave Sun a letter, this one for Mikhail Kalinin, the chairman of the Presidium of the Supreme Soviet, stating that Sun was fully authorized to discuss all forms of assistance.[42] Although Sun's trip did bring some results,[43] the Soviet Union persisted in its refusal to send troops to China, giving as reasons that direct Soviet military involvement might lead Western countries to withdraw their aid, that it could lead to China's international isolation, and that it would provide further fuel to Japanese aggression, including in China.[44]

Sino-Soviet Negotiations during 1938

The year 1938 was a difficult one for China on the battlefield. It lost the key battle of Xuzhou, after which the Japanese were able to take North China and the regions along the Yangzi River from Shanghai to Wuhan in Central China. Off the battlefield, the international situation also deteriorated, with Hitler gaining in strength and the European countries continuing to appease him. While the Soviet Union continued to provide large amounts of material aid, it became even more reluctant to become involved militarily, other than when its own forces faced a direct Japanese military threat.

Germany had remained neutral after the outbreak of the war, and in the German Foreign Office there was support for China, in part because of substantial German financial and industrial interests in China. German ambassador Oskar Trautmann had tried to have Germany and Japan accept him as mediator to end the fighting between China and Japan. However, Hitler believed that Japanese success in East Asia would weaken Great Britain and the United States, as well as the Soviet Union.[45] He therefore sided with Japan, recognizing Manchukuo on February 20, 1938.

The next month, Germany invaded Austria. Churchill's appeals for a grand alliance involving the United Kingdom, France, and the Soviet Union fell on deaf ears. Prime Minister Chamberlain continued to pursue appeasement. Well aware that Britain would offer no help, in a February 26, 1938, meeting with the new Soviet ambassador to China, Ivan Luganets-Orelsky, Chiang renewed his plea for Soviet military involvement. "The recent developments in the West show that the aggression is strengthening," he argued. "Some nations that advocate peace cannot adopt a tough stance," and therefore it was up to the Soviet Union to help China "maintain the peace in the Far East."[46]

Chiang Kai-shek ordered Sun Ke, who was then in Europe, back to Moscow.[47] On May 19, Sun met with Deputy Foreign Commissar Stomonyakov, mentioning that British prime minister Neville Chamberlain and foreign minister Viscount Halifax were half-hearted about supporting China, while the new Edouard Daladier cabinet in France merely followed Britain's lead. Sun asked Stomonyakov to exploit any and all opportunities to persuade Britain to provide more substantial assistance to China and to increase the Soviets' own aid.[48] To Sun's suggestion that China and the Soviet Union adopt a coordinated foreign policy toward Britain and France, Stalin answered pragmatically that "we should not break up with Britain and France. . . . We should try to get whatever we can get from them." Stalin urged China to become self-reliant in terms of its war industries. China should built its own airplanes, he argued.[49] Stalin, however, again rejected the idea of Soviet participation in the war, pointing out that the Soviet army was tying down 400,000 Japanese soldiers in Manchuria.[50] Sun did succeed in negotiating an aid package to China with a value of US$50 million.[51] Chiang Kai-shek sent a telegram to Stalin to express gratitude and instructed Yang Jie to sign the treaty,[52] which stipulated that China would repay the loan not with money but with tea, leather, wool, silk, cotton, tung oil, herbs, tin, antimony, tungsten, nickel, zinc, and copper.[53]

Even a substantial military clash between the Soviet Red Army and the Japanese Imperial Army at Lake Khasan (Zhanggufeng) did not lead to active Soviet engagement in the war. The clash, in the summer of 1938, resulted from a boundary dispute, with Soviet forces occupying ground they claimed belonged to the Soviet Union. Although the Japanese initially ignored Soviet moves, the Kwantung Army attacked on July 29. The fighting ended on August 10, after Soviet forces had driven the Japanese away. Neither side wanted an escalation of the fighting. During the incident, Chiang Kai-shek instructed Yang Jie to inquire about Soviet intentions.[54]

In late August after the incident was already over, Luganets-Orelsky explained that the Soviet Union would intervene in the War of Resistance against Japan only if three conditions were met. The League of Nations would have to adopt a resolution authorizing action against Japan; Britain, the United States, and France would have to declare war on Japan; and Japan would have to launch a war against the Soviet Union. He reiterated that the Soviet Union believed that China would be able to sustain a long war by itself and that with foreign aid it would eventually defeat Japan.[55]

Chiang once more sent a personal letter to Stalin on August 26, immediately after he had learned that the Soviet Union remained unwilling to participate actively in the war:

Only the Soviet Union, which liberates oppressed nations, and Your Excellency, who leads the world in the fight for peace, have shown genuine empathy toward China, which is fighting Japan alone. . . . China and Russia share the responsibility to uphold world peace and justice. I firmly believe that the strengthening of Sino-Soviet cooperation will lead to the failure of Japan's aggression. I hope to work closely with Your Excellency to reach this goal.[56]

Stalin asked Luganets-Orelsky to pass on the following reply:

First, the Soviet Union believes that at present it should not disregard Britain and the United States and should not fight Japan without them. Britain and the United States have powerful navies. Unilateral action of the Soviet Union will make the Chinese situation worse, as Japan would claim that it was being attacked and ask for protection from Germany and Italy. Britain would conclude that the Soviet Union violates other nations and was using the opportunity to strengthen its influence in China and turn it into a Communist country.

Stalin reiterated the three conditions that had to be met before the Soviet Union would deploy troops to China. He also reaffirmed the Soviet Union's commitment to the Sino-Soviet Nonaggression Pact and its military aid program.[57]

The year 1938 saw two more attempts by Chiang Kai-shek to draw the Soviet Union into the war. The situation had become increasingly desperate as Japanese forces were sweeping away China's resistance along the Yangzi River and were nearing Wuhan, which the Nationalists had turned into a sort of Madrid, a last center of resistance. Chiang Kai-shek asked Luganets-Orelsky to inquire whether the Soviet Union was at least prepared to enter into discussions about joint military planning.[58] Following the fall of Wuhan, Chiang Kai-shek asked the Soviets to use their air force in Vladivostok to bomb Japanese military bases and cities. He argued that as a result, "the situation in East Asia would change drastically and be beneficial to both China and the Soviet Union."[59] The Soviets held firm to their policy of not being drawn into the war in China.

The Outbreak of War in Europe

The outbreak of war in Europe in 1939 made active Soviet involvement in the Sino-Japanese War even more unlikely. Open negotiations in the spring and early summer involving the Soviet Union, France, and Britain about a joint guarantee to secure peace in Europe faltered as a result of mutual suspicion about one another's real willingness to take up arms against Germany and Polish unwillingness to allow Soviet forces to march through Polish territory in case of war with Germany. At the same time, secret negotiations were taking place between Germany and the Soviet Union, which would lead to the famous Molotov-Ribbentrop Pact between Germany and the Soviet Union, signed on August 23, by which the two countries would divide Poland and the Baltic states between them.[60]

The day the agreement was signed, the new Soviet ambassador to China, Alexander Paniushkin, stated in Nanjing that the pact was a contribution to world peace.[61] The English-language newspaper *Shanghai Evening Post and Mercury* stated optimistically that after the treaty was signed, the Soviet Union would have no worry on its western front and therefore could march eastward freely.[62] However, on August 31, the day that the Molotov-Ribbentrop Pact was signed, the German army invaded Poland, while the Soviet Union annexed the Baltic states and a part of Poland.[63] Some researchers believed that Stalin gave the green light to German troops stationed along the Polish border.[64]

The implications of these developments for China were difficult to assess. On the one hand, the Molotov-Ribbentrop Pact could be seen as isolating Japan, as Germany clearly did not want war with the Soviet Union. At the same time, while the outbreak of war in Europe inevitably would reduce European financial aid for China, the Molotov-Ribbentrop Pact could also be read as reducing the likelihood of war between the Soviet Union and Japan, and even a settlement between the two countries. In discussions with the new Soviet ambassador to China, Paniushkin, Chiang asked for clarification. He asked what the Soviet Union would do if Hitler attacked France, whether he anticipated that Britain and Japan would sign a treaty, or whether the Soviet Union was contemplating a nonaggression pact with Japan.[65]

Sun Ke reported from Moscow that he found the Soviet Union's formal declaration of wanting to stay neutral in a European war unconvincing. He pointed out that the Soviets had in reality helped Germany invade Poland

and that in any case it had used its forces to seize territory in Poland and the Baltic states. But, he stated, the Soviet Union had bolstered its defenses in the west, suggesting that Soviet suspicions of ultimate German intentions remained strong.[66] With respect to the Soviet attitude toward Japan, Sun's belief was that the Soviets continued to regard the Japanese also as a threat. He counseled Chiang that as long as Japan did not attack the Soviet Union, there was no chance that the Soviets would join the war in China. He added that the Soviets feared that the United States and Britain hoped for a confrontation between Japan and the Soviet Union, to safeguard their interests in East Asia. The Soviets would therefore attack Japan only if the United States and Britain took active military steps against Japan. The Soviets Union's policy, according to Sun, was simply to buy time to improve its military forces in preparation for the inevitable day that war would break out.[67]

Sun argued that China should not ask the Soviets again for direct military intervention, but also that they continued to be prepared to provide financial and military aid. After meetings with Soviet leaders, Sun Ke told Chiang Kai-shek, "Soviet aid to China will, it seems, be limited to equipment and technological assistance. It is not possible for us to persuade the Soviet Union to join in our war with Japan."[68] In fact, on June 16, 1939, on behalf of the Chinese and Soviet governments respectively, Sun Ke and Mikoyan signed the Sino-Soviet Trade Treaty, whereby the Soviets provided a credit of US$150 million for Chinese purchases in the Soviet Union.[69]

After Pearl Harbor

The Japanese decision to begin the Southern Offensive in December 1941 radically changed the strategic situation in East Asia. It ended the debate among Japanese military planners about whether to join the Germans in attacking the Soviet Union or to move south and drive the United States and Britain out of East and Southeast Asia. The result was that the Soviet Union no longer had to fear a war on two fronts. It also meant that the United States and the United Kingdom were then fighting Japanese forces, thus removing one argument the Soviets had used to deny Chinese requests for active military assistance.

Chiang Kai-shek hoped to use the opportunity to convince the United States, Britain, and the Soviet Union to opt for an "Asia first" strategy. He argued that the Allies working together would be able to defeat Japan quickly and that they then would be able to concentrate all their forces against Germany. He pleaded for this in diplomatic telegrams, arguing that the involvement of the Soviet Union was essential.[70] However, Hitler had begun Operation Barbarossa against the Soviet Union in June 1941. For the Soviets, Germany became their most important enemy. Having to retreat in the face of the German onslaught, the Soviet Union did not want to disperse its military forces by opening a second front. For Britain, too, Germany was a more important enemy than Japan, while after some procrastination the United States too decided on a Europe first strategy. In a letter to Chiang Kai-shek, Stalin wrote that while he recognized China's contribution in the fight against their common enemies and that the Soviet Union would at some point take up arms against Japan, as Japan was likely to break its nonaggression pact, he also asked Chiang to understand that the Soviet Union could not at this point declare war on Japan.[71] Chiang Kai-shek would not again ask for Soviet military participation.

The Soviets did attack the Japanese Kwantung Army in China's Northeast, then still Manchukuo, precisely three months after the defeat of Germany, as Stalin had agreed with President Roosevelt and Prime Minister Churchill at Yalta and Tehran. The attack also followed the detonation of the first atomic bomb over Hiroshima and preceded by a day the second atomic bomb that destroyed Nagasaki. In less than two weeks, the Soviet army conquered not only China's Northeast but also parts of Inner Mongolia, northern Korea, southern Sakhalin, and the Kuril Islands, thus ensuring for itself a prominent postwar role in Northeast Asia.

The Nationalists paid a high price when the Soviets did finally engage the Japanese. A secret agreement had been concluded by Roosevelt and Churchill with Stalin in 1945 whereby the Soviets gained their approval to occupy the territories outlined above. The agreement also provided for Soviet control of Dalian and Lüshun (Port Arthur), Soviet access to the China Eastern and the South Manchurian Railways in Manchuria, and the maintenance of the status quo in Outer Mongolia. The historical rationale was that the Russians had held similar rights in Manchuria until the Japanese defeated Russia in 1905. Besides the Soviet participation in the war against Japan, Roosevelt's aim at Yalta was to secure Soviet participation in the new world order based on the United Nations.

On August 14, Molotov and Wang Shijie, China's representative, signed the Treaty of Friendship between the Republic of China and the Soviet Union in Moscow. This treaty provided that Nationalist China would recognize the status of Outer Mongolia following a referendum, and that in return the Soviet Union would recognize China's sovereignty over Manchuria, respect its territorial integrity, refrain from interfering in Xinjiang, and provide no aid to the Chinese Communists. If the Nationalists hoped that the Treaty of Friendship would make the best of a bad deal, they would be disappointed. The Soviets stripped Manchuria bare, removing much of its industrial plant while it also sheltered the Communists, who would build up their armies in Manchuria and whose campaign to defeat the Nationalists would begin there.

Nationalist China was one of the victors of the Second World War. One of its generals, Xu Yongchang, was present on the *USS Missouri*, which was moored in Tokyo Bay when Japan submitted its surrender document to the Allies. It was a founding member of the United Nations and, as one of the Big Four of the war, was given a permanent seat on the UN Security Council. But the secret Yalta agreements indicated that by the end of the war, its real status had greatly declined. Undermined by corruption, military exhaustion, a botched resumption of control of areas occupied by Japan, and ravaging inflation, the Nationalists quickly lost their grip. The Chinese Communists were victorious only four years later.

9 *Reshaping China*

AMERICAN STRATEGIC THINKING AND CHINA'S ETHNIC
FRONTIERS DURING WORLD WAR II

XIAOYUAN LIU

From the mid-nineteenth century, as part of the westernization of the culture of East Asian interstate relations, the Chinese conception of territoriality entered a long process of transformation from "imperial" to "national." This process included the extension of territories and their administration. It took place as the Western powers, modernized Japan, socialist Soviet Union, the ruling authorities in China, and ethnopolitical forces along China's peripheries collaborated or vied with one another in defining the "geo-body" of the Chinese state.[1] When the Communist Party took power in China in 1949, the ideologically charged international politics of the time assigned a color code to China: red.

Even kindergarten children know that a coloring book must have shapes for them to color in. Two cartographic images of China have evoked strong emotions from modern Chinese. One is a begonia leaf, the other a rooster. World War II decisively influenced the shape of China as it is today. The eradication of Japan's military empire in the Asia-Pacific region and inter-Allied wartime diplomacy were critical; they have already received careful scholarly scrutiny.[2] Previous studies have devoted much attention to China's "lost territories" and the status of former tributary states of the Chinese Empire (Korea, Manchuria, Outer Mongolia, the Ryukyus, Taiwan, Vietnam); they overlook a gray area—China's ethnic frontiers that blended domestic and foreign concerns. After all, "national" China took shape only after the "dependencies" (*fanshu*) of imperial China went their separate ways. In World War II, American policy makers' strategic thinking about China's peripheries had significance and influence, because of the wartime alliance between the two countries. Washington's wartime deliberations on China's ethnic frontiers also constituted an important background to intensified ethnopolitical struggles in postwar China.

European and Asian Minorities

During World War II, memories of the Great War and uncertainty about postwar stability caused serious concern in the US State Department's foreign policy planning. One issue after 1918 was the minorities problem in Europe. As defined by the State Department, a minority was a "group of people with a national consciousness distinct from that of the majority within a state, usually manifested by a difference of language and culture." In conceding that the minorities problem was "initially an internal problem," the State Department nevertheless believed that the problem could not be solved without the "evolution of a genuine multinational or un-national state in which citizenship is as separate from 'nationality' as it is from religion." What troubled officials were possible international ramifications of the problem in the immediate postwar years. If states were in constant fear that an aggressor state might use the minorities problem as a pretext for war, there would be no international peace and stability.

At the end of World War I, an international effort was made to solve the problem, which led to a "Wilsonian moment" to promote national self-determination in many countries.[3] The beginning of World War II in Europe in 1939 indicated that the solution had failed miserably. Conscious that the United States was in part responsible for the failure, Washington's political strategists wanted to do a better job the second time around. These considerations led the State Department to conclude that after the war an international organization ought to assume a dual responsibility: for maintaining a peaceful international environment to allow European states to implement their policies toward minorities, and for redressing dangerous situations caused by improper policies toward minorities. The State Department believed that the United States must play a leading role in such an organization, watching closely over how European states dealt with their minorities.[4] A policeman's role was prescribed for the United States in postwar European ethnopolitics.

By contrast, American policy makers never considered such an institutional approach for dealing with minorities problems in Asia. Asian politics seemed to have followed only one rule: power. China's minorities problem became an issue in Western governments' contemplation of Asian security after Japan invaded Manchuria in 1931. After the Mukden Incident, American and British diplomats in China agreed that the event had forced the Chinese government to change its attitude toward China's ethnic frontiers from apathy to anxiety. A British diplomat noted:

"The Mongols are always alive to the fact that they were once a great race and are eagerly awaiting the arrival of a new Genghis Khan to restore them to their former glory." The Chinese government therefore had better work out some arrangements with the Mongols to forestall Japanese conspiracies. Neither the United States nor the British government felt that anything could be done about the deteriorating situation along China's northern frontiers; even the Soviet Union, which had vital interests in the area, seemed unable to curb the Japanese other than by severing contacts between Inner and Outer Mongolia.[5] As far as the Western powers were concerned, during the 1930s Japan enjoyed freedom of action on China's northern peripheries. Before the start of the Pacific War in late 1941, many Americans accepted Japanese dominance in Manchuria and Inner Mongolia as the established status quo. Even well-informed individuals in official and academic circles could not see how China would be able to recover Manchuria and Inner Mongolia. They predicted that Manchuria would probably remain under Japan's influence, and Inner Mongolia would become a buffer zone between China, Japan, and the Soviet Union.[6] China would have to accept the Great Wall as its actual border in the north.

Pearl Harbor drastically altered the vision of postwar East Asia. In 1942, when the State Department started to organize its foreign policy planning operations, it drafted some questionnaires about postwar China. Inner and Outer Mongolia, Tibet, Xinjiang, and some other regions were listed in these questionnaires as the territorial problems that a liberated China would have to cope with. State Department officials expected that at the end of the war, difficulties regarding "several Chinese provinces comprising Inner Mongolia" would likely arise among China, Japan, the Soviet Union, *and* the Mongols.[7] Thus, from the outset, the State Department's policy planning projected Inner Mongolia as an international question, not a problem involving only the Chinese and the Mongols.

The State Department's reference to "Mongols" was intentionally ambiguous; the entity referred to obliquely as Outer Mongolia was neither independent nor subject to China's control. One definition of Outer Mongolia, given by the US Office of Strategic Services (OSS), was that it was a "colonial experiment" of the Soviet Union.[8] To officials of the State Department, this problematic territory, along with Xinjiang, Tannu Tuva, and Manchuria, were contested areas between China and the Soviet Union. Before the war ended, the State Department adopted a stand that although the American government must oppose any arrangement detrimental to Chinese sovereignty in Manchuria, it could accept solutions about the other three territories as long as they were reached through peaceful means. Actually, a prevalent view in Washington in the war years was that China could not realistically hope to recover Outer Mongolia.[9]

Even in the case of Manchuria, State Department officials entertained, for a while, an idea radically different from the Chinese government's conception of its sovereignty there. More than a year after the United States entered the war against Japan, a position paper by the Division of Far Eastern Affairs of the State Department proposed partition of Manchuria as a permanent solution to the Manchurian question. The paper argued that Manchuria had been a "cradle of conflict" in the past half century because none of the other races (Russians, Koreans, Japanese, Mongols) had completely accepted China's sovereignty over Manchuria. If the Manchurian borders were redrawn according to "ethnological principles," future troubles could be avoided. Allegedly, China would benefit from such arrangements in not only retaining the settled and most fertile lands and all of the 36 million Han Chinese in Manchuria; it would also regain its rights in the Guandong (Kwantung) Leased Territories and nearly all foreign railroads and mining concessions. What would be the cost to China? In the east, China would have to cede some 110,000 square miles of land to Korea. Another 165,000 square miles and its Mongolian inhabitants in the north and the west would also secede from China.[10]

In the summer of 1943, a similar exercise was conducted by the British Foreign Office's Research Department. The resultant memorandum speculated that the Soviet Union would have two options in expanding its influence in postwar Northeast Asia. Moscow might either encourage the Chinese Communists to set up a soviet republic in Manchuria or use Mongolian nationalism to create a Soviet-Mongolian bloc. The latter option had the advantage of using the nationality principle and therefore appearing less threatening to Anglo-American opinion. The Soviets would encourage Japanese-trained Mongolian armed forces and political groups in Inner Mongolia and Manchuria to join with Outer Mongolia in a strong movement to unify all Mongols in a single state, a Greater Mongolia. The memo noted that despite years of Sinicization, Inner Mongolia had a larger Mongol population than did Outer Mongolia. In northern Chahar and areas of western and northwestern Manchuria the Mongols were actually "ethnically preponderant" and could make territorial claims on "ethnographic grounds." Greater Mongolia could push southward to the Great Wall and eastward to the Yellow Sea, separating Chinese Manchuria from the rest of China. In such a scenario the modern industry and the railway system in Manchuria would help the Mongolian state achieve internal coherence. Because the scenario could drastically change the international landscape of Northeast Asia, the memo raised questions in the Foreign Office as to whether the Soviet Union really entertained such an intention and whether China would in any circumstances allow this to happen.[11]

When American and British officials hypothesized about the postwar conditions in Northeast Asia, they attached different significance to ethnicity. The State Department proposal for Manchurian partition intended, in a can-do spirit, to use the ethnic factor to macro-manage the trouble-some region, but the Foreign Office's somber prediction was that the issue of ethnicity in Inner Mongolia and Manchuria would only work to the Soviet Union's advantage. During the war, however, the Allies' policies were committed to promoting China as a strong and unitary power. Eth-nopolitical scenarios for China, by nature divisive, should not be pursued but should be discouraged.

At one of the State Department's policy planning meetings, this opinion was firmly expressed. "The question of Chinese unification is a key to the whole problem in considering security in the area [East Asia]."[12] To Ameri-can policy makers, the question of China's unity had three aspects. The first was internal political unification, meaning mainly the readjustment of the Guomindang (GMD)–Chinese Communist Party (CCP) relationship. Although American officials could not agree as to whether their govern-ment should commit itself to the GMD government to attain this goal, such a commitment did guide Washington's China policy during and after the war.[13]

The second aspect involved China's recovery of territories lost to Japan. In November and December 1943, at the Cairo Conference, President Franklin D. Roosevelt officially committed the United States to assisting China to recover these territories. In making such a commitment, Ameri-can policy makers also had America's commercial and strategic interests in mind. It was expected that after recovering Taiwan, the Chinese gov-ernment would grant the United States the right to use military bases on the island. Some officials even suggested that a "nationality factor" (the ethnic similarity between the aborigines of eastern Taiwan and the moun-tain tribes of the Philippines) be used as a lever in negotiating with the Chinese.[14]

The third aspect of China's unity was more complicated. It was a gray category involving the vast areas of Mongolia, Xinjiang, and Tibet. These territories were "gray" because any settlement would involve China's domestic and foreign affairs; Chinese sovereignty was incomplete or nomi-nal, and the Chinese government was in dispute not only with local people but also with two of the Allies, Britain and the Soviet Union.

A divergence between Chinese and American understandings of these issues appeared during the first few months of the Pacific War. When contemplating how the Western allies could strengthen China's resistance to Japan through psychological warfare, the US Joint Chiefs of Staff sug-gested that the morale of the Chinese government could be enhanced if the US government supported the restoration of Chinese territory, not just to the status quo before 1937 but to that before 1894.[15] The date 1894 meant China's recovery of the rights and territories lost to Japan after the first Sino-Japanese War (1894–1895). What the Americans had in mind were Taiwan and Manchuria; they seemed not to realize that to Chinese officials, the territory of 1894 meant the entire domain of the Qing Empire, including not only Taiwan and Manchuria but also Mongolia and Tibet, which were alienated from China after the overthrow of the Qing in 1911.

On these outlying territories, the United States government adopted the attitude of an interested bystander. Officials in Washington had no particular preference about their status as long as China, Britain, and the Soviet Union could work out some mutually acceptable understanding. During the war, China's disputes with Britain (over Tibet) and the Soviet Union (over Mongolia) must not hinder the common war effort. In treating these regions as part of China's relationship with Britain and the Soviet Union, the State Department had nothing particular to offer on the Han-Tibetan and Han-Mongolian relationships per se. The Tibetan and Mongolian questions were not considered in the framework of minorities problems. Though they devoted much time and energy to contemplating postwar settlement of the dependencies problem in Asia, officials never defined Tibet and Mongolia as such. In Asia, the State Department applied the dependency conception only to colonial possessions of the Western powers and Japan.[16]

The Roosevelt administration promoted China as one of the Big Four to assist the United States in counterbalancing Britain and the Soviet Union in the postwar years, and it sided with China in China's disputes with the other two powers. Washington's wartime China policy tended to bolster China's anti-imperialist nationalism. Washington appeared more sensitive than London to China's nationalist feelings about foreign influence in China. The obverse of this sensitivity was a calculated indifference toward the GMD regime's dealings with China's ethnic minorities. Washington worked to restore and safeguard China's territorial and administrative integrity, mainly in terms of eastern China.[17]

Only occasionally was American liberalism visibly affronted by the GMD government's official nationalism. The State Department's reaction to Chiang Kai-shek's *China's Destiny* was a case in point. After the book was released in 1943, State Department officials took it as evidence that a "virus of nationalism" existed in China and was "capable of becoming a cancer." The critique focused on the GMD regime's one-party authoritarianism against the CCP and liberal political forces in China and on its manifest ambition to become the leader of Asia. These tendencies convinced State Department officials that American policy must seek to direct Chinese nationalism into "healthy channels."[18] What was overlooked completely in this critique was the impact of Chiang's one-nation creed on China's ethnopolitical landscape, which treated ethnic groups in China as big or small "clan branches" of the Chinese nation (*zhonghua minzu*). A seasoned player in the Great Game for Inner Asia, London was more alert than Washington to developments on China's ethnopolitical front.

Chiang's book was more than propaganda. The GMD government directed local authorities in the borderlands to adopt Chiang's one-nation creed. The British consulate in Tihwa (Urumqi), Xinjiang, got wind of the directive. In February 1944, the British embassy in Chongqing transmitted the information to the Foreign Office with its own comments, a rather positive reading of Chongqing's new policy. The embassy suggested that Chiang's creed "represents a considerable advance, if not a radical departure from the views expressed by Dr. Sun Yat-sen on the subject of border races." Chiang's assertion of the common origin of all the races in China was intended to "establish the racial unity and equality of all the peoples living within the borders of the Chinese Republic." Although Chiang's arguments might be "jejune and unconvincing," "they nevertheless offer an historical justification for the policy now pursued by the Chinese Government of conciliation towards the border races as peoples of equal status with the Chinese." The embassy admitted that the same set of arguments could also be used to justify, "on the ground of family friendship and collaboration, a policy of economic and cultural penetration and political control which otherwise might have invited the stigma of imperialism."[19]

Officials at the Foreign Office did not share the embassy's sentiment. Annoyed by the Chinese government's wartime penchant for acting as a spokesman for Asian colonial peoples, Foreign Office officials believed that the GMD was hypocritical in denouncing European imperialism while "busy asserting imperial claims to dominate their non-Chinese neighbors, such as Mongolia and Tibet."[20] One of the Foreign Office commentaries on the embassy's dispatch ridiculed the ethnological arguments made in Chiang's book as "sheer nonsense" that "merely involve the whole issue of China's relations with these peoples in a cloud of humbug." Although under the new creed Chinese officials might behave better toward the non-Han groups, "on the other hand, the new theory disposes entirely of any possible claims of the Mongols or Tibetans to autonomy or separate national existence because it asserts them to be merely parts of the Chinese nation." To Foreign Office officials, this was as if the Nazis made a claim that all the Slavs were descendants of the German tribes and used it as a "better pretext" for conquering them.[21]

Whereas British officials might favor "any possible claims of the Mongols or Tibetans to autonomy or separate national existence," Washington tended to frown upon separatist tendencies in China's borderlands lest they hinder America's search for a strong and stable Chinese partnership in East Asia. The disagreement between the British embassy and the Foreign Office indicated the complexity of the matter. If taken out of the context of the GMD's assimilative policies toward the non-Han peoples in China,

Chiang's one-nation creed might be interpreted as an effort to promote interethnic equality through minimizing ethnic differences. Such a policy could find sympathizers within the US State Department. In the European context, policy planners of the State Department believed that after the war any valid solution of the minorities problem must work for the elimination of the stigma of "minorities," to place the problem on the "broader foundation of the protection of basic human rights."[22] The human rights idea, however, was not considered for China. Throughout the war, the GMD government and the United States never exchanged views on China's (or any other Asian country's) minorities problem. China's "internal" ethnopolitical problems were not even on the backburner of the wartime Sino-American partnership.

When Owen Lattimore was adviser to Chiang Kai-shek and gave advice to him on China's ethnopolitics in the second half of 1941 and 1942, he was not acting in accordance with official US policy, even though President Roosevelt himself recommended Lattimore to Chiang. Lattimore's advice to Chiang on China's ethnic frontier affairs was personal, neither solicited by Chiang nor encouraged by Washington.[23] More than three decades later, when recalling his service to Chiang in the early 1940s, Lattimore admitted that since he went to Chongqing as Chiang's personal adviser and not as "Roosevelt's man," he "must put loyalty to what I thought were the best interests of Chiang Kai-shek above everything else."[24] This loyalty to Chiang prevented Lattimore from being completely frank in offering his opinions. For instance, although he urged Chiang to suspend China's colonization policy in Inner Mongolia and to curtail the tyrannical behavior of provincial officials toward Mongols, Lattimore opposed an idea immensely popular among Mongols, that Inner Mongolia be organized into a single autonomous territory. His suggestion was intended to "make the Mongols actively patriotic toward China," whereas the autonomy idea contradicted the GMD government's demand for "general increase of political unity" in China. Lattimore stressed that the solution of the Inner Mongolia question must go hand in hand with general democratization in China. Democracy for the Inner Mongols could help the Chinese government attract Outer Mongolia back to China.[25]

After he returned to the United States and became director of the Pacific Bureau of the Office of War Information in late 1942, Lattimore expressed different ideas to his American audience. In a 1943 memorandum on Mongolia, prepared for the Council on Foreign Relations' confidential series "Studies of American Interests in the War and the Peace," Lattimore observed that Mongolia had never belonged to China in history and that the current Chinese government would have no chance to "recover" the Mongolian People's Republic by force. As for political antagonisms in Inner Mongolia, Lattimore's analysis suggested that the situation there was more complex than the "racial antagonism" fostered by Mongol elites, Chinese politicians, and Japanese intruders. Beneath this claim, another level of antagonism existed "at which the common people, both Mongol and Chinese, react in resentment against the princes, priests, generals, and magistrates whose pawns they are, but without knowing exactly what to do about it."[26] This socioeconomic insight was important, but its relevance to American foreign policy was unclear. In the postwar years the Chinese Communists would use these lower-level antagonisms in manipulating Mongolian nationalism.

Lattimore's remarks would not have pleased the GMD leaders. In devoting a substantial portion of his *China's Destiny* to China's interethnic question, Chiang showed that he took the non-Han peoples and their territories seriously. Yet despite Lattimore's confidence in Chiang's open-mindedness, GMD ethnopolitics continued heading in a direction opposite to Lattimore's recommendations. The GMD not only extolled China's traditional assimilation policy but also advocated a one-nation creed that threatened to eradicate non-Han ethnic identities in China.

The Colors of China's Three Corners

In his talks with Chiang Kai-shek, Lattimore pointed out several times that China's century-old struggle against the unequal treaty system had been won; now it was time for China to take care of its "three corners," the northeast, northwest, and southwest. He warned that if the minorities in these areas were oppressed by China, they would "recoil" toward Russian and British influence. Contending that China's traditional assimilation policy had failed, Lattimore especially warned Chiang that the Soviet Union's "outstanding success" with its own minority nationalities could be a lure to China's minorities.[27]

Lattimore was prescient about how the ethnic aspect of great-power politics in Asia would unfold, but his repeated calls for attention to the Inner Asian frontiers came from a lonely voice in China and the United States. In May 1942, while still Chiang's adviser, Lattimore made a trip to the United States. He wrote to Chiang and predicted that once Japan and the Soviet Union were at war with each other, China's interests in Manchuria, Mongolia, and Xinjiang would be significantly affected. Since Washington knew almost nothing about these interests, Lattimore explained, he could help China better if he stayed in Washington, using his expertise to prevent misunderstandings of Inner Asia there.[28] Lattimore's view of the US government's or, more precisely, the State Department's lack of knowledge about China's ethnic frontiers was on the mark. In 1942 he was, however, way ahead of the progress of the war in suggesting that Inner

Asian geopolitics be a priority in Washington's China policy. To American policy makers, Moscow's intentions in northeastern and northwestern China were matters to be dealt with only when the war in the Pacific was won. Two years later, these issues *were* on Roosevelt's mind when he sent Vice President Wallace to China with Lattimore.

The Wallace Mission to China (June 1944) was one of the mysteries that gave Roosevelt the reputation of a sphinx. American journalists and the Chinese government were still trying to find out the purpose of the mission even after Wallace's party arrived in Chongqing.[29] Roosevelt's insistence on Lattimore's inclusion in the mission, which went to China by way of the Soviet Far East and Inner Asia, was based on the latter's expertise in these areas. He wanted Lattimore to help Wallace find a way to prevent Chinese-Soviet friction along their borders in the future. On his first day in Chongqing, Wallace made a vague suggestion to his hosts that self-government be granted to those minority nationalities that had not so far enjoyed it. To sensitive Chinese ears, their guest implied the Mongols and the Muslim groups in Xinjiang.[30] Yet in China, Wallace soon became immersed in more urgent issues, such as the GMD government's difficult military situation and its quarrels with the CCP, the central concerns in his postmission report to President Roosevelt. The report did make the point that after the war China could not realistically hope to resume sovereignty in Outer Mongolia because the region was under strong Soviet influence, which might even attract the Inner Mongols. As for Lattimore's contribution to his mission, Wallace later would claim that Lattimore was involved mainly in handling "publicity matters in China" and offered Wallace "no political advice at any time sufficiently significant to be recalled now."[31]

At a time when Washington was focused on the prospect of great-power politics in postwar East Asia and contemplated the issue from America's strategic position in the Pacific, Lattimore's expertise in Inner Asian ethnopolitics had only marginal usefulness to the US government. Only once, in August 1942, did the State Department seek information from Lattimore about the Chinese government's view on postwar issues. He briefed the State Department on the GMD regime's intentions regarding postwar Japan, the colonial problem of Asia, the CCP, and China's industrialization. He also called State Department officials' attention to China's three corners, though with an overstatement that the "future area of China's industrial and economic development will probably be in a triangle based on Yunnan, Sinkiang [Xinjiang], and Mongolia, rather than along the coast."[32]

The State Department was indeed interested in China's three corners, but what the State Department was really looking for was information that Lattimore could not provide: Moscow's intentions toward China's northern and northwestern frontiers, that is, whether they would turn "red" or stay "gray." So far, the Soviet Union's nonbelligerency in the Asia war had allowed Moscow to conceal its policy objectives even from its wartime allies. Washington's political strategists were mystified about Soviet intentions in Asia in general, and in Northeast Asia in particular. State Department officials went in different directions in hypothesizing about Soviet Asia policy.

In August 1943, officials of the Far Eastern Division sought help from their colleagues in the European Division, who supposedly had reliable information about Moscow's war aims in Europe. The resultant Far Eastern Division memorandum speculated that at the war's end Moscow would follow identical policies in the Far East and Europe, to create "sovietized governments among the peoples of Inner Mongolia, Manchuria, Korea," and other areas in the western Pacific.[33] Yet two months later, when planners considered the issue again, the Soviet factor in the postwar Far East seemed less alarming. So far as the Mongolia question was concerned, they did not expect any serious problems: whereas the Soviets would not abandon their position in Outer Mongolia, the Chinese government would be realistic and be satisfied with maintaining its "nominal sovereignty" there. State Department planners expected even fewer problems in Inner Mongolia. Since the area had been "increasingly assimilated to nearby Chinese provinces," a unified China should be able to control these areas effectively after the war.[34]

Although not expecting the ethnicity element in Sino-Soviet frontier relations to pose a serious challenge to US foreign policy, the State Department was troubled by a different scenario: the Soviets might use the CCP as an instrument to exploit prevalent anti-Western emotion in China and Asia. According to the OSS, Soviet policy seemed to point in this direction. In early 1944, a similar concern led John Paton Davies Jr. (US embassy, Chongqing) to urge Washington to send a military observer group to Yan'an before the Soviets entered the war against Japan and possibly turned North China into a Soviet satellite.[35] Officials of the Far Eastern Division agreed that in the event of the Soviets' entry into the Pacific War, the Western allies would not be able to prevent the Soviet Red Army from occupying many parts of Northeast Asia. By early 1945, the State Department was convinced that the Soviet Union would be plotting in Inner Mongolia, Manchuria, and Xinjiang, but Moscow's behavior would be contingent on its general relationship with China: "The real question in Chinese-Russian relations is not so much territorial as political; that is, the Russian attitude toward the Communist-Kuomintang [Guomindang] problem."[36] The distinction made by American officials between a "territorial" and a "political" character of the issues between China and the Soviet Union was revealing. Although the United States could afford to be a bystander on the shape of the Chinese state, it would not stand by if the Soviet Union tried to change the color of Chinese politics.

Despite the importance that American policy makers attached to the CCP question, hardly any officials in Washington pondered the significance of the CCP's own ethnopolitics for America's China policy. John Service went to Yan'an as part of the US Army's observer group. He collected information of major significance through his interviews with CCP leaders, and in late 1944 he sent a series of reports to the State Department. Service's reports tried to drive home the point that the CCP was not a mere tool of Moscow. In one report, Service observed that in the past several years the CCP leaders had made efforts to "get away from slavish attempts to apply Russian communism to China. . . . In fact, they are imitating nobody. Their emphasis is on being Chinese."[37] Years later, in the McCarthy era, Secretary of State Dean Acheson would dismiss Service from the Foreign Service for his alleged sympathy toward the CCP. Acheson believed that Service's understanding of the CCP would have been less naïve and fallacious had he had any knowledge of the Bolsheviks.[38]

Acheson's evaluation of Service failed to take into account the latter's characterization of the CCP ethnopolitics, which was based on his knowledge of Soviet theory and practice and did not attribute "Chineseness" to CCP policies toward ethnic minorities. In a report drafted in March 1945, Service asserted that despite its claim of identity with Sun Yat-sen's Three People's Principles, the CCP's ethnopolitical approach was actually identical to the Bolsheviks'. As if anticipating Acheson's allegation years later, Service asserted that "the best statement of the Chinese Communist policies can probably be found in direct quotations from Russian sources." More than half of his report consisted of quotations from Stalin's *Marxism and the National and Colonial Question*. Identifying the CCP with Stalinist dogma on the "national question," Service suggested that Yan'an was more progressive than Chongqing in this regard, though he also pointed out that China's unique ethnographic landscape might "delay or impede the workability of these policies in China." At the time, State Department planners tended to believe that Soviet practices regarding ethnic minorities were "in line with the evolution of Russian liberal thought."[39]

Contrary to Acheson's verdict, Service's evaluation of the CCP ethnopolitics proved too influenced by Soviet rhetoric to reveal the essence of the CCP's own practices. Service got his impressions mainly from an interview with Bo Gu. To Service, Bo's views were significant; he was a former chairman of the CCP and a current member of the CCP Politburo. He had been trained in Moscow. Service cited the "pro-Russian" Bo's testament as the most convincing evidence that ideologically the CCP had been naturalized.[40] Probably in the dark about internal frictions in the CCP leadership, Service failed to notice that Bo was no longer in the CCP's policymaking circle around Mao Zedong. Consequently, when Bo cited Stalinist doctrines as the CCP's attitude toward the minorities question, Service assumed that he was listening to an authoritative statement on the CCP policy. Service was one of the earliest Western observers of China who substituted reading Marxist-Leninist-Stalinist treatises for empirical analysis of the CCP's practices. His discounting of the CCP's self-identification with Sun Yat-sen's doctrines was a serious misjudgment, for in the war years the CCP embraced many of the official policy goals of the GMD government, including those on ethnic frontiers.[41]

One of Service's reports touched on the Mongolian question; again, his source was Bo Gu. According to Service, the CCP's view included these points: First, unity between the inner and outer halves of Mongolia was inevitable; Inner Mongols were attracted to living conditions in Outer Mongolia which, though still recognized by Moscow as part of China, practiced Soviet policies. Second, China could keep the two parts of Mongolia in China only if the Chinese government granted national autonomy and the right of secession to the Mongols in a federal system, and implemented democratization and economic improvement in Mongolian society. Third, currently there was no sign of improvement in the GMD policy, and the policy had hardened since the publication of Chiang's *China's Destiny.*[42]

Bo was misleading. In the war years, the CCP did not support minority nationalities' right of secession but promoted unity among all China's nationalities in a common struggle against Japan.[43] In maintaining the CCP's righteous stance about Outer Mongolia for the sake of criticizing the GMD, Bo concealed the difficulties that the CCP ran into with Inner Mongols in the war years. In early 1945, Raymond P. Ludden (second secretary, US embassy) visited the CCP base areas in the Shanxi-Suiyuan-Chahar region. He noticed that CCP cadres there tended to be more outspoken than those in Yan'an in criticizing the GMD government and expressing a desire for CCP expansion. They were proud of their accomplishment in organizing peasant resistance against the Japanese and confident about expanding CCP influence into new areas. They were not optimistic about CCP expansion into Manchuria, Suiyuan, and Chahar. Manchuria was under Japanese control; Suiyuan and Chahar had "serious difficulties" created by the "predominantly Mongolian" population's misgivings about the Chinese.[44]

This contradiction between Chinese Communism and Mongolian nationalism was completely missed by Service. Ironically, devoting much of his energy to discrediting GMD propaganda that the CCP was an instrument of Moscow, Service's characterization of CCP ethnopolitics dovetailed nicely with anti-CCP allegations made by the GMD government. In May 1945, reporting to the State Department from Xi'an, Edward

Rice (second secretary, US embassy) transmitted an allegation from a GMD source that the CCP was agitating among the Inner Mongols for Inner Mongolia's national self-determination through accession to Outer Mongolia. Rice found the allegation credible; the CCP was using the Inner Mongols' "powerful racial urge" to serve its own ends, to control Inner Mongolia, and to have a common border with the Soviet Union to get assistance from Moscow.[45]

Ever since the Long March, CCP leaders had hoped to open a corridor through Mongolia to the Soviet Union. The CCP pursued this goal without making pan-Mongol agitation among the Inner Mongols. For different reasons, the GMD and the CCP were both misleading Americans. Although American influence penetrated deeply into Chinese politics during World War II, American diplomats and policy makers remained clueless about the direction of China's ethnopolitics. When a new round of power struggle began in China after Japan's defeat, the CCP's main concern in Inner Mongolia was not how to get to the Soviet Union but how to keep the Inner Mongols as part of China, to maintain its own nationalist credentials and win a friendly ethnopolitical ally in its fight against the GMD government.[46]

In early 1945, the scenario described by Rice troubled Washington. The prospect of Soviet entry into the Pacific War moved the State Department to contemplate US action along China's northern borders. The State Department was especially troubled by possible negative reactions from the GMD government to Soviet entry into the Asian war through Inner Mongolia. In January, in preparing for Roosevelt's meeting with British and Soviet leaders at Yalta, the State Department drafted a series of position papers on the Far East. The first of these made reference to Inner Mongolia, pointing out that in the event of Soviet participation in the fight against Japan, Inner Mongolia's strategic location would make it a logical route for the Red Army's offensive. The GMD government, fearing that the Soviets would use the opportunity to establish contact with the CCP, had vowed to take preemptive action. Fearing that imminent events in the Far East would lead to political and military "embarrassment and difficulties," the State Department recommended American intervention. Either a uniform command of GMD and CCP forces should be established before Soviet entry, or, failing that, an "over-all American command of Chinese troops." The second course would be "highly advantageous" for it could prevent wartime political difficulties between the Chinese and the Soviets and serve as a "stabilizing influence" in China in the immediate postwar years.[47]

Neither of these arrangements materialized. While the State Department was drafting these policy memos, American mediation between the GMD and the CCP was already under way. As for the proposed US command of all Chinese forces, the Roosevelt administration could not broach the idea to the GMD regime *again;* it had done that already in the Stilwell Affair (1944), which marked the end of Washington's efforts to turn Chiang Kai-shek's army into an effective tool against Japan.[48]

The Roosevelt administration seemed not to understand the ambiguity of Outer Mongolia's international status until after Pearl Harbor. In early 1942, when contemplating a plan for launching air attacks against Japanese forces from Outer Mongolia, Roosevelt learned from the War Department that the plan could not be feasibly implemented because the territory was beyond the GMD government's authority. The Soviet Union would have to agree to open Outer Mongolia to the US Air Force. Obviously, Moscow's neutrality in the Asian war made such a decision unlikely. Later, aware of the stark contradiction between Moscow's determination to keep its Outer Mongolian buffer and the GMD regime's resolution to restore China's "original frontiers" and to extend its authority to "outlying provinces," the State Department and Roosevelt shared the view that Sino-Soviet conflict over Outer Mongolia must be averted. A border clash between Xinjiang and Outer Mongolia in the spring of 1944 indicated that such a conflict might break out any time. At first Roosevelt was so anxious about a crack in the alliance that he wanted to mediate between Moscow and Chongqing. Only cautionary advice from the State Department persuaded him to adopt a more detached position, advising Chiang Kai-shek not to rush into any action that might endanger the Allied war effort.[49]

The Yalta Conference changed America's impartiality in the Sino-Soviet dispute over Outer Mongolia and put a Washington stamp on Moscow's ticket. At the summit, to induce Joseph Stalin to agree on Soviet entry into the fight against Japan, Roosevelt and Churchill accepted Stalin's price tag, which included a status quo clause on Outer Mongolia in a secret agreement. The agreement became a precondition for the Sino-Soviet negotiations in Moscow in the summer of 1945, which resulted in the Chinese government's concession on Outer Mongolia's independence. This history is well-known.[50] At Yalta, Stalin used the ambiguous status quo to cover Outer Mongolia's "red" politics and separation from China. Roosevelt's endorsement of the Stalinist ambiguity had nothing to do with Mongolian ethnicity and everything to do with power politics. Before and after Yalta, Roosevelt consistently told Chinese officials that Stalin did not harbor any ambition for Outer Mongolia. Yet the Yalta agreement endorsed the geopolitical reality on the Mongolian Plateau and reflected Soviet strategic interests. After Yalta, the State Department began to suggest that America's China policy should seek readjustment of China's territorial claims in Outer Mongolia and Tibet. Promotion of "local autonomy" was part of the rationale, but the principal motive was to "accommodate British and Russian interests" in these territories.[51]

Roosevelt helped create the playground for forthcoming Cold Warriors in establishing geopolitical fault lines between Soviet and American influence. These lines were not all satisfactory to his successors. Before the war in Asia ended, officials in Washington, irritated by Moscow's expansion in Central Europe, had already begun to question the wisdom of the Yalta concessions that put Outer Mongolia and Manchuria on the Russian side of the line.[52] A new era of postwar international politics was about to dawn in Asia.

Politics of Color and Shape

The war years were about the shape of the Chinese state. Washington's wartime diplomacy helped China recover some of the lost territories and sustain its claim of sovereignty over much of the Qing territorial domain, but the same diplomacy also shared responsibility for perpetuating Outer Mongolia's independence from China. It is not far-fetched to suggest that the United States had a hand in changing the shape of China from a begonia leaf to a rooster. Ethnicity was a rare commodity in Washington's contemplation of its China policy. On the rare occasions that ethnicity did receive attention, it was treated as an appendage to great-power relations. This pattern in America's China policy did not change in the postwar years even though China entered a period of intensified ethnopolitical contention.

During the war, Stanley K. Hornbeck, chief of the State Department's Far Eastern Division, observed in an internal communication that if the Western allies could establish a partnership for collective security with both Russia and China, then "we would bridge the chasm between Occident and Orient *and* the chasm of 'colors.'"[53] International politics in postwar Asia, however, were characterized neither by such partnership nor such cultural and racial chasms. The endings of World War II in Europe and Asia, at different times, were pivotal events that marked not only the arrival of peace but also of new crises. Postwar international politics was color coded, but the basis for the coding was ideological, not cultural or racial.

In the shadow of the Cold War, policy makers in Washington and Moscow viewed China as one of the countries whose color was yet to be determined. Postwar China was a crowded political stage, in which great powers, Chinese political parties, and non-Han ethnopolitical forces were all players. Backed by their respective international allies, the GMD and the CCP competed in China proper to decide China's color, while the Mongols, Tibetans, Uighurs, and Kazaks intensified their own struggles on China's frontiers to alter China's shape. Washington's Soviet-centered perspective often led to misreadings of the dynamics internal to China.

In the initial postwar years, there were two prevalent themes in the United States' assessment of Moscow's China policy. One was that the Soviets would defer action in China to avoid collision with the United States in Asia but take a range of circuitous actions to expand their influence in China.[54] The second theme was, as they had in Europe, the Soviets would establish a cordon sanitaire along its Asian boundaries, establishing control in Manchuria, Inner Mongolia, and Xinjiang, areas referred by American officials either as potential Soviet "satellites" or part of a Soviet "defensive cordon."[55] The deferral strategy demanded that Moscow use forces native to China as agents of influence; the CCP's competition with the GMD in northern and northeastern China and non-Han groups' drives for autonomy in Manchuria, Inner Mongolia, and Xinjiang were all "fertile soil for Soviet intrigues."[56]

It was not new for American officials to identify the CCP with Moscow. When the Cold War began, however, the CCP's affiliation with the Soviet Union assumed a clear-cut and adverse significance to the United States. George Kennan pointed out that the CCP had maintained a "surprising degree of independence of Moscow" in sporting its own brand of Marxism and its own regime of "nationalist coloration."[57] The opposing opinion held that the CCP was "but a stalking horse for Soviet territorial and political expansion."[58] Colonel Ivan Yeaton, commander of the US Army Observer Group in Yan'an from July 1945 to April 1946, began his final report with a bald statement: "Communism is international!" In his view, the CCP and Moscow "are one and the same," and "the Soviet Union is guiding the destinies of one of its strongest satellites, the Chinese Communist Party, as it has in the past and will in the future."[59]

As long as Washington considered China in terms of international bloc politics, the debate about whether the CCP was a "satellite" or an "independent" ally of Moscow was academic. In an interbloc contest with the Soviet Union, Washington needed only to ascertain which side the CCP took. In early 1947, after General George Marshall's mediation effort failed, the US embassy in China concluded that the CCP's refusal to compromise with the GMD was motivated by "partisan interests" at the expense of China's "national interests," and that the GMD/CCP struggle was an "extension of the Soviet-American relations."[60]

This incorporation of China into the Cold War reflected the presentist perception and superpower mentality of American officials. By identifying the United States with the current GMD government, American officials saw all opposition forces in China, whether the CCP fighting to change the color of China or the frontier autonomy movements struggling to alter the shape of China, as ones "bearing all the hallmarks of Soviet inspiration."[61]

Lagging behind the Americans and still thinking in the old modes of China's treaty century and the Great Game, British officials pointed to lingering traces of the past in postwar China and found it hard to part with an old view that "all Chinese were Chinese." On the CCP-Moscow relationship, diplomats in China asked their colleagues in London to consider the "vital and vexed question of the extent to which the Chinese Communist leopard can divest himself of or avoid developing soviet spots." They cautioned that it would be "fool-hardy to ignore the historical fact of China's genius for implanting or super-imposing the native culture and way of life upon the foreign invader," and that the "inertia" of China "may emasculate even a force as virile as Communism."[62]

"Chineseness" was certainly an element in postwar China's ethnic frontiers. British officials did not believe that the Mongols were capable of political activism without Soviet agitation; a typical Mongol did not "know or care for 'isms'" and wanted "to be left alone with his wives, camels and herds, in a fertile oasis within easy hearing of the tinkling of lamasery bells."[63] British diplomats recognized that Inner Mongolia, along with Manchuria, might be the first battleground in a multilateral power struggle, but they predicted little difference between the GMD and the CCP approaches to the Inner Mongols: "[The] trouble is that the old Han idea that we [the non-Chinese] are all barbarians is dying hard and the men sent [by the CCP] to administer Mongolia will certainly have that idea about their tribesmen."[64]

Being allied with China for years and facing a serious challenge from the Soviet Union, American policy makers seemed ready to turn the page of history. Not so fast, the British told themselves. The rapid growth of American influence in China during World War II prompted Washington to see convergence between its "colored" perception of postwar world politics and the "central" status of the GMD government versus the CCP and the ethnic minorities on the frontiers. After 1949, the CCP's ascendance to power forced Washington off the stage in China, but it maintained the "central" status that the GMD government took with it to Taiwan. Along China's Pacific shores, America's "color" politics, that is, its anti-Communist policy, maintained a theoretical consistency with its commitment to the physical form of China set in World War II. By contrast, ever since the British replaced the Inner Asians as China's most dangerous barbarian intruders in the nineteenth century, the Huntingtonian theme (if anachronism is permissible) was embedded in the British version of China affairs. In the early years of the Cold War, British diplomats' obsession with "Chineseness" seemed archaic and of little policy relevance. The British view, however, contained elements of culture, ethnicity, and historical continuities. At least to historians, it may serve as a useful counterpoint to the typical, color-coded perceptions of world affairs during the Cold War.

10 Northeast China in Chongqing Politics

THE INFLUENCE OF "RECOVER THE NORTHEAST" ON DOMESTIC AND INTERNATIONAL POLITICS

NISHIMURA SHIGEO

During the first half of the twentieth century, China's political land-scape changed dramatically. Within this process of change, the Northeast Factor, that is, the ultimate fate of China's northeastern provinces, was tightly connected to both Sino-Japanese relations and to global political developments. In this essay, I suggest that while the Northeast Factor was concerned with one particular location, it was also deeply intertwined with Chinese regional politics, central government politics, East Asian regional politics, and global politics. The Guomindang (GMD) government invested so much of its political capital in the recovery of the Northeast that the issue could never be abandoned, nor could others be allowed to question whether the Northeast was an inalienable part of China.

In order to understand the position that the Northeast Factor occupied in central Chinese politics and in global politics, we must begin our search in 1941–1942 and continue it to the December 1, 1943, release of the Cairo Declaration. This document gave full Allied support for the Chinese war aim of recovering sovereignty over its northeastern provinces, which had been occupied by Japan (under the guise of the puppet state of Manchukuo) since 1931. But although the Cairo Declaration marked the full internationalization of the Northeast Factor, the path to this point was marked by conflict and disagreement. Thus, it is necessary to look at the contradictory phenomena of the time to analyze the creation of this new path. This article will trace the existence of the Northeast Factor in central and global politics, as well as analyze its political function from the standpoint of regional politics. I draw mainly on articles published in the Chongqing journal *Fangong banyuekan* (Counterattack bimonthly) as a source to analyze the role of the political discourse of "recover the

Northeast" in China's wartime capital during the years before the 1943 Cairo Declaration.

The desire of the Republic of China to recover sovereignty over the Northeast was clearly recorded in May 1936, when the text of the Republic's draft constitution listed the four provinces of the Northeast as Chinese territory. Other state actions after the advent of full-scale war between Japan and China in the wake of the July 1937 Marco Polo Bridge Incident provide further evidence of this desire. In May 1940, the Chinese government reorganized the local governments of the four northeastern provinces and appointed new provincial governors. In March 1942, the GMD held a meeting of high-level party cadres from the four northeastern provinces, and, in May 1942, it merged various popular organizations devoted to recovering the Northeast into one another.

During this series of political developments, particularly the reorganization and recombination of the various popular groups, there were many conflicts at the upper levels of the GMD leadership. Historian Chen Liwen has already revealed the origins of these conflicts.[1] However, I believe that a further look at the issue is needed, especially with regard to the role of popular groups. For example, what was the momentum behind the political discourse of "recover the Northeast" in *Fangong banyuekan* (Counterattack bimonthly); the journal was published between February 1938 and September 1945 by the General Association of Northeasterners for Resisting Japan (*Dongbei kang-Ri jiuwang zonghui*), an association under the influence of the Chinese Communist Party (CCP). At the same time, how did the notion of recovering the Northeast come to be accepted by people in general? In the political climate of Chongqing, how did this discourse become a political topic that attracted attention and slowly unified the opinions of citizens? As of yet, little progress has been made on such issues.

The popularization of this discourse developed against the backdrop of many domestic and foreign crises and conflicts. From a midlevel perspective focused on Chinese politics, the process by which the Northeast Factor slowly reached a breakthrough can be divided into three phases. The first began with Japan's Twenty-One Demands in 1915, which insisted on a dramatic increase in Japanese rights in the Northeast. The second began with the September 18, 1931, Mukden Incident, which resulted in the Japanese occupation of the Northeast. In the aftermath of this, the Northeast became a problem directly connected to China's own sovereignty as well as an increasingly complex regional problem. The third phase began with Japan's pre–Marco Polo Bridge Incident "plan to separate the Northeast" and the 1936 Xi'an Incident, in which military officers from the Northeast kidnapped President Chiang Kai-shek in order to force him to ally with the CCP to oppose the Japanese occupation of the Northeast. At this point, issues of nationalism and the power of the central government came into play. The history of the Northeast during this time moved along a tortuous path.

This article discusses a brief historical period around 1942; from the perspective of this period, we can see aspects of how the Northeast Factor manifested themselves in earlier phases. At this time, the international community attached little importance to the Northeast Factor in Chinese politics, instead seeing it as "a pawn for achieving certain ends." For example, at the December 1942 meeting of the Institute of Pacific Relations (IPR) in Canada, some delegates suggested that the Chinese Northeast should be ceded to "a certain Allied power [i.e., the Soviet Union]" after the end of the war. In the wake of this meeting, the Chinese media came to understand that China's claim to the Northeast was in danger of being undermined.[2]

Hu Shi, China's ambassador to the United States, reported the discussions at the IPR meeting to Chiang Kai-shek. In response, Chiang wrote on January 29, 1943, that "after the war we will recover Taiwan, the Northeast, and Outer Mongolia; any other nonsense from overseas doesn't need to be taken seriously." Likewise, Wang Zhouran, a native of the Northeast living in Chongqing who advocated for northeastern interests during the war, penned an article entitled "The True Crisis in the Northeast Is Here" that quoted Chiang's 1941 "Declaration on the Tenth Anniversary of the September 18 Incident" and argued that "the aim of this war is to save our compatriots in the Northeast and to recover the territory of the Northeast."[3] From this, we can see that the Northeast Factor had already become an issue of nationalism and that it had taken on an important function in politics. With the views of Chiang and Wang as a starting point, this article seeks to clarify the political discourse regarding the Northeast Factor from 1941 to 1943 and to investigate the international and domestic political background of the November 1943 Cairo Declaration.

The Soviet Union–Japan Neutrality Pact and Its Political Impact

The Soviet Union–Japanese Neutrality Pact and Joint Declaration, signed on April 13, 1941, had a profound impact on the government of China and on Chinese concepts of the Northeast Factor. This agreement, signed in Moscow by Japanese foreign minister Matsuoka Yosuke, Japanese ambassador to the Soviet Union Tatekawa Yoshitsugu, and Soviet commissar of foreign affairs Vyacheslav Michaelovich Molotov, announced that henceforth "both Contracting Parties undertake to maintain peaceful and friendly relations between them and mutually respect the territorial integrity and inviolability of the other Contracting Party." The joint declaration issued alongside the pact stated even more clearly that "Japan pledges to respect the territorial integrity and inviolability of the Mongolian People's Republic" and, in exchange, "the U.S.S.R. pledges to respect the territorial integrity and inviolability of Manchukuo [Manzhouguo]."[4]

Once word of this agreement reached Chiang Kai-shek, he commented that "the Soviet Union–Japanese pact includes a clause that recognizes the territorial integrity of Outer Mongolia and the puppet regime in Manchukuo; this is yet another example of the Soviets harming others in order to benefit themselves. It has not only harmed us but has also caused great damage to their international credibility."[5] China refused to recognize the independent existence of either Outer Mongolia or Manchukuo. This agreement between Japan and the Soviet Union directly impinged upon Chinese sovereignty. On April 14, Chinese foreign minister Wang Chonghui issued a statement saying that "the Northeast and Outer Mongolia are . . . Chinese territory, plain and simple. . . . We cannot recognize this agreement . . . and it is absolutely inapplicable to China."[6]

On April 15, US president Franklin Roosevelt, in a White House meeting with Chinese ambassador Hu Shi and Bank of China president T. V. Soong, announced that, despite this new development, "nothing had happened recently to change the [US] policy of aiding nations against which aggression had been committed."[7] Consequently, we can infer that US-China relations became closer in the wake of the Soviet Union–Japan pact, and that, when the final pre–Pearl Harbor US-Japan negotiations began in earnest, the Soviet Union–Japan pact played a significant role in the multilateral relations between Japan, the United States, the Soviet Union, and China.

On April 24, Chiang Kai-shek sent a memorandum to senior government and military leaders that analyzed the contents of the Soviet Union–Japan pact. First, Chiang noted, "The Soviet Union's plans against Japan were successful. This caused real harm to our enemy and increases the factors that will lead to their defeat because it has shaken the foundations of the German-Italian-Japanese Axis . . . because it increases their suspicions of Japan." This was a medium- to long-term prediction that Japan would fall into isolation. Second, "The unified defenses of the United States–United Kingdom–Australia–Netherlands grow stronger by the day. . . . The Japanese army has nine divisions stationed in the Northeast. . . . We estimate that at most they can transfer six for use in China." Third, "From the perspective of our foreign policy and our resistance to the enemy, this pact is extremely regrettable, because it [the Soviet Union–Japan pact] was unanticipated." With regard to this, Chiang Kai-shek vowed that "after defeating our enemy, we will reclaim our lost territory and restore our sovereignty" and swore that since "our sovereign territory absolutely cannot be abandoned," this new situation "does not jeopardize our overall war situation." Fourth, he pointed to the possibility that the pact could have direct and immediate military impact if, for example, Japanese divisions currently in the Northeast were redeployed to China proper. Even this, Chiang claimed, would "definitely not be sufficient to bring the war to a conclusion [in Japan's favor]." Fifth, he assured his readers that "the moment of our ultimate victory is approaching rapidly."[8] Obviously, the Soviet Union–Japan pact had a large impact on Chinese politics—yet after the pact was made, China's vision of the world situation indicated an understanding of Soviet strategy. Fixing its attention on the medium- to long-term, the Chinese government acknowledged that "our country's war aims presuppose that it is only within the development of the general global situation that our country can achieve final victory."

On June 22, 1941, Nazi Germany declared war on the Soviet Union, and the world situation changed yet again. During this turbulent period, a political mobilization meeting for the tenth anniversary of the Mukden Incident was held in Chongqing. At this time, "recover the Northeast" reemerged as a discourse and was redefined as a political topic. Chiang Kai-shek's "Message to the Chinese People," issued for the anniversary, repeatedly stressed the Northeast's signal importance to the issue of Chinese sovereignty. Chiang vowed to his country that "my determination to recover the Northeast is known to everyone at home and abroad (or perhaps here I should say the Soviets)."[9]

Chiang's public message redefined the Mukden Incident in two ways. The first was a rearticulation of the principle that the "recovery of the Northeast" was a Chinese war aim. This was expressed in Chiang's statement that "until we ensure that our compatriots in the Northeast have true freedom and fully recover the lost territories of the Northeast, our sacred War of Resistance will not cease." Second, he framed the "recovery of the Northeast" as a long-term goal that would be accomplished only after a long process involving changes in the global situation. Chiang had long seen the Northeast as the arena in which China's republican revolution would be completed. As he explained, "when I went to the Northeast in 1914 to agitate for the revolution, I had a chance to investigate conditions there and wrote in a report to Sun Yat-sen that "the three northeastern provinces are not the place of origin of the national revolution but instead are the revolution's ultimate destination. Because the fate of the Northeast is tied to the international situation in the Far East, it cannot be solved during the opening phases of the revolution but can only be fundamentally solved at the moment when the objectives of the national revolution are accomplished." The two statements put forth by Chiang can be summed up as "we must recover our lost lands in the Northeast and rescue our northeastern compatriots in order to wipe clean the humiliation and enmity of the era since the Mukden Incident."[10]

In a diary entry dated September 17, 1941, senior GMD official Wang Shijie wrote about the connection between the Northeast Factor and Chiang's political judgments: "Tomorrow is the tenth anniversary of the September 18th incident. Chiang has been promoting an expansion of propaganda efforts to explain in detail that our war aim is the absolute integrity of our territorial sovereignty." One or two years before, at a secret meeting of the People's Political Council, Chiang had offered a negative appraisal of national strategy and hinted that the purpose of the war was merely to restore the status quo ante to the Marco Polo Bridge Incident. Northeasterners could not help but be suspicious and fearful about this. "At the time, I strongly expressed the opinion that this idea could not be announced publicly. As a result, there is no open record of Chiang's talk on that day. In his proclamation on the following day, Chiang stated that until our territory was returned, the war would not end."[11]

From this we can conclude that Chiang had not abandoned his political judgment of 1939–1940 that restoration of the pre–Marco Polo Bridge situation would be an acceptable basis for a peace accord with Japan. Wang Shijie, at least, came to this conclusion. At the same time, we can deduce that the Northeast Factor had become the grounds for a sharp political confrontation between Chiang and political leaders from the Northeast. Whatever his previous judgments had been, however, in September 1941 Chiang publicly articulated a demand for restoration of China's pre–Mukden Incident boundaries.[12] Chiang Kai-shek's expressed predictions for the solution of the northeastern issues were founded on the discourse of "recovering the Northeast" and an appreciation of the importance of international conditions. Such a view highlighted the need to take a long-term view of the situation. This was particularly the case for the international conditions under which a favorable settlement might be achieved for China. The announcement of the Soviet Union–Japan pact helped propel the Northeast Factor to international prominence.

Beyond Chiang's own rhetoric, associations of northeastern compatriots in Chongqing announced that "now, as victory over Japan draws near, the recovery of the lost territories can be expected." At the same time, they emphasized that only "a return of all territories held before the Mukden Incident" could be seen as "ultimate victory."[13] The GMD-organized Northeastern Issues Research Institute, headed by Qi Shiying, produced a special issue of its journal, *Northeastern Monthly*, that commemorated the Mukden Incident's tenth anniversary. The issue was graced with a calligraphic inscription from Chiang that read: "Vow to reclaim our national territory! (*Shi Fu Jin'ou*)." It also ran an article by Chen Lifu, a powerful official in the central government, entitled "For There to Be a Southwest, There Must Be a Northeast." In this article, Chen proposed "using the strength of the Southwest to recover the Northeast," providing yet another indication that the Northeast Factor in the politics of the Nationalist government in Chongqing had gradually grown in importance.[14]

In conclusion, the above evidence allows us to re-envision the Northeast Factor during the turbulent year of 1941 as not purely an issue of local politics but an issue of increasing significance for the central government in Chongqing. The turning point for the issue was the proclamation of the Soviet Union–Japan pact and Chiang's emphasis on the Northeast Factor in his letter to Chinese citizens on the tenth anniversary of the Mukden Incident. On November 26, the Consultative Council in Chongqing affirmed the importance of the Northeast Factor on the national political stage. On the same day, Chiang telegraphed his ambassador to the United States, Hu Shi, ordering him to "inform the US government that it should not sacrifice China in order to reach an accommodation with Japan." Coincidentally, on the very same day, US secretary of state Cordell Hull demanded that the Japanese representative, Kichisaburō Nomura, begin negotiations with the United States. The Japanese considered this the beginning of the end of diplomacy, and, the following day, began the final move toward war with the United States, the United Kingdom, and the Netherlands. Hull had requested the removal of all Japanese land, naval, and air forces from China and French Indochina, as well as Japanese recognition of the Chongqing government. Hull, too, considered the "Empire of Manchukuo" a part of Chinese territory that must be evacuated by Japanese forces. From 1941 onward, the Northeast Factor had risen in importance on the international stage, too.

After the December 7, 1941, attack on Pearl Harbor and the outbreak of war in the Pacific, what would happen to the Northeast Factor?

The Road to the Cairo Declaration:
The International Situation and "Recover the Northeast"

What was the place of the Northeast Factor in the Pacific War from the perspective of the Allied powers? More specifically, how did the United States view the Northeast Factor? Moreover, what were the particular characteristics of the actions taken by Chiang Kai-shek?

THE CHIANG-CURRIE TALKS

During the first half of 1942, Sino-US relations were bedeviled by the reduction of US military aid and aircraft for the China Theater, while the conflicts between Chiang Kai-shek and his American chief of staff, Joseph Stillwell, intensified daily. To mend this growing rift, Chiang contacted President Franklin Roosevelt through the Chinese foreign minister, Song

Ziwen. In response, Roosevelt sent his personal envoy, Lauchlin Currie, to Chongqing for talks. This resulted in a temporary relaxation of the tensions between Chiang and Stillwell.[15]

In July and August 1942, Chiang met with Currie fourteen different times. At a meeting on August 3, Currie raised the subject of postwar China. According to Chinese notes taken at the meeting, Currie said that "some people in Washington think that, after the war, the Chinese Northeast should become a buffer state between Japan and the Soviet Union; there is already the impression in Washington that the Northeast will not be a part of China, even though [China specialist] Owen Lattimore has vigorously explained to various US government agencies that the Northeast is an inalienable part of China." Chiang retorted that "the Northeast is part of Chinese sovereign territory, and there is absolutely no room for discussion on this point—this is the fundamental point of our war with Japan. If this war were not a war aimed at the recovery of the Northeast, it probably could have been ended a long time ago." At the same time, he emphasized to Currie that this suggestion for a future buffer state is "truly unanticipated and disturbing news" and that "if this information were to spread to the Chinese people, the war effort could be affected or stopped." Over a year earlier, in February 1941, during talks in Chongqing between Chiang and Currie, Chiang had stated that "the recovery of the Northeast is a necessity, and this is a fundamental Chinese war aim," so Currie specifically explained that this was merely a case of "American misunderstanding."[16]

From Chiang's perspective, any such "extremely dangerous and mistaken ideas" required correction, so he repeated his declaration that China's fundamental war aim was to "exert all efforts to recover the four provinces of the Northeast." Chiang also pointed out that the condition in Japan's recent peace proposal that allowed Japan to retain the Northeast was absolutely unacceptable, as were any proposals for "joint Sino-Japanese management of the Northeast." "I absolutely reject these," he said, "because the Northeast is an inseparable part of China—this has long been my policy and there is no room for it to change." Moreover, he asked Currie to "convey these thoughts to President Roosevelt so that he can understand that the Northeast is a part of China. If this problem cannot be solved, then any beautiful rhetoric about equality and freedom is meaningless." Chiang had to acknowledge at this time that the Northeast Factor, though increasingly important in the Chinese Republic, had not yet become significant in the world at large. As a consequence, Chiang stressed to Currie that the English-language terms "Manchuria" and "Manchukuo" were absolutely not the "commonly accepted terms" and that they should be replaced with the phrase "Chinese Northeast" in order to increase popular awareness. Currie replied that even the president himself would "require some education."

Following the Chiang-Currie talks, the Office of Strategic Services (OSS), America's wartime intelligence agency, made a special announcement on September 18, 1942. Citing Henry Stimson's January 7, 1932, doctrine of nonrecognition of Manchukuo, the agency noted that "actual occupation of territory cannot create the right to possess that territory," thus reiterating that the United States "recognized the three northeastern provinces as Chinese territory." Chiang Kai-shek noted that "this is one of the issues I raised with Currie."[17]

THE NORTHEASTERN RESISTANCE ASSOCIATION

A GMD meeting of high-level cadres from the Northeast was held in March 1942. That May, four popular associations were combined to form the Northeastern Resistance Association (*Dongbei si sheng kangdi xiehui*) as part of domestic political preparations for the eventual recovery of the Northeast. On September 18 that year, on the eleventh anniversary of the Mukden Incident, the association issued a declaration that emphasized that "the territory of the Northeast is a part of our nation's land, and the people of the Northeast are of our race." At the same time, the declaration emphasized the international aspects of the situation, stating "the Northeast issue was not only the harbinger of the current global crisis but even more so is the key to world stability. The recovery of the Northeast will both increase human happiness and guarantee long-term global peace."[18]

The journal *Fangong banyuekan* (Counterattack bimonthly), published by the General Association of Northeastern Salvation, ran a special issue to commemorate the anniversary, running articles by Gao Chongmin, Wang Depu, Zhang Shenfu, Chen Xianzhou, Wang Huayi, Wang Zhuoran, and Chen Jiying. Wang Depu's article, entitled "Transforming the Meaning of Commemorating the Mukden Incident," argued that the September 18 anniversary was not simply a chance to memorialize "a day of tragedy and humiliation," but should also be seen as a day that would set China on a path to "eliminate the Japanese pirates" and, ultimately, "the revitalization of China and the restoration of world peace." Wang's vision slowly gained popular support, and at the same time, introduced the political topic of "constructing a new Northeast."[19]

Against this background, a series of important speeches were made at the Northeastern Resistance Association's meeting to commemorate the anniversary. Wu Tiecheng, a high-ranking GMD official, spoke on September 15 about "the connections between the Northeast, China, and the world," while on September 17 Sun Ke, the head of the Legislative Yuan, gave a speech entitled "The Northeast after the War." These speeches represented the increased public recognition of the Northeast Factor by the central authorities in Chongqing.[20] During his speech, Wu Tiecheng drew an analogy between the Chinese Northeast and the territories of Alsace-Lorraine, which were returned to France after the First World War. At the same time, he noted that at the time of the Mukden Incident, most global observers had little understanding of the true situation in East Asia. The Northeast, according to Wu, was not only of domestic importance in China but also intimately connected to the international situation.

Sun's comments focused on the "construction of a new Northeast" after the end of the war. This was part of a new political discourse. He touched upon a wide range of points that encompassed the future political, economic, and social organization of a Northeast reincorporated into the Republic of China. Sun contextualized his specific policy proposals within four general principles for the new Northeast: first, "the enactment of land reform policies in keeping with the principle of the people's livelihood;" second, "the implementation of collectivized agricultural cooperatives;" third, "the allocation of direct government investment in industrial revitalization in order to strengthen the industrialization of the Northeast;" and fourth, "the use of government aid to the poor in other parts of China to encourage immigration to the Northeast." He emphasized that these four principles rested on the premise of "recovering the Northeast and revitalizing China." Similarly, he reaffirmed Chiang Kai-shek's designation of the recovery of all pre–Mukden Incident territory as a war aim, thus further confirming that this policy had wide acceptance in Chongqing.

On what basis could political discussions of a "postwar Northeast" proceed? How was a "postwar Northeast" envisioned? Wang Zhuoran, once an adviser to Zhang Xueliang, asserted that, given the global situation in November 1942, "we can say that it is 99 percent certain that the Allied powers will be victorious." With this as a premise, though, he went on to ask a new question: "How will those of us northeasterners who have been exiled for the last eleven years return to our homeland, to the government of the Northeast, and to policymaking?" To deal with these issues, he suggested strengthening the government agencies responsible for the Northeast that had been established in Chongqing in May 1940. Wang Zhuoran further backed a proposal that had been made by Ma Manning, a delegate in the Consultative Council from Heilongjiang Province, that the government offices for the Northeast should be moved to Luoyang, where they would be closer to the territories they were intended to govern. According to Wang, "moving the seat of the northeastern provincial governments to the front line [i.e., Luoyang]," would "strengthen its functional ability," "allow it to concentrate and coordinate its power," and "bring it into accord with public opinion and spur unity."[21] Statements such as Wang's were emblematic of attempts at the time to make concrete policies and organizations for the Northeast.

The Quebec Meeting of the Institute
of Pacific Relations

The Institute of Pacific Relations held its eighth international meeting in Mont Tremblant, Quebec, from December 4 to 14, 1942. At this meeting, a statement was made to the effect that "a representative from an Allied power proposed that in order to ensure peace in the postwar world, the Northeast should be ceded to a certain Allied power."[22] Obviously, such a proposal was connected to earlier suggestions that the Northeast become a buffer state between Japan and the Soviet Union. Northeasterners in Chongqing, after hearing news of this proposal, were indignant, and the Northeastern Resistance Association held a discussion in December at the Sino-Soviet Cultural Cafeteria. The attendees all agreed that "inside such an insidious suggestion lie the seeds of future crises in the Northeast, and thus such talk needs to be rooted out entirely." Chiang Kai-shek himself noted that "recently I have again reiterated to the world that the Northeast and Taiwan must be returned to China and that Korea must be made independent. . . . I think that probably 100 percent of the Chinese people agree." Yet continued questions abroad indicated that international opinion was not as firm as Chiang's. As a result, Wang Zhuoran and other "exiled northeasterners" were sensitive to international opinion, yet Wang's judgment about "where the true crisis in the Northeast is located," was premised on the notion that China should not allow itself to be controlled by international forces.[23]

The January 6, 1943, edition of the newspaper *Dagongbao* ran an editorial entitled "Reading the US White Paper and Arguing That the Northeastern Provinces Are an Inalienable Part of China," which noted the political notion of "a postwar Northeast separate from China" had emerged among some people in the Allied powers. It argued that such an idea was based on three flawed premises: First, the contention that in order to maintain "balance in the Far East" some sort of international management of the Northeast would be necessary. If this were to happen, it would negate China's reason for fighting to restore "lost territories" and would violate the territorial integrity of China. Second, the suggestion that "the Northeast could be given to the Soviet Union, and in exchange China could be allowed to annex Vietnam" was condemned as problematic for the same reason. And, finally, the proposal to "return postwar sovereignty of the Northeast to China, but assign economic rights to Japan" was also condemned because the restoration of sovereignty needed to be unconditional, for fear that if economic rights were assigned to Japan, then "the Kwantung Army would soon run wild again."

The *Dagongbao* editorial emphasized that if this sort of idea was being entertained by some among the Allied powers, then it indicated that there were still significant misunderstandings concerning the Northeast. Thus, China needed to make clear that "if the Northeast is not recovered, China's war aims will not be accomplished" and that "the roots of this global war lie in the Chinese Northeast, and therefore the issue of the Chinese Northeast must receive a just and rational solution." The following day, the editorial in the *Dagongbao*, entitled "China Must Recover Taiwan—Taiwan Is Our Oldest Occupied Territory," drew a link between the status of Taiwan and that of the Northeast.

Such editorializing clarified the major political issues involved in enumerating Chinese war aims and highlighted the three major options for those aims: a restoration of Chinese territory to its limits before the first Sino-Japanese War of 1894–1895, a restoration of Chinese territory to its limits before the 1931 Mukden Incident, or a restoration to the status quo before the July 1937 Marco Polo Bridge Incident and the consequent outbreak of general war.

This series of incidents—from Currie's mention of a postwar Manchurian buffer state in his August 1942 discussions with Chiang Kai-shek to reports of the British delegates to the Mount Tremblant IPR conference in December 1942 proposing that Manchuria "either be ceded to the Soviets or to turned over to joint international management"—indicated that Allied visions of the "future of Manchuria" were still unsettled. OSS officer and Harvard historian John K. Fairbank, in a December 30, 1942, report to Lauchlin Currie, characterized the events at the IPR meeting as "a bombshell."[24]

Chinese newspapers published reports of the IPR meeting in April 1943.[25] On April 7, the Chinese delegation to the meeting included Shi Zhaoji (as lead representative) as well as Xia Guanlin, Zhou Gengsheng, Fang Xianting, Li Gan, and Xu Shuxi (who was appointed by the Chongqing government). Approximately 150 people attended the meeting; in addition to the Chinese delegates, attendees came from the United States, the United Kingdom, the Soviet Union, Canada, Australia, New Zealand, India, and the Philippines, among other countries. Unlike previous meetings of the IPR, this one featured a number of government representatives, although they supposedly attended in a purely unofficial capacity. In fact, however, many had strong connections to the center of decision making in their respective governments, such as US delegates Stanley K. Hornbeck and Maxwell M. Hamilton. According to the final report submitted by Chinese delegate Xu Shuxi (director of the Chinese Foreign Ministry's Department of West Asian Affairs), the conference voiced its support for the abolition of the unequal treaties between China and the United States and the United Kingdom that was scheduled to happen in January 1943, but it was unable to come to a decision about the future status of foreign concessions in Hong Kong, Macao, Kowloon, and Guangzhouwan (present-day Zhanjiang) or of the Yunnan-Vietnam railway. The conference favored the establishment of postwar structures to maintain the peace. The majority of delegates approved of disarming Japan after the war and prohibiting "warlords" from reentering Japanese politics, returning Taiwan and the Northeast to China, establishing an independent Korea, punishing war criminals, and assessing reparations. Differences between the Chinese and UK delegations about the postwar status of Taiwan and the Northeast had already been reported in the January 6, 1943, issue of the *Dagongbao*, but these differences were not yet widely known. On April 8, the paper reported that the conference report, *War and Peace in the Pacific*, had been published and that it included calls for Japanese disarmament and the return of the Northeast and Taiwan to China.

As the above indicates, the Chinese Northeast was the subject of some debate at the meeting; the goal of "recovering the Northeast" as a Chinese war aim was accepted by the United States and other international groups in 1942. Chiang Kai-shek's standpoint was, as he wrote on January 29, 1943, that "at this time, China is looking only for actual recompense for its injuries, meaning the recovery of Taiwan, the Northeast, and Outer Mongolia; any other suggestions aren't worth the paper they are written on." Song Meiling, during her visit to the United States, reiterated the same line in February 28, 1943, discussions with President Roosevelt.[26]

A month later, Chinese foreign minister Song Ziwen met with US assistant secretary of state Sumner Welles in Washington, DC, to inquire about US and UK attitudes toward "the future position of Manchuria." Welles confirmed that "both the US and the UK support the restoration of Chinese sovereignty over Manchuria" and that the future disposition of Soviet economic rights in Manchuria was a topic for bilateral Sino-Soviet negotiations. Welles averred, too, that the United States supported the return of Taiwan to Chinese rule. An international consensus on the place of the Northeast in China was rapidly solidifying.

The New US-China and UK-China Treaties and the Northeast

On January 11, 1943, the Republic of China signed new treaties with both the United States and the United Kingdom that discarded the "unequal treaties" that had been concluded in the previous century. Chiang Kai-shek hailed this as the realization of the century-long hope of the Chinese people to realize "the equality and freedom of the Chinese Republic" and "the success of the national revolution," and yet at the same time he pointed out that these were also the wartime goals of the Allied powers.[27] As an Allied power, China had now concluded an "equal treaty" with the

United States and the United Kingdom. Put another way, the international status of the Republic of China in wartime Asia had ascended to a new height. Obviously, these international conditions also lifted the discourse of "recovering the Northeast" to a new level within the political space of Chongqing.

Soon after he signed these new treaties, Chiang's book *China's Destiny* was published. It laid out a clear vision of a China that included the Northeast, Taiwan, the Penghu Islands, Inner Mongolia, Xinjiang, and Tibet as parts of China's sovereign territory. In September 1943, on the twelfth anniversary of the Manchurian Incident, a northeastern political figure named Mo Dehui released an essay of his own, entitled "Looking at the Future of the Northeast and *China's Destiny*." In this piece, Mo argued that Chiang's book provided a "powerful guarantee for the recovery and reconstruction of the Northeast."[28] In a similar vein, Wang Zhuoran made a series of proposals at the Consultative Council designed to implement concrete policies based on these goals. This included designating the Northeast as its own theater of war (complete with its own military commander), moving the exiled northeastern provincial government offices closer to the front lines, creating consultative political assemblies for the Northeast, and giving assistance to Korean resistance to Japanese rule on the Korean Peninsula.

Consequently, developing a concrete and detailed plan for the reconstruction of the Northeast became a major political topic in late 1943. Chen Xianzhou proposed "political work within the army" that would require coordination with northeastern troops that had been stationed south of the Great Wall. These troops, though "many had been scattered between the Yellow River and the Yangzi" still retained a "love of country and a desire to recover their homeland that was second to none." Such troops, Chen explained, should be concentrated on the battlefields of North China, where they could exert an influence on their compatriots north of the Great Wall in occupied Manchuria. Chen seconded Wang Zhuoran's proposal to move the agencies of northeastern government closer to the front lines, and he added suggestions of his own for the training of the party cadres, administrators, and technicians who would be needed after the war.[29]

Yet there was still uncertainty. To give one example, the authoritative voice of public opinion, the *Dagongbao*, said in an editorial on September 25, 1943, that "after the war, the national capital should be moved to the north," and discussed different forms that the victory might take. The editorial proposed that "if an incomplete victory is achieved, the status of the Northeast might be unclear." Under such a situation, the national capital should be moved to Xi'an. In the case of a "complete victory" that involved the return of the Northeast, the paper proposed Beiping as the capital. This seemed a dangerous indication that support might exist for a peace deal that would allow Japan to retain its Manchurian possessions. In direct response, Wang Zhuoran cited Chiang Kai-shek's 1941 affirmation of China's determination to reclaim the Northeast and retorted that "there is no way that our final victory will be 'incomplete.'"[30] Although this editorial pointed to the continued existence in 1943 of the idea of an "incomplete" Chinese victory in the war, this notion was obviously subject to criticism within the Chongqing political environment.

By the time that Cairo Conference between the Allied powers commenced in late November 1943, ideas of a "complete victory" were clearly dominant. In their personal discussions with President Roosevelt on November 23, Chiang Kai-shek and Song Meiling repeated China's demand for the return of all territories (including the Northeast and Taiwan) occupied by the Japanese. On November 26, during negotiations over the text of what would become the Cairo Declaration, the UK representative, Sir Alexander Cadogan, proposed that the statement "the Northeast, Taiwan and the Penghu islands must be returned to China" be revised to read "[these territories] ought to be vacated by the Japanese." W. Averell Harriman, the US negotiator, supported the position of Wang Chonghui, the Chinese delegate, that the wording remain unchanged. In the final version of the declaration, the relevant passage reads: "Japan shall be stripped of all the islands in the Pacific which she has seized or occupied since the beginning of the First World War in 1914, and that all the territories Japan has stolen from the Chinese, such as Manchuria, Formosa, and the Pescadores [the Penghu Islands], shall be restored to the Republic of China. Japan will also be expelled from all other territories which she has taken by violence and greed."[31]

On May 5, 1936, the Republic of China promulgated a draft constitution. The text was the product of several years of deliberations. During this process, the drafters confronted the issue of how to delineate the political territory of the Chinese nation-state in the text. In one early version, released in June 1933, the sovereign territory of the Republic of China was defined vaguely as "the actual territory held by China." A subsequent revision, in March 1934, replaced this with a list of thirty specific territories that composed China and added a stipulation preventing the cession of Chinese territory without the consent of China's legislature. These two proposals illustrated a debate that occurred among those drafting the constitution. Supporters of the 1934 version held that listing China's territory would allow the Chinese people to understand more about their nation and also serve to protect the territorial integrity of the country. Those who supported the more general 1933 statement, by contrast, believed that leaving the constitution vague would assist in the recovery of occupied Chinese territory without necessitating any revision to the constitution.[32]

During this debate in 1934, the Shanghai-based periodical *Heibai Bimonthly*, published by an association of northeasterners, ran its own systematic and historical analysis of the "listing" methodology. The commentator argued that "constitutions are a product of their times and, at this time, one-eighth of our country's territory is overrun by enemy forces and no longer belongs to us. . . . If we desire to recover this territory, we need to make everyone deeply aware of these lost lands." Furthermore, he noted, "The sacredness of the constitution must be preserved and the integrity of the constitution cannot be easily violated, so we should first devise a plan for the recovery of these territories. . . . This is the true meaning of this proposal for listing national territories in the constitution." He further emphasized that the listing of territories in the constitution would highlight the fact that responsibility for "planning for territorial integrity and unimpaired national sovereignty" lay with the citizens themselves.[33] The final draft issued in 1936 followed the model of the 1934 document and incorporated a list of Chinese territories by name. This list included the four northeastern provinces that had been occupied by Japan since 1931, as a sign that China did not recognize the Japanese actions. This list of Chinese territories survived a wartime revision of the draft constitution in March 1940.

As the path to victory over Japan became increasingly clear, the head of the Legislative Yuan, Sun Ke, proposed on April 5, 1945, that it was no longer necessary for the constitution to include this detailed list of Chinese territories. He reasoned that "according to the decision at Cairo in 1943, all of the territories seized by the enemy since 1895 must be returned to China, thus giving us a new assurance that we will recover our lost lands. After our victory, we will recover the Northeast, and so I think that a more general approach [to delimiting Chinese territory in the constitution] is more appropriate."[34] Thus, the final draft of the Republic of China's constitution, issued on November 30, 1946, reverted to the vaguer wording of the 1933 draft. The political function of the Northeast Factor that had been so consequential in Chinese legal and constitutional history since 1931 had finally reached its end. It had remained a central policy to the GMD throughout that time.

Part III

ENDING WAR

11 The Nationalist Government's Attitude toward Postwar Japan

WU SUFENG

The postwar treatment of Japan was decided by the United States, the Soviet Union, and the United Kingdom, and not by China, even though China was one of the Allies. At the Cairo Conference of Allied leaders in late November 1943, Chiang Kai-shek had raised the question of reparations and proposed that all Japanese property in China, private as well as public, should be handed to China as compensation, something that was later included in the 1952 peace treaty between Japan and the Republic of China and would come about.[1] However, at Cairo the Allies made few decisions about postwar Japan, other than agreeing that Japan had to surrender unconditionally. It was only at the Yalta Conference of February 1945 and at the Potsdam Conference in late July 1945 that more substantive decisions were made about the postwar order in East Asia. China was not officially represented at either conference. However, Chiang's views were known, including his belief that it was up to the Japanese people to decide the position of the Japanese emperor.

Chiang Kai-shek's general policy was to "repay aggression with kindness" (*yide baoyuan*). Iechika Ryoko has argued that Chiang Kai-shek announced this policy before Japan's surrender to prepare the ground for a postwar Sino-Japanese alliance to counter the likely efforts of Britain, the United States, and the Soviet Union to rebuild their former positions in Asia or carve out new ones. Huang Tzu-chin has maintained that Chiang Kai-shek hoped for Japan's assistance in countering the Soviet Union and suppressing Communism in China.[2] This article examines the information and advice that was made available to Chiang Kai-shek from around the world as he formulated his views on the treatment of Japan after the war. An analysis of these communications suggests that Chiang's policy formulations derived from assessments of changes in international relations around the world and not just in East Asia. The purpose of the article is to make Chiang's views clear and to demonstrate that his aim was to secure a limited role for China in determining the postwar shape of East Asia, despite China's weakness. Although he suffered serious setbacks and had to endure many indignities as a consequence, he was successful, something that would have long-lasting consequences, as now has become clear.

The Position of the Japanese Emperor

During the Cairo Conference in 1943, Roosevelt raised the issue with Chiang Kai-shek of Japan's postwar constitution. Chiang replied that the political influence of Japan's militarists should be eliminated and that "politically aware progressive Japanese elements" should decide the form of Japan's constitution. The free will of the Japanese people should be decisive, according to Chiang.[3] Chiang Kai-shek may have believed that he had convinced Roosevelt, but in reality Roosevelt had reservations about the desirability of retaining the Japanese emperor.

In early 1945, Wei Daoming, the Chinese ambassador to the United States, became aware that the Institute of Pacific Relations had come to the conclusion that Britain and the United States held different views about the postwar treatment of Japan. The IPR believed that Britain, a constitutional monarchy, would probably advocate the retention of the Japanese emperor. Britain also hoped to maintain Japanese living standards so that Japan would be able to rejoin the Pacific economy quickly. However, the United States proposed to abolish the position of the emperor. Believing that the Japanese people deserved to be punished, the United States was not interested in supporting Japanese living standards.[4] On January 27, 1945, Shao Yulin met with Joseph Grew, the most influential voice in the US administration about Japanese affairs. Grew was US ambassador to Japan at the time of Pearl Harbor and undersecretary of state for East Asian affairs afterward. Grew mentioned to Shao that he personally supported Chiang Kai-shek's proposal to respect the free choice of the Japanese people with respect to the position of the emperor. Concerning Japan's unconditional surrender, Grew held that there should be an agreement among all Allies, including the Soviets.[5]

In March 1945, during the conference to plan for the establishment of the United Nations, the United States proposed to disarm Japan and disband the Japanese armaments industry. The United States worked out a draft agreement and gave it to Chiang Kai-shek, who expressed his full agreement.[6] The United States, convinced that the participation of the Soviet Union in the war against Japan would be essential, took the initiative in organizing the Yalta Conference, which took place February 4 to 11, 1945. There Roosevelt, Stalin, and Churchill discussed the creation of an organization to maintain world peace as well as the military planning for offensives against Germany and Japan. In order to bring the war against Japan to a quick end, Roosevelt hoped to gain Stalin's agreement to move his armies to East Asia after the defeat of Germany and to join the war against Japan. In return, Roosevelt accepted Stalin's demands for privileges such as access to the Manchurian railroads, which had been built with Russian assistance before the Russo-Japanese War, as well as the right to use Dalian and Lüshun, two warm-water ports in China's Northeast, which would give the Soviet Union's navy access to the Pacific.

The secret Yalta agreements would have enormous consequences for postwar relations in East Asia. But the Nationalist government did not know about them, while Japan was making efforts to prevent Soviet participation in the war against it. When the Nationalist government learned that secret agreements had been made at Yalta on March 15, it set out to discover their contents and dispatched Song Ziwen, the minister of foreign affairs at that time, to begin negotiations with the Soviets.[7] However, it is possible that the Nationalist government shifted its attention to US and British intentions for postwar Japan, as attention was now switching to the planning for the San Francisco conference to establish the United Nations. The Nationalist government wanted to make use of the period to gain favorable treatment for China, stabilize East Asia, and boost its international status by making proposals about Europe.

Representatives from various countries convened in San Francisco from April 25 to June 1945 to establish the United Nations. On April 11, Peng Keding, the Nationalist representative, stated in a report to Chiang Kai-shek that no high expectations should be had about the conference. He argued that China's proposals should deal with East Asia rather than Europe. He suggested that China should propose that Japan be asked to compensate China for war damages and that the equipment of the Imperial Japanese Army and Japan's arsenals should be given to China as part of its war reparations. With respect to Germany, China as a victorious ally should insist on a statement that Germany should repay China for illegal seizures of Chinese property in the past. But Peng added that he believed that China should ask for more only if other countries agreed. He finally suggested that China should make a number of proposals for postwar relief, but not just for China so as to avoid appearing to be concerned only about its own country.[8]

A report from Song Ziwen, interim Executive Yuan director and foreign minister, shows that Peng's hopes were unlikely to be realized. On May 7, Song Ziwen wrote a memorandum stating:

The United States went to war with Japan originally in support of China. Now that the war in Europe is over, army and navy officials as well as members of Congress only want to defeat Japan as quickly as possible. They no longer are interested in supporting China to make it a powerful nation in East Asia.[9]

In the past, American president Franklin Roosevelt had been willing to listen to and take into account proposals by the Nationalist government about the treatment of Japan. But in the spring of 1945, China counted for much less.

On August 10, Japanese emperor Hirohito issued a diplomatic note, passed on by the Swiss government to China, the United States, Britain, and the Soviet Union, stating that Japan was willing to accept the articles enumerated in the Potsdam Declaration and surrender unconditionally. It requested that the position of the Japanese emperor would not change.[10] The next day the Chinese ambassador to Britain, Gu Weijun, visited the British deputy foreign minister. He inquired whether the British government had made any decision about Japan's offer and the statement in it about the Japanese emperor. The British deputy foreign minister answered that during the British-American discussion, the United States made the following proposal:

1. From the day that Japan surrenders, the Supreme Allied Command will control the powers of the Japanese emperor and the government of Japan.
2. The cease-fire document shall be signed by the Japanese emperor and the Japanese supreme military commander.
3. The Japanese emperor shall order that all Japanese forces everywhere will obey Allied orders in handing over their weapons.
4. Upon the signing of the cease-fire document, all Allied prisoners of war and all Allied residents in Japan shall be released immediately and be shipped away by the Allies.[11]

Gu was told that Britain was in general agreement with the American proposals but that it believed that Emperor Hirohito did not need to sign the cease-fire document. It would be sufficient if the Japanese emperor empowered the Japanese supreme commander to sign it. He was furthermore told that after Britain and the United States reached agreement, they would ask for Chinese and Soviet opinions and then respond to Japan. Gu inquired about Allied plans for the occupation of Japan. The British deputy foreign minister stated that a great number of soldiers would be needed and that as they were to occupy the main Japanese islands, they would need an appropriate amount of weapons and equipment. Gu suggested that a meeting of the foreign ministers of the United States, Britain, the Soviet Union, France, and China should convene a meeting for detailed discussions about postwar arrangements for East Asia.[12]

On August 14, on behalf of the Allies, the American secretary of state, James F. Byrnes, handed a note in reply to Emperor Hirohito's message to Max Grassli, the Swiss chargé d'affaires, which gave instructions for Japan to follow upon its surrender. The Japanese were to report the time when they ordered the termination of all military operations to the supreme Allied commanders in charge of the forces fighting Japan. Japan was to send emissaries to the supreme Allied commander to notify him of the location of Japan's forces and their commanders. They were to have all necessary authority to implement orders given to them by the supreme Allied commanders, who would formally receive the Japanese surrender when they and their troops arrived at designated places.[13] The next day, Japan announced its surrender. Nothing further was said about the position of the emperor.

The Response to the New Order in East Asia

Before Yalta, Japan's intelligence did its best to find out as much as possible about Allied intentions and took active steps to make clear to Britain and the United States that defeating Japan would not be easy—certainly not in China—as well as to prevent the Soviet Union from joining them. Dai Li, the head of one of the two intelligence services of the Nationalists, secured information about Japan's troop movements from the Japanese military headquarters in Shanghai. After January 18, Japanese Imperial Headquarters had decided to strengthen fortifications along the Chinese coast and reinforce troops on Hainan Island and in Hong Kong. Japan also transferred fifteen marine brigades to the command of the Japanese fleet in China. The purpose of these steps was to seek a decisive battle between the Japanese Combined Fleet and British and American naval forces. Japanese forces in China were ordered to destroy joint US-China special forces, prevent the Nationalist army's counteroffensive, and forestall Allied landings on the China coast.[14] At Yalta, the weekly intelligence estimates of the US Joint Intelligence Committee provided a great amount of evidence about Japan's strong reaction to the conference.

A February 4, 1945, report to Chiang Kai-shek by Shang Zhen, a senior Nationalist general and at the time the Chinese military attaché in Washington, said that a semiofficial Japanese spokesman had indicated that Japan was willing to make maximum concessions to the Soviet Union to prevent its withdrawal from the Sino-Soviet Nonaggression Pact. Influential figures outside the military had become worried after the Allied liberation of the Philippines. They did not want the Soviet Union to assist Britain and the United States in East Asia. The Japanese spokesman believed that although Roosevelt and Churchill were concerned about the situation in

East Asia and wanted to receive Soviet assistance, Stalin's primary objective at the conference was to resolve disputes in Europe, especially about Poland. His personal opinion was that Stalin would not do anything more than recognize Japan as an aggressor state. Although Japanese officials, according to this spokesman, were certain about this assessment, they nonetheless wanted to reach an understanding with the Soviet Union. They were willing to cancel the Axis and, more importantly, the anti-Comintern pacts and even terminate anti-Communist policies in Japan. They hoped that in return the Soviet Union would continue to observe the Soviet-Japanese Nonaggression Pact.[15] Japan was taking active steps to appeal to the Soviet Union and prevent the United States from reaching its objective.

Nevertheless, Yalta caused the Japanese to be concerned about their future prospects. According to a Chinese report of February 12, cautious older Japanese believed after the Allies had landed in the Philippines that Japan should make contact with China to bring about an early end to the Sino-Japanese War so that Japan would retain the strength to confront the Soviet Union. Japanese military commanders, on the other hand, thought that although the situation had turned against Japan, it should drag out the war and wait for a change of fortune in the future. Young hard-line military officers, according to this report, favored continuing the war, so that even if Japan would lose, China would be utterly destroyed. These officers intended to make contacts with the Chinese Communist Party and support it to ignite civil war in China and so lessen pressure on Japan. The report counseled Chiang that China should take steps to prevent such a plot.[16]

Based on the information available to it, the Nationalist government concluded that there was a real possibility that the Japanese were genuinely interested in ending the war. Dai Li's intelligence of a Japanese cabinet meeting of February 6, 1945, suggested that both Japanese prime minister Kuniaki Koiso and foreign minister Mamoru Shigemitsu had expressed their pessimism about the future. They believed that after Germany surrendered, Japanese-Soviet relations would break down and that America would land forces in China. Dai Li's conclusion was that the Japanese navy and key figures in the Japanese cabinet all favored peace and that only young hard-line military officers were unwilling to give up.[17]

This background explains why the initial response of the Nationalist government to the Yalta Conference was to seek clarity about US and British attitudes toward Japan and why they disregarded the nature of the agreements with the Soviet Union. On February 4, Kong Xiangxi, who was in the United States as Chiang Kai-shek's personal representative, submitted a report together with Shang Zhen, the military attaché. The report mentioned that Roosevelt's trusted adviser, Harry L. Hopkins, had stated that the Allies had to occupy Germany and Japan to prevent them from rearming and waging war again, as powerful persons would not accept defeat.[18] Hopkins's statement revealed that the intention of the United States and Britain was to occupy Japan for a substantial period.

When Chiang Kai-shek met with US general Charles M. Cooke, who was on his way back from Yalta, Cooke's unusual manner led him to suspect that at Yalta China had been sold out.[19] But it does not seem that he took active steps to find out what precisely had taken place. Staff from the Chinese Foreign Ministry discussed with US government officials only the Soviets' stance toward participation in the war against Japan. For instance, Kong Xiangxi stated that Harry Hopkins had mentioned to him that the Soviet-Japanese Nonaggression Pact would expire at the end of April and that the Soviet Union was bound to do something with respect to East Asia. Hopkins had further stated that the United States and Britain wanted to stabilize the world and secure international cooperation, for which further guarantees would be necessary. He also mentioned that the United States, Britain, and the Soviet Union had discussed the postwar treatment of Germany, and that with respect to the normalization process in European countries, they had decided that national referendums would decide their constitutional arrangements, which would be a victory for the democratic system. Hopkins stated that the San Francisco Conference might discuss the postwar treatment of Germany, but that he would like to know China's views.[20] He mentioned the Soviets' actions only in passing, focusing on the topic of the stabilization of the world after the war.

On February 22, the Chinese ambassador to the United States, Wei Daoming, reported that American officials were only superficially positive about the Yalta Conference, and that in reality they were disappointed. They indicated that although they had made maximum concessions, Soviet support had been secured only with the greatest difficulty. The Soviet Union obviously wanted Communist-controlled governments in Europe. US officials were extremely worried about what attitude the Soviets might take in the future toward other issues, including the relationship between the Soviet Union and China's Northeast. To reach a compromise with the Soviet Union, some American government officials even proposed to give up the Northeast in exchange for Soviet participation in the war against Japan. According to Wei Daoming, the United States had generally believed that a close connection existed between the issue of the Northeast and peace in East Asia. US policy should decide whether the Northeast should be restored to China or fall under the Soviet influence. Fortunately, according to Wei, *Fortune* magazine argued that the United States should stick to its traditional policy of supporting China's territorial integrity and sovereignty. Wei considered this a useful correction to unfortunate comments in the American press.[21]

According to Wei Daoming, some politicians in Congress maintained that European issues would always be destabilizing and that American policy should be to switch its focus to the Pacific. They advocated that the United States cooperate with the Nationalist government. Wei Daoming thought that the significance of the Pacific region in US policy would be enhanced, even though the United States would not withdraw from Europe altogether.[22]

On March 4, Shang Zhen reported a discussion he had with William D. Leahy of the US Joint Chiefs of Staff. Shang had asked Leahy whether the Soviets would join the war in the East and whether the Soviet Union would declare war on Japan at the time of the San Francisco Conference. Leahy replied that he was optimistic about Soviet participation, and he believed that soon there would be a major change for the better in the military situation. However, Leahy explained, the timing of the Soviet participation had to be a secret because a difficult situation would emerge if Japan decided to attack the Soviets first. Leahy also stated that the Soviet Union was not a member of the Allied Joint Staff, that President Roosevelt hoped to fulfill the promise of US landings on the China coast, and that the US navy would also move toward its objectives. The problem was that there were insufficient troops. Therefore, according to Leahy, if the war in Europe could be brought to a conclusion quickly, the landings on the China coast would then soon go ahead. Leahy personally regarded Hong Kong and Guangdong as the best places for a US landing, but others had different opinions.[23]

It appears that Nationalist officials in the United States did not realize that something was afoot. Even though Wei Daoming had reported that the future status of the Northeast would be decided by US policy, the implications seem not to have been realized. This changed only on March 15. On that day, Wei Daoming reported that he had learned the contents of a conversation between Roosevelt and Stalin.[24] Stalin had demanded that the Manchurian railways be placed under international trusteeship, with sovereignty belonging to China but the Soviet Union owning the North Manchurian Railway. Stalin had demanded that Lüshun or Dalian become their ice-free port. Roosevelt had replied that the Soviet Union could lease Lüshun but that China should have sovereignty. When Chiang Kai-shek learned of this, he was utterly furious and concluded that Roosevelt had sold out China, and that China's hopes for the War of Resistance against Japan had come to nothing.[25]

On August 6 and 9, 1945, the United States dropped atomic bombs over Japan. On August 7, Chiang Kai-shek attempted to secure an advantageous position to take back China's Northeast. He sent a telegram to Song Ziwen, the Executive Yuan director then in Moscow conducting negotiations for a Sino-Soviet treaty of friendship. Chiang demanded that "all industries with all their equipment in the Northeast must be turned over to China as part of Japanese war reparations. Before a treaty is concluded, you must come to an agreement with the Soviets about this point and make a declaration."[26] However, the Soviet rejection of this demand made this impossible.

On August 9, the Soviet Union declared war on Japan. Chiang Kai-shek met with senior government leaders. They agreed that while China would soon be victorious, it should make preparations to confront the Soviet Union to avoid China being completely sacrificed as a result of the changes occurring in Asia.

The Japanese Surrender

On July 25, 1945, Patrick Hurley, the US ambassador to China, passed on a message from President Truman to Chiang Kai-shek about the Potsdam Declaration, which he hoped to announce soon. He hoped that Chiang would be able to give his assent in the shortest possible time. The Potsdam Declaration demanded Japan's immediate unconditional surrender; adding that otherwise it would face "prompt and utter" destruction."[27] Chiang Kai-shek had no objection to the wording of the declaration, other than the omission of China in the first clause. He requested that it should read "We—the president of the United States, the president of the Nationalist government of the Republic of China, and the prime minister of Great Britain," rather than just the US president and the British prime minister.[28] Chiang Kai-shek was in no position to suggest any other changes, as all decisions had already been made. The order in which the countries were named reflected Chiang's opinion of the United States and Britain.

On August 10, the Nationalist commander in chief learned that Japan had indicated that it was willing to accept the Potsdam Declaration, as it would do formally two days later. He Yingqin immediately issued an instruction to Japan's supreme commander in China, Okamura Yasuji, ordering him to direct his troops to cease all military activities, stay were they were, not destroy any materiel, safeguard transport facilities, and maintain order and discipline while awaiting instructions from national army commanders. He Yingqin insisted on a reply within twenty-four hours. In instructions to China's military forces about Japan's surrender, he stated that they should prepare for possible Japanese obstruction and that the Japanese should not be allowed to surrender to anyone else or hand their weapons to military commanders other than those so designated by him. He further ordered them to establish contact with Chinese forces that had collaborated with Japan, to urge them to return to the Nationalists.[29]

On the same day, Xu Foguan, an official in Chiang Kai-shek's personal staff office, submitted recommendations for dealing with the Japanese surrender, which had come earlier than China, or the Allies, had expected and therefore had caught everybody unprepared. "We must first of all ensure that we gain the spiritual fruits of victory," he wrote, and "so smash the morale of the Communists and traitors." Xu warned that "the Communists in Japanese-occupied areas will do their utmost to make the Japanese surrender to them, incorporate their forces, and establish contact with the Soviet army marching southward." He feared that they "will rebel openly, calling for our overthrow" as they already had secured North China. But he also believed that victory, if handled properly, would enable the Nationalists to "bring about a big change" and get the whole country onside.

Specifically, Xu advised that the Nationalists should immediately announce the appointment of high-level officials to take charge of areas occupied by the Japanese and fly them there forthwith. The Nationalists should also send leading figures to Yan'an to begin talks about political unity, something that should be announced in the press. The National Consultative Conference, which had non-GMD members, should be called into session to discuss postwar affairs and rehabilitation.[30]

The next few days saw intensive planning for the takeover from Japan. On August 11, Peng Keding suggested that China should proceed immediately to take over Japan's arms and munitions without waiting until an agreement about procedures had been reached with the Allies, as they themselves had done in Germany. He suggested that officials able to get along with the Japanese should be sent to China's Northeast, to Korea, and to areas within China to conduct negotiations with them, promising good treatment so as to prevent them from fleeing. Military confrontations with the Japanese should be avoided so that China's forces would not sustain further losses. Messages should be broadcast over the radio, and flyers should be dropped by airplanes to reassure the Japanese. Peng further suggested that China's priority should be to take Beiping and points along the Shanghai-Nanjing Railroad. Troops, if necessary parachute regiments, should be sent to the Northeast to establish links with Soviet forces to prevent them from occupying the area. Peng advised Chiang that China should insist on participation in the occupation of Japan. He wanted the Japanese navy to become a war prize for China.

Peng suggested that Japan should be forced to provide substantial amounts of compensation, with China receiving at least 75 percent of all compensation paid by Japan. China should receive "all of Japan's light and heavy industry." Japanese technical experts should be forced to provide assistance in rebuilding China, and Japanese railroads and modern means of communications should be handed to China. Japanese prisoners of war should be put to work in repairing China's roads. All Japanese materials and possessions in China that had a military value should be handed to China. Peng expected that Japan would soon be overwhelmed by famine. As European experiences had shown that food would secure the allegiance of the local population, he argued that Japanese prisoners of war and Japanese refugees should be treated well.[31]

Japanese troops in China made their own preparations for surrender. Yasuji Okamura sent a delegate to talk face to face with Zhou Fohai, the Executive Yuan deputy director of the Nanjing government that had been led by Wang Jingwei. He asked Zhou Fohai to pass on to Dai Li, with whom Zhou had been in touch for some time, the message that while "he had received no instructions from Tokyo, he would not oppose the order of the emperor once it was delivered. Zhou said that Okamura had indicated that the entire army was unanimous that it would only surrender to Chiang Kai-shek and would under no circumstances surrender to Britain or the United States."[32] Okamura further revealed that the Japanese cabinet had decided to make public the negotiations that had led to surrender in the hope that this would bolster morale. It would instruct the media in Japan to emphasize that "it is of utmost importance to have understanding for the emperor's will" and to call for unity in meeting the difficulties that this unprecedented situation in history had created. The cabinet had also proscribed any mention of Communist revolution.[33]

There are dangers in reconstructing history on the basis of intelligence reports and internal news analyses. We do not know the full record, nor were the sources necessarily reliable. They might even have been planted to mislead their recipients. Chiang Kai-shek, though, had no option but to base his views on the information available to him, and his assessments of their usefulness.

Several points seem clear. Chiang's essential policy was to insist on compensation by Japan for the damage inflicted on China, a compensation that was geared to helping China rebuild after war. At the same time, perhaps under the influence of China's tradition of benevolent government, he favored an attitude of generosity and insisted that the Japanese should choose their form of government themselves. While the United States considered seriously the abolition of the position of the Japanese emperor, it did not press an issue about whose merits neither China nor Britain were convinced.

China's policy toward Japan was articulated in the context of internal Allied and especially US policy, with Nationalist officials in the United States trying to get as much information about the US stance toward postwar Japan as possible. It is clear that they were caught off guard by Roosevelt's decisions about China's Northeast at Yalta. Before Yalta, they had paid little attention to the Soviet Union, but afterward they wanted to negotiate with the Soviet Union immediately to limit the negative consequences for China of the US and British belief that handing the Northeast to the Soviet Union was a price worth paying for Soviet involvement in the war against Japan.

The Nationalists had in reality little impact on Allied policy. Like Yalta, the Potsdam Declaration came as a surprise. All Chiang could do was to ensure that his name, as China's highest political authority, was inserted into the text. By that time, the essential decisions had already been made, including the ones that Japan would be occupied for a long time, that revenge would be restricted to the punishment of war criminals, that disarmed soldiers would be repatriated immediately, and that war reparations would be limited to payments in kind. It seems that for Chiang Kai-shek, recognition of China as one of the victorious countries, having defeated Japan along with Britain and the United States, was a most important concern.

China's position at the end of the war was such that he could not have done much more. The Ichigo Offensive of 1944 had seen Japanese forces cut through China's defenses and occupy vast areas of Nationalist-controlled territory. The little faith that had remained in China's ability to contribute actively to the defeat of Japan evaporated, and some began to fear that the Nationalists would yet be knocked out of the war. With US forces encountering determined Japanese opposition in their battles with the Japanese as they fought their way to the Japanese homeland, it is not surprising that US leaders, seeking the quickest possible end to World War II, decided that the help of the Soviet Union had to be called in, even though many knew, and were appalled by, Soviet behavior in Eastern Europe. The only thing that Chiang could do was to continue to insist on the recognition of China as one of the victorious countries and secure a minimum involvement of China in the negotiations about the postwar fate of Japan and the future shape of East Asia.

12 Postwar Sino-French Negotiations about Vietnam, 1945–1946

YANG WEIZHEN

Before World War II, China and France had good diplomatic relations. In May 1930, the two countries signed a Special Treaty Concerning Bilateral Relations. The treaty stipulated that military equipment and armaments for the Chinese government would be free from duty when passing through Vietnamese territory. As chapter 1 by Marianne Bastid-Bruignere demonstrates, the treaty was highly beneficial to China during the first year of the Sino-Japanese War. Then by mid-1938 as the situation in Europe deteriorated, France moved toward a more neutral position regarding the war in China. Limitations began to be put on armament shipments passing through Vietnam to Kunming. In September 1939, after war broke out in Europe, France went further and temporarily halted the shipments to China via Vietnam.

After the German occupation of France in the summer of 1940, Japan forced the French viceroy in Vietnam to shut down Sino-Vietnamese trade altogether. In September of that year, this was formalized with the signing of a Vietnam-Japan treaty. The French viceroy in Vietnam was forced to permit the stationing of Japanese troops in Vietnam and the use by Japan of three air bases in northern Vietnam. Needless to say, these measures seriously threatened the security of southwestern China. In July 1941, the French puppet government and Japan signed another agreement, this one for the joint defense of Indochina. According to this document, Japan had the right to exercise military authority in Vietnam. In effect, France lost control. Thereafter, in order to maintain the semblance of a colonial presence in Vietnam, the French continued to meet Japanese demands, obviously at the cost of China's interests.[1] Six months later, in December 1941, the Pacific War broke out. Chiang Kai-shek considered the French puppet government in Vietnam as under the control of the Axis and unfriendly to China. Therefore, he ordered the Chinese ambassador to France, Wei Daoming, not to return to France. Sino-French diplomatic contact for all practical purposes was terminated.[2]

In January 1943, the French puppet government asked the Chinese government to evacuate its embassy in Paris. In February, France acquiesced to the Japanese military occupation of the Guangzhou Bay area and the transfer of various French concessions in Beiping, Tianjin, Shanghai, Wuhan, and Guangzhou to the jurisdiction of the Nanjing puppet government led by Wang Jingwei. For the Nationalist government, this was the last straw. On August 1, it announced the formal termination of diplomatic relations with the French government and on August 27 recognized the French National Liberation Committee led by Charles de Gaulle in North Africa. France was liberated from German occupation in August 1944. The provisional French government moved back to Paris and formed a new government, which the Chinese recognized in October. But it was not long before serious differences emerged between the two governments over Vietnam.

The histories of China and Vietnam have been closely intertwined. In the nineteenth century, both were invaded by world powers. Therefore, the Chinese Nationalist Party and Nationalist government had always been sympathetic to Vietnam's aspirations for independence. Supporting Vietnam's independence was one diplomatic objective of the Chinese government and the Nationalist Party. But it was only after the Sino-Japanese War broke out, and especially after the Pacific War began with Pearl Harbor in December 1941, that China began to play a greater role in Vietnamese affairs.

On December 31, 1941, following the suggestion of the US-British Joint Command, Roosevelt proposed Vietnam as part of the China Theater with Chiang Kai-shek as overall commander. Shortly thereafter, the Nationalist government notified the French puppet government in Hanoi that Chinese troops would enter Vietnam if necessary.[3] The Chinese military in particular was concerned about Vietnam. On March 23, 1942, Legislative Yuan director Sun Ke publicly asked Roosevelt and Winston Churchill to include in the Pacific Charter a guarantee recognizing the independence of Vietnam, India, Korea, and the Philippines.[4] In November 1943, Chinese, British, and American leaders met at Cairo, where Chiang Kai-shek reached an understanding with Roosevelt. China and the United States would jointly help Vietnam to gain independence after the war. Chiang Kai-shek claimed that China had no ulterior ambitions regarding Indochina. But Roosevelt believed that the people of Indochina were not prepared for independence. Therefore, he raised with Chiang Kai-shek the possibility of putting Indochina under international trusteeship and postponing the independence of the Indochinese people for twenty or thirty years.[5]

Roosevelt was determined to prevent France from returning to Indochina as a colonial ruler after the war. However, while China favored Vietnamese independence, the United States wanted an international trusteeship for Annam, as Vietnam was called at the time. The Chinese ambassador to Britain, Gu Weijun (Wellington Koo), recalled in his memoirs a discussion with Roosevelt at the White House on May 4, 1943, half a year before the Cairo Conference, in which Roosevelt stated:

Indochina should not be returned to France. After France governed that place for a century, people's lives there were even worse than they had been in the past. The place should be managed temporarily by China, the United States, and perhaps a third country until complete independence at a later date.[6]

Afterward during the Tehran Conference between the United States, Britain, and the Soviet Union in November 1943, Roosevelt and Stalin talked about postwar France. Stalin submitted that since France had collaborated with Germany, the French should not enjoy special privileges or the restoration of colonial rule over Indochina. President Roosevelt agreed completely.[7] A year later, at Dumbarton Oaks in October 1944, Roosevelt told Gu Weijun: "The United States does not care about Indochina; China should take care of Indochina."[8] These exchanges illustrate both Roosevelt's attitude toward Vietnam and China's support for postwar independence.[9]

On March 9, 1945, the Vietnam Incident occurred when the Japanese army stationed in Vietnam suddenly attacked the French puppet authorities. Viceroy Jean Decoux was arrested, and most of his French-Vietnamese troops surrendered. The remainder (about 5,000 soldiers) retreated north across the border into Yunnan Province. Chiang Kai-shek observed at the time that this was a positive development for China but one that also brought dangers. At a meeting with his military and political advisers to discuss the situation in Vietnam, he stated: "We must remain concerned about the military situation in Vietnam. Our army needs three months to redeploy troops. However, the Japanese have the ability to pull troops back from Burma, Thailand, and Southeast Asia and concentrate/deploy them in Vietnam in less than three months."[10]

Meanwhile, the new French ambassador to China, Zinovi Pechkoff, asked the Nationalist government to treat the 5,000 former puppet French-Vietnamese soldiers who were in southern Yunnan Province as Allied troops and recognize General Sabattier as their commander. He asked that the army be incorporated under the overall command structure of the China Theater. The Chinese Ministry of Military Operations rejected the proposal as coming from ex-puppet troops and their commander.[11] On

May 11, 1945, however, Chiang Kai-shek indicated that he would agree if France met three conditions. France had to agree to work out unresolved issues between China and Vietnam, such as the future treatment of overseas Chinese in Vietnam; it had to compensate China for losses incurred because of the surrender of authority to the Japanese; and it had to provide a guarantee of the security of southwestern China and recognition of Vietnam's international status.[12]

On August 10, 1945, after Japan announced its surrender, the Chinese Supreme Command ordered First Front Army commander Lu Han to lead his troops into Vietnam to accept the surrender of Japanese troops north of the sixteenth parallel.[13] The First Front Army had been responsible for monitoring the movement of Japanese troops in Vietnam and intervening in Vietnam if necessary. With the conclusion of the war, the army assumed the task of moving into northern Vietnam.[14] On August 20, Lu Han received orders to enter Vietnam and accept the Japanese surrender. On August 23, a telegram was forwarded to him from Chiang Kai-shek stipulating the date he should enter Vietnam.[15] On September 1, Lu Han attended a preparatory conference at Zhijiang in Hunan Province chaired by army chief commander He Yingqin. He Yingqin passed on the following central government instructions: Lu Han was ordered to prepare for the establishment of a provisional military government to occupy northern Vietnam.[16] The First Front Army's key responsibilities were as follows: First, the army would accept the Japanese army's surrender, disarm Japanese soldiers, and return them to Japan. Second, the army would establish a military government to manage civil affairs. Third, the French-Vietnamese army in Yunnan Province would remain there awaiting orders. The army would not be allowed to enter Vietnam. Individual soldiers could voluntarily return to Vietnam without arms.[17]

On September 9, 1945, Yin Jixun, the vice chief of staff for the First Front Army in charge of the troops preparing to march into Vietnam, flew with his staff to Hanoi to set up a command office. The expeditionary force was large in scale. However, heavy rain made transport and resupply difficult. Once in Vietnam, they encountered difficulties because the League for the Independence of Vietnam, led by Ho Chi Minh, blocked the advance of the Chinese troops.[18] After surmounting these difficulties, around September 20, the First Front Army reached defense perimeters around Hanoi. On September 14, General Lu Han had flown into Hanoi from his headquarters in Yunnan. He settled in the former French viceroy's mansion and presided over various issues relating to the acceptance of the Japanese surrender. At 10 a.m. on September 28 in a formal ceremony, Lu Han accepted the Japanese army's signature on the surrender document for regions to the north of the sixteenth parallel in Vietnam.[19] After the ceremony, troops of the First Front Army were redeployed to various locations. Thus commenced the military occupation of northern Vietnam.

General Long Yun, the warlord and governor who had controlled Yunnan since the 1930s, saw the establishment of a provisional military government in northern Vietnam by Lu Han as an ideal opportunity to expand his regional influence by means of the long-term occupation of northern Vietnam.[20] In addition to dispatching all the troops of the First Front Army led by Lu Han, he dispatched to Vietnam as well the provisional Nineteenth Division, led by Long Shengwu, and the provisional Twenty-Third Division, led by Pan Shuoduan. Arguing that almost all his troops were in Vietnam, he planned to ask the central government for permission and funding to train new troops and thus expand his power.[21] As we shall see, when the Nationalist government began to adjust its policy toward Vietnam because of the international environment, it met strong opposition from regional military authorities like Long Yun and Lu Han.

After Japan surrendered, the League for the Independence of Vietnam, led by Ho Chi Minh, started the so-called August Revolution. It seized major cities, occupied territories, and declared independence, establishing a new government of the Democratic Republic of Vietnam on September 2, 1945.[22] Chinese documents confirm the existence of strong anti-French feeling. One observer declared, "Vietnamese shared a profound hatred of the French. Nobody dares to fly a French flag. Captured French military officers had to be protected by the enemy [that is, the Japanese army]; otherwise, they would be killed.[23] Another said, "Ho Chi Minh has established the Vietnamese provisional government in resolute opposition to France. He prohibits the hanging of the French national flag. He has the full support of the Vietnamese people."[24]

The Allied Supreme Command had settled postwar issues such as the Japanese army's surrender in Indochina according to agreements made at the Potsdam Conference. China and Britain would split the responsibility for accepting the Japanese surrender; in the north, the Chinese were to do so, and in the south, the British would act for the Allies. The French were to be excluded. But the French were confident that a British occupation of southern Vietnam would enable them to recover colonial rule under the cover of British trusteeship. They believed that the clash of British and French interests in North Africa and the Middle East would mean that the British would not want more problems with France over Vietnam.[25] Moreover, Britain wished to retain its colonies in Asia, giving both countries a common interest in maintaining colonial rule. China, however, was different.

Needless to say, the French wanted their forces to participate in accepting the Japanese surrender of northern Vietnam along with the Chinese. On August 30, such a proposal was rejected politely by the Americans and in firm language by the Chinese as a violation of the Potsdam agreements.[26] At this point, the French government went to work diplomatically on the Americans. De Gaulle went to Washington, DC, and raised the subject directly with Truman, whom he saw as more pragmatic and amenable to argument than Roosevelt. De Gaulle objected to American contacts with Ho Chi Minh. He left Washington feeling reassured that the Americans were softening (because of the political situation in Europe) and would not prevent the French from reestablishing colonial authority in Vietnam.[27]

At the same time, the Nationalist government began to alter its policy toward Vietnam and the French. As the First Front Army prepared to enter Vietnam to accept the Japanese surrender, the Nationalist government's Executive Yuan organized an Advisory Team of the Executive Yuan to go to Vietnam. Six bureaus (for foreign affairs, the military, fiscal policy, the economy, transportation, and grain) and the Secretariat each sent one representative. The team entered Vietnam with the First Front Army and prepared to function as the highest administrative body in northern Vietnam and to assist Lu Han in the management of relevant issues. Consequently, at a session on September 18, the Executive Yuan passed a fourteen-article document, "Principles for Occupying Military and Administrative Facilities in Vietnam." It required the adoption of a neutral stand of noninterference toward relations between France and Vietnam. A French delegation would be permitted to attend the surrender ceremony and participate with observer status in the activities of the Chinese occupation government. The Executive Yuan instructed the Advisory Team to be prepared to return Vietnam to the French.[28]

As a matter of fact, when the Sino-Japanese War ended, the Chinese government's Executive Yuan had little awareness of the importance or complexity of the issues concerning Vietnam. For instance, when Ling Qihan received orders to join the Advisory Team in Vietnam as Foreign Ministry representative, he met with the Executive Yuan Political Affairs Bureau director, Xu Daolin. Xu Daolin responded: "Your mission for this trip is very simple. When the Japanese army surrenders to the Chinese army, the Chinese army simply turns over the posts to the French army. In two or three months, you could fulfill your mission. It is really nothing remarkable."[29]

This episode demonstrates that the central government really had a mistaken, misinformed view of the issues concerning Vietnam.

What lay behind the Executive Yuan's passive policy toward Vietnam was the Foreign Ministry's good relations with de Gaulle since at least

1944. For instance, in October 1944, when meeting with Pechkoff, the new French ambassador to China,[30] French records indicate that Chiang Kai-shek assured France that the Chinese government had no interest in Indochina.[31] In August 1945, when France demanded that China allow the 5,000 French soldiers who retreated to China to return to Vietnam, there was a favorable diplomatic response from Chongqing. On August 17, the Chinese Foreign Ministry handed the French diplomat in China the following note:

The Chinese Foreign Ministry greets the French Foreign Ministry. Concerning the French embassy's memo asking China to permit the 5,000 French soldiers who have retreated to China to return to Vietnam, the Chinese government approves. It has asked the Chinese army general in command to inform the French troops to prepare for departure. The Chinese government understands that in the Vietnamese territories where China accepted Japanese surrender, French troops and other French military forces or affiliated troops should coordinate with Chinese troops under the China Theater commander or his designated representative.[32]

Moreover, in addition to giving permission for French representatives to attend the surrender ceremonies, the Foreign Ministry followed up with an even stronger statement on September 7 that essentially recognized France's special status in Vietnam.

The period of Chinese occupation of Vietnam will terminate after France sends troops to assume positions, and China hopes that the period should not exceed three months. . . . China occupies Vietnam purely to accept Japanese surrender and to take over military posts. The number of Chinese troops should not exceed what is needed to take over Japanese positions. This should be decided clearly, and the French should be notified.[33]

Finally, activities and statements at the time by Executive Yuan director Song Ziwen and Foreign Minister Wang Shijie supported the French. In Washington, Song made a formal promise to Charles de Gaulle that China would not interfere in Indochina.[34] On September 18, Chinese foreign minister Wang Shijie attended the conference of foreign ministers of five nations in London. He also talked with the French foreign minister about the situation in Vietnam. According to Wang Shijie, "France asked China to allow French troops stranded in Yunnan Province to return to Vietnam. I stated that I would send a telegram to my government. Meanwhile, I expressed my hope that France would give some guarantees toward the political prospects for Vietnam."[35] On the next day (September 19), Song Ziwen arrived in France for a visit. Accompanied by Chinese ambassador to France Qian Tai, Song Ziwen met with Charles de Gaulle. When de Gaulle mentioned that in northern Vietnam, Lu Han and his occupation army had adopted measures harmful to France, Song Ziwen promised that the Chinese government would stop these measures and pull out Chinese troops from Indochina.[36] These episodes demonstrate the naïveté of the Chinese central government and its Foreign Ministry.

In his diary, the Chinese foreign minister, Wang Shijie, made clear his reasons for opposition to the Chinese army's occupation of Vietnam over the long-term.[37]

In Vietnam China has stationed eight divisions. The military expenditure is huge and cannot be financed locally. China has repeatedly expressed that China has no territorial ambition toward Vietnam. So Chinese troops should pull out as soon as the Japanese surrender is complete. I repeatedly suggested to Chiang Kai-shek that China should keep to its plan of pulling out Chinese troops early. In terms of China's relations with France and Vietnam, China is in a position to propose resolutions to the crisis that are reasonable, having no territorial ambition or hostility to the various sides.[38]

Wang Shijie was also taking into account changes in the international and domestic situations. Internationally, the American position was shifting. There were conflicts at that time between China and Britain over Hong Kong. He did not want to see hostilities with France concerning Vietnam interfere with other difficult diplomatic negotiations. To make matters worse, before the Japanese surrender, the Soviet Union declared war on Japan and marched into Northeast China. After the Japanese surrender, China and the Soviet Union had signed treaties of friendship and alliance. Yet the Soviet army still occupied Northeast China and was not pulling out. If at that time China did not pull out its army from Vietnam, why should the Soviet army be forced to pull out from Northeast China?[39] Moreover, the complexity of the situation in Vietnam far exceeded the Chinese government's capabilities. China should get out rather than fall into a trap.

In terms of the domestic situation, with the conclusion of the Sino-Japanese War, a lot of problems needed to be dealt with concerning acceptance of the Japanese surrender in China and organizing the demobilization of Chinese soldiers. The likelihood of a Nationalist-Communist civil war was also looming. In North China and Northeast China, a lot of soldiers were urgently needed to accept the surrender of over a million Japanese troops. So why were nearly 200,000 Chinese soldiers standing idle in Vietnam? Moreover, the Chinese army in Vietnam "was not disciplined and reportedly engaged in selling opium and buying gold."[40] All these factors caused the Foreign Ministry to advocate pulling Chinese troops out of Vietnam.

Needless to say, the passive stance and actions toward France of the Executive Yuan and the Foreign Ministry differed sharply from the attitude on the ground of the Chinese military and the Yunnan regional commanders after the war. As we shall see, these differences had a huge impact on the course of Sino-French negotiations over the future of Vietnam.

*   *   *

Unlike the administrative and foreign affairs branches of the government in Chongqing, the Chinese military began to take a serious notice of developments in Vietnam after December 1944, when the China Theater army headquarters moved to Kunming in Yunnan Province. At the same time, the military mission in Vietnam was put directly under the command of the army headquarters. He Yingqin stayed in Chongqing as the army's commander in chief.[41] After the Vietnam Incident of March 1945, the Chinese military became truly alarmed. He Yingqin came to Kunming from Chongqing to organize troops for military intervention in Vietnam. The Fourth War Zone commander, Zhang Fakui, received orders to prepare to enter Vietnam for combat.

The army headquarters (and the Chinese military in general) had always taken a hard-line stance about disputes concerning Vietnam. In particular, they were dissatisfied with the French authorities in Vietnam for assisting the Japanese army in blocking the Sino-Vietnamese transport line as well as for seizing military supplies that China had left in storage in Vietnam.[42] Moreover, along the Sino-Vietnamese border, Chinese and French military units had frequently skirmished. Needless to say, by the end of the war the Chinese military was opposed to the return of French authority in Vietnam.[43]

On August 16, 1945, the commander of the French units marooned in Kunming, General Alessandri, met with Xiao Yisu, who was the Chinese army headquarters chief of staff. He asked the Chinese army headquarters to assist the French army in returning to Vietnam to accept the surrender of the Japanese army. Xiao Yisu stated that the matter had been decided by the Allied Supreme Command; accepting Japanese surrender was the responsibility of China and Britain. He had heard nothing about the involvement of the French army in the matter and therefore rejected Alessandri's demand.[44]

Alessandri also had discussions with Chen Xiuhe, who was the Chinese army headquarters Kunming office director. He wanted to send French airplanes to Hanoi to make contact with the Japanese authorities. Chen Xiuhe immediately reported this to He Yingqin, who ordered the Chinese air force in Kunming to seize the French airplanes so as to prevent them from flying to Vietnam secretly. Moreover, he ordered that while the Chinese army was accepting the surrender of the Japanese army in Vietnam, the French-Vietnamese army units in Yunnan Province must await further instructions. They should not be allowed to cross the Sino-Vietnamese border.[45]

In order to circumvent the tough stance of the Chinese military, the French appealed to the Chinese Foreign Ministry in Chongqing to support their position and obtained a document requesting the release of the French airplanes and permission for the French army to enter Vietnam. On August 18, Deputy Foreign Minister Wu Guozhen sent Chiang Kai-shek a telegram to that effect.[46] Resolution of the issue this way was beyond the authority of the Foreign Ministry, and their telegrams were ignored by Chinese army headquarters. In a long-distance phone call to Foreign Minister Wang Shijie, General He Yingqin emphasized the need to avoid being used by France as well as the need for various government bodies to hold to a united position.[47] On August 25, Chinese army headquarters sent a telegram to General Alessandri stating that he could attend as a private person the ceremony in which Chinese military authorities accepted the Japanese surrender. But French troops should stay at their current posts and await further instruction. They should not enter Vietnam without an order from the Chinese army headquarters.[48]

On September 1, the Chinese Foreign Ministry sent another telegram to He Yingqin repeating the request that French troops, commander Alessandri, and the airplanes be permitted to go to Vietnam. This time it added that the request had been reported to Chiang Kai-shek and had received his approval.[49] The Chinese army headquarters adjusted its attitude slightly but did not change its tough stance.

The Chinese military's stance at that time was as follows: French army commander Alessandri could accompany the Chinese and American commanders to Hanoi. He could attend the surrender ceremony as an observer. Alessandri could stay in Hanoi, but he could not set up a staff department or command. Movements of the French army were to obey the orders from the Chinese occupation army commander, Lu Han. After the Chinese army had occupied northern Vietnam, if the French army returned to Vietnam, its status would be a subordinate one, rather than as an occupation army. The Chinese army chief commander would not allow French officials to fly with French airplanes. Alessandri had to rely on the Americans for transport to Vietnam.[50]

Despite these restrictions, the French greatly valued the permission for Alessandri to attend the surrender ceremony in Hanoi. It signaled that France had fought Japan as a member of the Allies and thus was entitled to return to Indochina and restore French colonial rule. On September 11, Alessandri flew from Kunming to Kaiyuan, where the First Front Army was stationed. He asked to meet with Lu Han to talk about the trip to Vietnam. Lu Han kept him waiting for three days, and then on September 14 flew to Vietnam without meeting Alessandri.[51] Alessandri, understandably irritated with the Chinese authorities, reached Hanoi finally on September 19 in an American airplane.

Locally in Yunnan, popular opinion was even more hostile to France. For years the people of Yunnan had been angry about French discrimination against Chinese people in Vietnam and along the Kunming-Hanoi railway.[52] Local officials vigorously opposed the idea of France's return to Vietnam. In early August 1945, Governor Long Yun sent Chiang Kai-shek the following telegram:

After the Sino-Japanese War broke out, when China moved its national capital to Sichuan Province, the French authority in Vietnam declared neutrality. Then it allowed the Japanese army to land in Haiphong and to threaten southwestern China. Furthermore, it signed military and economic agreements with Japan. It failed to uphold justice and broke its promises. Essentially, it cooperated with Japan in doing harm to China. I heard that the French army that retreated to Yunnan Province is demanding to return to Vietnam. Newspapers report that the French government asked the United States to allow France to take part in the negotiations concerning the Far East. These two important issues are closely associated with the treatment of Vietnam in the future. I ask Your Excellency to reject the French demands. The First Front Army has received orders and advanced. It will reach Hanoi soon. In order to avoid conflicts, at present, China should not allow the French army stranded in Yunnan to return to Vietnam. French participation in the negotiations concerning the Far East would adversely affect China's policy toward Vietnam. I hope that you will reject the request from France.[53]

On August 16, Long Yun sent another telegram to Chiang Kai-shek, arguing that China must not allow France to continue its colonial rule over Vietnam. He argued that with the Allies' victory, now was the time to insist on Vietnamese independence. This option corresponded, Long maintained, to the American aim of bringing liberty to all and building world peace. Therefore, he suggested, the Chinese army should seize the opportunity of entering Vietnam and occupying northern Vietnam. "After China fully occupies northern Vietnam, China can cooperate with France in the economic realm, enough to mollify Charles de Gaulle."[54] Chiang Kai-shek was careful in his reply to Long Yun's telegram:

I entirely agree with your thoughtful opinion. However, the central government believes it inappropriate to reject the French army's request to return to Vietnam. It has therefore given its approval. France's request to join the negotiations concerning the Far East is not of significance. We will win if our army enters Hanoi and Haiphong first. Please do not worry.[55]

Chiang Kai-shek's words and the central government's decisions did not deter General Lu Han. His hatred of the French was deep-seated. During the war, Lu Han's troops often skirmished with the French-Vietnamese puppet army. Lu Han had refused to host the French-Vietnamese troops that had retreated into Yunnan in March 1945. He Yingqin sent a telegram asking Lu Han to follow the instructions of the central government. And he asked the Chinese army headquarters Kunming office director Chen Xiuhe to go to the First Front Army command at Kaiyuan to discuss the matter with Lu Han face to face. At this point, Lu Han agreed to arrange for the French-Vietnamese troops to stay in Mengzi.[56] But he continued to take a tough stance toward France, arguing with He Yingqin and seizing the airplane that General Alessandri had planned to use to fly to Vietnam. Lu Han posted bulletins to publicize Chiang Kai-shek's speeches that showed sympathy to Vietnamese people and supported Vietnam's independence.[57]

On September 19, 1945, Ling Qihan, the representative of the Advisory Team from the Foreign Ministry stationed in Vietnam, submitted a report, complaining about Lu Han's attitude:

Commander Lu Han is dissatisfied with the central government's stance. In particular, he is critical of the measures taken by the Foreign Ministry. There are great disagreements between the central government and local authority. It seems that an urgent telegram should be sent to Chief Commander He Yingqin at the army headquarters. We should ask He Yingqin to select a person who is familiar with Vietnam to go to the central government to explain the situation. Otherwise, even if the central government and France have reached agreement, the Yunnan government might not accept it. Then France would blame China for administrative discord and for not faithfully executing the agreement.[58]

On September 22, at the occupation army's headquarters in Hanoi, Lu Han met with the Vietnam Advisory Team from the Executive Yuan. He expressed great dissatisfaction with the fourteen articles in the "Principles for Occupying Military and Administrative Facilities in Vietnam" drafted by the Executive Yuan and mentioned earlier. He argued that these principles virtually gave up Vietnamese sovereignty to France. They differed greatly from the rules concerning acceptance of the Japanese surrender in Vietnam made by the army headquarters. He demanded that Advisory Team director Ling Qihan explain why the central government had changed the policy. And he asked Ling Qihan to go back to Chongqing immediately to ask for instructions from Chiang Kai-shek.[59] The central government often had conflicts with local authorities, so Lu Han's refusal to accept or implement many of the central government's policies concerning Vietnam was not unusual. Regardless of French diplomatic protests, the Chinese military and Foreign Ministry clearly were at odds over Vietnam policy. This led to disagreements between the central government and local authorities as well.

The Foreign Ministry tried repeatedly to get Chiang Kai-shek to intervene and instruct Lu Han to follow the central government's orders.[60] China was to maintain control of the Lao Cai–Hanoi–Haiphong railway but not oppose local authorities or prevent the French army from entering Vietnam.[61]

Throughout, Lu Han (backed by Chinese military authorities above him) remained firm, permitting General Alessandri to attend surrender ceremonies only in a private capacity.[62] On September 28, at the ceremony in the grand hall of the occupation army command headquarters, the national flags of China, the United States, Britain, and the Soviet Union were hung around the hall, but the French flag was not displayed. General Alessandri arrived ten minutes before the ceremony started. He protested and met with Lu Han in person to demand that the French national flag be hung in the grand hall. Lu Han rejected the demand, replying that France was neither among the four powers of the United Nations nor a signatory to the Potsdam Declaration. Alessandri became furious and left.[63] A few days later, the French ambassador in Chongqing submitted a formal protest.[64] Unfazed, at the end of the surrender ceremony, Lu Han made the following announcement describing his mission as the leader of the occupation forces:

I am not a conqueror or oppressor of Vietnam. Instead, I am a friend and liberator of the Vietnamese people. I am responsible for administrative and military affairs north of the sixteenth parallel north. . . . Before the Japanese invaders are sent home and before law and order is restored, I hold the supreme power, which I am willing to wield when necessary.[65]

Then, suddenly, Lu Han's anti-French resolve in Vietnam was undercut by events in Kunming. On October 3, 1945, Long Yun, Lu Han's patron and the governor of Yunnan, was overthrown by military forces loyal to Chiang Kai-shek.[66] The event stripped Lu Han of power, and the capacity to manage affairs in Vietnam. He had to retreat rapidly, drastically changing the nature of Sino-French negotiations over Vietnam.

On September 10, 1945, after meeting with the French deputy foreign minister, Wang Shijie proposed the following concerning Vietnam to Chiang Kai-shek:

I plan to inquire with the American secretary of state whether the United States will ask France to provide guarantees about Vietnam's future autonomy or independence. According to our analysis, China's demands toward Vietnam are the following:

1. Control of the part of the Yunnan-Vietnam railway located in China shall be transferred to China to compensate for China's losses in Vietnam.
2. Immigrant Chinese in Vietnam shall receive most-favored-nation treatment or the same treatment as French people.
3. Chinese goods exported or imported through the Yunnan-Vietnam railway shall all be free from duty.
4. .Haiphong shall be a free port.

With the American secretary of state, I believe that we can enter into negotiations with the French on the basis of the above points. I personally believe that now is an appropriate time to negotiate with France, as our army simply cannot stay in Vietnam for the long-term.[67]

The Executive Yuan director and foreign minister both proposed that the Chinese army be pulled out of Vietnam. With the overthrow of Long Yun, opposition from the Chinese military and local authorities decreased. After repeated appeals from Foreign Ministry officials, Chiang Kai-shek finally decided to act. In the evening of October 30, 1945, Chiang Kai-shek held a banquet for the French ambassador to China, who was leaving his post. With reference to Vietnam, Chiang Kai-shek stated that China was planning to withdraw its army from Vietnam and hoped that France could resolve disputes in Vietnam peacefully."[68] The Chinese government was now on a course to implement its policy toward Vietnam as outlined in the Foreign Ministry document above.

There was, of course, another factor at work behind the evolution of Chinese Vietnam policy and the triumph of the Foreign Ministry's point of view. During the war, the Nationalist government was willing to support Vietnam's independence movement. However, with the conclusion of the Sino-Japanese War, conflicts between the Nationalist and Communist Parties intensified. Vietnamese Communist Party leader Ho Chi Minh was too close to the Chinese Communist Party. Chiang Kai-shek was well aware that the French government was as opposed to Communism as his was. Moreover, a French Expeditionary Corps was on its way to Vietnam. The Chinese army was afraid of becoming entangled in French-Vietnamese conflicts. Thus, China reconsidered its policy toward France and its support of independence for Vietnam. After prolonged negotiations, France agreed to give up its privileges in China in exchange for the withdrawal of Chinese troops from Vietnam. On February 28, 1946, China and France signed the Sino-French agreement concerning Vietnam.

Chinese foreign minister Wang Shijie was relieved. In his diary on February 28, he wrote:

In the afternoon, the French ambassador, Meyrier, and I signed various Sino-French treaties, including the agreement concerning Vietnam. This has been my major achievement over the past few months. I did not suggest that the Chinese army should stay in Vietnam for long, and I proposed that the Chinese army should pull out of Vietnam as early as possible. And I insisted that France should sign a treaty with China to resolve the treatment of overseas Chinese in Vietnam, to make Haiphong a free port, and to return the part of the Yunnan-Vietnam railway located in China to China. All these items are listed in the Sino-French agreement. After signing the treaty, I made a speech to urge France and Vietnam to hold negotiations to resolve disputes peacefully. Meanwhile, I expressed to the French ambassador that China was willing to mediate the French-Vietnamese disputes.[69]

Not surprisingly, the Chinese military was unhappy and did not agree with Wang Shijie or approve of the agreement of February 28. It was dissatisfied with the Foreign Ministry's soft stance toward Vietnam and the French. When the actual transfer of military authority over Vietnam from China to France took place in the spring of 1946, difficulties ensued, including military clashes between Chinese and French troops in the Haiphong area.[70]

In short, the Chinese Nationalist government's immediate postwar policy toward Vietnam was beset with internal contradictions. From the surrender of Japanese troops in northern Vietnam to the departure of Lu Han, there were serious disagreements between the Executive Yuan and the Foreign Ministry on one side and military commanders at both central and regional levels on the other. A major problem was the semiautonomous military power wielded by Long Yun and his protégé, Lu Han. Long and Lu saw the occupation of northern Vietnam as an extension of their sphere of influence and as a source of wealth. At one point, 200,000 Chinese troops (mostly from Yunnan) were in northern Vietnam. Chiang Kai-shek was also not interested in promoting an independence movement led by the Communist Ho Chi Minh. In early October 1945, Chiang was able to defeat Long Yun militarily and establish his authority over Chinese troops in Yunnan and northern Vietnam. China thereafter spoke with a single voice, and its policy moved in a direction more accommodating to French interests. The Chinese and French reached an agreement on February 28, 1946, in which France gave up concession areas and extraterritorial rights in Shanghai, Tianjin, Hankou, and Guangzhou. In exchange, China agreed to withdraw troops from northern Vietnam, ceding occupational authority to the French. The Chinese military was unhappy and at times clashed with French troops during its withdrawal. The policy of ceding authority over northern Vietnam to France would have an enormous impact on future developments in Vietnam.

13 The 1952 Treaty of Peace between China and Japan

HANS VAN DE VEN

When the Sino-Japanese War ended, the situation in East Asia was more like that of Europe after World War I than after World War II. After World War I, the peacemakers who gathered in Paris in 1919 had to deal with the collapse of Austria-Hungary and the Ottoman Empire, the emergence of many new nations in Europe, and a revolution that had succeeded in Russia and threatened to spread west. They had to do so while economies across the continent had collapsed with the result that substantial segments of Europe's population lived in deep poverty. Many people suffered from malnutrition and some faced starvation. In addition, the barbarity of World War I had shattered Europe's nineteenth-century pride and confidence. No one wanted to go back to the prewar status quo.[1]

The questions that World War II raised in East and Southeast Asia were at least as complicated, and perhaps even more so. When on August 15 Japan accepted the demand, made in the Potsdam Declaration of July 26, 1945, for an unconditional surrender to the Allies, the one thing then clear was that Japan's bid to establish its supremacy over East and Southeast Asia was over. But many other questions remained: What would happen to the British, French, and Dutch Empires? If, for instance, the French empire were to be wound up, what countries would retake its place, and what would be their borders? What would be the role of the United States, drawn deep into Asian politics because of the Pacific War? Or, for that matter, the Soviet Union, which occupied China's Northeast (Manchuria) in the last weeks of the war? If the European economy was in tatters in 1919, its populations had the skills, and its societies, the institutions to make recovery possible, even though that would not prove easy. World War II had ravaged the economies of East and Southeast Asia, with a number of areas in China, Vietnam, and India suffering severe famines. Political and trading systems had collapsed, currencies had become worthless, and much of what little industry there had been was destroyed, all combining to make economic recovery extraordinarily difficult. World War II had empowered Communist and left-wing national liberation movements across the region, with the result that civil war threatened in several places. The difficulties facing those who had to make decisions about Asia's future were inhumanly complex.

The treaties that formally ended World War II in Asia were the 1951 San Francisco Peace Treaty and the 1952 Treaty of Peace between the Republic of China and Japan. Although their titles echoed the Versailles Peace Treaty, they derived not from any optimism about laying a secure basis for a long-lasting peace. The Paris model had ceased to command respect; some of its provisions were thought to have contributed to the outbreak of World War II, including the severe reparations imposed on Germany. In reality, the treaties resulted from the United States' effort to establish a US-dominated Cold War front line along Asia's mainland.

Yet the two treaties have proved durable, putting into place the essential structure of international relations that continues to prevail in East Asia. At the same time, many of the issues that bedevil those relations can be traced back to the two treaties, including the unresolved issue of the status of Taiwan, the disputes about the Senkaku, or Diaoyutai, Islands, the question of whether Japan has sufficiently apologized for its wartime misdeeds, and the continuing demands for Japan to make more war reparations. If it is clear that the treaties have bequeathed on East Asia a series of significant problems, it is also the case that their limited ambition and their purposeful ambiguity has at times proved productive. They have, for instance, been able to accommodate the United States' abandonment of its Cold War strategy in East Asia and its normalization of relations with the People's Republic of China (PRC).

The exercise to excavate the debates and diplomacy that led to the conclusion of the two treaties, as I will do in this essay, is useful for a number of reasons. First, it allows us to recover the differing visions at the time of East Asia's postwar shape. Second, even though Chiang Kai-shek had a weak hand, in the negotiations leading up to the signing of the Taipei Treaty, he was able to assert his view of a China-centered East Asia. The Taipei Treaty formed the culmination of Chiang's strenuous wartime efforts, illustrated in many chapters in this volume, to give China a central position in international and East Asian affairs. In the long run, it would of course be the PRC rather than the Republic of China that profited from Chiang's endeavors. Finally, important issues that bedevil diplomatic relations in East Asia today, including the status of Taiwan, have their origin in the way that peace was formally concluded. The two treaties have been largely ignored by historians. Yet they were, and continue to be, constitutive of the East Asian political order and hence deserve far greater attention.

A Cold War Treaty

Following the victory of the Chinese Communists in China in 1949 and the outbreak of the Korean War the year after, US policy makers came to the conclusion that Communism in East Asia was best contained by ending the US occupation of Japan, firmly tying Japan to the United States, and arranging a series of interlocking agreements about mutual defense and economic cooperation with as many East and Southeast Asian states as it could corral. John Foster Dulles was the man in charge of making this structure come about, which he did during an intensive year of diplomatic activity, while at the same time pioneering shuttle diplomacy. Dulles would become US secretary of state in the Eisenhower administration, when he advocated a policy of confronting Communism aggressively, including in Vietnam. However, under President Truman, Dulles's position was that of "special consultant to the secretary of state," Dean Acheson. US policy at that time had the more limited aim of stabilizing the Korean War at the thirty-eighth parallel, avoiding armed conflict with the People's Republic of China, and creating a "US defensive line" consisting of "Japan-Ryukyus-Philippines-Australia and New Zealand."[2]

A peace treaty that ended the state of war between Japan and the countries of East and Southeast Asia with which it had been at war and that restored sovereignty to Japan was fundamental to the United States' strategy. In early January 1951, Dulles formulated the following principles for the San Francisco Peace Treaty:[3] it should end the state of war between Japan and the Allies; force Japan to renounce sovereignty over Korea, Taiwan, and Penghu; agree to a UN trusteeship for the United States over Liuqiu (Ryukyu Islands and Okinawa); require Japan to apply for UN membership; and because that application might be blocked by the Soviets, contain a clause requiring Japan to adhere to Article 2 of the UN Charter, that is, to use only peaceful means to resolve conflicts with other countries. Dulles, who had attended the Paris Peace Conference, insisted that Japan should not be compelled to make war reparations.

The reason that China was not represented at San Francisco was because the United States and Britain, its helpmate in convening the peace conference, could not agree on whether Beiping should speak for China, as Britain wanted, or whether Taipei should do so, as was the hope of the United States. Britain had recognized the People's Republic in China, in part because considerable sympathy for the Chinese Communists existed among South and Southeast Asian states, and these were important to

Britain's efforts to build up its Commonwealth and so rescue something from its prewar empire. As the United States recognized, the Nationalists, who had fled to Taiwan, were generally unpopular, "seriously complicating," as one National Security Council paper stated, the United States' aim of denying Taiwan to the People's Republic, as was part of its strategy.[4] Britain suggested as a solution the inclusion of an accession clause in the San Francisco Peace Treaty and leaving it to the Far Eastern Committee to decide which China should be allowed to sign the treaty. The Far Eastern Committee had been established by the Allied foreign ministers meeting in Moscow in December 1945 to oversee the implementation of the Potsdam Declaration in Japan. That proposal was unacceptable to the United States because it was likely that it would be outvoted in that committee.

The US-UK disagreements about Chinese representation and the status of Taiwan nearly doomed the treaty. Britain argued that "a formula should be worked out for deciding what should be done with Formosa and Pescadores, rather than leaving the matter up in the air."[5] Dulles rejected that and stated that he was not willing to go any further than to leave open the status of Taiwan and Penghu: "At present we were only providing that Japan should relinquish its claim to Formosa and that we were not attempting to indicate what the final settlement of the Formosa problem should be."[6] When Britain continued to insist that the PRC should at least be consulted and broached the idea of convening its own peace conference in conjunction with Commonwealth countries, the United States threatened to break off negotiations. Faced with the United States' strong stance, Britain agreed to accept that "the treaty should merely require Japanese renunciation of sovereignty, leaving future status to be decided later."[7] The issue would continue to sour US-UK relations. Following the signing of the San Francisco Peace Treaty, the British foreign minister, Herbert Morrison, and Dulles flew back to Washington together. Morrison told Dulles that Britain would not ratify the treaty if anything "was done to crystallize the Japanese position toward China before it came into force."[8] Here then is the treaty origin for the idea that the status of Taiwan would remain unresolved.

US officials thought that Labour prime minister Attlee was "distrustful of US influence in Japan."[9] That was true, but Attlee was also genuinely concerned about the intensifying Cold War and was seeking ways to dampen it, for instance by involving the Far Eastern Committee. In addition, as the US ambassador to London, Walter Gifford, commented, "Britain wanted a Treaty of greater detail which faces up to all the issues."[10] It demanded the inclusion of a clause on war guilt, as normal practice for peace treaties, and it wanted Japanese gold reserves to be used for war reparations. It also argued that Japanese assets in Swiss banks should be seized, as these consisted of UK funds that had been handed to the Red

Cross for the relief of POWs and civilian internees in Japanese camps but which Japan had never passed on.[11] Britain further called for the destruction of "excess" Japanese shipping and the proscription of "undesirable" political parties.[12]

Attlee was not alone in his opposition to the US approach to the peace treaty. On August 23, 1951, the US chargé d'affaires to India, M. K. Kirpilani, informed the US State Department that India had decided to decline the United States' and the United Kingdom's invitation to attend the conference because of the United States' "continued occupation of the Ryukyu and Bonin Islands, failure to restore Formosa to China, and provision that US troops stay as part of a US-Japanese defensive agreement."[13] K. P. S. Menon argued in the Indian cabinet that India would "build up considerable good will" with Beiping if it refused to attend the peace conference and that "the whole of South Asia and the Far East would acclaim India," including, eventually, Japan.[14] Menon served as high commissioner to Britain between 1947 and 1952, after which he became the head of the Indian delegation to the United Nations. Jawaharlal Nehru, the prime minister, indicated that he wanted a separate peace conference involving only Asian countries,[15] something that made Britain's idea of a peace treaty organized by the Commonwealth a nonstarter. India signed a separate treaty with Japan on June 9, 1952, in which both parties were treated with strict equality.[16]

Dulles's insistence that Japan should not pay war reparations provoked widespread anger. Dulles was motivated by the example of the damage done by the war reparations imposed on Germany after World War I and the dire straits of the Japanese economy. Dulles refused to go any further than requiring Japan to hand back property acquired illegally in a given country during the war and to "make available the services of the Japanese people" to assist countries to repair the damage done by its forces, provided that these countries would provide the necessary raw materials and that exchange rate costs were carried by them.[17] The Philippines government believed this approach to war reparations was demeaning, as it implied that the Japanese were more highly skilled than its own citizens and because it would allow Japan to maintain a substantial presence in the Philippines and so "prolong Philippine colonial dependency."[18]

The Nationalists in Taiwan also objected to relinquishing claims for reparations. A Nationalist memorandum to Dulles stated that "the Chinese people suffered and sacrificed longer and more extensively than the people of any other invaded country. It would be entirely consonant with the principles of justice to insist upon adequate war reparations."[19] However, the reality was that, driven from mainland China, the Nationalists were in no position to deliver any reparations paid by Japan to its victims living there. Making a virtue out of necessity, Taipei indicated that it was willing to waive reparations "provided that other governments do likewise." Its concern was that if China was the only country that waived reparations, it would be seen as having a lesser status than the other Allies. Taipei also insisted that the US agree to assist China in recovering Japanese war loot from Japan and to transfer to China "property and assets in Japan that belonged to the puppet regime of 'Manchukuo' and the Bank of Taiwan."

The San Francisco Peace Treaty was signed on December 8, 1951, at the War Memorial Opera House, after a brief conference. Its main provisions were that Japan abandoned any claim to Korea, Taiwan, the Penghu Islands, Hong Kong, the Kuril Islands, the Spratly Islands, and Sakhalin. The Bonin and Ryukyu Islands were placed under US trusteeship. No mention was made of the Senkaku Islands, or the Diaoyudao Islands as the PRC government refers to them or the Diaoyutai Islands as the Taiwanese government does, an apparent oversight, with the result that they have become a major flashpoint in disputes between Taiwan, the PRC, and Japan. The treaty affirmed that Japan accepted the judgments of the Tokyo War Crimes Tribunal and committed Japan to adhere to the UN Charter.[20] While the treaty did not require Japan to make war reparations, except in the case of maltreated prisoners of war, it did provide for the confiscation of Japanese government, business, and private assets in the countries it had occupied.

The Soviet Union was represented at the San Francisco Peace Conference by Andrei Gromyko, the Soviet representative to the United Nations. Gromyko attended the conference to put on record the Soviet Union's objections to it. He called Dulles a "warmonger," argued that the treaty could not be regarded as a general peace treaty because the Soviet Union had not been consulted, dismissed it for turning Japan into a US military base, and attacked it for the injustice it did to China.[21] Zhou Enlai, the PRC's foreign minister, denounced it on August 15—the sixth anniversary of Japan's surrender—along similar lines, adding that the failure of the treaty to return sovereignty over Taiwan to China amounted to the US occupation of part of China's "sovereign territory."[22r]

These criticisms were exaggerated, but their essential argument was right: the San Francisco Peace Treaty was a Cold War treaty, designed to ensure the United States' dominance in the western Pacific. Only forty-eight countries signed it, consisting mostly of US allies in Europe, the Middle East, and South America, not all of whom, or even many, had actually fought Japan. The treaty ensured the diplomatic defeat, for the moment, of alternative visions of Asia's future, including Britain's version based on its Commonwealth, India's one of an Asia of independent nonaligned countries, and Moscow's and Beiping's version of a Communist Asia. It restored sovereignty to Japan, thus providing clarity about its future, but it also left a great many issues undecided, including the status of Taiwan. Together with the Korean War, it put in place the Cold War structure that in many ways continues to dominate East Asia's international relations.

The Cairo Declaration

So far, we have not heard much about Chinese visions of Asia's postwar future, unsurprisingly so given that both Taipei and Beiping were excluded from the San Francisco Peace Conference. A good deal has been written about the foreign policy of the Chinese Communists, who were fundamentally opposed to, and paranoid about, Western influence in China. They allied China to the Soviet Union to secure Soviet protection, consolidate China's revolution, learn from Soviet industrial and managerial models, and profit from Soviet aid and advisers, while at the same time restricting its influence in China.[23] What the Nationalists wanted has been studied much less, on the assumption that they had ceased to matter very much. However, Nationalist thinking was not as irrelevant as all that; it shaped the San Francisco Peace Treaty, and of course also the Taipei Treaty, in quite fundamental ways.

At the heart of Nationalist thinking was the restoration of a China-centered Asia, a goal to which the Nationalists under Chiang Kai-shek dedicated considerable energy during World War II. Chiang Kai-shek articulated this view at the Cairo Conference of November 1943, the only Allied wartime conference in which the Nationalists participated. The conference took place November 22 to 27, 1943, and dealt mainly with two issues, namely Allied operations in 1944 and postwar arrangements for East Asia. The first issue was largely decided by Churchill, Roosevelt, and Stalin during meetings they had in Tehran from November 28 to December 1 and where Chiang Kai-shek was not present. While afterward Roosevelt and Churchill returned to Cairo for further discussions, Chiang was by then on his way back to China. During the first round of discussions at Cairo, Roosevelt cultivated Chiang Kai-shek, to Churchill's chagrin, because he believed that China should become the pillar of the postwar order in East Asia. An examination of the Cairo Declaration and the discussions Chiang Kai-shek had with Roosevelt at a time that thinking about postwar Asia was beginning to take shape at the highest levels of government, is useful in excavating the indirect but substantial impact of the Nationalists on the postwar order in East Asia.

Chiang Kai-shek's diary gives some indication of Chiang's thinking prior to and during the Cairo Conference about his views of Asia's future, the appropriate way to handle Japan after its defeat, and the war reparations that Japan should be compelled to make. Chiang's diary makes clear that he possessed clear views about China's postwar borders and about how East Asia should be reconstituted after the war. While he envisioned the windup of European empires, he naturally did not want to do anything to undermine the alliance on which victory over Japan depended.

On November 3, Chiang discussed for the first time in his diary in detail the items he intended to raise with Roosevelt and Churchill at Cairo. These included issues of immediate military importance, such as the idea that the United States, the United Kingdom, and China should organize a joint military staff. With respect to the treatment of Japan after the war, Chiang wrote that "China should take over all public and private property acquired by Japan in China (on territory occupied since the 18 September [1931] Incident)."[24] He also wanted acceptance of his belief that Japan should hand over most of its military materiel, including naval vessels and airplanes, to China. Finally, he planned to demand the restoration to China of sovereignty over Hong Kong and Kowloon, in return for which he wrote that he would agree to turn Hong Kong into a free port.[25] At this point, then, for Chiang the Japanese occupation of China's Northeast was the important historical dividing line. Territories occupied by Japan subsequently were to be restored to China. He made no mention of either Korea or Taiwan.

A subsequent briefing paper of the staff office of the Military Affairs Commission was more explicit about China's territorial demands. It insisted that China should gain control of Taiwan, Penghu, Lüshun, Dalian, the South Manchurian and China Eastern Railroads, and Liuqiu. With respect to the latter, the paper added that Liuqiu could be internationalized or be made into a demilitarized zone. Chiang appears to have considered this and to have decided that he should not insist on the return of Liuqiu to China because "the historical position of Liuqiu and Taiwan in our history is different. Liuqiu is a kingdom, and its status is similar to Korea's, so I have decided not to raise the issue of Liuqiu. However, the independence of Korea is something that I should raise."[26] Chiang from then on held to that position. On November 21, he noted in his diary that "the Northeast [Manchuria] as well as Taiwan and Penghu should be restored to China. Japanese public and private property in China and merchant vessels should be used as part of Japanese war reparations."[27] He added that he would avoid raising issues sensitive to his wartime partners. "If the United States raises the issue of Hong Kong and Kowloon, Tibet, and overseas Chinese, I will state our position of principle, but I will not engage in debate."[28] It appears that out of concern for maintaining good relations with Britain, he dropped his demands about Hong Kong and Kowloon.

At Cairo, Chiang Kai-shek and Roosevelt talked for nearly four hours on November 23. In line with the position he had adopted, Chiang argued, according to his diary, "with respect to territorial issues, the four eastern provinces [Manchuria/the three eastern provinces/the Northeast], Taiwan, and Penghu must be returned to China."[29] He asked Roosevelt to support his proposal for the future independence of Korea and Vietnam. As Wang Hui has made clear, Roosevelt asked Chiang a number of times whether China wanted possession of Liuqiu.[30] Chiang declined, arguing, according to his diary, that Liuqiu should be administered jointly by the United States and China, as "Liuqiu had come to belong to Japan before the 1894–1895 Sino-Japanese War" and also "to put the United States at ease"; Chiang probably believed that the United States wanted control over an island in the western Pacific.[31] Chiang and Roosevelt also discussed the occupation of Japan. Chiang rejected Roosevelt's proposal that China take the lead role, arguing that China lacked sufficient forces.[32] While that was true, having America lead the Allied occupation served Chiang's purpose of keeping the United States involved in East Asia after the war.

Chiang and Roosevelt discussed other topics, including the future con-stitution (国体) of Japan. Although the United States wanted the abolition of the imperial system, Chiang argued that the issue "should be resolved by progressive newly awakened elements in Japan" after the war, because "it was not good policy for a victorious country to meddle with a country's basic constitution" and because "the Japanese imperial system has taken on a natural position in the psychology of the Japanese people. Westerners do not necessarily understand this, but Chinese, who similarly are East-erners, have a rather better comprehension of this."[33] This stance, as well as Britain's reluctance to support the idea that Japan should become a republic, informed the Potsdam Declaration, which stipulated that "we do not intend that the Japanese shall be enslaved as a race or destroyed as a nation" and called for a government "established . . . in accordance with the freely expressed will of the Japanese people."[34]

At Cairo, then, Chiang Kai-shek acted as the spokesman for the nation-alist aspirations not just of China but also for the populations of Vietnam and Korea, and even Japan, and spoke as if China should have a promi-nent say in the affairs of all countries in the region. There was something ironic in this: it was as if the less power the Nationalists in Chongqing possessed, the larger the international role Chiang Kai-shek claimed. As we shall see, during the Taipei Treaty negotiations, Chiang would prove more concerned about maintaining that position than the precise words used to describe the status of Taiwan. Chiang's position was, of course, quite rational. If not by 1945, then certainly by 1950 the Republic of China could claim a significant international role only on the basis of its symbolic status as having led China's resistance to Japan in World War II. That status brought with it such important benefits as a seat in the UN Security Council.

In justifying China's territorial claims, Chiang implicitly articulated an important historical view. In declining sovereignty over the Liuqiu Islands,

Chiang argued that Japan's *sonderweg,* its departure from a normal developmental path that culminated in its brutal militarism, had begun with the 1894–1895 Sino-Japanese War. Finally, in insisting that Westerners did not understand the Japanese but that he as an Easterner did, Chiang alluded to a fundamental commonality in Japanese and Chinese cultures, even though Japan and China were engaged in a war to the finish.

No one reading the Cairo Declaration could have had any inkling of this background. All it stated was that "Japan shall be stripped of all the islands in the Pacific which she has seized or occupied since the beginning of the First World War in 1914, and that all territories that Japan has stolen from the Chinese, such as Manchuria, Formosa, and the Pescadores, shall be restored to the Chinese" and that Korea "shall become free and independent."[35] The declaration is as remarkable for its silences as for what it did say. At a time when maintaining a unified stance was of the utmost importance to the Allies, it is unsurprising that differences were covered up. However, sparse as it is, the Cairo Declaration, including the use of "stolen," a word that likely would not have been used if Western lawyers alone had drafted it, reveal that Chiang Kai-shek's thinking helped to give it shape. It is also clear that the position Chiang articulated was a compromise between his fundamental views about the proper place of China in Asia, his postwar strategy for realizing them, and the more immediate aim of maintaining good relations with his wartime allies.

The Taipei Negotiations

We are now in a position to consider the Taipei Treaty in the international, textual, and historical contexts in which it was concluded and to compare it to the San Francisco Peace Treaty. Important differences existed between the two. If at San Francisco Japan was prepared to be treated as a defeated country, in Taipei it acted as if it saw the Nationalists as just the local rulers of a small territory with which it was prepared to establish neighborly relations but nothing more. Like Britain, Japan had every reason to be concerned about the United States' Cold War strategy. Before the war, Japan had prospered economically because of its investment in and trade with China and Southeast Asia. If the Cold War fault line would be drawn as the United States proposed, Japan would have to find alternative markets elsewhere. At the same time, Japan could ill afford to alienate the United States. To sign a treaty with Taipei as a local government appeared to offer a way of satisfying the Americans while at the same time avoiding recognizing the Nationalists as representing all of China, thus keeping open the possibility of developing relations with mainland China. This approach would prove too clever by half. Because of the Cold War, Japan would not be able to restore relations with the PRC until the 1970s, while at the same time it gained itself a reputation of refusing to face up to its wartime behavior.

The Taipei Treaty was brevity itself. It consisted of fourteen short articles without subclauses. Attached were a protocol, stated to be an integral part of the treaty, and three diplomatic notes between Yeh Kung-ch'ao, representing the Republic of China, and Isao Kawada, the Japanese plenipotentiary. Besides stating that Japan relinquished its rights to Taiwan and Penghu, the treaty proper declared that "the state of war between the Republic of China and Japan" would terminate when the treaty came into force; it declared "null and void" all treaties between Japan and China concluded before December 9, 1941 (the war having formally been declared on December 8 in Asia); it committed both parties "to be guided by Article 2 of the UN Charter"; it committed both Japan and the Republic of China to conclude agreements about maritime trade, civil air transport, and fisheries; and finally it declared that the inhabitants of Taiwan and Penghu (the Pescadores island chain) would be regarded as nationals of the Republic of China. The main point of the protocol was that China waived "as a sign of magnanimity and goodwill" its claim on compensation for war damages. The most important diplomatic note was a statement by Yeh confirming Isao's "understanding" that the treaty was "applicable to all the territories which are now, or which may hereafter be under the control of [the Republic of China's] Government."[36]

The San Francisco Peace Treaty bound Japan to sign a peace treaty with any country with which it had been at war and which wanted such a treaty. That did not necessarily compel Japan to sign a peace treaty with the Nationalists, as their defeat by the Chinese Communists could be read as meaning that they had lost the right to represent China. As we have seen, Britain pressed the United States not to compel Japan to sign a peace treaty with Taipei but to let it make up its own mind. Prime Minister Yoshida Shigeru resisted US pressure to choose Taipei. At San Francisco, Shigeru told Dean Rusk, the US assistant secretary of state for Far Eastern affairs, that "he had been trying to think of some "contribution" Japan might make to the common cause of bringing peace and stability to East Asia . . . as a repayment for the enormous generosity and forbearance the Americans had shown during the occupation."[37] Rusk concluded that Yoshida was preparing him for a Japanese decision not to sign with Taipei. [38]During debates in the Japanese Diet about the issue, Yoshida faced pressure from pro-Communist Diet members as well as business interests to develop good relations with Beiping. He stated that "Japan has been given the right to determine which partner to sign a peace treaty with. Although we have that right, we must be careful . . . not to intervene in China's internal affairs," as this would be a form of "aggression."[39]

The intervention of Dulles was necessary to end Yoshida's procrastination. On December 13, 1951, he handed Yoshida a memorandum which stated that "the US Senate, Congress, and American people generally will insistently want to know whether Japanese Government intends to pursue foreign policies in Asia generally compatible with those of the United States."[40] He then went on to say that the Nationalist government "is recognized as the lawful government of China by the United States; . . . it has a seat, voice, and vote in the UN, including a Security Council vote over Japanese prospective membership; it has jurisdiction over Formosa and a large Chinese army. . . . It is suggested that Japanese interest might best be served if Japanese Government were to negotiate with National Government." This was clear as a bell.

Besides the United States' Cold War strategy, Dulles had two other reasons to push Yoshida to begin negotiations with Taipei. The first was the US Senate, which, mobilized by the China lobby, threatened to decline to ratify the San Francisco Peace Treaty unless Japan concluded a peace treaty with Taipei. Furthermore, Chiang Kai-shek, understandably livid about his exclusion from the San Francisco Peace Conference, contemplated denouncing the San Francisco Peace Treaty. He wrote in his diary that if Japan did not sign a peace treaty with Taipei, "China will continue to exert all its rights in Japan."[41] That meant that it would continue to act as an occupying power of Japan, a status it had as a member of the Committee of Far Eastern Affairs that formally oversaw MacArthur's activities, although he paid little attention to it. That would have been awkward. Yoshida replied to Dulles on December 24, agreeing to enter into negotiations with Taipei for a bilateral treaty "applicable in all territories which are now, or which may hereafter be, under the control of the Republic of China."[42] If Japan could not avoid a treaty with Taipei, it wanted to make sure that the treaty's applicability was limited to the areas the Nationalists actually controlled.

The Taipei negotiations lasted a relatively short time but were nonetheless acrimonious and at several times came close to collapse. The overt points of contention were the name of the treaty, the formulation to be used to describe its territorial scope, the wording of China's agreement to forego war reparations, and definitions of the nature of the war. At the start of the negotiations, Yeh Kung-ch'ao submitted a draft treaty that was essentially a copy of the San Francisco Peace Treaty, an approach that had been discussed first with the United States and had its approval. It included statements about the independence of Korea, the Japanese relinquishment of the Kuriles and part of Sakhalin, Japan's agreement to carry out the judgments reached by the Tokyo War Crimes Tribunal, the restoration to China of Taiwan and Penghu, Japan's agreement to give up all its rights and possessions in China, and the restoration of sovereignty to the

people of Japan. Had this approach been accepted by Japan, the Nationalists would have been seen to be acting as one of the victorious allies and
representing all of China.

The Japanese rejected Yeh's approach. When asked in the Diet whether
"the government wanted to link arms with the Taiwanese government
already rejected by the Chinese people," Yoshida replied that "the government sees the Taiwan government as having effective authority and
wants a treaty with it merely in pursuit of our good neighbor policy."[43] He
remarked, "At present the Taiwan government holds actual power over
some regions, and it is on the basis of this reality that we will sign a treaty
about peaceful relations with them."[44] To Japan, the treaty would be no
more than an agreement with a local power about some practical issues
such as trade.

Yoshida's attitude dismayed Chiang Kai-shek. He noted in his diary on
January 16 that Yoshida's letter to Dulles "was probably written for the
deliberations in the US Senate about the multilateral peace treaty; once
they approve it, we cannot be sure that he will not delay our treaty forever.
Yoshida is a slippery bureaucrat without any higher ambition for the cooperation of the peoples of East Asia. We should have no illusions."[45] On February 19, he wrote, "It is truly detestable that Yoshida continues to state
in the Diet that with the Taiwan government there will be a limited local
treaty."[46] Chiang saw Japan's attitude as evidence that it had not reformed
its militarist ways. "Japan's attitude toward the peace treaty is aimed at
destroying the status of China, it insults the Chinese government, and it
seeks to use this peace conference to wreck China's status and our rights
as one of the Allies."[47] "They are flaunting their position, deploying once
more their threatening attitudes. The old habit of insulting China—they
cannot change it."[48]

The different views about the treaty led to trouble even before the negotiations began. At a meeting on February 9, 1951, between Yeh and the
head of the Japanese Overseas Office in Taipei, Yeh was told that Japan
objected to calling the treaty a peace treaty because Yoshida's letter to
Dulles had provoked strenuous opposition in Japan and that in any case
"his letter had not mentioned the words 'peace treaty.'"[49] In addition, Isao's
letter of credentials could not be changed, it was argued, because Emperor
Hirohito had signed it.[50] Chiang agreed to proceed with the negotiations
without a change to Isao's letter of credentials after Kimura promised that
Japan would "voluntarily" produce a letter explaining that Isao had the
powers to sign a treaty of peace. At the same time, he drew up guidelines
for Yeh, which insisted that the treaty should "not injure our status as one
of the Allies" and "should not infringe our rule over Taiwan," while it also
should not contain anything detracting from the usefulness of Taiwan and
Penghu as a base from which to retake the mainland.[51]

At their first meeting, Yeh and Isao agreed in public to refer to the negotiations in Chinese as "the Chinese-Japanese Peace Conference" (中日和会), in Japanese as "the Conference for a Sino-Japanese Treaty," and in English as "the Sino-Japanese Peace Conference."[52] The issue of the title of the treaty remained subject to controversy almost to the end. On March 4, Chiang stated in his diary that he suspected that Japan wanted "to wait for the emergence of a third government in China and to recognize that," while "seeing Taiwan as a newly emerged country like India," with whom it would have a "treaty of friendship."[53] The issue was finally put to bed when on March 12 Isao agreed as Japanese plenipotentiary that the treaty would be called "The Peace Treaty between the Republic of China and Japan" (中华民国与日本间之和平条约).[54]

Yet Japan was determined not to be treated as a defeated country that was responsible for the war. At a first informal meeting on February 23, Isao stated that "between the draft treaty submitted by the Chinese side and what the Japanese side expected . . . there are clear differences."[55] He explained that the Japanese would be hugely disappointed if the "clauses with relevance to a defeated country appeared in the text" as in the San Francisco Peace Treaty.[56] In conformity with this stance, in his opening remarks at the first meeting of the negotiations, Isao was not willing to go further than to offer regrets for the war, without making clear which country was responsible. He stated that "in the past there repeatedly have occurred unfortunate incidents between China and Japan not in accord with the genuine desire of the citizens of both countries," a situation which he declared to be "regrettable" (惋惜).[57] Here, then, is one origin for the still highly contentious issue of Japan's apology for the war.

Chiang ordered Yeh to make clear to Isao that "China suffered fourteen years of aggression by Japan. It lost 30 million lives and an inestimable amount of public and private property was destroyed. The wording and clauses proposed by the Japanese [for the treaty] are, however, an even greater insult than their fourteen years of military invasion. . . . If the Nationalist government could be brought down by bullying, then the Republic would have been destroyed by Japan thirty years ago."[58] At the conference, Yeh reiterated these points in a long tirade, ending with the assertion that Japan's aggression had resulted in the Communist conquest of China.[59] However, he then went on to say that the Nationalists were in fact willing "not to mention the issue [of war guilt] in consideration of the feelings of the Japanese people,"[60] as long as a peace treaty was signed and Japan recognized the Republic of China's status as one of the victorious allies. For Chiang, that was the critical point.

Given Japan's stance, it is unsurprising that Japan objected to acknowledging a moral duty to make war reparations. Yeh's draft treaty followed the San Francisco Peace Treaty by including a clause that recognized

Japan's obligation to offer compensation for the "damages and suffering" (损害与痛苦) it had inflicted, but then waived them.[61] Isao rejected
this, arguing that "stipulations regarding reparations do not belong in the
treaty,"[62] because "the treaty between China and Japan must have as its
objective future good relations between the two countries and friendly
feelings between our citizens."[63] Isao remarked,

We have always believed that we have left huge assets behind in the mainland of
your country. In US dollar terms, their value reaches to several billion. To use
these assets for making compensation is enough. Your demand for service reparations contradicts your repeated declarations about a policy of generosity toward
Japan.[64]

Following a good deal of discussion, the two sides agreed to include
in the treaty the statement that "as a sign of magnanimity and goodwill
toward the Japanese people, the Republic of China voluntarily waives the
benefit of the services to be made available by Japan pursuant to Article
14(a)1 of the San Francisco Peace Treaty."

The definition of the territorial scope of the treaty was unsurprisingly
one of the most difficult issues faced by the negotiators of both sides in
Taipei. One point of debate was whether the relevant statement would be
part of the treaty proper, as the Japanese wanted, or whether it would be
handled in an exchange of notes, as the Nationalists wanted, and as did
happen. The precise wording was debated at length. The Chinese proposed

The Treaty of Peace signed today between the Republic of China and Japan shall
be applicable to all the territories under the sovereignty of each party. It is, however, understood that in view of the fact that a part of the territories under the
sovereignty of the Republic of China is at the present time under the occupation of
the Communists, the terms of the treaty shall, in respect of the Republic of China,
be applicable to all the territories which are now and may hereafter be brought
again under the control of the government of the Republic of China."[65]

It was the English version of the text that was discussed because it was
regarded as authoritative.

If the phrasing quoted above had been used, it would have meant that
Japan explicitly recognized the Republic of China's sovereignty, not just
over Taiwan and Penghu but all of China. However, Isao rejected the
above phrasing. He offered two counterproposals, one of which made the
treaty applicable to "all the areas and all the territories under Chinese
sovereignty which are now or may hereafter be under the control of the
government of the Republic of China."[66] This acknowledged that Taiwan
was Chinese sovereign territory, but it also left open an interpretation that
the Republic of China merely controlled it rather than being its legitimate
government. The second appended the explicit statement that "nothing
in this note shall be construed to involve the issue of the sovereignty of

the Republic of China."[67] Chiang Kai-shek was not particularly bothered about the phrasing of this clause. On March 25, he recorded in his diary: "I convened a meeting of the Small Group for the peace treaty with Japan. As to the words for sovereignty [*zhuquan*] for the area to which the treaty is to be applicable, my view is that as long as Taiwan is regarded as our territory [*lingtu*], we do not have to argue much about the precise choice of words."[68] One Japanese proposal used *diqu*, perhaps best translated as "region."

The Japanese argued that since Prime Minister Yoshida had used "region" in his letter to Dulles, that word should be used, even if the word was not entirely appropriate.[69] In the end, the negotiators settled on "the present treaty . . . shall be applicable to all territories which are now, or which may hereafter be, under the control of its government." [70] The Chinese version used *lingtu* to translate "territory," but the Japanese one used *ryoiki*, a vaguer term.[71] Eiji Wajima, the head of the Asia desk of the Japanese foreign minister, explained in the Diet that in the Japanese interpretation, even "territory" did not mean "national" or "sovereign territory," and that the Japanese used *ryoiki* to leave no doubt about Japan's interpretation:

In common international practice some cases are found where the term "territory" is not so strictly interpreted as to mean "state territory." As it is used in the present treaty, the term is not to be taken so strict as to mean "state territory." It was from this point of view that we translated it into the Japanese term *ryoiki*. . . . Both parties agreed that it should be rendered *ling-t'u* (land) in the Chinese text.[72]

The difference in the Chinese and Japanese texts is best seen as evidence that both sides acknowledged the existence of the other's views without accepting it.

Throughout the negotiations, the key issue for Chiang was that the treaty should recognize his government as one of the Allies. He was willing to give way on just about all other issues as long as the treaty made that clear in some way. On March 5, a member of the Chinese delegation informed his Japanese counterpart that if Japan accepted Clause 21 of the treaty, which held that Japan would grant the Republic of China any benefits it also granted to other countries with whom it had concluded a peace treaty, China would give way on most other contentious points.[73] Although that clause did not appear in the treaty, the protocol did accord the Republic of China any rights and benefits with respect to customs duties, trade, navigation, and taxation that it had granted other countries with which it had been at war. That was deemed sufficient recognition of the Republic of China as one of the victors of World War II.

The final treaty made no reference to Korea, it said nothing about the Tokyo War Crimes Tribunal, and it stated merely that "the state of war between Japan and the Republic of China is terminated." It omitted any reference to Japan's war guilt and did not include a statement, as the original Chinese draft did, that the treaty restored sovereignty to the Japanese people. In many ways, the text did end up treating the Republic of China as a local government. Yet because the treaty had preserved his government's status as representing one of the victorious allies, it left Chiang Kai-shek convinced that he had struck a blow against the Communists. On April 27, he wrote in his diary,

I am disturbed and embarrassed. However, the peace treaty will be signed before the San Francisco Multilateral Peace Treaty comes into force tomorrow. Thus, my government has recovered its international position to a degree, and perhaps our rapid downward trend of the past few years will now turn around and improve. The greatest significance is that, although we are in a horrendous situation of bitter defeat, we have been able to sign a treaty of peace with Japan as one of the victors, and doubtless this is a major blow to the bogus Communist organization. Of course it cannot erase my responsibility for the defeat of the revolution.[74]

The peace treaty was signed hours before the San Francisco Peace Treaty came into effect. This avoided the possibility that Japan would walk away from the treaty once it had regained sovereignty while preserving the appearance, just about, that it had voluntarily signed the Taipei Treaty.

How, then, should we assess the San Francisco and Taipei peace treaties? Little mention was made by anybody of the Taipei Treaty until recently. The PRC government naturally ignored it. In Taiwan, the GMD for many years argued that it had sovereignty over all of China, not just Taiwan and Penghu. It based its claim not on the Taipei Treaty but on the Cairo and Potsdam Declarations; the so-called Nanjing Constitution, which was adopted in 1947 when the Nationalists still controlled what was then China's capital; and the Republic of China's membership in the UN as one of the Permanent Five. The Democratic Progress Party in Taiwan, which emerged as a major political force after the lifting of martial law in 1987, argued that sovereignty over Taiwan rests with the Taiwanese people and that Taiwan should be recognized as an independent state by virtue of the 1933 Montevideo Convention, which declared that a state was a juridical person in international law if it had a defined territory, a settled population, a government, and the capacity to conclude international treaties. Few other countries referred to the Taipei Treaty, as they regarded Taiwan under Chiang Kai-shek as a nasty dictatorship. It became impossible to do so after Taiwan normalized relations with the PRC in the 1970s. Hence, the treaty lapsed into oblivion.

In Taiwan, this changed only about five years ago. For the GMD, the insistence that the Republic of China was the legitimate government for all of China became an electoral liability. Most Taiwanese, including "mainlanders," do not want reunification with the PRC. In addition, the claim that Taiwan is the legitimate government of all of China leaves it with no prospect of breaking out of the international isolation imposed on it by the PRC. A different stance, therefore, was needed. In a series of newspaper articles, lectures, and academic papers, the historian Lin Man-houng argued that the Taipei Treaty had handed sovereignty over Taiwan and Penghu to the Republic of China and recognized that the populations living there were nationals of the Republic of China. Her argument was that the 1895 Treaty of Shimonoseki, concluded after the 1894–1895 Sino-Japanese War, had ceded sovereignty over Taiwan and Penghu in perpetuity to Japan. The Taipei Treaty, although it had not explicitly indicated that Japan ceded sovereignty to the Republic of China, had nonetheless done so, she argued, as otherwise the treaty would not make sense. The treaty explicitly confined the Republic of China's territory to just Taiwan and Penghu, and not all of China. Because it was an international peace treaty, according to Lin, it had a greater weight than any other treaty. Lin's conclusion was that as a result of the Taipei Treaty, the Republic of China exists, that its name is the Republic of China, and that Taiwan and Penghu are its sovereign territory. She has proposed that August 5, the day that the treaty came into force, should become a public holiday, that Taiwan should seek to reenter the United Nations as the Republic of China, and that the Taipei Guesthouse, where the treaty was signed, should be accorded a special status.[75]

While in office, President Ma Ying-jeo has somewhat gingerly lent his support to Lin's position. He has made her the director of the Academia Historica, Taiwan's national history office; he has participated in commemorations of the signing of the Taipei Treaty; and he has challenged Japanese representatives in Taiwan who continued to insist that Taiwan's status remains undecided. Unsurprisingly, his efforts have been largely of a symbolic nature, and no other country has yet felt able to respond to his initiative in any way. However, the new currency the Taipei Treaty has gained in Taipei suggests that at least there it has gained a new lease on life.

If the Taipei Treaty and the San Francisco Peace Treaty that underpinned it have largely done their work in silence, this does not mean that they have not been important. They have worked away in the background, like the operating software of a computer, hardly noticed yet critical. They laid the basis for the postwar political order in East Asia. The terseness of the Taipei Treaty and its adoption of purposeful ambiguity has enabled it to accommodate radical change, including the United States' recognition of the PRC government as the legitimate representative of China. The documents the PRC and the United States signed at the time, such as the Shanghai Communiqué, echo the Taipei Treaty in their brevity and their ambiguity. Neither side could refer to the Taipei Treaty, but they were clearly aware of it. There are many reasons why East Asia has remained at peace, but the San Francisco and Taipei treaties have played a role too. Coming after the Sino-Japanese War, the Chinese Civil War, and the Korean War, they brought to an end a period of instability in which East Asia could have gone in many different directions, perhaps more from general exhaustion than intent.

Let me end with the following anecdote. During the US occupation of Japan, a member of the MacArthur's headquarters promoted the idea that the Japanese should abolish *kanji*, and that the Japanese language should be romanized. This was anathema to the Chinese members of the Far East Commission. Shen Jinding, the number two in its office in Tokyo, feared that the elimination of *kanji* would destroy the shared cultural heritage of Asia. Shen became relaxed about the issue after a lunch with Yoshida. The occasion, attended by Japanese diplomatic officials Shen knew well from prewar days, was an elegant one, with French food, real coffee, and cigarettes. Yoshida told Shen that the Japanese cabinet would never agree to the romanization of Japanese. "Confucianism," he remarked, "was the main moving force behind the Meiji Reforms; to abolish characters would be inappropriate."[76] For now, the legacy of World War II continues to shape the East Asian world order in fundamental ways. However, other constructions are possible, and as the anecdote above suggests, older ones, including one derived from the notion of a shared cultural heritage, have percolated into the new reality, blunting the sharp divisions that the United States imposed. In the future, these may yet gain a new vitality.

Conclusion

STEPHEN R. MACKINNON

Chiang Kai-shek is the central figure of this book. His handling of wartime international relations dominates almost every chapter. Minimal attention is given to subjects about which the scholarly literature is abundant, such as the secret negotiations with the Japanese, diplomacy of the Wang Jingwei government, Yan'an's international maneuverings, and Chiang's contentious relationship with the United States after 1941. The diaries and other personal communications that recently became available make clear that Chiang was obsessed with winning international support—material and diplomatic—for China's war effort. Before 1941 he saw it as the key to his government's survival (and that of Free China). After 1942, besides continuing to demand more material aid, Chiang doggedly pursued the enhancement of China's international status as the war concluded and the Japanese were defeated.

It was the latter, Chiang's concern with China's postwar international status, that seems today to have been remarkably prescient and clear in articulation and consistency. He rejected the idea that the war in Asia was an adjunct or secondary theater to the European and North African conflicts. For him, the reverse was true. Anticipating the end of Western and Japanese colonial empires throughout East and Southeast Asia, Chiang saw the challenges to Chinese territorial sovereignty that this development would raise. Chiang and his wife, Song Meiling, clashed openly with Churchill, Roosevelt, and Indian leaders like Nehru over this issue—as Rana Mitter and Yang Tianshi show—and over China's legitimate role as the dominant power broker in Asia once the war was concluded. In retrospect, Chiang's essential analysis proved correct. The war reshaped the geopolitics of Asia and paved the way for China's rise as a world power. Put another way, from the perspective of the twenty-first century, we see the compelling logic behind Chiang Kai-shek's seemingly quixotic efforts in the 1940s to regain for China its rightful place as a great power on the global stage. Chiang's concerns in the 1940s are the dominant concerns today of the oligarchy in Beiping, whose diplomats represent the People's Republic at the United Nations and other world forums.

Chiang's efforts internationally during the war seemed unrealistic at the time, and long afterward, because, as is often noted, his government was isolated and losing its grip on the country domestically as the war dragged on. Inability to relieve the misery of the people (as in the Henan famine of 1943) and widespread corruption in Chongqing undermined the regime to the point that it fatally weakened Chiang internationally as well as domestically. This became abundantly clear when the Nationalist government tried to reestablish control of coastal China after the war. The sudden and ignominious conclusion to the civil war that followed came as a surprise in foreign capitals from Washington to Moscow, in part because of the Chiangs' wartime success in boosting the regime's international image.

The theme of the need to defend China's territorial sovereignty runs through many chapters. Chiang Kai-shek was concerned with reclaiming Chinese sovereign rights along borders to the southwest, the northeast, and the east. As Chang Jui-te's chapter makes clear, Chiang did not always draw a distinction between what was meant by the assertion of suzerainty versus claims of territorial sovereignty. But what is clear is that Chiang's aim was the reassertion of Qing Dynasty controls over Tibet, Manchuria, Mongolia, and Taiwan. This theme runs through the contributions of Chang Jui-te, Nishimura Shigeo, and Hans van de Ven.

Before 1941 Chiang resisted others in the leadership circle around him, like Kong Xiangxi, who favored greater accommodation with the Japanese as the more realistic survival path, as Tsuchida Akio explains in his analysis of Nationalist debates on the issue of whether to declare war. Minister Kong's argument in 1938 and early 1939 was that the Russians, British, Americans, and French were unreliable allies. Chiang Kai-shek vehemently argued otherwise. He saw the Allied alliance against the Axis powers as critical to China's survival. While refuting Kong Xiangxi, Wang Jingwei, and others, Chiang emerges in this book as more astute and skilled than previously thought in cajoling the United States, the Soviet Union, and Britain into providing more support—material, diplomatic, and in antifascist propaganda—than they otherwise intended.

To achieve his war aims internationally, as the essays show, Chiang became adept at playing off the Allied powers against one another: British versus French versus Americans versus Soviets. Cases in point are maneuvers for advantage and control over wartime Manchuria and Tibet, and postwar Vietnam. At another level, he cleverly maximized his regime's interests domestically by negotiating the Sino-Soviet pact of 1945, and eventually in a Cold War environment, the peace treaty of 1952, as is illustrated in Hans van de Ven's contribution.

Another feature of this volume is the absence of attention to Chiang's well-known troubled relations with the United States, China's most important ally during the latter stages of the war. The 1941 and 1942 trips of Roosevelt's special emissary, Laughlin Curry, to Chongqing are mentioned only a few times. The Stilwell matter and his eventual recall as theater commander in 1944 are on the sidelines. The one chapter, by Xiaoyuan Liu, that is concerned exclusively with relations with the United States breaks new ground concerning territorial sovereignty issues.

By taking the spotlight off the United States, light is shed on China's wartime relationships with the British, French, and Canadians. Doing so also brings out Chiang's overall global perspective. A Chinese-centered account of the relationship with the United Kingdom provided by Rana Mitter is a case in point. Chiang Kai-shek was consistently distrustful of the British, but at the same time he saw them as a vitally important ally. During his trip to India for talks with Nehru and Gandhi in 1942, he remained cordially tactful in dealing with British representatives in Delhi by avoiding direct confrontation over the independence issue.

The level of attention Chiang gave to international relationships, and his outsized rhetoric on the subject, raises the question of how successful Chongqing's foreign policy was during the war. What did Chiang's international maneuvers accomplish in concrete terms during the long *durée* from 1937 to 1945? This was the kind of question that Kong Xiangxi put to him in 1939, as related by Tsuchida Akio.

The chapters by Yang Kuisong, Li Yuzhen, and Wu Sufeng show that Chiang managed the tangled relationship with Moscow and Stalin with aplomb. Marianne Bastid-Bruguiere tells the remarkable and complicated story of the game being played between France, China, and the Japanese over access to Yunnan and the Vietnamese border. Before 1940 the railway between Hanoi and Kunming was a critical supply route for arms and supplies to the Chinese defending armies. From the mid-1930s on, the Chinese adroitly and cynically flattered and maneuvered the French as a colonial power into keeping the supply lines open. Once the war ended, as Yang Weizhen's chapter shows, Chiang overruled his regional commander and local militarist, Long Yun of Yunnan. His actions ultimately facilitated the handing back of northern Vietnam to the French. More important to Chiang than the nationalist sentiments of the Vietnamese was Allied support for the reconstruction of China—as well as political support in the coming civil war with the CCP.

The chapters show that for Chiang Kai-shek, what was fundamental to relations with the Allied powers internationally during the latter stages of the war was the defense of Chinese sovereignty as well as the insistence on China's recognition as a world power. This meant, if necessary, the acceptance of the residual presence of colonial powers and the downplaying of wartime anti-imperialist rhetoric or support of anticolonial independence movements, that is, acceptance of the French presence in Vietnam, as well as the British presence in India, Burma, and Malaysia.

Manchuria proved to be a kind of Achilles' heel in Chongqing's wartime foreign policy. The contradictions of Chiang's position were most evident in relations with Moscow. Chiang was forced grudgingly by Stalin to trade Soviet acceptance of Chinese sovereignty over the Northeast while accepting on the ground Soviet presence, special rights in Manchuria, and aid to the CCP.

In general, then, Chiang was rightfully distrustful of his Western and Soviet allies. In his single-minded pursuit of protecting China's interests in the postwar world, Chiang's myopic vision led at times to unexpected outcomes and trouble. The zealous commitment to assertion of Chinese sovereignty over Manchuria helps to explain Chiang's subsequent overemphasis on the strategic importance of the Northeast once war broke out with the Communists in 1947. When he lost Manchuria to the Communists in 1948, the loss militarily doomed his regime.

The majority of the chapters in this volume are authored by Japanese and Chinese scholars. They rarely cite Western-language sources, even when dealing with China's relations with the Western powers. The result is a forceful and detailed representation of Chiang Kai-shek and his associates in their effort to assert Chinese control over the Asian international environment. A sense of the latter, the international context, has been provided in the introduction but is left out of most individual chapters. There are advantages and disadvantages to such a narrow China-centered approach to the diplomacy of World War II. For example, in the chapter on Chiang and Nehru, essential background on the nature of the independence struggle against British colonial rule at this time—even the jailing of Nehru and Gandhi—is hardly mentioned or explained. The focus is entirely on Chiang's preoccupation with bringing Indian leaders into the war against Japan. From an Indian perspective, of course, this meant that China was willing tacitly to collude in the defense of the British Empire because of the Japanese invasion of Burma and southwestern China.

There is another book that needs to be written on the larger question about how to situate the Second World War more clearly in terms of its impact on the evolving web of twentieth-century Asian power relationships. How did the war change Asia's international environment? Work in this field is in its infancy. Two new studies on Asian wartime international relations draw contradictory conclusions. S. C. M. Paine, in *Wars for Asia*, views the international relations of the period largely in terms of strategic military results. In terms of outcomes, the Soviet Union as an Asian power was the clear winner. China emerged from the war too weak to fill the power vacuum left by the vanquished Japanese. The United States, too distracted by events in Europe, was soon to be bogged down in Korea and Vietnam. This left the Soviet Union free to exercise influence throughout Asia, from India to Korea.

A second study is a collection of essays edited by Shigeru Akita and Nicholas J. White, *The International Order of Asia in 1930s and 1950s*, which focuses on trade and economics. Essentially, the authors argue in a series of case studies that the war was an anomaly or, in Bruce Cuming's words, an "aberration." Intra-Asian trade patterns and cooperation of the prewar years simply resumed in the 1950s. The foundation for the miracle growth story of Asia in the late twentieth century was established in the mid-twentieth century through a variety of intra-Asian cooperative business networks (many of which were operative in the 1930s under the political umbrella of colonialism). China, excluded from the 1940s through 1960s because of war and revolution, would eventually recover the position as a trading nexus that it had enjoyed in the 1930s. Politically, by suggesting that by the 1950s the balance of power and competing interests in Asia returned to patterns previously in play in the 1930s, this is a more Japan-centered view of the impact of World War II on Asian power relations.

Regardless, our volume and the new studies by Paine, and by Akita and White, raise questions about how to understand an Asian-centered history of World War II. War as a catalyst for nationalist uprisings is an old theme repeated frequently when placing World War II in an Asian context. What about questions of sovereignty? Many of today's disputes in East Asian international relations are grounded in the war experience, as van de Ven argues. For China, the 1950–1952 Korean War, as well as the 1962 Indian and 1979 Vietnam conflicts, have roots in the Asian war experience of the 1940s. Was there an Asian balance-of-power matrix present in the 1930s that resurfaced in the 1950s and which, following China's rise as an economic powerhouse, has become China-centered today?

Like Germany in Europe, Japan reemerged as a dominant economic and political power by the 1980s. What was the nature of the changing relations between Asian countries (including nationalist movements) from the 1930s through the 1940s? Can one characterize indigenous Communist movements and their relationships with one another during the war as also transnational? Indonesian, Vietnamese, Korean, and Malaysian Communist leaders sought sanctuary in China during the war. How about the economic relationships across wartime Asia—and their impact on later developments? In Calcutta during the war, there was a miniboom of Chinese business activity. After 1949 it disappeared, and today it is back with renewed vigor.

These are the kinds of broader questions about the Asian context of wartime relationships, as opposed to China's relations with the United

States which dominated discussion by an earlier generation of scholars, that this book is intended to raise. The essays show how Chiang Kai-shek struggled throughout the war with a number of major issues—especially questions of sovereignty and the situating of China strategically as the preeminent postwar Asian power at international forums like the United Nations. From the perspective of Asian relations in the twenty-first century, Chiang understood the issues; his voice was prescient.

Notes

CHAPTER I

1. In China, of US$1.8 billion Western investment in 1936, France ranked second (US$180 million) behind the United States (US$220 million) but ahead of Germany (US$140 million) and Britain (US$108 million). Tôa kenkyûsho, *Rekkoku taishi tôshi to Shina kokusai shûshi* (Tokyo: Jitsugyô no Nihon sha, 1944), p. 76.

2. Sylvain Levi, *Indochine* (Paris: Société d'éditions géographiques, maritimes et coloniales, 1931), p. 7; Jacques Marseille, "L'investissement français dans l'empire colonial: l'ensuête du gouvernement de Vichy (1943)" [French investment in the colonial empire], *Revue historique,* no. 512 (October–December 1974), pp. 408–432.

3. Archives du ministère des affaires étrangères [French Ministry of Foreign Affairs Archives], Société des nations (hereafter MAE, SDN), 319/52, Consul Crépin (Shenyang) to Wilden, September 19, 1931; ibid., 319/143; Crépin to Wilden, September 22, 1931; ibid., 326/20; Crépin to Wilden, November 21, 1931; ibid., 319/33, Wilden to Briand, September 20, 1931.

4. MAE, SDN, 324/4, Wilden to Briand, September 7, 1931.

5. Ibid., 319/33, Wilden to Briand, September 20, 1931.

6. On Briand's feelings against Japanese expansionism, see the diary of journalist Geneviève Tabouis, *Ils l'ont appelée Cassandre* (New York, 1942), p. 56. See also reports of the French press on the Manchurian Incident in Marie-Thérèse Kobayashi-Moreau, "L'Incident de Mandchourie (1931) et la presse française" (MA thesis, Institute of Political Studies, Paris, 1968). A summary is found in Sun Xinhe, "La France et le conflit sino-japonais, 1931–1937" (PhD dissertation, Institute of Political Studies, Paris, 1990), pp. 81–95. Sun Xinhe's work is unfortunately fraught with errors resulting from inadequate sources and mistaken reading of the documents.

7. MAE, SDN, 319/174, Massigli's speech of September 22, 1931, at the Council of the League of Nations.

8. Ibid., 319/100, de Martel to Briand, September 23, 1931.

9. Ibid., 319/72, Berthelot, secretary general of the French Foreign Ministry, to Massigli, September 22, 1931.

10. Ibid., 319/214, Instruction of Briand to de Martel, September 25, 1931.

11. Ibid., 319/237, de Martel to Briand, September 25, 1931.

12. Ibid., 320/82, de Martel to Briand, October 7, 1931.

13. Ibid., 320/259, Martel to Briand, October 12, 1931.

14. Ibid., 320/115, Briand to Wilden, October 8, 1931; ibid., 320/103, Wilden to Briand, October 8, 1931.

15. Ibid., 321/155, Briand's speech to the league Council, Paris, October 16, 1931; ibid., 321/154, Briand to US secretary of state Stimson, Paris, October 16, 1931; ibid., 321/154, Japanese delegate's speech to the Council, Paris, October 16, 1931; ibid., 334/145, US representative Prentiss Gilbert's speech to the Council, Paris, October 16, 1931.

16. Attacks were continuous in the authoritative papers *Le Temps* and *Le Figaro.* MAE, SDN, 325/59; and ibid., 326/6, Briand to de Martel, November 21, 1931; ibid., 326/92, Briand to Claudel (French ambassador in Washington), November 24, 1931.

17. Ibid., 326/106, Wilden to Briand, November 25, 1931; 326/137, Briand to de Martel, November 26, 1931.

18. Ibid., 332/238, Berthelot to Massigli and Wilden, February 14, 1932.

19. Ibid., 330/220, Laval to de Martel, January 30, 1932.

20. Ibid., 331/104, Laval to Wilden, February 2, 1932; ibid., 331/100, French proposals to China on February 2, 1932.

21. Ibid., 332/59, Wilden to Laval, February 8, 1932; ibid., 332/204, Wilden to Laval, February 13, 1932.

22. On this plan, the most detailed study is Maurice Vaïsse, *Sécurité d'abord. La politique française en matière de désarmement. Décembre 1930–17 avril 1934* (Paris: Pédone, 1982).

23. MAE, SDN, 336/1, Wilden to Tardieu, March 15, 1932.

24. MAE, Asia, 675/115, Wilden to Laval, February 7, 1932; MAE, SDN, 333/177, Note no. 32/115 of the Foreign Ministry Press Service, February 1932.

25. MAE, SDN, 333/134, Claudel to Tardieu, February 20, 1932. Claudel was twice instructed to refute in Washington the "absurd rumors" with "utmost preciseness and energy." Ibid., 332/26, Tardieu to Claudel, February 1932; ibid., 33/155, Tardieu to Claudel, Paris, February 22, 1932. Again in March, the Japanese press claimed that France had congratulated the Manchukuo authorities on the founding of the new state. All French ambassadors received urgent instructions to deny the slander and make known that France had given no answer to the Japanese notification, in accordance with its principled stand on the respect of treaties and law. Ibid., 336/132, Léger to ambassadors in Nanjing, Tokyo, Washington, London, and Rome, March 23, 1932. On March 31, de Martel protested to the Japanese vice minister of foreign affairs that France could never recognize Manchukuo. Ibid., 336/233, de Martel to Tardieu, March 31, 1932.

26. The campaign stopped on February 27, 1932, when the US State Department declared to the *New York Times* that "it was known that France had no special arrangement with Japan and that French cooperation had been for the purpose of peace between China and Japan." Ibid., 334/29, Claudel to Tardieu, February 27, 1932.

27. Documents diplomatiques francaises 1932–1939, 1re série (1932–1935), [French diplomatic documents 1932–1939, first series (1932–1935), vol. 2 (November 15, 1932–March 17, 1933) (hereafter *DDF*) (Paris: Imprimerie nationale, 1966), p. 741, Asia-Oceania Desk for Foreign Affairs Minister Paul-Boncour, March 6, 1933.

28. MAE, SDN, 338/5, Tardieu to de Martel, April 26, 1932.

29. DDF series 1, vol. 1, p. 9, de Martel, July 8, 1932; ibid., p. 15, Herriot to de Martel, July 11, 1932.

30. Ibid., pp. 7–9, Massigli, July 9, 1932.

31. Ibid., p. 9.

32. Ibid., series 1, p. 136, Reynaud to Wilden, July 29, 1932.

33. Ibid., p. 275, Minutes of the conversation between General Araki, Japanese war minister, and Admiral Berthelot on board *Amiral Primauguet*, Tokyo, September 6, 1932, sent to Herriot by the War Ministry; ibid., p. 312, de Lens to Herriot, September 13, 1932.

34. DDF series 1, vol. 2, p. 741, Note of the Asia-Oceania desk for Foreign Minister Paul-Boncour, Paris, March 6, 1933.

35. Ibid., pp. 740–742. For a summary of the propaganda campaign and its impact on American diplomats, see J. C. Grew, *Ten Years in Japan*, p. 31. On its success in China and the United States, see *DDF 1932–1939*, series 1, vol. 1, pp. 350–352, Henry to Herriot, September 19, 1932; ibid., pp. 422–423, Wilden to Herriot, October 10, 1932. On Herriot's efforts to stop rumors, see MAE, Japan, 125/77, Note of the Ministry of Foreign Affairs in response to the question of the Communist deputy Gabriel Péri at the Chamber of Deputies, Paris, October 26, 1932; *DDF 1932–1939*, series 1, vol. 2, p. 11, Herriot to Claudel and Wilden, November 17, 1932.

36. DDF series 1, vol. 1, pp. 342–343, Henry to Herriot, September 17, 1932; ibid., p. 360, Massigli to Herriot, Geneva, September 22, 1932.

37. Foreign Relations of the United States (hereafter *FRUS*), *1932*, vol. 4, pp. 265–266, Edge to State Department, September 19, 1932.

38. DDF series 1, vol. 2, p. 22–26, Internal note of the Foreign Ministry, November 18, 1932. This note summarizes the real views on the French side, whereas the American and French diplomatic correspondence used by Reidfort reflect only soothing words meant for Americans.

39. Édouard Herriot, *Jadis. D'une guerre à l'autre, 1914–1936* (Paris: Flammarion, 1952), pp. 312–313. On the pact, "Du plan Briand au traité de non-agression franco-soviétique. Les relations franco-soviétiques au début des années trente: vers un rapprochement des deux États? (1930–1933)," in M. M. Narinskii, E. du Réau, et al., ed., *L'URSS et l'Europe dans les années 20* [*The Soviet Union and Europe in the 1920s*] (Paris: Presses de l'Université de Paris-Sorbonne, 2000), pp. 167–184.

40. DDF, series 1, vol. 2, p. 22–26, Internal note of the Foreign Ministry, November 18, 1932.

41. Ibid., p. 410, Note of the Ministry's LON desk, Paris, January 10, 1933.

42. Ibid., pp. 444–449, Asia-Oceania Desk, January 15, 1933; J. Dreifort, *Myopic Grandeur: The Ambivalence of French Foreign Policy toward the Far East, 1919–1945* (Kent, OH: Kent State University Press, 1991), p. 47, misses the point and thinks that there was no serious thought about the changes in Japan's policy and goals, and sees policy as based on short-sighted considerations.

43. MAE, SDN, 347/69, Note on the British government's consultation about the embargo, Paris, February 24, 1933; ibid., 351/51, Asia-Oceania Desk, March 9, 1933; *DDF 1932–1939*, series 1, vol. 2, p. 761, Fleuriau to Paul-Boncour, March 8, 1933.

44. DDF series 1, vol. 4, p. 470, Asia-Oceania Desk, Paris, October 2, 1933.

45. MAE, Asia 1918–1940, China, 659/90, Paris to Massigli, March 24, 1933; ibid., 114, Massigli to Paul-Boncour, July 18, 1933.

46. Ibid., series 1, vol. 11, p.148, Instruction to ambassador in Washington, June 20 1935.

47. Ibid., series 2, vol. 3, pp. 428–430, Asia-Oceania Desk for Secretary-General Léger, Paris, September 28, 1936.

48. MAE, E Series, Indochina-China-Japan, 549/3-3, 30/65, Mast's report to the general chief commander of troops of the Indochina Group, Tokyo, April 20, 1936.

49. Ibid., 30/70, Naggiar to Delbos, January 23, 1937.

50. Ibid., 30/79, Sato to Endo, February 15, 1937.

51. Ibid., pp. 302–303, Asia-Oceania Desk to Delbos, December 21, 1936.

52. DDF, series 2, vol. 6, pp. 370–371, Delbos to Corbin, July 13, 1937; Gu Weijun, *Gu Weijun huiyilu* (Beiping: Zhonghua shuju, 1985), , vol. 2, p. 408, does not mention that Gu had asked about a Nine Powers conference (perhaps it was not in his instructions) nor does it mention that the suggestion was made by Delbos.

53. Ibid., pp. 370–371, Delbos to Corbin, July 13, 1937.

54. Ibid., p. 431, Corbin to Delbos, July 21, 1937; ibid., pp. 363, 388, 416, 594, 854.

55. Paris was well informed of British hesitation. See *DDF* series 1, vol. 6, pp. 615–617, Cambon to Delbos, August 23, 1937.

56. DDF, series 1, vol. 6, pp. 697–698, Massigli's note on Gu Weijun's visit, Paris, September 6, 1937. This procedure was officially accepted by Gu in Geneva on September 15.

57. Ibid., pp. 761–762, Arsène-Henry to Delbos, September 12, 1937. The ambassador warned further that Japan might retaliate by attacking Hainan, a direct threat to Indochina.

58. Ibid., series 2, vol. 7, pp. 233–243, Note of the League of Nations Desk to Delbos, October 26, 1937.

59. Ibid., pp. 597–598, Note of the Asia-Oceania Desk, December 3, 1937.

60. Chen Sanjing, "Kangzhan chuqi Zhong Fa jiaoshe chutan" [Initial exploration of Sino-French negotiations in the early period of the War of Resistance], in Chen Sanjing, *Jindai Zhong Fa guanxi shi lun* [Modern history of Sino-French relations] (Taipei: Sanmin shuju 1993), pp. 241–261. Chen uses printed sources from the collection edited by Qin Xiaoyi, *Zhonghua minguo zhongyao shiliao chubian—dui Ri kangzhan shiqi* [Initial collection of important historical materials on the Republic of China—period of the War of Resistance against Japan] (Taipei: Dangshihui, 1981). Based on Yunnan local archives, two articles by Liu Weidong are also useful: "Kangzhan qianqi guomin zhengfu dui Yinzhi tongdao de jingying" [The National Government's management of the Indochina route in the early period of the War of Resistance], *Jindaishi yanjiu* [Modern history studies], 1998, vol. 5, pp. 119–148 (hereafter "Jingying"); and "Lun kangzhan qianqi Faguo guanyu Zhongguo jiedao Yuenan yunshu de zhengce" [French policy regarding transshipment of goods for China through Vietnam in the early period

of the War of Resistance], *Jindaishi yanjiu*, 2001, vol. 2, pp. 195–224 (hereafter "Zhengce").

61. DDF 1932–1939, series 2, vol. 7, pp. 418–419, Delbos to Arsène-Henry, November 13, 1937.

62. Ibid., pp. 39–40, Asia-Oceania Desk, Paris, October 5, 1937.

63. Ibid., p. 254, telegram from Tokyo of September 24, 1937, see footnote 2.

64. Ibid., p. 39, Asia-Oceania Desk, October 5, 1937.

65. Ibid., Ministry of Foreign Affairs to the Ministry of Colonies, October 1, 1937.

66. His argument is developed in Asia-Oceania Desk, October 5, 1937, in *DDF 1932–1939*, series 2, vol. 7, pp. 38–41.

67. Ibid., p. 226, Delbos to Arsène-Henry, October 25, 1937; ibid., p. 598, Asia-Oceania Desk, December 3, 1937. Discussion of the matter and its "illegality" in Liu Weidong, "Zhengce," pp. 197–203, is mistaken.

68. Ibid., series 2, vol. 8, p. 33.

69. Chen Sanjing, op. cit., pp. 244–245.

70. DDF 1932–1939, series 2, vol. 7, p. 226, Delbos to Arsène-Henry, October 25, 1937.

71. Ibid., pp. 254–255, Arsène-Henry to Delbos, October 27, 1937.

72. Ibid., pp. 263–264, Delbos to Arsène-Henry, October 28, 1937.

73. Ibid., pp. 284–285, Arsène-Henry to Delbos, October 30, 1937.

74. Ibid., pp. 363, 388, 416, 594, 854, Arsène-Henry, November 9, 11, 13, December 3, 1937, and January 10, 1938; ibid., p. 448, 904, Delbos, November 18, 1937, and January 13, 1938. Two French priests died in the Nanning bombing; Hirota told Arsène-Henry, who made an official protest, that the bombing was aimed at destroying war supplies from Indochina. Ibid., p. 875, Arsène-Henry to Delbos, January 12, 1938.

75. Ibid., pp. 901–903, Arsène-Henry to Delbos, January 13, 1938.

76. Ibid., Henry to Delbos, October 22, 1937.

77. Ibid., Delbos on his talks with Eden, Norman Davis, Spaak, and Litvinov, Brussels, November 6, 1937.

78. Ibid., p. 355–357, Henry to Delbos, November 7, 1937.

79. Ibid., pp. 364–365, Delbos to Henry, November 9, 1937.

80. Ibid., pp. 369–370, Henry to Delbos confirming a phone call to Léger, November 10, 1937.

81. Ibid., pp. 390–392, Henry to Delbos, November 11, 1937.

82. Ibid., pp. 430–431, Delbos to Corbin, November 16, 1937.

83. Ibid., pp. 656–657, Corbin to Delbos, November 19, 1937.

84. Ibid., pp. 926–930, Secret note of the Defense Ministry from Daladier to Delbos, January 7, 1938.

85. On this committee, see *Le Comité de l'Indochine, trente ans d'action* (Paris: Comité de l'Indochine, 1932).

86. DDF 1932–1939, series 2, vol. 8, pp. 32–33, Delbos to ambassadors in Tokyo and London, January 21, 1938. Contrary to Liu Weidong's view ("Zhengce," p. 210), the turn in French policy does not "follow" or "imitate" America and Britain in late 1938 but precedes them by almost a year. On the change in American and British policy, see B.A. Lee, op. cit., pp. 158–165.

87. DDF 1932–1939, series 2, vol. 8, p. 61–62, Arsène-Henry to Delbos, January 25, 1938.

88. Ibid., pp. 171–172, Daladier to Steeg, February 1, 1938. The National Defense Committee, was an ad hoc committee convened by the head of the cabinet; it included those ministers most concerned with defense matters together with the chiefs of staff of land, air, and sea forces, and some technical personnel.

89. Ibid., pp. 254–259, Note from the General Secretariat of the National Defense Council, February 8, 1938.

90. Ibid., pp. 390–394, Billotte, president of the Consultative Committee for Colonial Defense, to Steeg, February 17, 1938.

91. Ibid., pp. 413–417, military attaché (London) to Daladier, February 18, 1938.

92. DDF series 2, vol. 8, pp. 611–615, Note by the Air Force General Chief of Staff, March 28, 1938.

93. Ibid., pp. 671–672, Corbin to Delbos, March 8, 1938.

94. Ibid., p. 486, Delbos to Corbin, February 23, 1938; ibid., pp. 933–934, Paul-Boncour to Corbin, March 19, 1938.

95. Ibid., pp. 478–479, Arsène-Henry to Delbos, February 23, 1938; ibid., series 2, vol. 10, pp. 304–305, Bonnet to Mandel, July 7, 1938.

96. Ibid., series 2, vol. 10, pp. 698–699, Bonnet's instruction to Arsène-Henry, Paris, August 17, 1938; ibid., pp. 767–769, General Ugaki, Japanese minister of foreign affairs, to Bonnet, August 22, 1938.

97. Ibid., series 2, vol. 8, pp. 738–739, Delbos to Steeg, Paris, March 12, 1938; ibid., p. 855, Paul-Boncour to Moutet, March 16, 1938; ibid., series 2, vol. 10, p. 65, Army general staff proceedings of the weekly contact meeting with the Foreign Affairs Ministry, June 15, 1938.

98. Ibid., series 2, vol. 10, pp. 243–244, Bonnet to Arsène-Henry, July 1, 1938; ibid., pp. 253–254, Corbin to Bonnet, July 2, 1938; ibid., p. 268, Bonnet to Arsène-Henry, July 4, 1938; ibid., pp. 276–278, Bonnet to ambassadors in Washington, Rome, Berlin, London, Tokyo, and Shanghai, Paris, July 5, 1938; ibid., pp. 326–327, Bonnet to Arsène-Henry, July 9, 1938.

99. Ibid., 176–178, Bonnet to Mandel, June 24, 1938; ibid., pp. 196, Mandel to Bonnet, June 27, 1938.

100. M.F. Bourdin, "Le chemin de fer du Yunnan" [The Yunnan Railway] (unpublished doctoral thesis of Paris University Law Faculty, 1946), p. 86.

101. Liu, "Jingying," pp. 136, 139–140.

102. Bourdin, op. cit., p. 92.

103. Wang Shijie riji [Wang Shijie's diary] (Taipei: Zhongyang yanjiuyuan jindaishi yanjiusuo 1990), vol. 1, pp. 342–343, recording an August 20, 1938, talk with Nanjing Catholic bishop Yu Bin, just back from Hanoi where he met the governor general. In fact, Chinese cargo handling was so poorly organized that supplies were piling up on the Haiphong wharves. The first Soviet supplies, including airplanes in parts, which arrived in January 1938, were taken up and down to Yunnan and Guangxi border for five months because of contradictory orders. Liu, "Jingying," pp. 143–147.

104. B.A. Lee, op. cit., p. 162.

105. DDF, series 2, vol. 8, pp. 116–117, Note of the league desk on Delbos's talks with Eden in Geneva, January 28, 1938.

106. Ibid., pp. 148–149, Henry to Delbos, January 30, 1938; ibid., pp. 160–161, Delbos to Henry, January 31, 1938.

107. Ibid., pp. 165–166, 182–184, Lagarde, delegate to the league's Council, to Ministry of Foreign Affairs, February 1 and 2, 1938.

108. Ibid., pp. 506–513, Henry to Delbos, February 23, 1938; ibid., p. 729, Saint-Quentin to Delbos, March 11, 1938.

109. Ibid., p. 555, Avenol to Massigli, February 24, 1938; ibid., p. 560, Massigli to Avenol, February 28, 1938.

110. Chen Sanjing, op. cit., p. 248; Huang Qingqiu, *Faguo zhu Hua junshi guwentuan gongzuo jiyao* [A summary of the work of the French military mission to China] (Taipei: Guofangbu, 1968), p. 7.

111. DDF series 2, vol. 7, pp. 935–937, Georges to Daladier, May 28, 1938.

112. Ibid., pp. 943–945, Arsène-Henry to Bonnet, May 30, 1938.

113. Ibid., series 2, vol. 10, pp. 72–73, 100–102, 109–111, 265–266, Arsène-Henry to Bonnet, June 16, 19, 20, and July 3, 1938.

114. Ibid., pp. 111–113, Naggiar to Bonnet, June 20, 1938.

115. Ibid., pp. 135–137, Bonnet to Daladier, June 22, 1938.

116. Chen Sanjing, op. cit., pp. 249–250.

117. B.A. Lee, op. cit., pp. 131, 162–165.

118. Huang Qingqiu, op. cit., pp. 10–11.

119. Ibid., pp. 15–23.

120. Chen Sanjing, op. cit., p. 254.

121. Ibid., pp. 254–255. *Wang Shijie riji*, vol. 2, p. 101, entry of June 18, 1939.

122. Huang Qingqiu, op. cit., p. 32.

123. Evidence on this point is from the Chinese archives in Liu, "Jingying," pp. 125–130, 135–137, 139–141, 145–146.

124. Huang Qingqiu, op. cit., pp. 29–32.

125. DDF 1932–1939, series 2, vol. 10, pp. 614–615, Naggiar to Bonnet, August 9, 1938; ibid., pp. 667–669, Bonnet to French representatives in Tokyo, London, and Washington, August 14, 1938.

126. B. A. Lee, op. cit., pp. 159, 181.

127. Marc Meuleau, *Des pionniers en Extrême-Orient. Histoire de la Banque de l'Indochine 1875–1975* [Pioneers in the Far East: History of the Bank of Indochina] (Paris: Fayard, 1990), pp. 407–408.

128. Archives du service historique de l'Armée de terre, 2 N 147, Plan de défense générale de l'Indochine, Paris, October 1938.

129. J. Decoux, *À la barre de l'Indochine (1940–1945)* [At the helm of Indochina] (Paris: Plon, 1949), pp. 14–25, gives detailed testimony about the conference.

130. DDF 1939; *3 septembre-31 décembre* (Berne: Lang 2002), p. 39, Internal note, Paris, September 7, 1939.

131. Huang Qingqiu, op. cit., p. 24–26.

132. DDF 1939, pp. 228–229, Daladier's instruction to Cosme, Paris, September 24, 1939.

133. MAE, Papiers 1940, Papiers Baudouin, (hereafter MAE, Baudouin papers), vol. 5, pp. 9–14, Note for the Minister, Vichy, July 13, 1940.

134. DDF 1940, *Les armistices de juin 1940* (Berne: Lang 2003), pp. 22–23, Reynaud to Roosevelt, June 14, 1940; ibid., p. 39, Roosevelt to Reynaud, June 16, 1940.

135. MAE, Baudouin papers, pp. 28–29, 37, 133, Saint-Quentin to Baudouin, June 15, 16 and 22, 1940.

136. Ibid., pp. 898–899, Baudouin to ambassadors in Shanghai, Tokyo, and Bangkok, July 1, 1940.

137. Decoux, op. cit., pp. 65–66. On the Japanese side, see J. W. Morley, ed., *Japan's Road to the Pacific War. The Fateful Choice: Japan's Advance into Southeast Asia, 1939–1941* (New York: Columbia University Press, 1980), pp. 159–163.

138. Claude Hesse d'Alzon, "L'armée française d'Indochine pendant la seconde guerre mondiale, 1939–1945" [The French army in Indochina during the Second World War], in Paul Isoart, ed., *L'Indochine française 1940–1945* (Paris: Presses universitaires de France, 1982), pp. 77–83.

139. Centre des archives d'outre-mer, GGI CM 949, Catroux to Minister of Colonies, June 24, 1940, and Catroux to Governor General in Tananarive, June 25, 1940.

140. Georges Gautier, *9 mars 1945, Hanoï au soleil de sang. La fin de l'Indochine française* [Hanoi in the blood sun] (Paris: Société de production littéraire, 1978), pp. 21–22.

141. Decoux, op. cit., pp. 68–72.

142. J. W. Morley, op. cit., pp. 163–167.

143. MAE, Baudouin papers, 5/9–14, Note for the Minister, Vichy, 1940.

144. Ibid., 4/133 and 141, Saint-Quentin to Baudouin, July 7 and 14, 1940.

145. Ibid., 5/15–16, Baudouin to Arsène-Henry, July 26, 1940; 5/19–22, Arsène-Henry to Baudouin, August 2, 1940; 5/24, Baudouin to Arsène-Henry, August 2, 1940.

CHAPTER 2

1. Documents on British Policy Overseas (hereafter DBPO), series 1, vol. 8 (Britain and China 1945–1950), chap. 2, 1946, pp. 56–64, October 18, 1946.

2. DBPO, series 2, vol. 21 (Far East 1936–1938), chap. 3, pp. 368–369, October 5, 1937.

3. DBPO, series 2, vol. 21, chap. 4, pp. 470–471, November 11, 1937.

4. Ibid.

5. DBPO, series 2, vol. 21, chap. 6, pp. 664–665, January 24, 1938.

6. Ibid., pp. 664–665, January 24, 1938.

7. Ibid., pp. 679–680, February 2, 1938,

8. Ibid., pp. 685–686.

9. Ibid., pp. 689–690.

10. Ibid., pp. 744–746, April 29, 1938.

11. Hans van de Ven, *War and Nationalism in China, 1925–1945.*

12. Aron Shai, *Britain and China, 1941–47* (Macmillan, 1977), p. 23.

13. C. A. Bayly and Tim Harper, *Forgotten Wars: The End of Britain's Asian Empire* (Penguin, 2007).

14. DBPO, series 1, vol. 8 (Britain and China, 1945–1950), chap. 1, pp. 1–24, July 7, 1945, sec 31.

15. Ibid., sec. 2.

16. Ibid., sec. 15.

17. Odd Arne Westad, *Cold War and Revolution* (Chapel Hill, 1993).

18. DBPO, series 1, vol. 8 (Britain and China, 1945–1950), sec. 21, 23.

19. Ibid., sec. 28f.

20. DBPO, series 1, vol. 1 (Potsdam Conference, July–August 1945), chap. 1, pp. 156–161, July 10, 1945, sec. 9.

21. DBPO, series 1, vol. 2 (Conference 1945, London, Washington, Moscow), pp. 1–5, August 11, 1945.

22. DBPO, series 1, vol. 1 (Potsdam Conference), pp. 1141–1143, August 1, 1945.

23. DBPO, series 1, vol. 2 (Britain and China, 1945–1950), pp. 24–26, August 30, 1945.

24. DBPO, series 1, vol. 8, chap. 1, pp. 1–24, note 25/4, July 7, 1945.

25. DBPO series 1, vol. 8, chap. 2, pp. 38–41, March 1, 1946.

26. DBPO, series 1, vol. 2 (Conference 1945, London, Washington, Moscow), p. 189, September 16, 1945.

27. Ibid., pp. 292–294, September 22, 1945.

28. Ibid., pp. 323–325, September 23, 1945.

29. DBPO series 1, vol. 2 (Conference 1945, London, Washington, Moscow), chap. 1, pp. 506–509, October 27, 1945.

30. DBPO, series 1, vol. 3 (Britain and America, Negotiation of the US loan, 1945), pp. 310–313, November 8, 1945.

31. DBPO, series 1, vol. 2 (Conference 1945, London, Washington, Moscow), pp. 755–766, December 18, 1945.

32. DBPO, series 1, vol. 8 (Britain and China, 1945–1950), chap. 1, pp. 1–24.

33. Ibid., pp. 33–34, November 1, 1945.

34. Ibid., pp. 35–37, December 27, 1945.

35. DBPO, series 1, vol. 8 (Britain and China, 1945–50), chap. 2, pp. 46–49, June 11, 1946.

CHAPTER 3

This chapter is an abridged version of a paper in Chinese published in *Zhongyang Yanjiuyuan Jindaishi Yanjiusuo Jikan* [Bulletin of the Institute of Modern History, Academia Sinica], vol. 67 (March 2010), pp. 59–96. The author thanks the publisher for permission to translate this article into English.

1. Zhang Yuxin, Zhang Shuangzhi, eds., *Minguo Zangshi Shiliao Huibian* [Compilation of historical documents on Tibetan affairs in republican China] (Beiping: Xueyuan Chubanshe, 2005), vol. 1, p. 213; Zhang Ling'ao, *Wo zai Jiang Jieshi Shicongshi de rizi* [My days at the staff office of Chiang Kai-shek] (Taipei: Zhouzhi Wenhua Shiye Gufen Youxian Gongsi, 1995), p. 142.

2. Chen Xizhang, "Xizang Congzheng Jilu" [Brief record of political activities in Tibet], in Historical Documents Editorial Office, *Wenshi Ziliao Xuanji* [Selec-

tion of cultural and historical documents] (Beijing: Wenshi Ziliao Chubanshe, 1981), vol. 79, pp. 116–117; Zhang Ling'ao, *My Days at the Staff Office,* p. 142.

3. Zhang Yuxin, Zhang Shuangzhi, eds., *Historical Documents on Tibet,* vol. 7, pp. 118, 213.

4. British Mission in Lhasa to the Political Office in Sikkim, November 26, 1944, India Office Records, L/P&S/12/4218, cited in Hsiao-ting Lin, *Tibet and Nationalist China's Frontier: Intrigues and Ethnopolitics, 1928–49* (Vancouver: UBC Press, 2006), p. 148.

5. Shen is mentioned in the following works: Alastair Lamb, *Tibet, China and India, 1914–1950: A History of Imperial Diplomacy* (Hertfordshire: Roxford Books, 1989), pp. 328–336, 493–497; Zhou Weizhou, ed., *Yingguo Eguo yu Zhongguo Xizang* (Britain, Russia, and China's Tibet) (Beijing: Zhongguo Zangxue Chubanshe, 2000), pp. 553–560; Lu Zhaoyi, *Ying Diguo yu Zhongguo Xizang bianjiang* [British Empire and China's Tibet frontier] (Beijing: Zhongguo Zangxue Chubanshe, 2001), pp. 465–467; Chen Qianping, *Kangzhan Qianhou zhi Zhong Ying Jiaoshe (1935–1947)* [Sino-British negotiations before and after the Sino-Japanese War (1935–1947)] (Beiping: Sanlian shudian, 2003), pp. 185–193; Li Yuquan, "Zhu Zang Banshichu de Shezhi, Gongneng yu Yingxiang: Jianlun Guomin Zhengfu de Xizang Zhengce" [The establishment, function, and impact of the Tibet Office: Discussion of the national government's Tibet policy] (Taipei: Chinese Culture University History Department, master's thesis, 2004), pp. 22–25, 114–115; Deng Ruiling, Doje Cedain, Chen Qingying, Zhang Yun, and Zhu Qiyuan, *Yuan yilai Xizang Difang yu Zhongyang Zhengfu Guanxi Yanjiu* [The Relationship between Tibet and the central government since the Yuan Dynasty] (Beijing: Zhongguo Zangxue Chubanshe, 2005), pp. 1207–1222; Sherab Nyima (Guo Weiping), Su Faxiang, *Meng Zang Weiyuanhui Dang'an zhong de Xizang Shiwu* [Tibetan affairs in the Archives of the Mongolian and Tibetan Affairs Commission] (Beiping: Zhongyang Minzu Daxue Chubanshe, 2006), pp. 42–43 (hereafter *MZWYH*); Hsiao-ting Lin, *Tibet,* pp. 148–151; Zhang Yongpan, *Ying Diguo yu Zhongguo Xizang (1937–1947)* [The British Empire and China's Tibet (1937–1947)] (Beijing: Zhongguo Shehui Kexue Chubanshe, 2007), pp. 138–156.

6. Zhang Yongpan, *The British Empire and China's Tibet,* pp. 191–204.

7. Lin Xiaoting, "Erzhan Shiqi Zhong Ying Guanxi Zai Tantao: Yi Nanya Wenti wei Zhongxin [Discussion of Sino-British relations during World War II: With South Asian issues at the center]," *Jindaishi Yanjiu* [Research on modern history] vol. 4 (2005), p. 39.

8. Hsiao-ting Lin, *Tibet,* p. 148.

9. Li Yuquan, "The Tibet Office," pp. 113–114.

10. Republic of China Archives, 0592/4410.01–15.

11. Hsiao-ting Lin, *Tibet,* p. 148.

12. Republic of China Archives, 0592/4410.01–05. Kong Qingzong was from Sichuan, as were most of his staff members. Wu Zhongxin was from Anhui. He brought many Anhui people to Tibet. These two groups quarreled and split the Tibet Office. A British official in Lhasa reported that Kong did not get along with other government officials in Tibet. Hsiao-ting Lin, *Tibet,* p. 242.

13. Dai Jitao was a disciple of the Panchen Lama. In 1936, as the Executive

Yuan head, Dai worshiped the Panchen at a public Buddhist ceremony in Nanjing. The MTAC director, Wu Zhongxin, was Dai's revolutionary comrade. He often consulted Dai, who was said to be the actual head of the commission.

14. Zhou Xuanhua, *Caizheng yu Waijiao de Gongzuo Huiyi* [Memoirs of fiscal and diplomatic work] (Taipei, 2006), pp. 65–66.

15. Zhang Ling'ao, *My Days at the Staff Office*, p. 139.

16. Ibid., pp. 140–141.

17. Chen Xizhang, "Political Activities in Tibet," p. 117; Zhang Ling'ao, *My Days at the Staff Office*, pp. 142–143; Li Yuquan, "The Tibet Office," p. 25.

18. Chen Xizhang, "Political Activities in Tibet," pp. 120–121.

19. Zhang Ling'ao, *My Days at the Staff Office*, pp. 142–143; Zhou Xuanhua, *Memoirs of Fiscal and Diplomatic Work*, p. 69.

20. MZWYH, vol. 3, pp. 17–21.

21. Ibid., pp. 11–15.

22. The gifts were classified into three categories. First-tier gifts included gold watches, Hunan embroidery, and jade. They were given to the Dalai Lama, the regent, the king of Sikkim, and other dignitaries. They were worth 50,000 yuan per recipient. In total they cost 400,000 yuan. Second-tier gifts included embroidery, Sichuan silk, pocket watches, and crystal glasses, worth 20,000 yuan per recipient. In total they cost 800,000 yuan. Third-tier gifts included cloth and tea. They were worth 5,000 yuan per recipient. In total they cost 300,000 yuan. The total cost of gifts for 108 recipients was 1,500,000 yuan. *MZWYH*, vol. 13, pp. 371–374.

23. Gifts from British officials in Lhasa to the Dalai Lama included picture books and bicycles. See Alex McKay, *Tibet and the British Raj: The Frontier Cadre, 1904–1947,* (Dharamsala: Library of Tibetan Works and Archives, 2009), 157.

24. Zhang Ling'ao, *My Days at the Staff Office*, p. 143.

25. Melvyn C. Goldstein, *A History of Modern Tibet, 1913–1951: Demise of the Lamaist State* (Berkeley: University of California Press, 1989), p. 524.

26. Zhang Yuxin, Zhang Shuangzhi, eds., *Historical Documents on Tibet*, vol. 7, pp. 231–232.

27. Chen Xizhang, "Political Activities in Tibet," p. 119; Zhang Ling'ao, *My Days at the Staff Office*, p. 144; Liu Shengqi, "Wo Jin Zang de Di Yi Ke" [My first lesson after I entered Tibet], in Historical Documents Research Committee at the Tibet Autonomous Region Chinese People's Political Consultative Conference, eds., *Xizang wenshi ziliao xuanji* [Selection of Tibetan historical documents] (Lhasa: Xizang Renmin Chubanshe, 1984), vol. 4, p. 73.

28. Zhang Yuxin, Zhang Shuangzhi, eds., *Historical Documents on* Tibet, vol. 7, p. 232.

29. Lamb, *Tibet, China and India*, p. 328.

30. Zhang Yuxin, Zhang Shuangzhi eds., *Historical Documents on Tibet*, vol. 7, pp. 243–244.

31. Lamb, *Tibet, China, and India*, p. 329. In his memoir published after his retirement, Gould praised Shen Zonglian as "a patriot with wide views." See B. J. Gould, *The Jewel in the Lotus: Recollections of an Indian Political* (London: Chatto and Windus, 1957), p. 241.

32. Gould, *The Jewel in the Lotus,* p. 528. Zhang Yongpan, *The British Empire and China's Tibet,* pp. 141–143.

33. *Dagonghao* (Chongqing), August 13, 1944.

34. MZWYH, vol. 12, p. 250; Zhang Ling'ao, *My Days at the Staff Office* p. 145.

35. MZWYH, vol. 13, p. 378–382.

36. Gould, *The Jewel in the Lotus, pp.* 530–531.

37. Ibid., pp. 406–407.

38. Chen Qianping, *Sino-British Negotiations,* pp. 188–189.

39. Gould to the Government of India, November 1, 1944; Government of India to the India Office, November 15, 1944, Oriental and India Office Collections, L/PS/12/4217, cited in Lin Xiaoting, "Discussion of Sino-British Relations," p. 53.

40. Chen Qianping, *Sino-British Negotiations,* pp. 185–193.

41. Robert Ford, *Capture in Tibet* (London: Harrap, 1957), p. 215.

42. McKay, *Tibet and the British Raj,* pp. 155–156.

43. MZWYH, vol. 13, p. 327.

44. Ibid., pp. 428–429.

45. Xu Baiyong, "Shilun Minguo shiqi Yingguo dui Zhongguo Xizang de Wuqi Gongying" [Discussions on British Arms Supply to China's Tibet during the Republic], *Zhongguo bianjiang shidi yanjiu* [Research on the history and geography of China's frontiers], March 2007, pp. 72–81.

46. McKay, *Tibet and the British Raj,* p. 157.

47. Zhang Yuxin, Zhang Shuangzhi, eds., *Historical Documents on Tibet,* vol. 7, p. 273.

48. Historical Documents Research Committee at the Tibet Autonomous Region Chinese People's Political Consultative Conference, ed., *Xizang wenshi ziliao xuanji* [Selection of Tibetan historical documents] (Lhasa: Xizang renmin chubanshe, 1984), vol. 5, pp. 85–92.

49. Chen Xizhang, "Political Activities in Tibet," p. 122.

50. Zhang Yuxin, Zhang Shuangzhi, eds., *Historical Documents on Tibet,* vol. 7, pp. 273–275.

51. Gould, *The Jewel in the Lotus,* p. 530.

52. Li Youyi, "Xizang Wenti zhi Fenxi" [Analysis of Tibet issues], *Bianzheng gonglun* [Comments on frontier administration], vol. 7, no. 3 (September 1948), p. 1.

53. Chiang Kai-shek, *Zhongguo zhi Mingyun* [China's destiny] (Taipei: Zhongyang Wenwu Gongyingshe, 1965), p. 7.

54. H. E. Richardson, *Tibet and Its History* (London: Oxford University Press, 1962), p. 166.

55. Chen Xizhang, "Political Activities in Tibet," pp. 125–128; Li Yuquan, "The Tibet Office," p. 35.

56. Chen Xizhang, "Political Activities in Tibet," p. 128.

57. Li Yuquan, "The Tibet Office," p. 58.

58. Liu Shengqi, "Wo Xuexi Zangzu Shi de Jingguo" [My experience of studying the history of the Tibetans], *Zhongguo Xizang* [China's Tibet], vol. 3, no. 3

(2002), p. 48; Liu Shengqi, "Rezhen Shijian Jianwenlu" [Witness to the Reting Incident], *Zhongguo Zangxue* [China Tibetology], vol. 4 (1996), pp. 84–100.

59. Tsung-lien Shen and Shen-chi Liu, *Tibet and the Tibetans* (Stanford: Stanford University Press, 1953).

60. A. Tom Grunfeld, "Developments in Tibetan Studies in China Today," *China Quarterly*, vol. 115 (September 1988), p. 462.

61. Li Youyi, "Analysis of Tibet Issues," p. 4.

62. Zhang Ling'ao, *My Days at the Staff Office*, p. 45.

63. Hsiao-ting Lin, *Tibet*, p. 170.

64. Zhang Ling'ao, *My Days at the Staff Office*, p. 146.

65. In winter 1944, Chiang Kai-shek ordered the former warlords Yang Sen and Pan Wenhua in Sichuan to get rid of Liu Wenhui by force. Yang Sen obeyed the order, but Pan refused, on the grounds that if the central government had evidence that Liu Wenhui had committed treason, he should be put on trial. Chiang and Yang sent many telegrams urging Pan to act, but Pan was unmoved. Finally Chiang Kai-shek had to give up the plan. *Chengdu wenshi ziliao* [Chengdu cultural historical documents], vol. 4 (1988), pp. 200–201.

66. Zhang Ling'ao, *My Days at the Staff Office*, p. 147.

67. MZWYH, vol. 6, p. 308.

68. Gould, *The Jewel in the Lotus*, pp. 538–543.

69. Ibid., p. 544.

70. Zhang Yuxin, Zhang Shuangzhi, eds., *Historical Documents on Tibet*, vol. 7, pp. 299–300.

71. Dorje Ngodrub Changngopa, "Xizang Difang Zhengfu Pai Daibiaotuan Weiwen Tongmengguo he Chuxi Nanjing Guomin Daibiao Dahui Neimu" [The inside story behind the Tibetan authority's delegation to pay respects to the Allies and to participate in the National Representative Conference], *Xizang wenshi ziliao xuanji* vol. 2, pp. 1–3; Lamb, *Tibet, China and India*, p. 459. For the letters from the Dalai Lama and Tibetan Regent Taktra to President Truman, see United States Department of State, *Foreign Relations of the United States, 1947*, vol. 7, *The Far East: China* (Washington, DC: Government Printing Office, 1972), pp. 592–593.

72. Dorje Ngodrub Changngopa, "The Inside Story," p. 3.

73. Zhang Yuxin, Zhang Shuangzhi, eds., *Historical Documents on Tibet*, vol. 7, pp. 298–299.

74. Dorje Ngodrub Changngopa, "The Inside Story," pp. 3–4.

75. Ibid., p. 4.

76. Chen Xizhang, "Political Activities in Tibet," p. 131.

77. Dorje Ngodrub Changngopa, "The Inside Story," p. 6.

78. Gould, *The Jewel in the Lotus*, p. 554.

79. Dorje Ngodrub Changngopa, "The Inside Story," p. 7.

80. Bai Chongxi Xiansheng Fangwen Jilu [Interviews with Mr. Bai Chongxi] (Taipei: Academia Sinica, 1984), pp. 851–852. Bai was Muslim, and he was often asked to deal with non-Han peoples.

81. National Representative Conference Secretariat, ed., *Guomin Dahui Shilu* [Record of the National Representative Conference] (Nanjing: National Representative Conference Secretariat, 1946), pp. 368–415.

82. Dorje Ngodrub Changngopa, "The Inside Story," pp. 7–8.

83. Ibid, p. 7; Yuan Yicheng, *Zhixian Riji* [Diary of the drafting of the constitution] (Taipei: Commercial Press, 1970), p. 66.

84. Constitution of the Republic of China (Taipei: Executive Yuan News Bureau, 1983), Article 168.

85. Dorje Ngodrub Changngopa, "The Inside Story," p. 9.

86. Zhang Yuxin, Zhang Shuangzhi, eds., *Historical Documents on Tibet*, vol. 7, p. 402.

87. Dorje Ngodrub Changngopa, "The Inside Story," p. 9.

88. Zhang Yuxin, Zhang Shuangzhi, eds., *Historical Documents on Tibet*, vol. 7, pp. 403, 405.

89. Gould, *The Jewel in the Lotus,* pp. 558–559.

90. Zhang Ling'ao, *My Days at the Staff Office*, p. 149.

91. The Historical Documents Editorial Office at the Historical Documents Research Committee at the National Committee of the Chinese People's Political Consultative Conference, ed., *Wenshi Ziliao Xuanji*, vol. 92, pp. 152–153.

92. Li Youyi, "Analysis of Tibet Issues," p. 34.

93. Liu Jiaju, *Kang Zang* [Xikang and Tibet] (Shanghai: Xin Yaxiya Yuekan She), 1932, p. 24.

94. Recent works on Western perception of Tibet are Peter Bishop, *The Myth of Shangri-La: Tibet, Travel Writing, and the Western Creation of a Sacred Landscape* (Berkeley: University of California Press, 1989); Alex McKay, *Tibet and the British Raj*; Thierry Dodin and Heinz Räther, eds., *Imagining Tibet: Realities, Projections, and Fantasies* (Boston: Wisdom Publications, 2001); Laurie Howell McMillin, *English in Tibet, Tibet in English: Self-Presentation in Tibet and the Diaspora* (New York: Palgrave Macmillan, 2001); Martin Brauen, *Dreamworld Tibet: Western Illusions* (Bangkok: Orchid Press, 2004); Dibyesh Anand, *Geopolitical Exotica: Tibet in Western Imagination* (Minneapolis: University of Minnesota Press, 2007); Gordon T. Stewart, *Journeys to Empire: Enlightenment, Imperialism, and the British Encounter with Tibet, 1774–1904* (Cambridge: Cambridge University Press, 2009). There is only one article on Chinese people's perception of Tibet: Martin Slobodnik, "The Perception of Tibet in China: Between Disdain and Fascination," *Furen Lishi Xuebao* [Fu Jen historical journal], vol. 17 (2006), pp. 71–109. Unfortunately, this article does not discuss the situation during the republican period. Stevan Harrell, "Introduction: Civilizing Project and the Reactions to Them," in Stevan Harrell, ed., *Cultural Encounters on China's Ethnic Frontiers* (Seattle: University of Washington Press, 1995), pp. 3–36; idem, "L'état C'Est Nous, or We have Met the Oppressor and He Is Us: The Predicament of Minority Cadres in the PRC," in Diana Lary, ed., *The Chinese State at the Borders* (Vancouver: UBC Press, 2007), p. 223.

95. Gray Tuttle, *Tibetan Buddhists in the Making of Modern China* (New York: Columbia University Press, 2005), pp. 51–52.

96. Kelsang Tsering, *Bianren Chuyan* [Superficial opinions of a frontiersman] (Chongqing: Xizang Wenhua Cujinhui , 1946), pp. 100–101.

97. Dibyesh Anand, "Strategic Hypocrisy: The British Imperial Scripting

of Tibet's Geopolitical Identity," *Journal of Asian Studies*, vol. 68 (2009), pp. 227–252.

98. Wang Jianlang, "Daguo Yiyi yu Daguo Zuowei: Kangzhan Houqi de Zhongguo Guoji Jiaose Dingwei yu Waijiao Nuli" [Power mentality and power behavior: China's global role and diplomatic efforts at the end of the Sino-Japanese War], *Lishi Yanjiu* (Historical research), vol. 6 (2008), p. 130.

99. Lin Xiaoting, "Discussion of Sino-British relations," pp. 47–55.

100. Sechin Jagchid, *The Last Mongol Prince: The Life and Times of Demchugdongrob, 1902–1966* (Bellingham, WA: Center for East Asian Studies, Western Washington University, 1999), p. 68; Justin Tighe, *Constructing Suiyuan: The Politics of Northwestern Territory and Development in Early Twentieth-Century China* (Leiden: Brill, 2005), p. 229; Xiaoyuan Liu, *Reins of Liberation: An Entangled History of Mongolian Independence, Chinese Territoriality, and Great Power Hegemony, 1911–1950* (Stanford: Stanford University Press, 2006), p. 74.

101. Chiang Kai-shek, "Zhongguo Bianjiang Wenti" [China's frontiers], speech in Nanchang, March 7, 1934, in Qin Xiaoyi, *Important Materials*, vol. 12, pp. 108–109.

102. Ibid., vol. 11, pp. 172–173.

CHAPTER 4

1. On November 20, 1935, Comintern personnel reached the Red Army in Baoan (Shaanxi). The army used its homemade transmitter to communicate with the Soviet Union for the first time on June 16, 1936.

2. Yang Kuisong, *Xi'an Shibian xintan: Zhang Xueliang yu Zhonggong guanxi zhimi* [A new study on the Xi'an Incident: The secret relations between Zhang Xueliang and the CCP] (Nanjing: Jiangsu renmin chubanshe, 2007), chaps. 1–5.

3. "Luo Mao guanyu Hongjun zuozhan yuanze zhi Zhou Bo Lin dian" [Telegram on the Red Army's combat guidelines from Luo Fu (Zhang Wentian) and Mao Zedong to Zhou Enlai, Bo Gu, and Lin Biao], August 1, 1937, *Mao Zedong wenji* [Works of Mao Zedong] (Beiping: Zhongyang wenxian chubanshe, 1999), vol. 2, p. 1.

4. "Luo Mao guanyu Hongjun canjia Kangzhang de zuozhan renwu yu bingli shiyong yuanze gei Zhu Zhou Bo Lin Peng Ren de dianbao" [Telegram on the Red Army's combat task and principles for use of military force from Luo Fu and Mao Zedong to Zhu De, Zhou Enlai, Bo Gu, Lin Biao, Peng Dehuai, and Ren Bishi], August 5, 1937, ibid.

5. "Mao Zedong guanyu Bai Huang fang'an hanyou jida yinmou jianjue buneng tongyi gei Zhou Ye de dianbao" [Telegram that the plan by Bai and Huang had great conspiracy could never be agreed by Zhou Enlai and Ye Ting], August 18, 1937, ibid.

6. "Mao Zedong guanyu shixing duli zizhu de shandi youji fangzhen gei Peng Dehuai tongshengdian" [Telegram about the guideline of conducting independent guerrilla warfare in mountainous areas from Mao Zedong to Peng Dehuai], September 21, 1937, *Mao Zedong wenji*, vol. 2, pp. 19–20.

7. Georgi Mikhailovich Dimitrov, *Jimiteluofu riji xuanbian* [Selections of the

diary of Georgi Dimitrov], trans. Ma Xipu, Yang Yanjie, Ge Zhiqiang, et al. (Guilin: Guangxi shifan daxue chubanshe, 2002), p. 60.

8. Yang Yunruo and Yang Kuisong, *Gongchan guoji he Zhongguo geming* [The Comintern and the Chinese Revolution] (Shanghai: Shanghai renmin chubanshe, 1985), pp. 435–437.

9. "Jimiteluofu zai Gongchan Guoji Zhiweihui Shujichu taolun Zhongguo wenti huiyi shang de fayan" [Speech of Dimitrov at the Comintern Executive Committee Secretariat conference for the China issue], August 10, 1937, in *Gongchan Guoji guanyu Zhongguo geming de wenxian ziliao*, vol. 3, pp. 26–27; "Gongchan Guoji Zhiweihui Shujichu guanyu Zhongguo wenti de jueyi" [Resolution of the Comintern Executive Committee Secretariat conference for the China issue], October 10, 1937, ibid.

10. Dimitrov, op. cit., pp. 60–61.

11. "Wang Ming zai Zhonggong Zhongyang Zhengzhiju huiyi shang de baogao" [Report of Wang Ming at the CCP Central Committee Politburo Conference], December 9, 1937, *Mao Zedong wenji*.

12. "Mao Zedong zai Zhonggong Zhongyang Zhengzhiju huiyi shang de fayan" [Speech of Mao Zedong at the CCP Central Committee Politburo conference], December 12, 1937, *Mao Zedong wenji*.

13. Luo Fu (Zhang Wentian), "Gonggu Guo Gong hezuo, zhengqu Kangzhan shengli" [Consolidate Communist-Nationalist cooperation, struggle for the victory in the Sino-Japanese War], *Jiefang ribao* [Liberation daily], vol. 28, December 21, 1937; "Mao Zedong deng guanyu Hongjun zai youjun quyunei ying jianchi Tongyizhanxian yuanze de zhishi" [Instructions from Mao Zedong and others that the Red Army should stick to the United Front principle in the areas of the allying troops], December 24, 1937, *Mao Zedong wenji*.

14. Ye Qing, "Guanyu zhengzhi dang pai" [On political parties], *Xue lu* [Blood road], vol. 2, 1938.

15. "Chen Zhou Bo guanyu Jinchaji Bianqu tongdian shi zhi Shujichu bing zhuan Zhu Peng Ren Liu dian" [Telegram about the border area of Shanxi, Chahar, and Hebei from Chen Shaoyu, Zhou Enlai, and Bo Gu to the Secretariat, also forwarded to Zhu De, Peng Dehuai, Ren Bishi, and Liu Shaoqi], January 28, 1938, *Mao Zedong wenji*.

16. Yang Yunruo and Yang Kuisong, op. cit., pp. 449–450.

17. "Zhonggong Zhongyang zhi Guomindang linshi quanguo daibiao dahui dian" [Telegram from CCP Central Committee to the Nationalist Provisional National Congress], March 25, 1937, *Mao Zedong wenji*.

18. "Zhonggong zhongyang dui Guomindang linshi quanguo daibiao dahui de tiyi" [Proposal of the CCP Central Committee to the Nationalist Provisional National Congress], March 24, 1937, *Mao Zedong wenji*.

19. "Ren Bishi daibiao Zhonggong Zhongyang dui Gongchan Guoji baogao dagang" [Report outline from the CCP Central Committee representative Ren Bishi], April 14, May 17, 1938, *Mao Zedong wenji*.

20. Wang Jiaxiang, "Huiyi Mao Zedong tongzhi yu Wang Ming jihui zhuyi luxian de douzheng" [Memoir of Comrade Mao Zedong's struggle against the

Wang Ming opportunism political line], *Renmin ribao* [People's daily], December 27, 1939.

21. Wang Jiaxiang, "Guoji zhishi baogao" [Report on Comintern instructions], September 1938, in *Wang Jiaxiang xuanji* [Selected works of Wang Jiaxiang] (Beiping: Renmin chubanshe, 1989), pp. 138–142.

22. Mao Zedong, "Lun xin jieduan" [On the new stage], October 12–14, 1938, in *Mao Zedong junshi wenji* [Military works of Mao Zedong] (Beiping: Zhongguo renmin jiefangjun zhanshi chubanshe, 1981), p. 185.

23. "Zhongguo Gongchandang kuoda de Liuzhong quanhui zhi Jiang Jieshi weiyuanzhang dian" [Telegram from the expanded CCP Sixth Committee to Military Committee chairman Chiang Kai-shek], November 5, 1938, *Mao Zedong wenji*; "Zhongguo Gongchandang kuoda de liuzhong quanhui genju Mao Zedong tongzhi baogao tongguo de jueyian" [Resolution of the expanded CCP Sixth Committee based on Comrade Mao Zedong's report], November 6, 1938, ibid.

24. "Chen Shaoyu deng guanyu yige dadang wenti yu Jiang Jieshi tanpan qingkuang xiang Zhongyang de baogao" [Report from Chen Shaoyu and others to the CCP Central Committee concerning the negotiation with Chiang Kai-shek about one big party], December 13, 1938, *Mao Zedong wenji*.

25. Dimitrov, op. cit., p. 95.

26. Yang Kuisong, *Mao Zedong yu Mosike de enenyuanyuan* [Gratitude and resentment between Mao Zedong and Moscow] (Nanchang: Jiangxi renmin chubanshe, 2005), p. 99.

27. "Mao Zedong zai Zhonggong Zhongyang Zhengzhiju huiyi shang de fayan" [Speech of Mao Zedong at the CCP Central Committee Politburo], May 7, 1939, *Mao Zedong wenji*.

28. Mao Zedong, "Fan touxiang tigang" [Anti-surrender outline], June 10, 1939, *Mao Zedong wenji*, vol. 2, pp. 205–222.

29. Mao Zedong, "Dierci Diguozhuyi zhanzheng jiangyan tigang" [Outline for a speech on the second imperialist war], September 14, 1939, *Mao Zedong wenji*.

30. "Gongchan Guoji zhiweihui zhuxituan guanyu Zhonggong daibiaotuan baogao de jueyi" [Resolution of the CCP delegation's report by the Comintern Executive Committee Presidium], February 1940, *Mao Zedong wenji*.

31. "Jiang Jieshi zhi Sidalin dian" [Telegram from Chiang Kai-shek to Joseph Stalin], September 29, 1940, in Shao Lizi, "Chushi Sulian de huiyi" [Memoir of the visit to the Soviet Union], in *Wenshi ziliao xuanji* [Selections of literary and historical documents], vol. 60, p. 186.

32. Ibid., pp. 185–186.

33. Vasily Ivanovich Chuikov, *Zai Hua shiming* [Mission to China: Memoirs of a military adviser to Chiang Kaishek], trans. Wan Chengcai (Beiping: Xinhua chubanshe, 1980), pp. 34–36.

34. "Mao Zedong zhi Jimiteluofu, Mannuyiersiji de xin" [Letter from Mao Zedong to Dimitrov and Manuilsky], November 4, 1940, *Mao Zedong wenji*.

35. Yang Yunruo and Yang Kuisong, op. cit., p. 518; Dimitrov, op. cit., p. 115.

36. "Zhonggong Zhongyang Shujichu guanyu Huazhong gexiang zhengce de zhishi" [Instructions on various policies in central China by the CCP Central Committee secretariat], December 13, 1940, *Mao Zedong wenji*; "Zhonggong Zhongyang guanyu shiju yu zhengce de zhishi" [Instructions on the current situa-

tion and policies by the CCP Central Committee], December 25, 1940, ibid.; "Mao Zhu Wang guanyu cici yanzhong de touxiang weiji yi bei zhizhi zhi Peng Zuo Nie Peng Liu Deng deng dian" [Telegram from Mao Zedong, Zhu De, and Wang Ming to Peng Dehuai, Zuo Quan, Nie Rongzhen, Peng Zhen, Liu Bocheng, Deng Xiaoping, and others concerning suppressing the serious danger of Nationalist surrender], December 19, 1940, ibid.

37. Dimitrov, op. cit., pp.121–122.

38. Ibid., p. 122.

39. Ibid., pp. 123–124.

40. "Mao Zedong guanyu Jiang Jieshi fabu 117 mingling hou Guogong guanxi bianhua ji wo zhi duice zhi Zhou Enlai, Peng Dehuai, Liu Shaoqi dian" [Telegram from Mao Zedong to Zhou Enlai, Peng Dehuai, and Liu Shaoqi concerning the changes in Communist-Nationalist relations after Chiang Kai-shek issued the 117 command and our countermeasure], January 20, 1941, *Mao Zedong wenji.*

41. "Zhongyang guanyu dangqian shiju de juedui" [Decisions of the current situation by the CCP Central Committee], January 29, 1941, China Central Archive, *Wannan Shibian Ziliao xuanji* [Southern Anhui Incident, Selections of documents] (Beiping: Zhonggong Zhongyang Dangxiao chubanshe, 1982), pp. 197–220.

42. Dimitrov, op. cit., p. 126.

43. "Mao Zedong guanyu Rikou jingong xingshi de fenxi zhi Zhou Enlai dian" [Telegram from Mao Zedong to Zhou Enlai concerning the analysis of the Japanese enemy's offensive], February 7, 1941, *Mao Zedong wenji.*

44. "Mao Zedong, Zhu De, Wang Jiaxiang guanyu muqian fangzhen wenti zhi Peng Dehuai dian" [Telegram from Mao Zedong, Zhu De, Wang Jiaxiang to Peng Dehuai concerning the current policy], May 18, 1941, *Mao Zedong wenji.*

45. "Mao Zedong guanyu tuanji duidi wenti gei Zhou Enlai de zhishi" [Instruction from Mao Zedong to Zhou Enlai concerning getting united to fight the Japanese enemy], May 14, 1941, *Mao Zedong wenji.*

46. Dimitrov, op. cit., p. 142.

47. "Gongchan Guoji wei Zhonggong tigong caizheng zizhu qingkuang zhi kaocha" [Investigation of the financial aid from the Comintern to the CCP], in *Dangshi yanjiu ziliao* [Party history research materials] (2004), vols. 1 and 2.

48. Dimitrov, op. cit., pp. 146–147.

49. "Mao, Zhu, Wang, Ye guanyu cong zhanlue shang peihu Sujun zuozhan wenti gei Peng Dehuai dian" [Telegram from Mao Zedong, Zhu De, Wang Ming, and Ye Jianying to Peng Dehuai concerning cooperating the Soviet Army's combat strategically], July 2, 1941, *Mao Zedong wenji.*

50. "Mao Zedong guanyu Sulian zhanju jianqu wenti zhi Zhou Enlai dian" [Telegram from Mao Zedong to Zhou Enlai concerning the eventual stabilization of the Soviet war situation], July 6, 1941, *Mao Zedong wenji.*

51. "Mao Zedong guanyu bangzhu Sulian Hongjun women jue qu guangfan youjizhan de fangzhen zhi Zhou Enlai dian" [Telegram from Mao Zedong to Zhou Enlai concerning helping the Soviet Red Army and our decision to conduct extensive guerrilla warfare], July 15, 1941, *Mao Zedong wenji.*

52. Dimitrov, op. cit., pp. 148–149.

53. "Zhonggong Zhongyang junwei guanyu Kangri genjudi junshi jianshe de zhishi" [Instructions of the Communist Party Central Military Committee concerning the military construction of the anti-Japanese bases], November 7, 1941, *Mao Zedong wenji*.

54. Yang Yunruo and Yang Kuisong, op. cit., pp. 539–540.

55. Mao Zedong, "Fandui zhuguan zhuyi he zongpai zhuyi" [Against subjectivism and sectarianism], September 10, 1942, in *Wenxian yu yanjiu* [Documents and research] (1985), vol. 1; "Mao Zedong zai Zhongguo Gongchandang diqici daibiao dahuishang guanyu xuanju wenti de jianghua" [Mao Zedong's speech concerning election at the CCP Seventh Committee congress], May 24, 1945, *Mao Zedong wenji*.

56. Zhang Ruxin, "Xuexi he zhangwo Mao Zedong de lilun he celue [Studying and mastering the theory and strategy of Mao Zedong]," *Jiefang ribao*, February 19, 1942.

57. "Zhonggong Zhongyang Zhengzhiju guanyu Zhongyang jigou tiaozheng he jingjian de jueding" [Decisions of the CCP Central Committee Politburo concerning the adjustment and reduction of Central Committee organs], March 20, 1943, *Mao Zedong wenji*.

58. Dimitrov, op. cit., p. 198.

59. "Lun Gongchanguoji de jiesan [On the dissolution of the Comintern]," *Jiefang ribao*, May 28, 1943.

60. "Mao Zedong, Zai Yan'an ganbu dahui shang guanyu Gongchanguoji jiesan de baogao" [Report on the dissolution of the Comintern at the Yan'an Cadre Conference], *Jiefang ribao*, May 28, 1943.

61. "Zhonggong Zhongyang Zhengzhiju jiu Wang Ming dengren cuowu xingzhi wenti de jueyi" [Resolution on the nature of the mistakes made by Wang Ming and others by the CCP Central Committee Politburo], November 29, 1943, *Mao Zedong wenji*.

62. Dimitrov, op. cit., pp. 267–268, 273–274.

CHAPTER 5

1. Three of Canada's post-1975 ambassadors to China were born and raised in China—Ralph Collins, John Small, and Arthur Menzies. All spoke fluent Chinese. For the missionary/bureaucrat connection, see Jack Granatstein, *The Ottawa Men: The Civil Service Mandarins, 1935–1957* (Toronto: Oxford University Press, 1982).

2. Alvyn Austin, *China's Millions* (Grand Rapids: Eerdmans, 2007) discusses the strange and engaging history of the CIM.

3. Rosario Renaud, *Suchow: Diocese de Chine* (Montreal: editions Bellarmin, 1955).

4. Dong Linfu, *Cross Culture and Faith: The Life and Work of James Mellon Menzies* (Toronto: University of Toronto Press, 2005).

5. Menzies's house in Anyang has been turned into a museum, and his archaeological achievements are recognized at the Archaeological Research Station just outside the town.

6. Roger Bowen, *Innocence Is Not Enough: The Life and Death of Herbert*

Norman (Toronto: Douglas and McIntyre, 1986); and James Barros, *No Sense of Evil: Espionage, the Case of Herbert Norman* (Toronto: Deneau, 1986).

7. The Axis powers and Vichy France had relations with Wang Jingwei's collaborationist government in Nanjing.

8. Hans Van de Ven, "Stilwell in the Stocks: The Chinese Nationalists and the Allied Powers in the Second World War," *Asian Affairs*, vol. 34, no. 3 (November 2003), pp. 243–259.

9. Simon Winchester, *The Man Who Loved China* (New York: Harper, 2009).

10. J. K. Fairbank, *Chinabound* (New York: Harper and Row, 1982).

11. Robert Payne, *Chungking Diary* (London: Heinemann, 1945).

12. Han Suyin, *Destination Chungking* (New York, 1942).

13. K. P. S. Menon, *Delhi-Chungking: A Travel Diary* (London: Oxford University Press, 1947); and *Twilight in China* (Bombay: Bharatiya Vidya Bhavan, 1972). Menon was intrepid. He reached his post by traveling on horseback through the Karakorums, via the Hunza Valley and then along the northern edge of the Taklamakan Desert.

14. Oliver Lindsay, *Battle for Hong Kong* (Spellamat: Staplehurst, 2004). The Hong Kong government has restored the sites where Canadians fought in Hong Kong, such as at Magazine Gap.

15. Zhongguo kangRi dazidian (Wuhan: Wuhan chubanshe, 1995), pp. 1073–1074. These include two Bethune tombs, the first in Tang xian, the second in Shijiazhuang (both in Hebei Province).

16. Vancouver Historical Society, Newsletter, vol. 46, no. 6 (March 2008).

17. Odlum to MacKenzie King, August 1945, MacKenzie King Correspondence, National Archives of Canada, 349143.

18. Bethune died of septicemia after he cut his finger while operating without protective gloves.

19. G. F. McNally, "Odlum: Canada's First Ambassador to China" (Edmonton, University of Alberta thesis, 1976), p. 9.

20. Roger Odlum, *Victor Odlum* (Vancouver, 1995), pp. 129–130.

21. Victor Odlum Papers, December 1939, National Archives of Canada.

22. Kim Richard Nossal, "Relations with China in the 1940s," in *An Acceptance of Paradox* (Toronto: Canadian Institute of International Affairs, 1982), pp. 39–55.

23. Odlum, *Victor Odlum*, p. 176.

24. McNally, "Odlum," p. 152.

25. K. P. S. Menon, *Twilight in China*, p. 161.

26. Alvyn Austin, *Saving China: Canadian Missionaries in the Middle Kingdom, 1888–1949* (Toronto: University of Toronto Press, 1986), pp. 273–274.

27. Odlum, *Victor Odlum*, p. 243.

28. Stephen Endicott, *Rebel out of China* (Toronto: University of Toronto Press, 1980).

29. David Lethbridge, *Bethune: The Secret Police Files* (Salmon Arm: Undercurrent Press, 2003).

30. Selected Works of Mao Zedong, online version.

31. Lethbridge, *Bethune*, p. 102.

32. Scott Monroe, *McClure: The China Years* (Markham: Penguin, 1979), pp. 215–236.

33. Monroe, *McClure*, pp. 230–231.

34. In the 1930s the cult of the Virgin Mary, the Marian Cult, was at its height in the Roman Catholic Church in Quebec.

35. Diana Lary, "Faith and War: Canadian Jesuits and the Japanese Invasion of China," *Modern Asian Studies*, vol. 39, no. 4 (2005), pp. 825–852.

36. E. G. Perrault, *Tong: The Story of Tong Louie, Vancouver's Quiet Titan* (Vancouver: Harbour Publishing, 2002), p. 99.

37. Wing Chung Ng, *The Chinese in Vancouver* (Vancouver: University of British Columbia Press, 1999), p. 19.

38. Denise Chong, *The Concubine's Children: Portrait of a Family Divided* (Toronto: Penguin, 1994), pp. 139, 2.

39. See Colleen Leung's documentary *Letters from Home* (National Film Board of Canada, 2001).

40. Alexander Woodside heard his sermons as a child at the Bloor Street United Church in Toronto and vouches for his oratory.

41. Ted Allen and Sydney Gordon, *The Scalpel, the Sword* (London: Hale, 1954). The film *Bethune; The Making of a Hero* appeared in 1990. There are a number of other Canadian biographies of Bethune; the most recent are Adrienne Clarkson, *Norman Bethune* (Toronto: Penguin, 2009); and Roderick and Sharon Stewart, *Phoenix: The Life of Norman Bethune* (Montreal: McGill Queens Press, 2011).

42. Chalmers Johnson, *Peasant Nationalism and Communist Power: The Emergence of Revolutionary China* (Stanford: Stanford University Press, 1962). Johnson's thesis that the war was a key factor in the CCP's rise to power, once denigrated, is now in favor again.

43. The campaign is being pursued in Canada by Father Bernard's nephew, Professor Prosper Bernard. *De l'autre cote de la terre: la Chine* (Montreal: Sciences et culture, 2000).

CHAPTER 6

1. Convention Relative to the Opening of Hostilities, signed at The Hague in 1907, Article 1; see Lassa Oppenheim, *International Law: A Treatise,* 7th edition (London: Longman, 1952), vol. 2. Also see definitions in Waijiao xuehui (ed.), *Waijiao Dacidian* [Dictionary of foreign relations] (Shanghai: Zhonghua Press, 1937), pp. 637-638; and Tachi Sakutaro, *Shina Jihen Kokusaihou Ron* [International law regarding the China Incident] (Tokyo: Shokado, 1938), chap. 1; Shinobu Junpei, *Senji Kokusaihou Kougi* [Lectures on the law of war] (Tokyo: Maruzen, 1941), vol. 1; Taoka Ryoichi, *Kokusaihou III* [International law III] (Tokyo: Yuhikaku, 1959).

2. Kato Yoko, *Mosaku Suru 1930 Nendai* [1930s: A decade of search] (Tokyo: Yamakawa Publishing, 1993), pp. 68–71.

3. Second Chinese Historical Archive, comp., *Kangri zhanzheng zhengmian zhanchang* [Documents: Front battle lines of the Sino-Japanese War] (Nanjing: Jiangsu Guji Chubanshe, 1987), vol. 1, p. 260, command, July 9, 1937.

4. Li Yunhan, ed., *Jiang weiyuanzhang Zhongzheng kangzhan fanglüe shou-gao huibian* [President Chiang's personal communications during the war of resistance] (Taipei: Zhongguo guomindang dangshiweiyuanhui, 1992), p. 14.

5. Minutes, in Second Historical Archive (Nanjing), ed., *Minguo dang'an* [Quarterly journal of Republican Archives], no. 2 (1987), pp. 6–7.

6. Wang Shijie riji [Diaries of Wang Shijie] (Taipei: Institute of Modern History, Academia Sinica, 1990), vol. 1, p. 66.

7. Report no. 7, July 16, *Minguo dang'an*, no. 2 (1987), p. 10.

8. Report no. 14, July 24, ibid., p. 16.

9. Zongtong Jiang Gong sixiang yanlun zongji [Complete thoughts and speeches of President Chiang Kai-shek] (Taipei: Guomindang dangshi weiyuan hui, 1984), vol. 14, pp. 597–604.

10. Qin Xiaoyi et al., comp., *Zhonghua minguo zhongyao shiliao chu-bian—duiri kangzhan shiqi* [Preliminary compilation of the important historical documents of the Republic of China: Period of the Sino-Japanese War] (Taipei: Guomindang dangshi weiyuanhui, 1981), part 2, vol. 2, p. 67.

11. Report no. 18, July 28, *Minguo dang'an,* no. 3 (1987), p. 6.

12. Wang Shijie riji, vol. 1, pp. 84–85, entry for August 5–7, 1937.

13. Wang Zizhuang riji [Diaries of Wang Zizhuang] (Taipei: Institute of Modern History, Academia Sinica, 2001), vol. 4, p. 214, entry for August 2, 1937.

14. Wang Shijie riji, vol. 1, p. 87.

15. Ibid., vol. 1, p. 88.

16. *Zhongyang ribao*, August 15, 1937.

17. *Da Gong Bao*, October 4, 1937, cited in *Guowen zhoubao*, vol. 14, no. 41 (October 25, 1937), pp. 35–36.

18. Lugouqiao shibian qianhou de Zhongri waijiao guanxi [Sino-Japanese diplomatic relations around the Marco Polo Bridge Incident] (Taipei: Guomindang dangshi weiyuanhui, 1966), pp. 346–349. Documents compiled by Waijiao wenti yanjiu hui [Society for study of foreign policy questions].

19. Ibid., pp. 226–233.

20. Ibid., p. 241. Foreign Ministry telegram to embassy in the United States, December 9, 1937.

21. Ibid., pp. 235–240.

22. Ibid., pp. 245–252.

23. Diaries of Chiang Kai-shek, Hoover Institution, Stanford University, Box 39, Folder 20, entry for January 15, 1938.

24. Memorandum of conversation by the secretary of state, January 26, 1938, in Department of State, *Foreign Relations of the United States: Diplomatic Papers 1938,* Washington, DC: United States Government Printing Office, 1954, vol. 3, pp. 54–55 (hereafter FRUS, 1938–1943).

25. Wang Shijie riji, vol. 1, p. 191, entry for February 26, 1938.

26. Tsuchida Akio, "Rokoukyo Jiken to Kokuminseifu no Hannou" [Chinese Nationalist government's response to the Marco Polo Bridge Incident], in *Chuo Daigaku Keizai Gakubu Souritsu 100 Shunen Kinen Ronbunshu* [Essays com-

memorating the one hundredth anniversary of the founding of the faculty of Economics, Chuo University] (Hachioji: Chuo University, 2005).

27. Chen Yan, *Kangri zhanzheng shiqi zhongguo waijiao zhidu yanjiu* [Research on the Chinese diplomatic system during the Sino-Japanese War] (Shanghai: Fudan Daxue chubanshe, 2002), pp. 77–82.

28. Notes of Counsellors' meeting (canshi shi), Institute of Modern History, Academia Sinica, Taipei, 301-01—03-001. See also *Minguo dang'an*, 1995, no. 1, pp. 51–56. Chiang's prediction proved wrong. Japan never formally declared war.

29. Gaimusho Chosho [Research Report, Japanese Foreign Ministry], "Sensen Mondai no Sai Kentou" [Reconsidering the problem of declaration of war], in *Shina Jihen Kankei Kokusaihouritsu Mondai* [Issues relating to international war regarding the China Incident], vol. 4, Gaimusho Jouyaku-kyoku dai 2 ka [Second Section, International Treaties Bureau, Japanese Foreign Ministry], August 1938, Japan Center for Asian Historical Resources (JCAHR), reference code: B02030677800.

30. "Chen Bulei xiansheng riji gao" [Chen Bulei's diary in draft], vol. 3, entry for October 14, Academia Historica, Taipei, general no. 134, shiliao, 0161.40/7540.01-03.

31. Feng Yuxiang riji [Diaries of Feng Yuxiang] (Nanjing: Jiangsu guji chubanshe, 1992), vol. 5, pp. 276–277; *Zheng Tiangu huiyilu* [Memoirs of Zheng Tiangu] (Los Angeles: Zheng Damin, 1978), pp. 332–333.

32. Weng Wenhao to Hu Shi, October 21, in Hu Shi, *Hu Shi laiwang shuxinxuan* [Selected letters and papers of Hu Shi] (Hong Kong: Zhonghua shuju, 1983), vol. 2, p. 383; and Guo Tingyi, *Zhonghua minguo shishi rizhi* [Chronological history of the Republic of China] (Taipei: Institute of Modern History, Academia Sinica, 1979), vol. 3, October 22–24, 1938.

33. Qin Xiaoyi et al., vol. 1, pp. 121–124.

34. Diaries of Chiang Kai-shek, Hoover Institution, Stanford University, Box 39, Folder 29, entries for October 27, 28, 1938.

35. Zongtong Jiang Gong, vol. 37, pp. 177–179.

36. Telegram, October 30, 1938, in Jiang Zhongzheng dang'an [Chiang Kai-shek archive], Taibei Guoshiguan, handwritten (kangzhan shiqi), 002010300017050.

37. Zongtong Jiang Gong, vol. 30, pp. 301–306.

38. "Chen Bulei riji," vol. 3, entry for November 1, 1938.

39. November 1, 1938, in Chen Mushan, *Zong handian shiliao guan kangzhan shiqi de Jiang Wang guanxi* [Relations between Chiang Kai-shek and Wang Jingwei during the Sino-Japanese War: Evidence from letters and telegrams] (Taipei: Taiwan Xuesheng shuju, 1995), p. 141. This book cites a lot of Wang Jingwei archival materials that are stored in the Bureau of Investigation, Ministry of Home Affairs (Neizheng bu), Taiwan.

40. Ibid., p. 137.

41. Guomin canzhenghui jishi [Deliberations of the People's Political Council] (Chongqing: Chongqing chubanshe, 1985), vol. 1, pp. 311, 335–337.

42. Chen Mushan, op. cit., pp. 138–139, 140, 142. Chiang also sent a telegram to Hu Shi, his ambassador in the United States, asking him to query the US government about responses to a Chinese declaration of war. See "Chen Bulei riji," vol. 3, entry for November 3.

43. Sir A. Clark Kerr to Viscount Halifax, November 17, 1938, in Great Britain, Foreign Office, *Documents on British Foreign Policy, 1919–1939,* Third Series (London: H.M.S.O., 1949–1961), vol. 8, pp. 216–218. Rumor had it that the British ambassador visited Chiang in Hunan primarily to pass on peace proposals from Japan. See Johnson to Hull, November 5, 1938, FRUS, 1938–1943, p. 372; *Zhou Fohai riji* [Diaries of Zhou Fohai] (Beiping: Zhongguo shehui kexue chubanshe, 1986), p. 177, entry for October 28.

44. Nihon Gaiko Nenpyo narabini Shuyo Bunsho Ge, p. 401.

45. Tao Xisheng to Hu Shi, December 31, 1938, in *Hu Shi laiwang shuxin xuanji,* vol. 2, p. 398.

46. "Weng Wenhao riji xuan" [Selections from Weng Wenhao's diary], in *Jindaishi ziliao,* vol. 103 (March 2001), pp.111–112. Weng notes a speech by Kong on November 7.

47. Weng Wenhao rji xuan, p. 112, entry for November 10.

48. Telegram November 11, 1938, original in Jiang Zhongzheng dang'an, in *Geming wenxian dui Ying waijiao* [Collection of documents relating to foreign relations with England], Academia Historica, Taipei, 002020300039009; see also Chen Mushan, op. cit., pp. 165–166.

49. Qin Xiaoyi et al., op. cit., part 4 [Wartime diplomacy], vol. 2, pp. 29–31.

50. Chen Mushan, op. cit., pp. 143–145.

51. Feng Yuxiang riji, vol. 5, pp. 528 and 536, entries for October 29 and November 13, 1938.

52. Nationalist Party Central Committee, ed., *Zhongguo guomindang diwujie zhongyang zhixing weiyuanhui changwu weiyuanhui huiyi jilu* [Collected records of meetings of the Standing Committee, Central Executive Committee, elected at the Fifth Congress of the Nationalist Party] (Taipei, n.d.), pp. 353–354.

53. Wang Shijie riji, vol. 2, p. 176.

54. Second Historical Archives of China, op. cit., part 5, vol. 2, pp. 76–78, note 4.

55. Wang Shijie riji, vol. 3, pp. 20–21, for Wang's private thoughts on the matter.

56. Second Historical Archives of China, op. cit., part 5, vol. 2, pp. 78–79.

57. Second Historical Archives of China, op. cit., part 5, vol. 2, pp. 79–83.

58. Wang Shijie riji, vol. 3, pp. 28–29.

59. Qin Xiaoyi et al., op. cit., part 3 [Wartime diplomacy], vol. 1, pp. 146–152.

60. FRUS, Japan, 1931–1941, vol. 2, pp. 768–780.

61. December 1, 1941, United Press wire story from Chongqing.

62. Wang Shijie riji, vol. 3, pp. 200–202.

63. Chiang Kai-shek archives, Guoshiguan, Taipei, wartime archive no. 002-080103055004.

64. Qin Xiaoyi et al., op. cit., part 3 [Wartime diplomacy], vol. 3, p. 41.

65. Wang Shijie riji, vol. 3, pp. 203–204.

66. Zhongyang ribao, December 8, 1941.

67. Hull to Gauss, Chongqing, December 9, 1941, FRUS, 1941–1944, p. 739; Qin Xiaoyi et al., op. cit, part 3 [Wartime diplomacy], vol. 2, pp. 88–89.

68. National Government Archives, 07–089, Academia Historica, Taipei, vol. 3, pp. 204–205.

69. Memorandum of Conversation by Welles, December 10, 1941, FRUS, 1941–1944, p. 741; Qin Xiaoyi, et al., op. cit., part 3 [Wartime diplomacy], vol. 3, pp. 44–45, and vol. 2, pp. 88–89.

70. Ibid., vol. 3, p. 42.

71. Ibid., vol. 3, p. 57.

72. Wang Shijie riji, vol. 3, p. 208.

73. FRUS, 1941–1944, pp. 751–752; Qin Xiaoyi et al., op. cit., part 3 [Wartime diplomacy], vol. 3, p. 66.

74. Roosevelt to Stalin, December 14, 1941, in FRUS, 1941–1944, pp. 752–753; Roosevelt to British ambassador (Halifax), December 14, 1941, in FRUS, 1941–1944, p. 753.

75. Qin Xiaoyi et al., op. cit., part 3 [Wartime diplomacy], vol. 3, pp. 82–92.

76. Stalin to Roosevelt, n.d., transmitted by the Soviet ambassador, in FRUS, 1941–1944, pp. 760–761.

77. Roosevelt to Chiang, December 29, 1941, in FRUS, 1941–1944, pp. 763–764; Qin Xiaoyi et al., op. cit., part 3 [Wartime diplomacy], vol. 3, p. 98.

78. Chiang to Roosevelt, December 24, 1941, in FRUS, 1941–1944, p. 762; Qin Xiaoyi et al., op. cit., part 3 [Wartime diplomacy], vol. 3, pp. 794–795.

CHAPTER 7

1. "The New China," signed June 15, 1939, *National Herald*, June 18, 1939, and reprinted in *China, Spain, and the War* (Allahabad, 1940), pp. 11–15, and here quoted from J. Nehru, *Selected Works of Jawaharlal Nehru* (New Delhi, 1976), vol. 9, pp. 266–267. Hereafter cited as Nehru, *Selected Works*.

2. "Huanying Nihelu shi" [Welcome Mr. Nehru], *Central Daily News* [Zhongyang ribao], August 23, 1939, p. 2.

3. "Zhong Yin lishi de xin yizhang" [A new chapter in the India-China history], *Central Daily News*, August 24, 1939, p. 2. See also Nehru, *Selected Works*, vol. 10, p. 101 for a similar statement.

4. *Central Daily News*, August 26, 1939, p. 2.; Nehru, *Selected Works*, vol. 10, p. 101.

5. "Jiang Jieshi riji" [Diary of Chiang Kai-shek] (unpublished manuscript), Hoover Institution, Stanford University (hereafter CKS diary).

6. Record, August 28, 1939, Jiang Jieshi zongtong dang'an [Archive of President Chiang Kai-shek], Guoshiguan [Academia Historica], Tejiao dang [Special archives], CD 08A-01786.

7. CKS diary, August 28, 1939.

8. Nehru, *Selected Works*, vol. 10, pp. 102–104.

9. Jiang Jieshi zongtong dang'an [Archive of President Chiang Kai-shek], Guoshiguan [Academia Historica], Taipei. This record is also in Zhongguo Guomindang dangshiguan [Chinese Nationalist Party History Bureau], no. Special 13, 1–14, with the title "Nihelu xiansheng fazhan Zhong Yin guanxi yijianshu yiwen jieyao" [Sketch of the translation of Mr. Nehru's opinions on develop-

ing India-China relations], with slightly different wording; see also the original English text in Nehru, *Selected Works*, vol. 10, pp. 106–108, August 29, 1939.

10. Chen Lifu, *Zhu Jiahua baogao* [Report of Chen Lifu and Zhu Jiahua], October 6, 1939, Zhongguo Guomindang dangshiguan [Chinese Nationalist Party History Bureau], Taipei, Archive no. Special 13, 1–2. See also J. Nehru, *A Bunch of Old Letters* (Bombay, 1958), pp. 405–406, November 11, 1939, letter from Zhu Jiahua.

11. CKS diary, September 2, 1939.

12. Central Daily News, September 6, 1939, p. 3.

13. Huang Zhaoqin dian [Telegram from Huang Zhaoqin], Guoshiguan [Academia Historica], Taipei, in Tejiao dang [Special archives], CD 01790.

14. Nehru, *Selected Works*, vol. 10, p. 86; on the book, see also ibid,. vol. 10, pp. 84–100.

15. Zhongguo Guomindang dangshiguan [Chinese Nationalist Party History Bureau], Archive no. Special 13, 1–5.

16. "Dai Yuanzhang fang Yin qian shouhan zhailu" [Selections of the letters before executive branch head Dai Jitao's visit to India], Guoshiguan [Academia Historica], CD 08A-01786. Also see *Dai Jitao yu xiandai Zhongguo* [Dai Jitao and modern China] (Taipei: Guoshiguan, 1989), pp. 430–432.

17. Letter 1, October 15, 1939, Guoshiguan [Academia Historica], CD 08A-01786.3. For letter to Nehru, see Nehru, *A Bunch of Old Letters*, p. 452, October 18, 1940.

18. Guo Taiqi zhi Chongqing Waijiaobu dian [Telegram from Guo Taiqi to Ministry of Foreign Affairs in Chongqing], October 26, 1940, Guoshiguan [Academia Historica], CD 08A-01786.

19. Jiang Jieshi fu Guo Taiqi dian [Chiang Kai-shek's telegram back to Guo Taiqi], October 30, 1940, Guoshiguan [Academia Historica], CD 08A-01786.

20. Qin Xiaoyi, comp., *Zhonghua Minguo zhongyao shiliao chubian: dui Ri Kangzhan shiqi* [Preliminary compilation of important historical documents of the Republic of China: During the Sino-Japanese War], part 3, *Zhanshi waijiao* [Wartime diplomacy] (Taipei: Zhongguo Guomindang Zhongyang weiyuanhui dangshi weiyuanhui, 1981), vol. 3, p. 407.

21. Nihelu laihan [Letter from Nehru], Guoshiguan [Academia Historica], CD 08A-01786; and Nehru, *Selected Works*, vol. 11, pp. 515–516, December 17, 1940.

22. Shang xingqi fanxing lu [Notes on the reflections of last week], CKS diary, January 2 and 3, 1939.

23. CKS diary, January 23, 1942; "Kunmian ji" [Notes on frustration and encouragement] (draft), vol. 70, Guoshiguan [Academia Historica] (hereafter "Kunmian ji").

24. CKS diary, February 1, 1942; "Kunmian ji," vol. 70.

25. Tang Zong, *Zai Jiang Jieshi shenbian banian* [Eight years of working at Chiang Kai-shek's side] (Beiping: Qunzhong chubanshe, 1991), p. 255.

26. CKS diary, February 10, 1942; "Kunmian ji," vol. 70.

27. Qin Xiaoyi, op. cit, pp. 364–365.

28. CKS diary, February 11 and 13, 1939; "Kunmian ji," vol. 70.

29. Shang xingqi fanxing lu [Notes on the reflections of last week], CKS diary, February 14, 1942.

30. Qin Xiaoyi, op. cit, p. 365.

31. CKS diary, February 15, 1942.

32. Qin Xiaoyi, op. cit, pp. 376–377.

33. CKS diary, February 16, 1942; "Kunmian ji," vol. 70.

34. Qin Xiaoyi, op. cit., pp. 405–411.

35. Ibid.

36. CKS diary, February 19, 1942. For Gandhi's view of the visit, see *Collected Works of Mahatma Gandhi* (New Delhi, 1979), vol. 75, pp. 333–334, 341–342, 346. Gandhi was likewise unimpressed and dismissive of Chiang Kai-shek.

37. Qin Xiaoyi, op. cit., p. 430.

38. CKS diary, February 20, 1942; "Kunmian ji," vol. 70.

39. Ibid.

40. Qin Xiaoyi., op. cit., p. 449.

41. Ibid., p. 452.

42. Shen Shihua zhi Jiang Jieshi dian [Telegram from Shen Shihua to Chiang Kai-shek], May 26, 1942, Guoshiguan [Academia Historica], Tejiao dang [Special archives], 00482.

43. Qin Xiaoyi, op. cit., pp. 458–460. See Shen Shihua zhi Chongqing Junweihui dian [Telegram from Shen Shihua to the Military Committee in Chongqing], Guoshiguan [Academia Historica], Tejiao dang [Special archives], 00482. This message was conveyed to Shen Shihua through Nehru's secretary.

44. "Kunmian ji," January 28, 1942. See also CKS diary, July 28 and 29, 1942.

45. Guoshiguan [Academia Historica], Tejiao dang [Special archives], 00482.

46. Qin Xiaoyi, op. cit., pp. 439–440.

47. Song Meiling zhi Juli dian [Telegram from Madame Chiang to Laughlin Currie], Guoshiguan [Academia Historica], Tejiao dang [Special archives], 00482.

48. Song Meiling zhi Juli dian [Telegram from Madame Chiang to Laughlin Currie], Guoshiguan [Academia Historica], in Tejiao dang [Special archives], 00483, 0172.

49. Central Daily News, August 15, 1942, p. 2. Original English in Nehru, *Selected works*, vol. 12, p. 482, August 8, 1942.

50. "Chen Bulei riji" [Diary of Chen Bulei], August 10, 1942, Guoshiguan [Academia Historica.

51. CKS diary, August 10, 1942.

52. "Fangwen Yindu: [Visit to India], Guoshiguan [Academia Historica], Tejiao dang [Special archives], 00482.

53. Tang Zong, *Zai Jiang Jieshi shenbian banian* [Eight years of working at Chiang Kai-shek's side], p. 298.

54. CKS diary, August 10, 1942.

55. "Women duiyu Yindu wenti de guancha" [Our observations of the India problem], *Central Daily News*, August 11, 1942, p. 2.

56. Qin Xiaoyi, op. cit., pp. 477–481.

57. CKS diary, August 11, 1942.

58. Gu Dashi ma dian [Telegram from Ambassador Wellington Koo], Guoshiguan [Academia Historica], Tejiao dang [Special archives], 00485, 0232.

59. Yu (Tan Boyu) shang Song Ziwen cheng [Letter from Tan Boyu to Song Ziwen], July 10, 1942, Song Ziwen dang'an [Song Ziwen archive], 46-6, Hoover Institution, Stanford University. See also scattered suggestions in "Jiang Jieshi riji" for the year 1942. For details on the German feelers in 1942 and other connections, the author (Yang Tianshi) has written three well-documented and as yet unpublished papers:

1. "Gen deguo haishi gen ying, mei zhan zaiyiqi" [Stand with Britain/the United States or with Germany?]
2. "Jujue he gong yindu, zushao deri huishi yinduyang" [Refusal to invade India and obstruction of German-Japanese intentions in the Indian Ocean];
3. "Jiang Jieshi yu deguo neibu tuifan xidele de dixia yundong" [Chiang Kai-shek and contacts with the overthrow-Hitler underground movement].

60. CKS diary, August 24, 29, and 30, 1941; "Kunmian ji," vol. 70.
61. Zalu [Miscellaneous notes], CKS diary, 1943.
62. "Weiyuanzhang baogao Kailuo Huiyi qingxing" [Chairman Chiang Kai-shek's report on the Cairo Conference], in "Guofang zuigao weiyuanhui di 126 ci changwu huiyi jilu" [Record of the Supreme National Defense Committee no.126 general meeting], December 20, 1943, Zhongguo Guomindang dangshiguan [Chinese Nationalist Party History Bureau], Taipei. This report is in *Guofang zuigao weiyuanhui changwuhuiyi jilu* [Record of the Supreme National Defense Committee general meetings], vol. 5, p. 825, with a lot of omissions.
63. Shang xingqi fanxing lu [Notes on the reflections of last week], CKS diary, July 10, 1949.
64. Dashi biao [Record of significant events], CKS diary, 1950.
65. Shang xingqi fanxing lu [Notes on the reflections of last week], CKS diary, April 27, 1951.

CHAPTER 8

1. He Hanwen, *Zhong E Waijiao Shi* [Sino-Russian diplomatic history] (Shanghai: Zhonghua shuju, April 1935), pp. 428–431; *Dokumenty Vneshnej Politiki SSSR* (Документы внешней политики CCCP) [Compilation of Soviet foreign policy documents] (Moscow: Politizdat, 1969), vol. 15, pp. 680–683 (hereafter SFPD).
2. Fang Lianqing et al., comp., *Xiandai Guoji Guanxi Shi Ziliao Xuanji* [Compilation of historical documents of modern international relations] (Beiping: Higher Education Press, 1959), p. 335.
3. Qin Xiaoyi et al., comp., *Zhonghua Minguo Zhongyao Shiliao Chubian: Dui Ri Kangzhan Shiqi* [Preliminary compilation of important historical materials of the Republic of China: Sino-Japanese War period] (Taipei: The Chinese Nationalist Party Central Committee Party History Committee, 1981), vol. 3, no. 2, pp. 640–641.
4. SFPD, vol. 16, pp. 406–407.
5. Zhang Qiyun, *Xian Zongtong Jianggong Quanji* [Complete works of the late President Chiang Kai-shek] (Taipei: China Culture University, 1984), p. 154.
6. SFPD, vol. 19, pp. 35–36.
7. Ibid., vol. 17, p. 643.

8. Ibid., pp. 640–641.

9. Stomonyakov stated that he needed time to think it over. Ibid., vol. 17, p. 643.

10. Li Yunhan, *Xi'an Shibian Shimo Zhi Yanjiu* [Research on the Xi'an Incident] (Taipei: Jindai Zhongguo Chubanshe, 1985), pp. 11–22.

11. Zhou Tiandu, Zheng Zemin, Qi Fulin, and Li Yibin, *Cong Songhu Kangzhan dao Lugaoqiao Shibian* [From the (1931–1932) resistance war at Shanghai to the Marco Polo Bridge Incident] (Beiping: Zhonghua Shuju, 2002), vol. 2, p. 546; Li Xin, ed., *Zhonghua Minguo Shi* [History of the Republic of China], vol. 3, no. 2; Pan Hannian zhi Wang Ming Xin [A letter from Pan Hannian to Wang Ming] (July 1, 1936), in K. Anderson et al., eds., *VKP(b), Komintern i Kitaj* (ВКП(6), Коминтерн и Китай) [The All-Russia Communist Bolshevik Party, the Comintern, and China], vol. 4, no. 2, pp. 1052–1053.

12. Chen Mingshu's Nineteenth Route Army was defeated by the Japanese at Shanghai. In May, after the signing of an armistice agreement, Chiang Kai-shek transferred Chen's forces to Fujian Province. Chen Mingshu then resigned and moved abroad. See Jin Yilin, "Chen Mingshu yu Jiang Jieshi Guanxi Chutan," in *Minguo Dang'an* [Republican Archives], vol. 1 (2007), pp. 117–125; and Wu Minggan, *1933nian Fujian Shibian Shimo* [The history of the Fujian Incident] (Wuhan: Hubei People's Press, 2006).

13. Anderson et al., *The All-Russia Communist Party,* pp. 1039–1040.

14. Ibid., p. 1061.

15. Ibid., pp. 1060–1063.

16. G. M. Adibekov, K. M. Anderson, and M. M. Shirinja, *Politburo TsK RKP(b)-VKP(b) i Komintern 1919–1943; dokumenty* (Политбюро ЦК РКП(6)-ВКП(6) и Коминтерн 1919–1943; документы) 1919–1943; документы) [Politburo of the Central Committee of the Russian Communist Party/All-Russia Communist Bolshevik Party and Comintern; documents] (Moscow: Rosspen, 2004), p. 735.

17. Anderson et al., *The All-Russia Communist Party,* p. 1068.

18. Dimitrov answered., "I did not know this issue." Then Stalin asked a person to send this telegram to Dimitrov. Georgi Dimitrov, *The Diary of Georgi Dimitrov,* ed. Ivo Banac (New Haven: Yale University Press), 2003. Translated into Chinese by Ma Xipu, Yang Yanjie, and Ge Zhiqiang (Nanning: Guangxi shifan daxue chubanshe [Guangxi Normal University Press], 2002), p. 50.

19. *Pravda,* December 16, 1936.

20. Translation Office of the Institute of Modern History at the China Academy of Social Sciences, comp., *Gongchan Guoji You Guanyu Zhongguo Geming de Wenxian Ziliao* [Comintern documents related to the Chinese revolution] (Beiping: China Social Sciences Press, 1989), vol. 3, p. 11.

21. Jiang Tingfu, *Jiang Tingfu huiyilu* [Memoirs of Jiang Tingfu] (Taipei: Zhuanji wenxue chubanshe, 1979), pp. 197–199.

22. Rossijskij Gosudarstvennyj arhiv social'no-politicheskoj istorii (Российский Государственный архив социально-политической истории) [Russian State Archive of Social and Political History], Institut Dal'nego Vostoka Rossijskoj Akademii Nauk (Институт Дальнего Востока Российской Академии Наук) [Far East Institute of the Russia Academy of Sciences], Vostochno-aziatskij seminar Svobodnogo Universiteta Berlina (Восточно-азиатский семинар Свободного Университета Берлина)

[East Asian Department at Free Berlin University], comp., *VKP(b), Komintern i Kitaj* [The Comintern and China] (Moscow, 2003), vol. 4, no. 2 (1931–1937), p. 1016.

23. Chinese Communist Party Central Committee Secretariat, *Liuda Yilai Dangnei Mimi Wenjian* [The Chinese Communist Party's secret documents since the Sixth Party Congress] (Beiping: Renmin chubanshe, 1980), p. 788.

24. Translation Office of the Institute of Modern History at the China Academy of Social Sciences, comp., *Gongchan Guoji Guanyu Zhongguo Geming de Wenxian Ziliao* [Comintern documents related to the Chinese revolution] (Beiping: China Social Sciences Press, 1989), vol. 3, pp. 14–16; Chinese Communist Party Central Committee Secretariat, *The Chinese Communist Party's Secret Documents since the Sixth Party Congress*, pp. 792–802; *Dokumenty vneshnej politiki SSSR* (Документы внешней политики СССР) [Compilation of Soviet foreign policy documents] (Moscow: Politizdat, 1976), vol. 20, pp. 155–157.

25. Rong Mengyuan and Sun Caixia, eds., *Zhongguo Guomindang Lici Daibiao Dahui ji Zhongyang Quanhui Ziliao* [Documents of the Chinese Nationalist Party conferences and Central Committee plenums] (Beiping: Guangming Ribao Chubanshe, 1985), part 2, p. 435.

26. Rong Mengyuan and Sun Caixia, eds., *Documents of the Chinese Nationalist Party Conferences*, part 2, p. 436.

27. The Soviet Communist Party Central Committee Politburo decided that it would permit Chiang Kai-shek's son to return to China. C. L. Tikhvinskij (Тихвинский) et al., *Russko-Kitajskie otnoshenija 20 veka* (Русско-Китайские отношения XX века) [Russian-Chinese relations in the twentieth century] (Moscow: Pamjatniki istoricheskoj mysli, 2000), vol. 4, no. 1, p. 40.

28. Ibid., p. 44.

29. Ibid., p. 40.

30. Party History Office of the Chinese People's Liberation Army Political Institute, *Zhonggong Dangshi Cankao Ziliao* [Reference documents for Chinese Communist Party history], vol. 8, p. 34.

31. *Jiang Zongtong Milu* [Secret record of President Chiang Kai-shek] (Taipei: Central Daily Newspaper, 1974), vol. 11, p. 74.

32. Gu Weijun, *Gu Weijun huiyilu* [Memoirs of Gu Weijun], trans. into Chinese by the Institute of Modern History at the China Academy of Social Sciences (Beiping: Zhonghua Shuju, 1985), vol. 2, p. 592.

33. Yang Jie led a Chinese delegation to receive Soviet weapons. SFPD, vol. 20, pp. 474–475. Chiang Kai-shek asked Yang Jie and Zhang Chong to negotiate with the Soviet Union about getting Soviet airplanes. Qin Xiaoyi et al., *Preliminary compilation of important historical materials of the Republic of China: Sino-Japanese War period*, vol. 3, no. 2, p. 465.

34. Ibid., p. 334.

35. Ibid., p. 137.

36. Tikhvinskij et al., *Russian-Chinese Relations in the Twentieth Century*, vol. 4, p. 136.

37. Voroshilov had a bad impression of Yan Xishan, the warlord in control of

Shanxi. Yang Jie stated to him that Yan Xishan was determined to resist Japanese aggression, although Yan Xishan's army was not determined. Ibid., p. 138.

38. Ibid., pp. 152, 157.

39. Ibid., p. 155.

40. Ibid., pp. 164–165.

41. Ibid., p. 166.

42. The letter from Lin Sen to Kalinin, November 27, 1937, is in the Russian Federation president's archive. Ibid., p. 166.

43. Sun Ke brought a letter from Song Qingling to Mrs. Kalinin. The letter did not reach Mrs. Kalinin, as she was in prison during the Great Purge. Ibid., p. 590; SFPD, vol. 21, p. 43.

44. Tikhvinskij et al., *Russian-Chinese Relations in the Twentieth Century*, vol. 4, p. 199.

45. Institut Vseobshchej istorii (Институт Всеобщей истории) [Institute of general history], Akademija Nauk SSSR (Академия Наук СССР) [USSR Academy of Sciences], *1939 God: Uroki Istorii* (1939 год: уроки истории) [Year 1939: Lessons from History] (Moscow, 1990), p. 36.

46. SFPD, vol. 21, pp. 88–89.

47. Qin Xiaoyi et al., comp., *Sun Zhesheng xiansheng wenji* [Collected works of Mr. Sun Zhesheng] (Taipei: The Chinese Nationalist Party Central Committee Party History Committee, 1990), vol. 2, pp. 263–267.

48. SFPD, vol. 21, pp. 277–280.

49. Tikhvinskij et al., *Russian-Chinese Relations in the Twentieth Century)*, vol. 4, p. 249.

50. Ibid., p. 249.

51. Qin Xiaoyi et al., comp., *Preliminary Compilation of Important Historical Materials of the Republic of China: Sino-Japanese War Period*, vol. 3, no. 3, p. 495.

52. Telegram from Chiang Kai-shek to Stalin and Molotov concerning the US$160 million loan, in Tikhvinskij et al., *Russian-Chinese Relations in the Twentieth Century*, vol. 4, p. 253; Qin Xiaoyi et al., *Preliminary Compilation of Important Historical Materials of the Republic of China: Sino-Japanese War Period*, vol. 3, no. 2, p. 501.

53. Chen Jiagu, *Zhonggu Guojia Guanxishi Ziliao Huibian (1933–1945)* [Compilation of documents of Sino-Soviet relations (1933–1945)] (Beiping: Social Sciences Documents Press, 1997), pp. 91–93.

54. Telegram from Chiang Kai-shek to Yang Jie, July 27, 1938, in Qin Xiaoyi et al., *Preliminary Compilation of Important Historical Materials of the Republic of China: Sino-Japanese War Period*, vol. 3, no. 2, p. 342.

55. Tikhvinskij et al., *Russian-Chinese Relations in the Twentieth Century*, vol. 4, pp. 283–284.

56. Ibid., pp. 288–290.

57. Telegram from Soviet deputy foreign commissar to Luganets-Orelsky concerning the Soviet leader's response to Chiang Kai-shek's request for aid, September 8, 1938, in SFPD, vol. 21, p. 482.

58. Telegram from Soviet ambassador Luganets-Orelsky to the Soviet Foreign

Ministry, September 24, 1938, in Tihvinskij et al., *Russian-Chinese Relations in the Twentieth Century*, vol. 4, p. 329.

59. Cited in Chen Jiagu, *Compilation of Documents of Sino-Soviet Relations*, p. 354.

60. The reasons are complicated. Ministerstvo inostrannyh del SSSR (Министерство иностранных дел СССР) (USSR Foreign Ministry), comp., *Dokumenty i Materialy Kanuna Vtoroj Mirovoj Vojny* (Документы и материалы кануна второй мировой войны) [Documents and materials on the eve of World War Two] (Moscow: Politizdat, 1981), vol. 2, pp. 398–389; Ju. Fel'shtinskij (Ю.Фельштинский), *Oglasheniju podlezhit- SSSR i Germanija 1939–1941* (Оглашению подлежит- СССР и Германия 1939–1941] [Subject to disclosure: The Soviet Union and Germany: 1939–1941] (Moscow: Workers Press, 1991), p. 6.

61. Tihvinskij et al., *Russian-Chinese Relations in the Twentieth Century*, vol. 4, p. 486.

62. *Zhongyang ribao* [Central Daily News], August 25, 1939, p. 3.

63. Fel'shtinskij, *Subject to Disclosure: The Soviet Union and Germany: 1939–1941*, p. 6.

64. Ibid., p. 7.

65. Chiang Kai-shek asked Alexander Paniushkin. He said that he received this information from the Associated Press. Tikhvinskij et al., *Russian-Chinese Relations in the Twentieth Century*, vol. 4, p. 487.

66. Qin Xiaoyi et al., *Works of Mr. Sun Zhesheng*, vol. 4, p. 83.

67. Ibid., p. 81.

68. Ibid., p. 82.

69. The treaty was exchanged and approved in Chongqing on March 16, 1940. Wang Tieya, *Zhongwai Jiu Yuezhang Huibian* [Compilation of China's international treaties] (Beiping: Sanlian, 1982), pp. 1139–1146. The Nationalist government was to use this loan to purchase industrial products and industrial equipment in the Soviet Union. The annual interest rate was 3 percent. China was to pay back the loan in ten years from 1942. The appendix of the treaty stipulated that China could pay back the loan in kind, using tea, fur, wool, antimony, zinc, nickel, tungsten, silk, cotton, tung oil, copper, herbs, and leather.

70. Following the order of Chiang Kai-shek, Li Weiguo passed on this stance to the American ambassador and Soviet ambassador. Tikhvinskij et al., *Russian-Chinese Relations in the Twentieth Century*, vol. 4, pp. 671–672.

71. Qin Xiaoyi et al., *Preliminary Compilation of Important Historical Materials of the Republic of China: Sino-Japanese War Period*, vol. 3, no. 2, p. 392.

CHAPTER 9

1. See Charles S. Maier's seminal discussion of territoriality in "Consigning the Twentieth Century to History: Alternatives for the Modern Era," *American Historical Review*, vol. 105, no. 3 (June 2000), pp. 807–831. For an original discussion of *geo-body*, see Thongchai Winichakul, *Siam Mapped: A History of the Geo-body of a Nation* (Honolulu: University of Hawaii Press, 1994).

2. Important studies are John W. Dower, *War without Mercy: Race and Power in the Pacific War* (New York: Pantheon, 1986); John W. Garver, *Chi-*

nese-Soviet Relations, 1937–1945: The Diplomacy of Chinese Nationalism (New York: Oxford University Press, 1988), Akira Iriye, *Power and Culture: The Japanese-American War, 1941–1945* (Cambridge: Harvard University Press, 1981); Xiaoyuan Liu, *A Partnership for Disorder: China, the United States, and Their Policies for the Postwar Disposition of the Japanese Empire, 1941–1945* (Cambridge: Cambridge University Press, 1996); W. Roger Louis, *Imperialism at Bay: The United States and the Decolonization of the British Empire* (New York: Oxford University Press, 1978); Michael Schaller, *The U.S. Crusade in China, 1938–1945* (New York: Columbia University Press, 1979); Christopher Thorne, *Allies of a Kind: The United States, Britain, and the War against Japan, 1941–1945* (Oxford: Oxford University Press, 1978); Christopher Thorne, *The Issue of War: States, Societies, and the Far Eastern Conflict of 1941–1945* (New York: Oxford University Press, 1985); Barbara W. Tuchman, *Stilwell and the American Experience in China, 1911–1945* (New York: Macmillan, 1970); and Tang Tsou, *America's Failure in China, 1941–1950* (Chicago: University of Chicago Press, 1963).

3. Erez Manela, *The Wilsonian Moment: Self-Determination and the International Origins of Anti-colonial Nationalism* (Oxford: Oxford University Press, 2007).

4. "The problem of minorities in Europe," October 7, 1944, Harry N. Howard Papers, Box 3, CAC-250, Truman Library, Independence, MO; "The Problem of Minorities," March 26, 1945, ISO-245, ibid..

5. Dispatch from the British Legation in Peking to the Foreign Office, No. 1390, October 23, 1933, L/P&S/12/2287, India Office Records, British Library; Ingram to Sir John Simon, January 17, 1934, and enclosures, ibid.; H. M. Military Attaché at the Peking Legation to the Foreign Office, April 28, 1934, and enclosures, ibid.

6. "Draft agenda for meeting on inquiry Part IV," March 23, 1939, and appendix, Philip C. Jessup Papers, Box A122, folder IPR Annexes No. 21-40, Library of Congress; Lattimore to Yarnell, April 29, 1941, Stanley K. Hornbeck Papers, Box 449, Hoover Institution, Stanford, CA; Yarnell to Lattimore, April 29, 1941, ibid.

7. "China," n.d. (1942), Records of Harley A. Notter, Box 11, National Archives, College Park, MD.

8. Hornbeck to William Langer, April 15, 1943, enclosure, "Summary of Outer Mongolia and Tannu Tuva survey by Office of Strategic Services, February 23, 1943," Hornbeck Papers, Box 300.

9. "Sino-Russian Problems in the Post-War Settlement," October 4, 1943, Notter Records, Box 119, PG-34; "Summary Report of Vice President Wallace Visit in China," July 10, 1944, Franklin D. Roosevelt Papers/PSF, Box 27, FDR Library, Hyde Park, NY.

10. Division of Far Eastern Affairs to Division of Political Studies, "Partition of Manchuria," March 13, 1943, General Records of the United States Department of State Central Files: China: 893.01 Manchuria/1673, National Archives, Washington, DC (hereafter GRDS).

11. "The U.S.S.R. and the Possibility of a 'Greater Mongolia,'" August 3, 1943, Fo371/35860, The National Archives, London.

12. ST Minutes 21, July 2, 1943, Notter Records, Box 79.

13. Davies to Hopkins, December 31, 1943, Roosevelt Papers/PSF, Box 27; Davies to Hopkins, November 16, 1944, ibid. Davies (second secretary, United States embassy, Chongqing) made the point that the Americans held a "congenial fiction" in identifying Chiang Kai-shek with China.

14. "Military Government in the Far East," February 5, 1944, Notter Records, Box 109, CAC-66a; "Indications of Contact with President on Post-war Matters," n.d., ibid., Box 54; ST Minutes 16, May 7, 1943, ibid., Box 79.

15. "Joint Psychological Warfare Committee: Suggested China Plan," March 16, 1942, Records of Joint Chiefs of Staff, microfilm reel 13, JPWC3, National Archives, Washington, DC.

16. "Official Policy and Views Affecting the Post-War Settlement in the Far East," September 30, 1943, Notter Records, Box 58, P-241a.

17. Memorandum for the President, "Unconditional Surrender of Japan and Policy toward Liberated Areas in the Far East in Relation to Unconditional Surrender," June 29, 1945, Hopkins Papers, Box 169–171: Big Three Conference Agenda (Potsdam) July 1945, Georgetown University Library, Washington, DC.

18. Division of Far Eastern Affairs to Secretary of State, September 2, 1943, Hornbeck Papers, Box 70.

19. Seymour to Eden, February 5, 1944, and enclosures, Fo371/41654, The National Archives, London.

20. Minutes on communication from Jones to Broad, April 28, 1942, Fo371/31702, ibid.

21. Seymour to Eden, February 5, 1944, and enclosures, Fo371/41654, ibid.

22. "The problem of minorities," March 26, 1945, Howard Papers, Box 3, ISO-245.

23. For a detailed account of Lattimore's appointment and service to Chiang in 1941 and 1942, see Robert P. Newman, *Owen Lattimore and the "Loss" of China* (Berkeley: University of California Press, 1992), pp. 55–96. Newman's otherwise informative account leaves out Lattimore's ethnopolitical advice to Chiang.

24. Lattimore, Memorandum to Chiang Kai-shek, June 30, 1976, Lattimore Papers, Box 28, Library of Congress.

25. Lattimore, Memorandum on Inner Mongolia, n.d. (August 1941), ibid.

26. "Studies of American Interests in the War and the Peace: Territorial Series: Memorandum on Mongolia and the Peace Settlement, 8 June 1943," No. T-B 63, ibid.

27. Lattimore to Lauchlin Currie, July 27, 1941, Lattimore Papers, Box 27; Lattimore's note on a conversation with Wong Wen-hao (Weng Wenhao), November 2, 1942, ibid.; Lattimore's note on a conversation with Chu Chia-hua (Zhu Jiahua), November 7, 1942, ibid.; minutes of the conversation between Chiang Kai-shek and Lattimore on July 31, 1941, ibid.; Lattimore's note on a conversation with Chiang Kai-shek, December 5, 1941, ibid.

28. Lattimore to Chiang, May 3, 1942, *Zhonghua Minguo zhongyao shiliao chubian; Dui Ri Kangzhan shiqi* [Preliminary compilation of important historical records of the Republic of China; the period of the War of Resistance against Japan] (Taipei: Dangshi weiyuanhui, 1981), vol. 3, no. 1, pp. 744–745 (hereafter, ZZSC).

29. Liu Kai to the Ministry of Foreign Affairs, April 12 and 14, 1944, ZZSC, vol. 3, no. 1, pp. 859–860; T. V. Soong to Chiang, May 13, 1944, ibid., pp. 860–861; Wei Daoming to Chiang, May 15, 1944, ibid., p. 861; Newman, *Owen Lattimore*, p. 115.

30. Newman, *Owen Lattimore*, p. 108; Wang Shijie, *Wang Shijie riji* [Diaries of Wang Shijie] (Taipei: Zhongyang Yanjiuyuan Jindaishi Yanjiusuo, 1990), vol. 4, pp. 338–339.

31. Wallace to Harry Truman, September 19, 1951, and enclosure, "Summary Report of Vice President Wallace's Visit in China," July 10, 1944, Roosevelt Papers/PSF, Box 27.

32. "Principal Points of a Report by Owen Lattimore on China and Chinese Opinion on Postwar Problems," August 21, 1942, Notter Records, Box 60, T Document 44.

33. "U.S.S.R. Aims in the Far East," August 19, 1943, Hornbeck Papers, Box 396, FE memo.

34. "Possible Soviet Attitudes towards Far Eastern Questions," October 2, 1943, Notter Records, Box 119, PG-28.

35. Ibid.; "Russia and the Far Eastern Settlement," July 22, 1944, OSS Report, vol. 6 (microfilm reel 3), R & A No. 2211.1, National Archives; John Davies Jr. to Hopkins, January 23, 1944, enclosure, "Observers' Mission to North China," Hopkins Papers, Box 334.

36. Hornbeck to Secretary of State, July 18, 1944, Hornbeck Papers, Box 396; State Department to the officer in charge of the American Mission, Chungking (Chongqing), February 12, 1945, Top Secret General Records of Chungking Embassy, China, 1943–1945, Box 1, National Archives and Federal Records Center, Suitland, MD.

37. Joseph W. Esherick, ed., *Lost Chance in China: The World War II Dispatches of John S. Service* (New York: Random House, 1974), pp. 309, 313.

38. Ibid., pp. xvii-xviii; Dean Acheson, Post-Presidential Oral History Project, Truman Library, Independence, MO.

39. Service's memo "Policy of the Chinese Communists toward the Problem of National Minorities," March 16, 1945, 893.00/3–1645, GRDS; "Nationality Policy in the Soviet Union," February 24, 1945, Howard Papers, Box 3, PIO-Preliminary.

40. Esherick, *Lost Chance in China*, p. 311.

41. I discuss this subject in *Frontier Passages: Ethnopolitics and the Rise of Chinese Communism, 1921–1945* (Washington, D.C., and Stanford: Woodrow Wilson Center Press and Stanford University Press, 2004).

42. Memo by Service "Communist Views in Regard to Mongolia," March 16, 1945, 893.00/3–1645, GRDS.

43. Mao Zedong, "On the new phase," October 12–14, 1938, *Zhonggong zhongyang wenjian xuanji* [Selected documents of the Chinese Communist Party Central Committee] (Beiping: Zhonggong zhongyang dangxiao chubanshe, 1992), vol. 11, pp. 557–662 (hereafter ZZWX).

44. George Atcheson Jr. to the Secretary of State, February 16, 1945, enclosure, memo from Ludden, "Communist plans for expansion," 893.00/2–1645, GRDS.

45. Rice to the Secretary of State, May 21, 1945, 893.00/5–2145, GRDS.

46. I have discussed this subject in *Reins of Liberation: An Entangled History*

of Mongolian Independence, Chinese Territoriality, and Great Power Hegemony, 1911–1950 (Washington, D.C., and Stanford: Woodrow Wilson Center Press and Stanford University Press, 2006), especially pp. 115–280.

47. Memorandum, "Far East: (1) China: (a) Political and Military Situation if U.S.S.R. Enters War in Far East," n.d., Hopkins Papers, box 169–171; State Department to the United States Embassy, Chungking, February 8, 1945, enclosure 5, "Memorandum for the President," January 9, 1945, Top Secret General Records of Chungking Embassy, 1945, Box 1.

48. Schaller, *The US Crusade in* China, pp. 147–176.

49. War Department to President Roosevelt, January 28, 1942, Roosevelt Papers/PSF, Box 2; note by Harry Hopkins on a conversation with Winston Churchill, November 1943, Hopkins Papers, Box 331; "Chinese war and peace aims," March 1, 1944, Notter Records, Box 10, p. 254a; "Outer Mongolia," October 23, 1944, Box 115, CAC-297, ibid; memorandum for the president, April 7, 1944, Roosevelt Papers/MRF, box 10; FDR to the Secretary of State, April 7, 1944, ibid.; The President to Generalissimo Chiang Kai-shek, April 8, 1944, ibid.

50. Garver, *Chinese-Soviet Relations*, pp. 209–228; Liu, *A Partnership for Disorder*, pp. 242–286.

51. "Formosa," April 1943, Notter Records, Box 63; May 15, 1944, ibid., Box 110, PWC-195; Division of China Affairs memo, "Policy with respect to China," April 18, 1945, Records of the Division of Chinese Affairs, Box 10, National Archives, Washington, DC.

52. Grew to the Secretary of State, July 13, 1945, *Foreign Relations of the United States: Diplomatic Papers, 1945* (Washington, D.C.: G.P.O., 1969), vol. 7, pp. 934–938 (hereafter FRUS); Harriman to the Secretary of State, August 11, 1945, ibid., p.152.

53. Hornbeck to Secretary of State, 20 September 1943, Hornbeck Papers, Box 378.

54. "Russian political aims in China," May 15, 1945, OSS Report vol. 6 (microfilm reel 4); George Kennan (chargé d'affaires, US embassy, Moscow) to the Secretary of State, January 10, 1946, FRUS, 1946, vol. 9, pp. 116–119.

55. Kennan, loc. cit.

56. "Union of Soviet Socialist Republic: Policy and Information Statement," May 15, 1946, Clifford Papers, Box 15, Truman Library, Independence, MO.

57. Kennan, loc. cit.

58. Weigle to Drumright, May 4, 1946, Records of the Division of Chinese Affairs, 1945–1950, Top Secret Subject File, 1945–1950, Box 12.

59. "Report on Tour of Duty at Yan'an by Col. Ivan D. Yeaton," May 9, 1946, Records of the Division of Chinese Affairs, Subject Files, 1944–1947, Box 11.

60. Ambassador Stuart to the Secretary of State, January 6, 1947, FRUS, 1947, vol. 7, pp. 6–12; Memorandum from John Melby (Second Secretary, US embassy, Chongqing), n.d., FRUS, 1947, vol. 7, pp. 678–682.

61. State Department memo, "Union of Soviet Socialist Republics: Policy and Information Statement," May 15, 1946, Clifford Papers, Box 15.

62. Leo. H. Lamb to M. E. Dening, May 25, 1948, FO 371/69534, The National Archives, London.

63. Lamb to A. L. Scott, October 14, 1946, and Scott's comments, November 6, 1946, FO 371/53674, ibid.; memorandum of Far Eastern Department, "Mongolia," August 7, 1945, FO 371/46286, ibid.

64. G. A. Wallinger to J. H. Watson, 3 January 1947, FO 371/63420, ibid.

CHAPTER 10

1. Chen Liwen, *Cong Dongbei Dangwu Fazhan Kan Jieshou* [Analyzing the return of the Northeast through the development of party work] (n.p.: Dongbei Wenxian Zazhi She, 2000), chap. 3.

2. Sheping [Editorial], *Dagongbao*, January 1, 1943.

3. *Fangong banyuekan* [Counterattack bimonthly], vol. 13, pp. 1–2 (February 25, 1943).

4. Nihon Gaikō Nenpyō Narabini Shuyō Bunsho [Chronology of Japanese foreign affairs with documents] (Tokyo: Hara Shobō, 1966), vol. F, pp. 491–492.

5. Zongtong Jiang Gong Dashi Changbian Chugao [Draft chronology of major events in President Chiang's life] (Taipei, 1978), vol. 4, no. 2, p. 671, entry for April 13, 1941.

6. *Zhongyang ribao* [Central Daily News], April 15, 1941.

7. Frank Kluckhohn, "Roosevelt Holds Ships: Protection Required by Law," *New York Times*, April 16, 1941. A Chinese-language version of this statement can be found in *Zhongyang ribao*, April 17, 1941.

8. Draft Chronology of President's Chiang's Life, vol. 4, no. 2, pp. 674–684.

9. Ibid., pp. 723–724.

10. *Zhongyang ribao*, September 18, 1941.

11. Wang Shijie, *Wang Shijie Riji* [Diary of Wang Shijie] (Taipei: Zhongyang Yanjiuyuan Jinshisuo, 1990), vol. 3.

12. On this point, see the systematic analysis offered in Yang Tianshi 楊天石, "Lun 'Huifu Lugouqiao Shibian Qian Yuanzhuang' yu Jiang Jieshi 'Kangzhan Daodi' zhi 'Di'" [On "Restoring the status quo before the Marco Polo Bridge Incident" and the "End" in Chiang Kai-shek's "All-out resistance to the end"], in *Kangzhan yu Zhanhou Zhongguo* [Wartime and postwar China] (Beiping: Zhongguo Renmin Daxue chubanshe, 2007), pp. 295–327.

13. *Zhongyang ribao*, September 18, 1941.

14. *Dongbei Yuekan* [Northeastern monthly], vol. 4, p. 1 (September 18, 1941).

15. See chapter 5 of Nishimura Shigeo, ed., *Chūgoku Gaikō to Kokuren no Seiritsu* [Chinese diplomacy and the founding of the United Nations] (Kyoto: Hōritsu Bunkasha, 2004).

16. Qin Xiaoyi, ed., *Zhonghua Minguo Zhongyao Shiliao Chugao: Dui Ri Kangzhan Shiqi: Di 3 Bian: Zhanchi Waijiao* [Important historical materials of the Republic of China, draft edition: vol. 3: The war against Japan, wartime diplomacy 1] (Taipei: Zhongguo Guomindang shangyang weiyuanhui dangshi weiyuanhui, 1981), vol. 3, no. 1, pp. 677–684.

17. Draft Chronology of President Chiang's Life, vol. 5, no. 1, pp. 197–198, entry for September 18, 1942.

18. *Zhongyang ribao*, September 19, 1942.

19. *Fangong Banyuekan*, vol. 12, pp. 2–3 (September 18, 1942).

20. Wu's speech can be found in *Zhongyang dangwu gongbao* [Central party affairs gazette], vol. 4, p. 19 (October 1, 1942); Sun's can be found in *Fangong banyuekan*, vol. 4, p. 24 (December 16, 1942).

21. *Fangong banyuekan*, vol. 12, p. 16 (December 25, 1942).

22. *Dagongbao*, January 5, 1943.

23. *Fangong banyuekan*, vol. 13, no. 1–2 (February 25, 1943).

24. United States Department of State, *Foreign Relations of the United States: Diplomatic Papers, 1943—China* (Washington, DC: Government Printing Office, 1943), Document 893.9111/47, pp. 843–844.

25. Due to limited space, a detailed discussion of the conference will not be included in this essay. The official record of the meeting can be found in *War and Peace in the Pacific: A Preliminary Report of the Eighth Conference of the Institute of Pacific Relations on Wartime and Postwar Cooperation of the United Nations in the Pacific and the Far East, Mont Tremblant, Quebec, December 4–14, 1942* (New York: International Secretariat of the Institute for Pacific Relations, 1943). The author would like to thank Professor Sasaki Yutaka of Soai University for sharing this material with him.

26. Draft Chronology of President Chiang's Life, vol. 5, no. 2, pp. 286–287, entry for March 1, 1943.

27. Chiang Kai-shek, "Zhong-Mei, Zhong-Ying Pingdeng Xin Yue Gaocheng Gao Quanguo Jun Min Shu" [Letter to the nation on the new, equal treaties with the United States and United Kingdom] (January 12, 1943), http://www.chungcheng.org.tw/thought/class07/0017/0002.htm, accessed August 9, 2011.

28. *Fangong banyuekan*, vol. 14, pp. 2–3 (September, 1943).

29. Ibid.

30. Wang Zhuoran, "Shengli Bu Xu You Zhekou," *Fangong banyuekan,* [Counterattack bimonthly], vol. 14, p. 4 (October 15, 1943).

31. "The Cairo Communiqué," http://www.ndl.go.jp/constitution/e/shiryo/01/002_46/002_46tx.html, accessed August 9, 2011.

32. Duansheng, "Ping Lixian Yundong ji Xiancao Xiuzheng An" [A critique of the proposed constitution], *Dongfang zazhi* [Eastern miscellany], vol. 13, p. 19 (September 10, 1934).

33. Wang Zhujun, "Xianfa Chugao Zhong zhi Lingtu Guiding Wenti" [Issues relating to the delineation of sovereign territory in the draft constitution]," *Heibai banyuekan* [Black and white semimonthly, vol. 1, no. 10 (March 30, 1934).

34. Sun Ke, "Wu Wu Xian Cao Jiantao zhi Shouhuo" [Lessons learned from the 1936 draft constitution]," repr. in Hu Chunhui, ed., *Minguo Xianzheng Yundong* [Constitutional movements in the Chinese Republic] (Taipei: Zhongzheng shuju, 1978), p. 1010.

CHAPTER 11

1. *Jiang Zhongzheng Zongtong Dang'an* [Archives of President Chiang Kai-shek], November 23, 1943, Academia Historica, Taipei (hereafter Chiang Kai-shek Archives), 002–060100–00182–023.

2. Huang Zijin, *Zhongyang Yanjiuyuan Jindaishi Yanjiusuo Jikan* [Journal of

the Institute of Modern History at Academia Sinica], vol. 45 (September 2004), pp. 143–195.

3. "Zhonghua Minguo 33 Nian Yuandan Gao Quanguo Junmin Tongbao Shu" [Open letter to Chinese soldiers and civilians on the New Year of 1944], Qin Xiaoyi, comp., *Xian Zongtong Jianggong Sixiang Yanlun Zongji* [Compilation of former president Chiang Kai-shek's thoughts and speeches] (Taipei: China Cultural Service, 1984), http://www.chungcheng.org.tw/thought/default.htm.

4. Wei Daoming Dian Jiang Jieshi [Telegram from Wei Daoming to Chiang Kai-shek], January 16, 1945, Tejiao Dang'an [Special Archives], Chiang Kai-shek Archives, 002–080200–00301–005.

5. Wei Daoming Dian Jiang Jieshi [Telegram from Wei Daoming to Chiang Kai-shek], January 31, 1945, Tejiao Dang'an [Special Archives], Chiang Kai-shek Archives, 002–080200–0301–018.

6. Chiang Kai-shek Archives, 002–060100–00210–006.

7. Wu Sufeng, "Jiang Zhongzheng Juece Guocheng Zhong de Song Ziwen Juese Fenxi (1945–1949)" [Analysis of Song Ziwen's role in the decision-making process of Chiang Kai-shek], in *Zhanhou Dang'an yu Lishi Yanjiu: Di Jiu Jie Zhonghua Mingguoshi Zhuanti Yanjiu Taolunhui Lunwen Ji* [Postwar archives and historical research: Papers of the Ninth Special Conference on the History of the Republic of China] (Taipei: Guoshiguan, 2008).

8. Peng Keding Dian Jiang Jieshi [Telegram from Peng Keding to Chiang Kai-shek], April 11, 1945, Chiang Kai-shek Archives, 002–090103–00001–098.

9. May 7, 1945, Chiang Kai-shek Archives, 002–060100–00200–007.

10. The letter read:

In obedience to the gracious command of His Majesty the Emperor, who, ever anxious to enhance the cause of world peace, desires earnestly to bring about a speedy termination of hostilities with a view to saving mankind from the calamities to be imposed upon them by further continuation of the war, the Japanese government several weeks ago asked the Soviet government, with which neutral relations then prevailed, to render good offices in restoring peace vis-à-vis the enemy powers. Unfortunately, these efforts in the interest of peace having failed, the Japanese government, in conformity with the august wish of His Majesty to restore the general peace and desiring to put an end to the untold sufferings entailed by war as quickly as possible, has decided upon the following.

The Japanese government is ready to accept the terms enumerated in the joint declaration which was issued at Potsdam on July 26th, 1945, by the heads of the governments of the United States, Great Britain, and China, and later subscribed to by the Soviet government, with the understanding that the said declaration does not comprise any demand which prejudices the prerogatives of His Majesty as a sovereign ruler.

The Japanese government sincerely hopes that this understanding is warranted and desires keenly that an explicit indication to that effect will be speedily forthcoming.

August 10, 1945, Chiang Kai-shek Archives, 002–060100–00203–010.

11. Gu Weijun Dian Jiang Jieshi [Telegram from Wellington Koo to Chiang Kai-shek], August 11, 1945, Chiang Kai-shek Archives, 002–090105–00015–002.

12. Ibid.

13. August 14, 1945, Chiang Kai-shek Archives, 002–060100–00203–014.

14. Chiang Kai-shek Archives, 002–060100–00197–003.

15. Shang Zhen Dian Jiang Jieshi [Telegram from Shang Zhen to Chiang Kai-shek], February 4, 1945, Chiang Kai-shek Archives, 002–080107–00002–010.

16. Wei Yongcheng Dian Jiang Jieshi [Telegram from Wei Yongcheng to Chiang Kai-shek], February 12, 1945, Chiang Kai-shek Archives, 002–090200–00022–347.

17. February 20, 1945, Chiang Kai-shek Archives, 002–060100–00197–020.

18. Shang Zhen Kong Xiangxi Dian Jiang Jieshi [Telegram from Shang Zhen and Kong Xiangxi to Chiang Kai-shek], February 4, 1945, Chiang Kai-shek Archives, 002–080107–00002–010.

19. Chiang Kai-shek stated, "The American military's attitude to me turned from contempt to respect. I am increasingly worried about the respect. Does the Yalta Conference generate a secret treaty that betrayed China's interests?" February 14, 1945, Chiang Kai-shek Archives, 002–060100–00197–014.

20. Kong Xiangxi Dian Jiang Zhongzheng [Telegram from Kong Xiangxi to Chiang Kai-shek], February 20, 1945, Chiang Kai-shek Archives, 002–080107–00002–010.

21. February 22, 1945, Chiang Kai-shek Archives, 002–060100–00197–022.

22. Ibid.

23. March 4, 1945, Chiang Kai-shek Archives, 002–060100–00198–004.

24. It was not until March 26, 1945, that Chiang Kai-shek asked Song Ziwen to confirm the news in the *New York Post* that the plan concerning the treatment of postwar Japan drafted by the American secretary of the treasury Henry Morgenthau contained the clause "Whether Northeast China should be returned to China or fall under Soviet influence should be decided based on Soviet action in the Far East." Chiang Kai-shek realized the severity of the situation and tried to learn the content of the secret Yalta agreements. Jiang Jieshi Dian Song Ziwen [Telegram from Chiang Kai-shek to Song Ziwen], March 26, 1945, Chiang Kai-shek Archives, 002–090106–00017–194.

25. March 15, 1945, Chiang Kai-shek Archives, 002–060100–00198–015.

26. August 7, 1945, Chiang Kai-shek Archives, 002–060100–00203–007.

27. Letter from Patrick J. Hurley to Chiang Kai-shek, July 25, 1945, Chiang Kai-shek Archives, 002–020300–00027–001.

28. Ibid.

29. August 10, 1945, Chiang Kai-shek Archives, 002–060100–00203–010.

30. "Xu Foguan Cheng Jiang Jieshi" [Report from Xu Foguan to Chiang Kai-shek], August 10, 1945, Chiang Kai-shek Archives, 002–080103–00066–006.

31. Peng Keding Dian Jiang Jieshi [Telegram from Peng Keding to Chiang Kai-shek], August 11, 1945, Chiang Kai-shek Archives, 002–090105–00015–149.

32. "Dai Li Zhang Zhen Deng Cheng Jiang Jieshi [Report from Dai Li, Zhang Zhen, et al. to Chiang Kai-shek], August 13, 1945, Chiang Kai-shek Archives, 002–080103–00066–007.

33. "Dai Li Cheng Jiang Jieshi" [Report from Dai Li to Chiang Kai-shek], August 16, 1945, Chiang Kai-shek Archives, 002–030300–00027–020.

CHAPTER 12

1. Jiang Yongjing, *Hu Zhiming zai Zhongguo* [Ho Chi Minh in China] (Taipei: Zhuanji Wenxue Chubanshe [Biographical literature press], 1972), pp. 178–180.

2. Jiang Zhongzheng Zongtong Dang'an: Geming Wenxian: Kanluan Shiqi Zhongyao Wenjian Fenan Jibian [Archives of President Chiang Kai-shek: Revolutionary documents, compilation of important documents of the Chinese Civil War], vol. 50, *Dui Fa Yue Waijiao* [Diplomacy toward France and Vietnam], no. 16, p. 4 (hereafter *Geming Wenxian*); and "Gaishu" [Brief statement], *Dui Fa Yue Waijiao* [Foreign Policy toward French Indochina] (March 1945–January 1, 1950), Academia Historica, 2020.40.

3. Jiang Yongjing, *Ho Chi Minh*, p. 179.

4. Ibid., p. 153.

5. Foreign Relations of the United States: The Conferences at Cairo and Tehran, 1943 (Washington, 1961), p. 485, available at http://digicoll.library.wisc.edu/cgi-bin/FRUS/FRUS-idx?id=FRUS.FRUS1943CairoTehran; *Geming Wenxian*, no. 16, p. 4b; "Foreign Policy toward French Indochina," Academia Historica, 2020.40.

6. Gu Weijun, *Gu Weijun huiyilu* [Wellington Koo memoirs], trans. into Chinese by the Institute of Modern History at the China Academy of Social Sciences (Beiping: Zhonghua Shuju, 1987), vol. 5, pp. 282–283; *Foreign Relations of the United States, 1944* (Washington, 1965–1967), vol. 3, p. 773.

7. Foreign Relations of the United States: The Conferences at Cairo and Tehran, 1943, p. 485.

8. Gu Weijun, *Memoirs*, vol. 5, pp. 577–578.

9. For details about the Chinese Nationalist government's support for Vietnam's independence movement during the Sino-Japanese War, see Jiang Yongjing, *Ho Chi Minh*, chs. 8 and 9, pp. 119–176. After Roosevelt died in April 1945, Harry Truman assumed the presidency and policy changed, with the US stance gradually leaning toward France and becoming less supportive of Vietnam's independence. See Archimedes Patti, *Why Vietnam?* (Berkeley: University of California Press, 1982); and David Marr, *Vietnam, 1945: The Quest for Power* (Berkeley: University of California Press, 1997).

10. Jiang Zhongzheng Zongtong Dang'an [Archives of President Chiang Kai-shek], March 11, 1945, 002060100198011002, Academia Historica, Taipei.

11. Telegram from Xu Yongchang to Chiang Kai-shek, May 11, 1945, in *Geming Wenxian*, vol. 16, p. 4b; "Foreign Policy toward French Indochina," Academia Historica 2020.40.

12. Ibid.

13. The China Theater Supreme Command formed the First Front Army led by Lu Han by merging local troops in Yunnan Province with central army troops at the end of the Sino-Japanese War to launch strategic counteroffensives.

14. Yang Jiajie, ed., "Diyi Fangmianjun Kangzhan ji zai Yuebei Shouxiang Jiaofang Jishi" [Record of the First Front Army's anti-Japanese resistance, its

acceptance of the Japanese surrender in Vietnam, and its movement into northern Vietnam], in Yunnan Tongzhi Guan [Yunnan History Bureau], comp., *Xu Yunnan Tongzhi Changbian* [Extended and revised Yunnan gazetteer] (Kunming: Yunnan Shengzhi Bianzuan Weiyuanhui Bangongshi [General Office of the Yunnan History Compilation Committee], 1985), vol. 10, p. 103. Yang Jiajie was the director of the third bureau at the First Front Army command.

15. Yang Jiajie, "The First Front Army's Anti-Japanese Resistance," p.122.

16. Yunnan Sheng Zhengzhi Xieshang Huiyi Yunnan Lishi Bianzuan Weiyuanhui [Historical Documents Research Committee of the Yunnan Province Committee of the Chinese People's Political Consultative Conference], comp., *Yunnan Wenshi Ziliao Xuanji* [Selections of Yunnan historical documents] (Kunming, 1962), vol. 1, p. 12.

17. Chen Xiuhe, "Kangzhan Shenglihou Guomindang Jun Ru Yue Shouxiang Jilu" [The Nationalist Army's entrance into Vietnam and its acceptance of the Japanese surrender], in Zhengzhi Xieshang Huiyi Lishi Yanjiu Weiyuanhui [Historical Documents Research Committee of the National Committee of the Chinese People's Political Consultative Conference], *Wenshi Ziliao Xuanji* [Selections of cultural and historical documents] (Beiping, 1960), pp. 16–17. At that time, Chen Xiuhe was the director of the Kunming office of the Chinese army headquarters. He personally took part in the Sino-French negotiations concerning Vietnam.

18. Yang Jiajie, "The First Front Army's Anti-Japanese Resistance," p. 122; Jiang Yongjing, *Ho Chi Minh*, pp. 228–231.

19. Yang Jiajie, "The First Front Army's Anti-Japanese Resistance," pp. 122–125; Historical Documents Research Committee of Yunnan Province, *Selections of Yunnan Historical Documents*, vol. 47, pp. 326–327.

20. Historical Documents Research Committee of Yunnan Province, *Selections of Yunnan Historical Documents*, vol. 3, pp. 1–2.

21. Long Shengwu Xiansheng Fangwen Jilu [Long Yun's memoirs] (Taipei: Institute of Modern History at Academia Sinica, 1991), pp. 90–91; Historical Documents Research Committee of Yunnan Province, *Selections of Yunnan Historical Documents for Yunnan*, vol. 3, pp. 1–2.

22. Xie Lifu, *Yuenan Zhanzheng Shilu* [True record of the Vietnam War] (Beiping: Shijie Zhishi Chubanshe, 1994), vol. 1, pp. 25–27. See also David Marr, *Vietnam, 1945*.

23. Zhuang Zhihuan Deng Zhi Waijiaobu Dian [Telegram from Zhuang Zhihuan et al. to the Foreign Ministry], September 22, 1945, "Waijiaobu Dang'an: Wo Paizhu Yuenan Zhanlingjun An" [Chinese Foreign Ministry Archives: Our Army of Occupation in Vietnam], Academia Historica, 172-1/0601-1.

24. Chen Xiuhe, "The Nationalist Army's Entry into Vietnam," p. 18.

25. For British-French conflicts in Syria and the Middle East after World War II, see Winston Churchill, *The Second World War*, vol. 6, *Triumph and Tragedy*; and Charles de Gaulle, *Mémoires de Guerre*, vol. 3, *Le Salut, 1944–1946* (Paris, 1959). De Gaulle's memoir covers Vietnam extensively.

26. Waijiaobu Dang'an: Yuenan Rijun Touxiang an [Chinese Foreign Ministry Archives: The surrender of Japanese forces in Vietnam], Academia Historica, 172-1/0590.

27. Charles de Gaulle, *Mémoires de Guerre*, vol. 3, *Le Salut, 1944–1946*, pp. 208–215, 228–232.

28. "Our Army of Occupation in Vietnam," Academia Historica, 172–1/0601–1; Zhu Xie, *Yuenan Shouxiang Riji* [Diaries relating to the acceptance of the Japanese surrender in Vietnam] (Shanghai: Commercial Press, 1946), pp. 2–4; Ling Qihan, *Zai Henei Jieshou Riben Touxiang Neimu* [The inside story of the acceptance of Japan's surrender in Hanoi] (Beiping: Shijie Zhizhi Chubanshu, 1984), pp. 130–131.

29. Ling Qihan, *The Inside Story*, pp. 4–5.

30. In August 1943, the Nationalist government terminated diplomatic relations with the French Vichy puppet government and took back the right of managing the Chinese part of the Yunnan-Vietnam railway. It recognized de Gaulle's Free French government. So Pechkoff came to represent the political regime of Free France.

31. Charles de Gaulle, *Mémoires de Guerre*, vol. 3, *Le Salut, 1944–1946*, p. 229.

32. "Surrender of Japanese Forces in Vietnam," Academia Historica, 172–1/0590.

33. "Our Army of Occupation in Vietnam," Academia Historica, 172–1/0601–1.

34. Charles de Gaulle, *Mémoires de Guerre*, vol. 3, *Le Salut, 1944–1946*, pp. 229, 564–567.

35. Wang Shijie, *Wang Shijie Riji* [Diaries of Wang Shijie] (Taipei: Zhongyang Yanjiuyuan Jindaishi Yanjiusuo, 1990), vol. 4, p. 178, entry for September 19, 1945.

36. Charles de Gaulle, *Mémoires de Guerre*, vol. 3, *Le Salut, 1944–1946*, pp. 564–567; Ling Qihan, *Inside Story*, pp. 38–39; Wu Jingping, *Song Ziwen Zhengzhi Shengya Biannian* [Chronology of Song Ziwen's political life] (Fuzhou: Fujian Renmin Chubanshe, 1998), p. 477.

37. Yang Weizhen, "Cong Wang Shijie Riji Kan Zhanhou Zhong Fa Yuenan Jiaoshe (1945–1946)" [Sino-French negotiations concerning Vietnam as seen from the *Diaries of Wang Shijie* (1945–1946)], *Jindai Zhongguo* [Modern China], vol. 161 (2005), pp. 38–47.

38. Wang Shijie, *Diaries*, vol. 4, pp. 198–199, entry for October 22, 1945.

39. Ibid., vol. 4, p. 298, entry for April 5, 1946.

40. Ibid., vol. 4, p. 223, entry for November 30, 1945.

41. Chen Xiuhe, "The Nationalist Army's Entry into Vietnam," p. 14.

42. Zhang Xianwen, ed, *Kangri Zhanzheng de Zhengmian Zhanchang* [The War of Resistance battlefields at the front] (Zhengzhou: Henan Renmin Chubanshe), vol. 3, p. 875.

43. "Xing Senzhou Baogao" [Report from Xing Senzhou], in Jiang Yongjing, *Ho Chi Minh*, p. 186. Xing Senzhou was the director of the Chinese Nationalist Party's office in Vietnam. The office was located on the Yunnan border.

44. Zhang Xianwen, *War of Resistance Battlefields*, vol. 3, p. 874.

45. Chen Xiuhe, "The Nationalist Army's Entrance into Vietnam," p. 15.

46. Telegram from Wu Guozhen to Chiang Kai-shek, August 18, 1945, in

Geming Wenxian, no. 16, p. 4b; and "Foreign Policy toward French Indochina," Academia Historica, 2020.40.

47. Chen Xiuhe, "The Nationalist Army's Entrance into Vietnam," p. 16.

48. Telegram from General Commander He Yingqin to French General Alessandri, August 25, 1945, "Surrender of Japanese Forces in Vietnam," Academia Historica,172–1/0590.

49. Ibid.

50. Intelligence from the American First Front Army to Lu Han, September 6, 1945, "Surrender of Japanese Forces in Vietnam," Academia Historica, 172–1/0590.

51. "Our Army of Occupation in Vietnam," Academia Historica 172–1/0601–1.

52. Selections of Yunnan Historical Documents, vol. 1, pp. 50–54; *Long Yun's Memoirs*, pp. 25–26.

53. Telegram from Long Yun to Chiang Kai-shek, August 15, 1945, in *Geming Wenxian*, no. 16, p. 4b; and "Foreign Policy toward French Indochina," Academia Historica, 2020.40.

54. Jiang Zhongzheng Zongtong Dang'an [Archives of President Chiang Kai-shek], August 16, 1946, Academia Historica, CD no. 09A-00387.

55. "Jiang Jieshi Pishi" [Instruction from Chiang Kai-shek], May 11, 1945, in *Geming wenxian*, no. 16, p. 4b; "Foreign policy toward French Indochina," Academia Historica, 2020.40.

56. Chen Xiuhe, "The Nationalist Army's Entry into Vietnam," pp. 14–15.

57. Report from Ling Qihan to the Chinese Foreign Ministry, September 19, 1945, "Our Army of Occupation in Vietnam," Academia Historica, 172–1/0601–1. See also Xie Benshu, Niu Hongbin, *Lu Han Zhuan* [Biography of Lu Han] (Chengdu: Sichuan Minzu Chubanshe, 1990), pp. 80–81.

58. Report from Ling Qihan to the Chinese Foreign Ministry, September 19, 1945, "Our Army of Occupation in Vietnam," Academia Historica, 172–1/0601–1.

59. Ling Qihan, *The Inside Story*, p.13.

60. Report from Ling Qihan to the Chinese Foreign Ministry, September 19, 1945, "Our Army of Occupation in Vietnam," Academia Historica, 172–1/0601–1.

61. Ling Qihan, *The Inside Story*, pp. 14–15.

62. Telegram from General Commander He Yingqin to Lu Han, September 15, 1945, "Surrender of Japanese Forces in Vietnam," Academia Historica, 172–1/0590.

63. Telegram from Lu Han to the Military Command Department, October 26, 1945, "Surrender of Japanese Forces in Vietnam," Academia Historica, 172–1/0590.

64. Memorandum from French ambassador Pechkoff to Song Ziwen, October 2, 1945, "Surrender of Japanese Forces in Vietnam," Academia Historica, 172–1/0590. Soon thereafter the hapless ambassador was replaced by Meyrier, who had once been consul general in Shanghai. Report from Dai Li to Chiang Kai-shek, October 21, 1945, in *Geming Wenxian*, no. 16, p. 4b; and "Foreign Policy toward French Indochina," Academia Historica, 2020.

65. Ling Qihan, *The Inside Story*, pp. 132–133.

66. Yang Weizhen, *Cong Hezuo dao Juelie: Lun Long Yun yu Zhongyang de*

Guanxi (1927–1949) [From cooperation to rupture: Long Yun's relations with the central government (1927–1949)) (Taipei: Academia Historica, 2000), pp. 216–248.

67. Telegram from Wang Shijie to Chiang Kai-shek, September 10, 1945, in *Geming wenxian*, vol. 50, no. 16, p. 4b; and "Foreign Policy toward French Indochina," Academia Historica, 2020.40.

68. Wang Shijie, *Diaries*, vol. 4, p. 203, entry for October 30, 1945.

69. Ibid., vol. 4, pp. 278–279, entry for February 28, 1946.

70. In 1946, Chinese and French troops clashed in Haiphong. *Zhonghua Junshi Xuehui Huikan* [Chinese Military History Association journal], vol. 9 (2004), pp. 251–291.

CHAPTER 13

1. Margaret MacMillan, *Peacemakers: The Paris Conference of 1919 and Its Attempt to End War* (London: John Murray, 2001) provides a lively description of the complex agenda with which the Paris Peace Conference had to deal.

2. "NSC Staff Study on US Objectives, Policies, and Courses of Action in Asia," *Foreign Relations of the United States, 1951: Asia and the Pacific*, vol. 6, no. 1, pp. 53–55, http://digicoll.library.wisc.edu/cgi-bin/FRUS (hereafter FRUS).

3. Memorandum, attached to Memorandum of Conversation, by the Special Assistant to the Consultant (Allison), January 12, 1951, in FRUS, pp. 795–796.

4. "NSC Staff Study," FRUS, p. 55.

5. Minutes: Dulles Staff Meeting, January 30, 1951, FRUS, p. 831.

6. Memorandum of Conversation, by the Special Assistant to the Consultant, January 12, 1951, FRUS, pp. 794–795.

7. Ambassador in the UK (Gifford) to the Secretary of State, June 5, 1961, FRUS, p. 1106.

8. Memorandum of Conversation, by the Consultant to the Secretary (Dulles), September 9, 1951, FRUS, p. 1343.

9. Ambassador London to Consultant to the Secretary, June 8, 1951, FRUS, p. 1109

10. Ibid., p. 952.

11. Ibid., pp. 831–832.

12. Deputy to Consultant (Allison) to Consultant to the Secretary, April 5, 1951, FRUS, p. 961.

13. Indian Chargé Kirpilani to Consultant to the Secretary, August 23, 1951, FRUS, p. 1288.

14. The Chargé in China (Steere) to the Department of State, September 24, 1951, FRUS, pp. 1356–1357.

15. Acting Secretary of State to Ambassador India, August 31, 1951, FRUS, pp. 1312.

16. Treaty of Peace between Japan and India, http://www.gwu.edu/~memory/data/treaties/India.pdf.

17. Article 14 of the Treaty of Peace with Japan (the San Francisco Peace Treaty). See http://www.taiwandocuments.org/sanfrancisco01.htm.

18. The Ambassador in the Philippines (Owen) to the Secretary of State, August 8, 1951, FRUS, pp. 1248.

19. See Memorandum of April 21 [1951], in "Japanese Peace Treaty: Working Draft and Commentary Prepared in the Department of State," June 1, 1951, FRUS, p. 1086.

20. "John Foster Dulles's Speech at the San Francisco Peace Conference," September 5, 1951, accessible on The World and Japan Database Project, http://www. ioc.u-tokyo.ac.jp/~worldjpn/documents/texts/JPUS/19510905.S1E.html.

21. "Gromyko's Statement on the Peace Treaty" and "Peace Treaty with Japan Signed; Gromyko Warns Step Risks War," *New York Times*, September 9, 1951.

22. "Zhou Enlai Waizhang Guanyu Ying Mei Dui Ri Heyue Cao'an he Jiujinshan Huiyi Shenming" [Foreign Minister Zhou Enlai's statement on the US-UK draft peace treaty with Japan and the San Francisco Conference], August 15, 1951, http://news.xinhuanet.com/ziliao/2004-12/15/content_2337746.htm.

23. Arne Westad, *Restless Empire: China and the World since 1750* (London: Basic Books), pp. 285–304.

24. Wang Hui, "Lengzhan de Yuzhou: Jiang Jieshi yi Kailuo Huiyizhong the Liuqiu Wenti" [A Cold War omen: Chiang Kai-shek and the issue of Liuqiu at the Cairo Conference," in *Kaifang Shidai* [Open Times], May 2009, p. 25.

25. Ibid., p. 25.

26. Ibid., pp. 25–26.

27. Ibid., pp. 25–26.

28. Chiang Kai-shek Diary, Hoover Institution, Stanford University, Box 42, Folder 10, entry for November 15 (hereafter Chiang Kai-Shek Diary). I am grateful to Dr. Lin Hsiao-ting for making excerpts of the diary available.

29. Entry of November 17, idem; and Wang Hui, "Cold War Omen," 27.

30. Wang Hui, "Cold War Omen," pp. 27–28.

31. Ibid.

32. Ibid.

33. Ibid.

34. Potsdam Declaration, July 26, 1945, http://www.ndl.go.jp/constitution/e/etc/c06.html.

35. "Cairo Declaration," in US Department of State, *A Decade of American Foreign Policy, 1941–1949: Basic Documents* (Washington: Historical Office, Department of State, 1950), p. 20; "Cairo Conference," http://www.taiwandocuments.org/cairo.htm.

36. Treaty of Peace between the Republic of China and Japan, signed April 28, 1952, in Taipei. See http://www.taiwandocuments.org/taipei01.

37. Memorandum of Conversation, by the Assistant Secretary of State for Far Eastern Affairs (Rusk), November 27, 1951, FRUS, p. 1416.

38. Ibid., p. 1417.

39. "Riben Shouxiang Jitian Mao zai Guohui de Shengming" [Statement of Japanese prime minister Yoshida Shigeru in the Diet], October 30, 1951, in Qin Xiaoyi, ed., *Zhonghua Minguo Zhongyao Shiliao: Duiri Kangzhan Shiqi: Di Qi Bian: Zhanhou Zhongguo* [An initial compilation of important documents of the

Republic of China: The period of the War of Resistance: vol. 7, Postwar China], vol. 7, no. 4, pp. 758–760 (hereafter ZYSL).

40. The US Political Adviser to SCAP (Sebald) to the Secretary of State, December 13, 1951, FRUS, pp. 1437–1438.

41. Chiang Kai-shek Diary, Box 49, Folder 12, entry for April 1, 1952.

42. "Riben Shaoxiang Jitian Mao Zhi Meiguo Guowuqing Dulesi Han Yiwen" [Translation of Japanese Prime Minister Yoshida Shigeru to US Secretary of State Dulles]," December 24, 1951, ZYSL, pp. 770–771.

43. "Riben Guohui Dui Zhong Ri Heyue zhi Bianlun" [The Diet debate about the Sino-Japanese peace treaty," ZYSL, p. 790.

44. Ibid., 789.

45. Chiang Kai-shek Diary, Box 49, Folder 16.

46. Chiang Kai-shek Diary, Box 49, Folder 16, entry for February 19, 1952.

47. Chiang Kai-shek Diary, Box 49, Folder 10, entry for February 23, 1952.

48. Ibid., entry for February 25, 1952.

49. "日方对于条约名称问题之意见" [The Japanese view on the issue of the title of the treaty], February 1952, in ZYSL, p. 775.

50. "Ye Gongchao Buzhang ji Mucu Silangqi Suozhang zhi Jiaoshi" [Negotiations between Foreign Ministers Ye Kung-ch'ao and Isao Kawada], February13, 1952, ZYSL, p. 780.

51. "Jiang Zongtong Tiaolun zhi Dui Ri Heyue Fangzhen" [The Policy toward the peace treaty with Japan as detailed by President Jiang], April 17, 1952, in ZYSL, p. 713.

52. "Zhong Ri Heyue Choubei Huiyi Jilu" [Record of preparatory meeting for the China-Japan Peace Conference], February 19, 1952, ZYSL, p. 795.

53. Chiang Kai-shek Diary, Box 49, Folder 11.

54. "Riben Dierci Tichu Yuegao" [Second draft for the treaty submitted by Japan], March 12, 1952, ZYSL, p. 885.

55. "Zhong Ri Hehui Di Yi Ci Fei Zhengzhi Huiyi Jianyao Jilu" [Brief record of the first informal meeting of the China-Japan Peace Conference], February 23, 1952, ZYSL, p. 811.

56. Ibid.

57. "Zhong Ri Hehui Di Yi Ci Huiyi Jilu" [Minutes of the first meeting of the China-Japan Peace Conference], February 20, 1952, ZYSL, p. 796.

58. Chiang Kai-shek Diary, Box 49, Folder 11, entry for March 29, 1952.

59. "Zhong Ri Hehui Di Er Ci Hiyi Jilu" [Minutes of the second meeting of the China-Japan Peace Conference], March 1, 1952, ZYSL, p. 821.

60. Ibid.

61. "Zhong Ri Hehui Di Liu Ci Fei Zhengshi Huiyi Jilu" [The sixth informal meeting of the China-Japan Peace Conference], March 7, 1952, ZYSL, p. 861.

62. Ibid.

63. "Zhong Ri Hehui Di Qi Ci Fei Zhengshi Huiyi Jilu" [The seventh informal meeting of the China-Japan Peace Conference], March 17, 1952, ZYSL, p. 888.

64. Ibid., p. 890.

65. "Zhong Ri Hehui Di Ba Ci Fei Zhengshi Huiyi Jilu" [The eighth informal meeting of the China-Japan Peace Conference], March 19, 1952, ZYSL, p. 904.

66. "Hu Qingyu Fu Daibiao yi Mucun Silangqi Shaouxi Tuanyuan Tanhua

Jianyao Jilu" [A brief record of the discussion between Vice Minister Hu Qingyu and members of the delegation led by Isao Kawada], March 22. 1952, ZYSL, p. 918.

67. Ibid., p. 919

68. Chiang Kai-shek Diary, Box 49, Folder 11, entry for March 25, 1952.

69. "Zhong Ri Hehui Di Ba Ci Fei Zhengshi Huiyi Jilu" [The eighth informal meeting of the China-Japan Peace Conference], March 19, 1952, ZYSL, p. 904.

70. Note from the Japanese plenipotentiary, Isao Kawada, to the Chinese plenipotentiary, Yeh Kung-ch'ao, April 28, 1952, http://www.taiwandocuments.org/taipei03.htm.

71. See photographs of the Chinese and Japanese versions of the text in Lin Man-houng, *Liewu, Jiaohuan, yu Rentong Weiji: Taiwan Diwei Xinlun* [Witch hunts, soul stealing, and crisis of identity: A new historical perspective of Taiwan's legal status] (Taipei: Liming Wenhua Gongsi, 2008), pp. 8–11.

72. Ng Yuzin Chiautong, "Historical and Legal Aspects of the International Status of Japan," (1972), http//www.wufi.org.tw/eng/intlstat.htm, p. 16. Ng was president of the World United Formosans for Independence.

73. For Yeh's statement, see "Zhong Ri Hehui Di Si Ci Fei Zhengshi Huiyi Jilu" [The fourth informal meeting of the China-Japan Peace Conference], March 5, 1952, ZYSL, p. 829. For the original clause, see "Wo Fang Suo Ti Zhong Ri Hehui Yuegao" [Preliminary draft for the China-Japan Peace Treaty submitted by US], ZYSL, p. 810.

74. Chiang Kai-shek Diary, Box 49, Folder 12, entry foor April 27, 1952.

75. Lin Man-houng, *New Historical Perspective*, 23.

76. Shen Jinding, "Canjia Zhu Ri Daibiaotuan de Huiyi" [Recollecting my membership of our delegation in Japan], ZYSL, p. 667.

CONCLUSION

Western sources, when cited, were added by the editors for greater clarity of statements by Western or Indian leaders.

Index